theory aside

theory aside

jason potts and daniel stout, editors

DUKE UNIVERSITY PRESS

Durham and London 2014

© 2014 Duke University Press
All rights reserved

Designed by Amy Ruth Buchanan
Typeset in Quadraat and Quadratt Sans
by Westchester Book Group
Cover art: Rafael Reveron-Pojan, *Piccolo-Paradiso*, 2009.
Rolled paper and thread, 95×20×16 cm. rafareve.blogspot.com

Library of Congress Cataloging-in-Publication Data
Theory aside / edited by Jason Potts and Daniel Stout.
pages   cm
Includes bibliographical references and index.
ISBN 978-0-8223-5670-7 (cloth : alk. paper)
ISBN 978-0-8223-5681-3 (pbk. : alk. paper)
1. Criticism.   2. Literature—History and criticism—Theory, etc.
I. Potts, Jason, 1967–   II. Stout, Daniel.
PN81.T446   2014
801'.95—dc23
2013048708

contents

INTRODUCTION On the Side: Allocations of Attention in the Theoretical Moment | *Jason Potts and Daniel Stout*, 1

PART I Chronologies Aside

1. Writing the History of Homophobia | *Eve Kosofsky Sedgwick*, 29
2. Late Exercises in Minimal Affirmatives | *Anne-Lise François*, 34
3. Comparative Noncontemporaneities: C. L. R. James and Ernst Bloch | *Natalie Melas*, 56
4. On Suicide, and Other Forms of Social Extinguishment | *Elizabeth A. Povinelli*, 78

PART II Approaches Aside

5. What Is Historical Poetics? | *Simon Jarvis*, 97
6. The Biopolitics of Recognition: Making Female Subjects of Globalization | *Pheng Cheah*, 117
7. Before Racial Construction | *Irene Tucker*, 143
8. Archive Favor: African American Literature before and after Theory | *Jordan Alexander Stein*, 160
9. What Cinema Wasn't: Animating Film Theory's Double Blind Spot | *Karen Beckman*, 177

PART III   *Figures Aside*

10. Hyperbolic Discounting and Intertemporal Bargaining | *William Flesch*, 199

11. The Primacy of Sensation: Psychophysics, Phenomenology, Whitehead | *Mark B. N. Hansen*, 218

12. Reading the Social: Erving Goffman and Sexuality Studies | *Heather Love*, 237

13. Our I. A. Richards Moment: The Machine and Its Adjustments | *Frances Ferguson*, 261

14. Needing to Know (:) Theory / Afterwords | *Ian Balfour*, 280

BIBLIOGRAPHY | 287

CONTRIBUTORS | 299

INDEX | 303

acknowledgments

This volume had the support of our home institutions, St. Francis Xavier University and the University of Mississippi, but it would have been impossible without the assistance of a number of people we are glad to have the chance to thank publicly. We are particularly grateful to Frances Ferguson, who backed this project from its inception and provided assistance in countless ways over the course of its production. Frances is awesome. Neil Hertz and Jonathan Arac were also early boosters, and we appreciate their support. Courtney Berger has been terrific to work with. We would like to thank her and Duke University Press's two anonymous readers for their many helpful comments and suggestions. We'd also like to thank: Jessica Ryan for seeing the manuscript through DUP's editorial process; Amy Buchanan for her art design; and Mark Mastromarino for indexing the collection. We are very grateful to Hal Sedgwick and Jonathan Goldberg for allowing us to include a previously unpublished essay by Eve Kosofsky Sedgwick; we are honored to have it as part of this collection and appreciate the work they did in locating it in her archive. We would also like to thank our many friends and teachers for their encouragement and engagement. Katie Arthur and Cristie Ellis patiently put up with us throughout this process and generously allowed us to benefit from their bright-minded insights at many turns.

This volume is dedicated to our parents, John and Lora Stout and Pat and John Potts, for their unflagging support and for encouraging us to think otherwise, even when it was clear it almost assuredly wasn't going to pay.

introduction

On the Side: Allocations of Attention in the Theoretical Moment

Jason Potts and Daniel Stout

There is a moment in Jane Elliott and Derek Attridge's introduction to their important 2011 collection *Theory After 'Theory'* to which we are deeply sympathetic. In the sixth paragraph of that essay, the editors decry cultural theory's "tendency to draw obsessively on the work of certain oracular figures." Suggesting that such figures are not a "necessary or consensual feature of the project of theory in the first place," they offer a version of theory capable of operating with a less static canon and no longer subject to the centralizing force of any narrow band of theorists.[1] Such an open-ended prospect is, of course, almost intuitively appealing. It would be hard not to choose intellectual flexibility and diversity over the static monumentality of a few defining figures. Who would want fewer options?

On some level, though, it must seem ironic that such a plea would need to be made at all, given the role that many theoretical approaches played in expanding the terrain of humanistic inquiry and fostering new connections across fields of research. There can be little dispute, anyway, that undergraduate and graduate students are now able to take seriously a host of topics and lines of inquiry that, even twenty years ago, would have seemed more or less impossible, or that this expansion has been in some significant part cultural theory's doing. Having underwritten the decanonization of the humanities by fostering a new and more rigorous self-consciousness about our operating assumptions, disciplinary categories, and institutional practices, it's noteworthy that cultural theory should itself now need to be freed from its obligations to the oracular gravity of a leading name.

But the easy irony here, that the theory that began by knocking down methodological orthodoxies should itself remain beholden to what one critic calls "master thinkers," is in fact only apparent.[2] The place of the proper name within the operations of cultural theory is, from our perspective, not so much a failure of self-consciousness—not a puzzling exception to theory's otherwise energetic canon critique—as it is a byproduct of the desire for the particularly radical forms of intellectual transformation that drove theory all along. The proper name hung around—and did so despite lots of eloquent skepticism about agency, authority, and the organization of knowledge—because the proper name satisfied theory's commitment to, in Terry Eagleton's phrase, "ideas of . . . incomparable value."[3] What High Theory offered in the guise of a singular name, in other words, was in fact a set of thoughts that was understood not merely to *add to* but to *fundamentally reconfigure* knowledge as we had (always "until now") known it. This is how, for instance, it was possible for a reading of "A slumber did my spirit seal" to arrive less as a contribution to our understanding of Wordsworth's oeuvre than as an essentially institutional intervention into some of our most basic practices and assumptions. Such strongly interventionist ambitions ensured that theory would operate, somewhat paradoxically, as a canon of singularities, a collection of intellectual incursions that were, by definition, without precedent. It is certainly true that this drive toward the "incomparable" meshed (all too) conveniently with the commodifying processes of a publishing industry eager for marquee names and an academic culture only too happy to let the star system constellate its distributions of value.[4] But to treat theory's seemingly counterintuitive attachment to the proper name as merely a sign of a slightly shady alliance with the very structures it should most oppose (capitalist industries, corporate universities) overlooks the degree to which the desire for unprecedented intellectual transformation itself built a tendency toward canonicity into theory from the very beginning.

The current conventional wisdom, of course, is that the rigidly canonical moment of High Theory has passed. Most commentators agree that Theory's operations have now been devolved to a less monolithic set of efforts loosely grouped by the decidedly lowercase "theory." From this perspective, the break with "oracular figures" that Elliott and Attridge mean to encourage is already under way. But if virtually everyone can see that theory is undergoing a salutary move away from singular names, it's all the more important to note that this devolution has not in fact diminished any of the demand for the paradigm-shifting work that helped Theory earn its capital T in the first place. Indeed the two desires—for less centralized theoretical canons and for more radical intellectual transformations—are often seen to be mutually supporting, as if the move away from oracular figures was simply the first, space-clearing step needed to initiate a new round of intellectual overcomings. It's with something like this understanding that Elliott and Attridge, only sentences after dispensing with "certain oracular figures," declare their ambition to chronicle a new set of "radical alterations." The aim is to replace "recent work" that has failed to be truly transformative—work, they say, whose "groundbreaking nature [is] more apparent than real"—with the sort of thing they've collected in their volume: work that "exceeds the terms of the present in a way that allows us to think something hitherto unthinkable." In their demand for the truly transformative, in their sense that one can reliably distinguish the truly groundbreaking from the illusory, and in their insistence that valuable theory deals in the "hitherto unthinkable," Elliott and Attridge resubscribe to the very model of intellectual progress that drove Theory's heyday. Their break with a canon of "oracular figures" in one paragraph does nothing to minimize the desire for oracular effects in the next. It's a peculiar turn maintained in their introduction's final sentence: "'Theory' is dead," they write, "long live theory."[5] Under this new dispensation Theory may be able to do away with the monarch, but it clearly also remains stubbornly attached to the model of monarchical succession that was the real problem in the first place. *Theory After 'Theory'* thus preserves the force of Theory, just now without the Theorist, the oracular effect without the "oracular figure."

We believe that the consequences of this compulsion toward radical transformation are not merely rhetorical. That fundamental change and paradigm shifts are now endemic to the way we have come to think about how theory shapes our understanding of intellectual work in the humanities in ways that have all kinds of practical consequences. What, we want to ask, would our intellectual landscape look like if we were less beholden to the idea of wholesale change? What if we were less committed to imagining cultural theory as an institution made up solely of breakthroughs?[6] What if we took more seriously, or embraced more fully, the break with the oracular that Elliott and Attridge propose? Is it possible, that is, not just to distance ourselves from the oracular *figure* but to orient ourselves away from oracularism as such? How might we begin to value different kinds of thoughts, both current and past, if we weren't so attached to a version of intellectual progress that, in order to look like progress at all, needed to obliterate all that was hitherto thinkable? What intellectual options has this demand for radical alteration left by the wayside?

It seems to us that our intellectual projects and interests have come to have extremely short shelf lives. This puts pressure on every aspect of scholarly life. Working academics struggle to publish before the flag under which they began their research has been captured and replaced with another. In the period we now know as "the moment of theory" theories came to replace one another with sufficient speed that obsolescence threatened to predate publication.[7] We hire new faculty on the basis of the topics a theory licenses, even as we can see our preferences already beginning to shift in ways that will raise questions about the new hire's research plans tomorrow. This is not an easy way to live (or work). We do not, to be sure, imagine an entirely depressurized profession or think that we should all operate as though our activities were entirely without stake. But we are concerned with how this desire for immediacy attenuates our interests. When we ask the question that lies behind an ambition like Elliott and Attridge's—What's thinkable today that wasn't thinkable yesterday?—we severely and unnecessarily restrict the shape and span of our intellectual attentions. The question presumes, for one thing, that we have somehow already "thought up" all of yesterday's thoughts, when it's not clear to us that we were ever operating with a comprehensive sense of the available options. And is it really true, as the question implies, that a thought thinkable a day or many days ago would, just by virtue of this historical quality (its "precedentedness," as it were) have ceased to have any real value? From our perspective, intellectual progress need not run on a model that is so insistently unidirectional or exclusively revolutionary. It is our view that the nearly constant "crisis" in which the humanities finds itself has as much to do with the way its allocation of attention—its lack of interest in anything but the hitherto unthought—constantly makes it seem that the well has run nearly dry as it does with the actual value of its activities at any given moment.[8] Indeed it is this cycle of feast-then-famine-then-feast that accounts for theory's curiously double condition: simultaneously moribund and monumental, politically impotent and ambitious, obsolete and an entrance requirement for a job in the academy.[9]

Instead of treating our academic fields like crowded social events, where we've scouted our next conversation before we've concluded the one we're in, we would prefer to see a looser and differently ambitious model of intellectual engagement, one that kept old conversations around longer or proceeded in ways more open to unscripted (and even potentially fruitless) encounters.[10] We would like to develop a less apocalyptic model of intellectual development, one more catholic and modest in approach. Of course, it's true that even this suggestion can't help but seem like another version of the demand for an intellectual sea-change. But by looking to stand aside from (rather than replace) existing models and thoughts and by thinking carefully and explicitly about the costs of attenuating our thoughts prematurely, the essays collected here feel out what a different kind of critical practice might look like.

This less linear view of cultural theory does not fit easily into the narrative arc that either traces or denies the development of theory's death rattle.[11] In any case, describing the theoretical corpus as though *alive* and *dead* were not only the relevant terms but the only available options has made it difficult, even for a voice as prominent as W. J. T. Mitchell's, to turn the discussion toward less rigid options. In fact his introduction to the 2004 special issue of *Critical Inquiry* on "the futures of criticism" makes for a particularly telling case study in this sort of strain, as it wants both to acknowledge the pervasive sense of Theory's crisis and, at the same time, to distance itself from those life-or-death options. On the one hand, Mitchell acknowledges that the symposium marks a decisive moment in Theory's fate: an unprecedented summoning of the editorial board ("This group had never before convened in the entire thirty-year history of the journal"). Their task, Mitchell explains, was to respond to "a moment of crisis for [*Critical Inquiry*]'s own mission, understood as an intellectual, interdisciplinary microcosm of a global crisis, and as a global mission for peace and justice." In fairly stark contrast to this "global mission," though, Mitchell spends a good portion of his introduction laying out his vision for what he calls "medium theory," a theory oriented toward more modest claims. "Medium theory," he writes, would "stand in contrast to what has been called high theory, the aspiration to total mastery, coherence, [and] explanatory power."[12]

We are all for this sort of thing. But it says a lot, we think, that Mitchell's vision has not exactly been widely endorsed.[13] Even Mitchell's own suggestion takes place in an introduction otherwise preoccupied with the vocabulary of intellectual crisis, death, and resurrection, and it arrives accompanied by his acknowledgment that medium theory is not likely to satisfy the assembled crowds on either side of the pro- or anti-Theory question. "Medium theory," he acknowledges, "is not going to be quite radical enough for some and probably too radical for others."[14]

On the still-too-radical side, we find the pointedly antitheoretical perspective of *Theory's Empire* (2005), edited by Daphne Pattai and Will H. Corral. Their introduction eagerly pursues the *Critical Inquiry* symposium as if it presented one final threat (that Theory might actually be revived) and one final lesson in the empty excess that, for them anyway, characterized life under Theory's imperial sway. For them, the gathering "of the founders and promoters of Theory" and their effort to "reinvigorate their propositions, including, in particular, their claims to be politically relevant," do nothing more than "confirm . . . the by-now entirely established nature of assertions about Theory" and make feeble apology for "their own excesses." The goal of *Theory's*

Empire is to sketch out a future for literary studies freed of such "tedious obligation[s]," one in which we might move away from questions of methodology and back to questions of pleasure. We ought, they argue, to return to our basic "affection for literature," our "delight in the pleasures it brings," and our "respect for its ability to give memorable expression to the vast variety of human experience."[15] For these editors, no theory—even medium theory—is a good theory.[16]

Accordingly even studiedly relaxed claims for theory's future, like those recently offered by Jonathan Culler, wouldn't satisfy Pattai and Corral. In fact the modest tone of Culler's recent reflections on theory's condition might particularly exercise Pattai and Corral, since it is precisely the extent of theory's dissemination into the basic operating procedures of many disciplines that enables Culler to rest assured that theory will remain indispensable, even if it therefore no longer counts as avant-garde.[17] Like Eagleton, who sees some value in theory's continuing in a fairly modest form (as "a reasonably systematic reflection on our guiding assumptions"), Culler treats theory as a set of established intellectual practices.[18] Theory, Culler admits, may now be "deprive[d]" it of its "glamor of novelty and notoriety" but that's in part because "it now seems widely accepted that any intellectual project has a basis in theory of some sort."[19] For Culler as for Eagleton, theory "remains as indispensable as ever."[20] As the breadth of Culler's phrasing suggests ("any intellectual project"), what he imagines is a theory so fully domesticated that it no longer remains the exclusive property of the professoriate. For Culler, it's not only that graduate students "need to be aware of theoretical debates in their fields and able to situate themselves and their work within changing intellectual structures of the professional landscape," but that undergraduates "ought to explore" theory "as one of the most exciting and socially pertinent dimensions of the humanities."[21]

Insofar as this outcome would ensconce theory in the core of humanities education, it's easy to see why Culler's vision would strike the editors of *Theory's Empire* as a regrettable fate. It may be less easy, though, to understand why this outcome would look not only insufficient to some of theory's biggest proponents but, much more strongly, like a repudiation of theory's fundamental project. But for those who believe that theory's mandate is exclusively to bring about wholesale and immediate interruption, emancipation, or transcendence, any theory that fits happily into given academic operations, any theory that is such an institutionally useful team player, is not going to seem like theory at all. For critics like Kenneth Surin, Michael Hardt, and Clarie Colebrook, for instance, the problem with recent theoretical interventions is that they are neither exciting nor socially or politically pertinent enough. Surin's introduction to the "Theory Now" special issue of *South Atlantic Quarterly* makes clear his sense that we occupy an exhausted present in which new oracles could not come fast enough: "The *problématique*, urgent for our time, of producing new emancipatory names to replace the ones that have become exhausted is, for me, a focal point of these essays." In Surin's view, theory's "exemplary vocation" is thus not only to name "this smiling or snarling beast who won't permit the aspiration for anything radically different" but to slay the dragon.[22] Hardt's contribution to the same discussion is even more emphatic than Surin's, arguing that critique's proven "inability... to fulfill its transformative promises" has produced a persistent "melancholy" among critical theorists. This melancholy, Hardt argues, can be rectified only by a move toward what he calls "militancy," a mode of thought distinguished from its more diluted sibling, "critique," by its ability to enact wholesale transformation. Where critique operates by smaller, local adjustment (in Hardt's words, critique aims "at the art of not being governed so much"), "militancy seeks... to govern differently, creating a new life and a new world."[23]

Demands like Surin's and Hardt's for radical difference, militant thought, and unprecedented worlds are put in especially stark terms in Colebrook's essay "Extinction Theory," which elevates a run-of-the-mill theoretical skepticism toward the human or the humanist into a literal principle. Theory, Colebrook suggests, should embrace the example of the many extinction narratives "regarding the possible or inevitable absence of humans" to purge itself of its lingering attachment to life (as in the "vital norms" of biopolitics) or those ideas (like "re-humanizing emancipation") that might serve the interests of actually existing humans. A mode of thinking that could consider "not simply the formal absence of a population but an actual disappearance" would, Colebrook argues, restore theory to its proper function, to be "destructive of the imagination" or the "imaginary."[24] For Colebrook, the only theory after Theory is a theory after humans.

What's common to Surin, Hardt, and Colebrook, then, is the position that theory's obligation is to identify a thought that remains beyond existing politics, social forms, or the human itself. In this sense, what they are urging is not merely that we adopt positions of constant self-reflection or self-critique but that we undertake a constant process of perpetual and self-willed extinction, successively discarding one present imaginary after another.

What this model of successive replacement has going for it, obviously, is the thrill of its sweeping power and its refusal of half-measures. It's easy enough to see the value in renewing the demand on us, as thinkers, to advance possibilities rather than to simply rehearse the available options. And it's hard not to wince at Eagleton's charge that those who can't "think up feminism or structuralism" are left to merely "apply such insights to *Moby-Dick* or *The Cat in the Hat*."[25] The reserves of intellectual energy to which views like Colebrook's (or Hardt's or Surin's) testify are considerable, and their principled refusal to be satisfied with the available set of options is, in and of itself, admirable. But the problem, as we see it, with construing this radicalism as theory's exclusive mission is that it puts an extraordinarily large burden on the present moment (even as it seeks to discard it).[26] For it is, after all, only from within the very immediate confines of our current "imaginary" that we might determine an idea's adequacy. Can we really trust ourselves this much? It's a real question, since the theory-as-wholesale-transformation model means that our determinations on any given issue—alive or dead, liberatory or complicit, emancipatory or not—can't help but have extremely high stakes. It is hard to imagine how, within this model, we would ever want to go back to a thought that seemed to have exhausted itself or to a prior moment that seemed to have offered a limited purview.

Given these reservations, it seems to us like a good sign that not everyone seeking change demands that it be quite so apocalyptic or imagines that the wholly new will necessarily be quite so readily identifiable. Peter Osborne's essay "Philosophy after Theory," for instance, strikes us as notable for its attempt to find an alternative to modes of intellectual advancement that do not simply transcend contemporary conditions. Osborne means to remind us that any "specific newness" necessarily stands in some sort of relation "to its negation of the old." But it's also the case that Osborne's critique ends up conserving the figures his own account ties to the forms of destructive negation he wants to resist in the first place (Nietzsche, Heidegger, Benjamin, and Deleuze). Osborne's final proposition is for "a renewed investigation of the underlying affinities between Hegel's and Nietzsche's thought" and a return to the "exemplary" work of Benjamin and of Deleuze and Guattari.[27] His essay thus seems to turn in a rather small circle in order to salvage the very oracular figures we were meant to give up. Like Osborne, Cary Wolfe's essay "Theory as a Research Program—The Very Idea" seems to move in two directions at once: both cautioning against and subscribing to the simplified appeal of the categorically new. In favor of the radical break, Wolfe argues that theory should not abandon its allegiance to "unconditional freedom" (its resistance to, "say, technical training and the development of applied knowledge") even as his engagement with the pragmatism of Barbara Herrnstein Smith and Richard Rorty acknowledges that "unconditionality is never entirely possible."²⁸ Theory's role, as Wolfe portrays it, is to function as an antidote to the conditioning power of disciplinary norms, carving out a space for the "unconditional freedom [that] is the *raison d'être* of the university" (even as that *raison* must lie on the other side of any actual *être*). "Professing theory," for Wolfe, thus comes to mean operating counter to the otherwise professionalizing missions of what he repeatedly calls "the corporate university."²⁹ But that it is Derrida who turns out to be the figure who best represents the promise of the "unconditioned" or the antidisciplinary only serves to underscore the degree to which theory has developed not only a curriculum but also a set of protocols as thoroughly codified as those involved in "technical training and the development of applied knowledge." Thus even as both of these accounts seem aimed at complicating the charismatic avant-garde-ism to which high theory seemed prone, there is also a strange conservatism in the persistence of both the oracular figure and the as-yet uncharted land (a renewed new, a different elsewhere) to which that oracle points.³⁰

What we are after is an alternative to *both* the apocalyptic model of radical replacement (where we start brand new) *and* the recursive return to a Derrida or a Hegel (where we simply start over). What's required, we think, is a version of theory that is able to reflect more openly and more substantially on the distribution of intellectual attention at any given moment. Both the apocalyptic and recursive models of theoretical activity effectively linearize the intellectual landscape, such that one can either (which is to say *only*) leap radically forward or restart from the old beginnings. Our wager here is that the resources that are available for thinking are less cut-and-dried than either of these models suggest; we're guessing that it can't be the case that absolutely new (which is what Surin wants) or tried and true (which is how Osborne and Wolfe shape the question) are really the only kinds of names (or thoughts) there are. Because our approach eschews both these forms of the oracular, it's obviously hard for us to "call for" something without seeming hypocritical. But what we're imagining here, and what we think the contributions we've collected exemplify, is a different (more modest and more flexible) attitude toward those things that we have, for whatever reason, set aside or to which we have remained indifferent. We want to be clear, though, that we don't see the drastically unequal distribution of attention as a moral failing. That things look the way they do is, in many cases, simply another sign that attention is necessarily scarce: people are busy; publication is finicky; translation is worse; and just framing a debate one way can—innocently—obscure other intellectual trajectories. Our argument, then, is not that we have been paying attention to the wrong figures. We have had good reason to be interested in the names and debates we all know. But we think that the set of options available to us at any one time are much more extensive than we have been able to appreciate or acknowledge. Grant Farred is right, in this sense, to suggest that we need to "train ourselves . . . to 'linger' over our thoughts, to extend them, to take our time with them."[31] But the question of patience extends not only to those thinkers or thoughts we already know but to those we do not. We're all for a patient reading of Derrida (in case anyone's flown through it). But we also suggest that our patience must become something more systematic, something like a genial skepticism toward the structures of our own attentions. The alternative to the contemporary condition is not, we think, an oracular void waiting to be filled but in fact already comprises the myriad interesting and immediately available details that are thinkers who did not gain instantaneous traction; thoughts that seemed to be without political promise; ideas that, for whatever reason, didn't fit the shape of an already recognized need. This collection does not seek the "unconditioned," in other words, but instead looks to focus more closely on the local possibilities that our desire for sweeping gestures and virgin territories cannot stoop to notice.

We think slowing ourselves down in this way is particularly important when it comes to theoretical concerns. A theoretical canon, we would suggest, is not subject to the same degree of external pressure as, for example, a literary canon. Whereas literature departments (like most humanities departments) respond in part to forms of human activity that take place outside of the academy, a department of theory (if there were such a thing) would respond largely to the forms of thought that it itself had generated. The pressure on a theoretical canon thus is primarily restricted to those who are already participating in it. This is not to say that there hasn't been social pressure on theory. The humanities, for example, have come under attack for teaching feminism, Marxism, deconstruction, Foucault, and so on. But it is telling that the pressure has tended to come in the form of a question about whether we should be "doing theory" at all—as if it were a closed and undifferentiated field—rather than about which theories we should be doing or about the processes that have led us to treat only certain thoughts as capable of standing in for theory in the first place. (Eagleton's dichotomy, between those who do theory and those who merely apply or practice theory, makes clear just how actively theory has operated as a restricted field within the already narrowed world of the academy.) The debates we have had—about Foucauldianism versus Marxism, say, or feminism versus psychoanalysis— are debates that existed for the most part only among theorists themselves and thus took place only among people whose work already fit one of a relatively few available models. Even our fights never really risked a radical numerousness of options. When Frank Kermode (to give a short example) recognized that the theory of canonicity and aesthetic evaluation he had been assembling did not fit any of the available positions in what had blossomed as the "canon wars," he was discovering that even debates (and even debates about canons) produce their own form of tunnel vision.[32] The fact that so many recent articles on theory's future cite Derrida is indicative of how tightly framed theory's own forms of self-reflection remain.[33]

Part of the work undertaken by the essays collected here is to illustrate some of the consequences of such institutional conditions. One essay charts how queer theory came to be hived off from one half of its intellectual roots in sociology. Another looks at the way a theory of voluntary action developed, at least initially, through an investigation of pigeons might impact our accounts of identity and reading alike. What essays like these offer is not another iteration of the oft-repeated call for "more" interdisciplinarity. Rather their goal is to acknowledge that correcting our natural insularity is, inevitably, a never-ending project *and* to provide a historically detailed sense of the options for rethinking any particular, local configuration. Doing this involves not only a form of self-scrutiny that calls our practices to account but an active will to go looking for trouble we didn't know we needed.

It's because we start from this particular set of concerns that we find two recent statements on theory particularly useful. The first, William Rasch's contribution to *Theory After 'Theory,'* argues that theory's job description is not limited to analyzing things that are out there in the world (a state apparatus, a discipline, an institution) but also includes thinking about *itself* as a system operating in the midst of other systems. In one sense, this reflexive, relentlessly contextualizing view lines up with the descriptions of theory offered by Wolfe, Osborne, and Farred, each of whom acknowledges what Wolfe calls theory's constant "conjuncture with forces that are disciplinary, institutional and even . . . 'ideological.'"[34] But where Wolfe's description of theory's "conjuncture with forces" sees theory as a heroic effort to produce unconditioned thought in the midst of contextualizing conditions, Rasch wants us to step outside "the mode of perpetual crisis, the demand [for] more critique, more education, more enlightenment."[35] His concern is that critical theory's proximity to "the battlefield" and "the barricades" may obscure the many ways in which our "various values do not cohere" or the way "norms once harmoniously united now 'tragically' conflict."[36] Such small-scale tensions, conflicts, and incoherencies tend to disappear under the myth-size struggles that dominate theory's storylines (between the now and the future, the thinkable and the unthinkable, the already institutionalized and the not yet available). Rasch's essay helps us see that a properly systemic perspective is not opposed to but in fact requires small-scale observation.

Rasch's call for an immanent description even of theory itself aligns closely with the notion of "working through" to which Rei Terada turns in her essay "The Frailty of the Ontic," the other recent statement about theoretical practice with which we want to note a particular affinity. The psychoanalytic notion of working through offers Terada a view of "the complexity of experience," in which a life appears as "a density that cannot be completely untangled." As opposed to standard "moral philosophy," whose "artificially normative conventions" presort certain phenomena (killing, crying, loving, etc.) as significant while determining other phenomena (the squeak of a bicycle, the sound of water on the roof, a passing smell) "insignificant for action," working through puts no necessary limits on what will get counted as important and what will be relegated to "mere" background. Working through deals with "the interaction of multiple registrations of different perceptions, which meet different degrees of resistance, and also with registrations of various kinds and levels: an internally differentiated, open-ended, always changing, maximally complex network of registrations, each of which potentially changes everything, albeit just a little bit and never necessarily for the good." Like Rasch, who wants a more micrological account of the tensions (or resistances) in our normative frameworks, Terada suggests our psychological and ontological landscapes ought to be credited with a similar complexity. Both views are designed to resist the tendency (a moral philosophical one, in Terada's terms) to simplify the world according to a "typecast" hierarchy of values.[37]

It's been our intention from our first conversations about this project (don't ask how long ago) to put something like the view Rasch and Terada propose into practice as a different way of thinking about both the history and the condition of theory. We were frustrated by the options we saw for thinking about theory's condition only in terms of its life or its death, and we saw in those options a continuation of the zero-sum notion of intellectual progress in which theory had specialized all along (i.e., unprecedented thoughts, emancipatory names).[38] In trying to posit an alternative to the question "What's next for theory?," we asked our contributors to consider alternative intellectual trajectories that may have lain dormant behind the large-scale replacements (structuralism by poststructuralism, feminism by queer theory, agency by ontology) that characterized theory's progress.[39]

Our basic thought was that at any moment of developmental crisis, the course of theory could have broken another way. What, we wanted to know, would some of those options have looked like?

Thinking about that way of framing the project now, one feeling we have is that it probably seems still more susceptible to notions of progress and replacement than we're entirely comfortable with. In defense of our earlier selves, though, we would note that it is just the case that it's very hard to talk about processes and transactions in ways that don't end up feeling like narrative progressions (in which an orphaned theory is returned to its inheritance, say) and that we're okay with that. The effort, this is to say, was not to reject sequence or progress or even "the new"; it was to dilute the hold they had on our intellectual attentions by asking people to move laterally and retroactively, to think specifically about what might already be out there. Because the project is committed to drawing alternative maps, we simply tried to characterize the kind of attitude or perspective we had in mind instead of asking authors to focus on any specific theoretical concern or subfield. And in keeping with that initial impulse, we would stress that the results presented here are necessarily exemplary. These are neither rescue missions (claims for what theory should have been) nor white papers (policy proposals for theory's future). They are, rather, examples of what theoretical work might look like if it bore more programmatic attention to what its own developmental logics leave aside.[40]

The body of the book is divided into three parts: "Chronologies Aside," "Approaches Aside," and "Figures Aside." Each of these is organized around a different valence of the question of aside-ness or adjacency. Part I houses a set of accounts that explicitly examine questions of chronological sequence, currency, nextness, or nowness. As even the titles of *Theory Now* or *Theory After 'Theory'* make abundantly clear, currency and sequence remain built in to the way we frame the very question of theory's condition (not to mention that question's answer). But how long is a moment? How singular is the now? When has the past fallen behind us? Is the future really in front of us?

The volume opens with Eve Kosofsky Sedgwick's previously unpublished essay on the history of homophobia. This piece (originally a paper presented, we think, as a short talk at Amherst) discusses the difficulties of writing alternative histories. Because, as Sedgwick points out, one is necessarily always operating with an already established archive of terms and relations and assumptions, it is not clear that one can simply up and decide to tell a different story or go looking for a hidden ideological history as if discursive operations had all the objective solidity of buried treasure. As best we can

Introduction: On the Side 13

tell, the paper's delivery preceded the publication of *Epistemology of the Closet* (1990), though the problems of archive, exclusion, and occlusion that work engages are clearly visible here in early form. The situation Sedgwick describes—in which one realizes that the knowledge required even to *pose* a historical question exists only in a differently configured knowledge bank—serves as a hallmark of both the challenges of the counterhistorical project we've attempted to undertake here as well as a lesson in the kinds of oblique movements necessary if it is to be undertaken at all.

Where Sedgwick is interested in the difficulty of moving between one archive and another—or even of knowing about the existence of one archive from inside another—Anne-Lise François examines the possibility of moving laterally across or more loosely among cultural objects. Drawing our attention to what she calls the "minimal affirmations" in the late work of Sedgwick, Roland Barthes, and William Empson, François offers a clear-eyed study in both the promises and a certain treacherousness of these open, minimally demanding, and antisuspicious aesthetics. While she finds much to admire in these thoughts, she also offers important considerations about "the place of this accepting, easy mode in a culture (both in the university and beyond) committed to de-skilling labor" and ensuring "the ever-readiness of cultural goods."

Natalie Melas takes up the question of the present as it has been treated (recently and not so recently) in postcolonial theory. While it may be difficult to think of a theoretical field that has devoted more attention to discontinuous, disrupted, and uneven chronologies, Melas argues that many current construals of postcolonial theory continue to rely on "particularly absolute teleological representation[s] of that past." In a remarkable discussion of Ernst Bloch and C. L. R. James, Melas suggests that these stubborn teleologies might be undone by remembering that "epochs are not closed in on themselves with absolute limits" and that "the historical time of modernity" therefore has a "multidirectional aspect" thanks to a "complex interplay between contemporaneity and noncontemporaneity."

Where Melas carefully draws our attention to the complexity of thinking in and of time, Elizabeth Povinelli demonstrates how critical theory's overriding concern with the production and management of life in contemporary liberal society has blockaded attention to the extinguishment of life that is, she argues, a necessary byproduct of forwarding any project. Povinelli asks, "What might the future of critical theory have been if it had distinguished its approach to power from the problem of the repressive forces but nevertheless allowed itself to acknowledge its own acts of altercide and suicide?" Drawing on Spinoza's conception of the *conatus*, Povinelli demonstrates that an ethics that attends both to the production and the extinguishment of life requires "the radical leveling of modes of being." If we are to redress the absence of any discussion of extinguishment in theories of multiplicity, she maintains, then we are going to have to avoid repeating the "generational debate between the repressive and productive hypotheses" and instead develop ethical and political theories that are "on the side of potentiality and yet ha[ve] a relation to the limits of plasticity."

One can immediately see the force of Povinelli's claim—that every advancement entails extinguishment—by considering the number of methodologies that fell to the wayside in a theoretical moment otherwise devoted to detailing the consequences of our methodological suppositions. Theoretical oracularism, in other words, did not simply restrict our attentions to a limited number of thinkers; it also prompted us to prioritize overwhelmingly those methodologies that could present themselves as directly overturning a previous model's common sense. Again the problem with this way of proceeding, as we see it, is that it effectively binarizes the question of method, reducing it to a face-off between those doing the overturning and those maintaining the status quo. The result is the false sense that methods are available in only two forms: the visionary and the blinkered. As a way of un-typecasting this drama, as Terada might put it, part II discusses a set of theoretical frameworks, and views on theoretical frameworks, in which overcoming is not necessarily synonymous with the conception of method.

Simon Jarvis, for instance, describes a "historical poetics" that he finds modeled theoretically in the work of Alexander Veselovsky and Theodor Adorno and practically (i.e., poetically) in the verse of Alexander Pope. For Jarvis, historical poetics ought to greatly expand our sense of what counts as poetic technique and "prosodic intelligence" by allowing us to see any stretch of verse as the product of multiple sets of constraints: "the constraint of making sense in English and the constraints selected by the poet's metrical art" and the vast history of verse practice that helps define the value of any poetic decision. By focusing on how even poetic virtuosity involves, and indeed requires a relationship to an established and evolving field of precedents, Jarvis suggests a model in which neither the development of poetry nor the practice of reading poetry would follow the hard angles of aesthetic or theoretical rupture.

Pheng Cheah criticizes the way our accounts of power have so often restricted themselves to seeing it as either "conferring or withholding . . . recognition in social relations." For Cheah, the recognition model offered by people like Judith Butler and others mistakenly slants our understanding of Foucault's notion of biopower in two directions: first, it orients us primarily toward questions of "the intersubjective constitution of consciousness" and, second, it causes power to seem to operate according to exclusively "prohibitive and repressive" models. Drawing on the considerable resources made available by the United Nations work on the material processes of globalization, Cheah argues that "the female subjects of globalization" can help us "come to terms with power's physical dimension." Doing so, Cheah argues, is essential since "we cannot adequately explain the tenaciousness of global capitalism or hope to resist it if we cling to the dogma that oppression primarily operates through forms of consciousness."

This focus on physical embodiment, on a resolutely material view of the human subject, also features in Irene Tucker's revisionary account of the history of racialized skin. Tucker returns to Kant's writing on race to argue to argue that racialized skin might serve an important philosophical, epistemological, and, above all, universalizing function. The hold the deconstructive or semiotic account of race has had on our thinking—under the grip of which we constantly remind ourselves that skin color is an empty signifier—has, Tucker argues, obscured an older vision in which a "race without racism" served to "announce a universal aspiration to a likeness that would allow us to escape the privation of our finitude as individual subjects."

Like Tucker's intervention in the history of our thinking about race, Jordan Stein also asks us to return us to an earlier moment to look at the way a single effort crystallized into two apparently opposed discourses. For Stein, the long-standing opposition in the study of African American culture between interpretive and bibliographic modes of study has truncated the possibility of our "learning from scholars working in cognate modes." Drawing our attention back to some of the early architects of African American studies whose work exhibited a "methodological pluralism," Stein argues that we would do well not to look for the "next big thing" but, more modestly, to encourage "disciplinary wholeness."

The kind of rapprochement Stein is proposing between the interpretive and the bibliographic arms of African American literary studies finds a parallel in Karen Beckman's suggestion that "the introduction of animation as a primary topic of concern for the discourse of film theory will not simply add new material . . . [but will] help to catalyze full-scale conceptual reorganizations." Long a neglected question in media studies (which preferred to specialize in "film"), animation not only offers a "a useful lens" for considering older work but, Beckman argues, is an increasingly important category in the contemporary digital context, whose "use of compositing and the frequent absence of continuous shooting threaten to jeopardize some of the central traits we associate with a cinema that defines itself in opposition to animation."

Part III takes up the case of specific figures who in various ways lay athwart (or beneath) the mainline of theory's development. William Flesch's discussion of George Ainslie's theory of hyperbolic discounting and intertemporal bargaining offers a relatively unknown but enormously useful vision of mental life, desire, and subjectivity. A variety of factors may have contributed to keeping Ainslie out of the light of theoretical attention, among them, the authority that psychoanalytic criticism already enjoyed on such questions and a prejudice in the humanities against what are perceived to be the "usually reductive and cheerless explanatory systems based on economics and experimental theory." But Ainslie's work is, Flesch contends, "as challenging, important, exciting, provocative, powerful, and far-reaching as anything you'll find in literary theory over the past two decades," and his account shows how Ainslie's theories of risk and reward, desire, and psychological bargaining might offer insight into both our literary and our intersubjective experiences.

If Flesch's essay shows how the devotion of our collective attentions to one current line of theoretical thought obscures our ability to recognize other valuable modes of inquiry (even those operating on the same general theoretical terrain), then Mark Hansen's essay provides an important case study for why we should be careful not to archive the thoughts of thinkers who seemed untimely in their own day. Hansen exploits the "unrealized potential" of Whitehead's metaphysics for current discussions of sensation and twenty-first-century media studies. Hansen radicalizes Whitehead's model of perception by reading it in the context of psychophysics, a move that allows him (in combination with a reading of Merleau-Ponty) to chart an alternative to post-Kantian philosophy that avoids integrating "sensation into higher-order forms of experience and/or linguistic or conceptual analysis." This theoretical rearrangement makes it possible for Hansen to address the twenty-first century as a time in which sensation is not exclusively phenomenological (taking place in human bodies). Rather he argues that the advent of digital devices and other new media technologies "comprises both an intensification of our properly human sensibility and an expansion of the domain of worldly sensibility" such that we can now capture and begin to understand the "extraperceptual" dimension of experience.

Hansen's interest in a notion of "generalized sensibility" informs the sociological focus of the final two essays in the collection. Heather Love argues that the shape of sexuality studies today reflects a "divide between the humanities and the social sciences," but that this divide "has not always been as strong as it now is." For Love, the work of Gayle Rubin and particularly Erving Goffman shows us how intertwined the humanities and social science genealogies of queer studies already are. In Goffman's work on stigma, Love finds a method that is "attentive to questions of mediating without losing track of the world, self-reflexive without turning in on itself entirely." She follows the legacy of Goffman's "descriptive, observational method" through the work of Philip Toynbee and Laud Humphreys and out into contemporary queer studies. Her claim is that these approaches, which combine the analytic procedures of close reading with the observational practices of postwar microsociology, not only offer queer studies methodological lessons for handling the "partial identifications" that take place through "quasi-universal and flexible categories" but also open up the possibility of forging "crucial alliances" between disciplines that have for too long seen themselves opposed.

Frances Ferguson's essay takes up questions of communication and agreement as they are made conspicuous (or conspicuously absent) in the sociological experiment in verbal behavior that was I. A. Richards's *Practical Criticism* (the compiled results of Richards's having asked students to respond to poems with no preparation or even the help of knowing the author's name). For Ferguson, the value of Richards's approach is that it steers us away from the sense that "reading literature [involves] signing a contractual agreement about what one would and would not notice." Unlike the bulk of the past half century of criticism, which has, Ferguson argues, organized itself around attaining agreement, the responses Richards collects from his students show just how unstable and variable our readings are, how often they differ from the readings of others, and how much variance there can be between even a single person's reading at different times. Richards's insight, as Ferguson describes it, was not only that psychology could not be separated from reading, but that, for just this reason, criticism had built into itself a tool for "tracking the fluctuating values of human behavior, including linguistic and literary behavior." In Ferguson's view, criticism thus comes to count as a "strongly ethical" activity insofar as its ability to keep tabs on the fluctuations in our responses to language and literature gives us the possibility of responding seriously to our own (and others') responses.

Taken as a whole, these essays demonstrate an orientation toward theoretical inquiry that is capable of opening up problems and conversations without having to insist that intellectual progress must always come at the cost of jettisoning our older ways of seeing. There is no doubt that the essays collected here are deeply ambitious: they address large, complicated categories (e.g., sensation, race, power, contemporaneity) and they take up thorny institutional and methodological questions (about poetics, close reading, bibliography, and the relations between academic disciplines). At the same time, though, each of these essays asks us to consider (and often to consider softening) the rigidity with which we have tended to frame intellectual work as a ceaselessly oppositional struggle. What stands out to us upon reading through these essays once more is their remarkable absence of insistence, their ability to offer alternatives without having to discover error at every turn.

We would be willing to see these collected essays as an attempt to make good on the desire Elliott and Attridge express for a theory that could do away with oracular figures. The truth, though, is that the oracular remains an occupational hazard even when one works hard to minimize its lures. It's certainly true, for instance, that many of these essays offer up a new lens for an old issue or focus on a thinker whose perspective seems valuable precisely because it allows us to move through some conceptual static in a way that can't help but feel like linear progress. As one essay puts it, "The only way through such difficulties is forward." Or, as we would put it, *any way through some difficulty is bound to feel like forward*.

But in feeling our way forward, we need not follow the editors of *The Structuralist Controversy*, who, when faced with "the exigencies of [their] present intellectual conjuncture," went directly after the "old sureties." We think the old sureties aren't that sure—and some aren't even that old. The shape of our attentions is neither consistent nor given, and it's only by radically limiting its range that we've been able to divine the before from the after, the obsolete from the current, or the tired surety from the trying exigency.[41] What the *Structuralist Controversy* editors did not foresee was the way their construal of the present as a "conjuncture"—as an ongoing collision between the old and the immediate, the before and the after—would itself generate the "systematic reference point[s]" around which "successive conceptual webs" get organized. One can see why one might want, as they did, to replace a Hegel who could center "conceptual webs" with "a conceptual system which aspires to be without center, without origin, or without end." But it would have been hard to see, only three years after the original conference, that the very figures (Derrida, Foucault, and Deleuze) who had transubstantiated Hegel from a center to a specter (who "still haunts us") would themselves shortly recenter our attentions.[42] Even harder to foresee would have been the

Introduction: On the Side   19

speed with which many of the participants in one of Theory's original "controvers[ies]" would themselves disappear from critical attention in relatively short order. "No symposium," said Richard Macksey, quoting Jean Hippolite's concluding remarks, "without its shadow." But shadows, in fact, stretch out far past those cast by the immediate light of the symposium. As the participant list makes clear, even many of those who contributed to the symposium are no longer familiar names. Looking back, we find that *The Structuralist Controversy* has as much to say about how our critical attentions inevitably become organized around certain figures—and just as inevitably transmute others into shadows—as it does about the status of the subject.[43]

In this sense, what *Theory Aside* proposes is not just a return to one of the animating principles of the structuralist controversy—that there are no structures without shadows—but a model for how we might keep this fact as a more constant presence in our intellectual work. The goal here is not to resurrect the theoretical past entire or to remake the theoretical present around the next big idea. The effort is rather to lay out a version of intellectual development that, by being willing to proceed less dramatically, less linearly, and less oligarchically, might also be able to reflect on its own inevitable blind spots more thoroughly and more patiently. Such a practice may, at bottom, require making more modest claims. And if it didn't seem so strangely self-canceling, we'd say that modest claims are exactly what this moment in critical history requires. Actually, we'll say it anyway.

Notes

1. Elliott and Attridge, "Introduction," 3.
2. Surin, "Introduction," 5
3. Eagleton, *After Theory*, 1.
4. For a discussion of the relations between theory's intellectual avant-garde-ism and the publishing industry's commodification, see Osborne, "Philosophy after Theory." For an account of the star system, see David Shumway, "The Star System in Literary Studies," PMLA 112 (January 1997): 85–100.
5. Elliott and Attridge, "Introduction," 4, 14.
6. Cultural theory, of course, is not the only institution that has sought to conceive itself almost entirely as a set of paradigm shifts. The desire to rethink from the ground up—to be a disruptive technology—is ubiquitous, visible in everything from TED Talks to think tanks like the Breakthrough Institute, which is set up to be something like an incubator for unprecedentedness. The Breakthrough Institute's mission was born out of a familiar sense of formal exhaustion—"We believe that today's political dysfunction reflects the exhaustion of older paradigms"—and offers an entirely formal rejuvenation:

"paradigm-shifting research and writing" that is "by its nature unpopular among the powerful defenders of the status quo." We would like to take our distance from this incessantly renovating Zeitgeist. We are, to be clear, not opposed to new ideas (or even transformations!), but we would also say that there is something particularly (and paradoxically) reductive in imagining that the world is neatly divided into "powerful defenders of status quos" and disruptive "paradigm shifters" or that one can immediately identify those thoughts that would (or would not) shift paradigms on inception. The institute's website is www.thebreakthrough.org (accessed 9 November 2012).

7. If the threat of obsolescence seems an unavoidable consequence of an insistence on academic progress (all ideas have shelf lives), in other words, it is important to see that Theory not only accelerated these normal operating conditions but, in its more or less serial replacements of one school by the next, acted as the agent of its own foreshortening. From this perspective, the steep curve of Theory's rise and the sharp curve of its dramatic obsolescence give Theory's narrative a storybook symmetry that is not at all accidental. It is rather an important reflection of the way a sense of an ending has been intrinsic to Theory's operations from its very beginning. In this light we might associate the theoretical moment less with a set of thinkers who share a method, however abstract, and more with the substitutive process by which one critical method replaces another.

8. For accounts of theory's decreasing energy, see Bruno Latour, "Why Has Critique Run out of Steam? From Matters of Fact to Matters of Concern," *Critical Inquiry* (2004): 225–48; Eagleton, *After Theory*; Jeffrey Williams, "The Death of Deconstruction, the End of Theory, and Other Ominous Rumors," *Narrative* 4.1 (1996): 17–35. Our thinking about how canons organize attention has been helped a lot by Jonathan Arac's study *Huckleberry Finn as Idol and Target* (Madison: University of Wisconsin Press, 1997), especially chapter 6, "Nationalism and Hypercanonization."

9. For a suggestion of Theory's increasing political quiescence, see one of the organizing propositions to which participants in *Critical Inquiry*'s symposium "The Future of Literary Criticism" were asked to respond: "It has been suggested that theory now has backed off from its earlier sociopolitical engagements and its sense of revolutionary possibility and has undergone a 'therapeutic turn' to concerns with ethics, aesthetics, and care of the self, a turn of which Lacan is the major theoretical symptom. True?" See Mitchell, "Medium Theory," 330. For the connection between Theory and employability, see Michael F. Berubé, *Theory, Jobs, and the Future of Literary Studies* (New York: New York University Press, 1997).

10. Maybe we will have to find new modes of proceeding anyway. The recent, and quite literally geographic, scaling-up of theoretical inquiry—from the national to the transnational to the planetary—does not seem as if it can continue forever. Barring something like interstellar theory, it seems inevitable that theoretical discourse will have to allow itself to undergo something like an inward turn. In this sense we will all be doing sustainability theory. For a recent set of considerations very congenial to our suggestions here, see Halberstam, *The Queer Art of Failure*, in particular her introduction "Low Theory" (1–25). Actually, we had hoped to include an essay by Halberstam, but, because of scheduling, it didn't work out. We remain supportive of her suggestion in the introduction to *The Queer Art of Failure* that theory might be reimagined as "an ambulatory journey though the unplanned, the unexpected, the improvised, and the surprising"

(15–16) and that such a project might entail looking below (for Halberstam) or beside (for us) not just High Theorists but the readily available models of what it means to have theoretical aspirations in the first place. Obviously, though, lowness and beside-ness aren't exactly synonymous. Our concern with the former would have to do with the way "low theory," by necessarily existing in direct opposition to some high theory, would also remain attached to the insurrectionist, all-or-nothing narratives of wholesale world-remaking that have come to define the theoretical almost entirely. So, if it were up to us, we'd put less weight on the oppositional notion of a "counterhegemonic form of theorizing," which doesn't in the end seem so "unscripted," and more on what Halberstam describes as the project of theorizing "alternatives within an undisciplined zone of knowledge production" (18). That last bit we like a lot.

11. As with the passing of any public and controversial figure, the depth of these sentiments may serve simply to measure Theory's social and intellectual importance over the second half of the twentieth century. To be sure, it is not every death that is covered (on several occasions) by the *New York Times*. See, for instance, Dan Edelstein, "Is Theory Dead?," *Republics of Letters*, 22 February 2009; Jennifer Howard, "The Fragmentation of Literary Theory," *Chronicle of Higher Education*, 16 December 2005; Stephen Metcalf, "The Death of Literary Theory: Is It Really a Good Thing?" *Slate*, 17 November 2005 (accessed 1 December 2011); Michael Cook, "The Death of Theory," *Salvo*, 12 August 2005; David Kirby, "Theory in Chaos," *Christian Science Monitor*, 27 January 2004; Dinitia Smith, "Cultural Theorists, Start Your Epitaphs," *New York Times*, 3 January 2004; Emily Eakin, "The Latest Theory Is That Theory Doesn't Matter," *New York Times*, 19 April 2003.

12. Mitchell, "Medium Theory," 324, 328, 332.

13. An MLA search for "medium theory" brings up no responses related to anything but media. A Google search brings up a limited number of responses to Mitchell's use of the term, but many of these citations come from Mitchell's own subsequent writing. The remainder deals almost exclusively with media in the technological sense, something that Mitchell certainly had in mind, but not something he'd imagined as the exclusive sense of the term. What's gotten lost in the move from medium to media, this is to say, is the emphasis on patience, modesty, and longer intellectual *durées* that he also meant to encourage. It's possible, of course, that people are doing medium theory so modestly, so mediumly, that they aren't even explicitly announcing it, but one might still expect to be able to trace these contributions a little more definitively in the literature on the current state of theory. Perhaps, though, things will still pick up for the sort of moderated stances Mitchell suggests. Stefan Helmreich, "What Was Life: Answers from Three Limit Biologies," *Critical Inquiry* 37.4 (2011): 696n72, for instance, in a gesture with which we very much agree, positions Mitchell's medium theory and "its calibration to moderate claims" against the "one foot after the other" form of intellectual progress modeled in *Theory After 'Theory'* and the "Theory Now" special issue of *South Atlantic Quarterly*.

14. Mitchell, "Medium Theory," 335.

15. Pattai and Corral, introduction, 3, 13, 14. The obfuscations the editors associate with Theory can now, they argue, be "replace[d]" by the presumably more durable virtues of "open discussion and logical argumentation" (7). In this sense, the unobjectionable and, at heart, salutary position from which *Theory's Empire* begins—that the unthoughtful application of Theory produces rote interpretations of objects governed by "the now-predictable categories of race, class, gender, and, later, sexuality" (8)—underwrites a

much more radical and conservative return to an earlier model of criticism's practice and aims. So while the editors disavow explicitly a retreat to "an ideal past (nonexistent, in any case) of literary studies" (7), they nevertheless second Frank Kermode's suggestion that we return to an earlier literary criticism that not only "could be taught" but, since it is "an influence for civilization and personal amendment," should be taught (9). The overriding hope, then, is for a future freed from the "textual harassment" (in the phrase Pattai and Corral quote from Howard Felperin) that "transmogrif[ies literature] into a cultural artifact" (8).

16. While we obviously disagree with Pattai and Corral's desire for a world without theory, we do find value in their claim that the canonization of theory wound up discarding ideas and texts that still had value. They note in particular "the exclusion of Schlovsky, Empson, Trilling and Steiner" as well as "Booth, Abrams, Ellis, Tallis and Vickers" from the Norton Anthology of Theory and Criticism. It would be interesting to do a short survey of graduate students and junior faculty to discover just how faint (or not) are the bells that these names ring.

17. Culler, for instance, cites queer theory as just one of theory's modes that continues to develop in interesting directions and notes that others, like narratology, have been revived under a new interest in cognitive-scientific approaches. See Culler, "Afterword," 223–24.

18. Eagleton, After Theory, 2.

19. Culler, "Afterword," 224.

20. Eagleton, After Theory, 2.

21. Culler, "Afterword," 224.

22. Surin, "Introduction," 7, 17.

23. Hardt, "The Militancy of Theory," 19, 33.

24. Colebrook, "Extinct Theory" 69, 70.

25. Eagleton, After Theory, 2.

26. It's important for us to point out that our problem with this radical-replacement model is not merely a kind of radicalism fatigue; it is that we are now almost programmed (by this very model) to want something else (as though theory were fashion). For a recent account of theory's radicalism fatigue, see Rey Chow, "When Reflexivity Becomes Porn: Mutations of a Modernist Theoretical Practice," in Elliott and Attridge, Theory After 'Theory,' 135–48. For Chow, this constant effort to strip the world down takes on a hollow, serialized violence she identifies as pornographic. We wouldn't put the complaint quite this way. Insofar as the forms of world-refusing we see in Hardt and Colebrook are driven by a demand for things to be otherwise, it may well be that what Chow sees as theory's "moralistic and chic" (146) negativity is a kind of optimism. Our concern, however, is that this optimism can take only one form: the destruction of this world in favor of another, the heralding of a thought not yet possible as opposed to a thought already thunk, and a commitment to a mode of futurity predicated on a confidence (one we do not share) that the present we are rejecting was the only one we could have had. The essays collected in part I of the present volume take up these questions of chronology, sequence, simultaneity, and so on.

27. Osborne, "Philosophy after Theory," 29–30.

28. Wolfe, "Theory as a Research Program," 46. Wolfe's focus on the inevitable disciplinarity of all intellectual work parallels closely Grant Farred's recent argument against

any form of interdisciplinarity that imagines it can simply transcend the category of disciplines. "It would be difficult," Farred writes, "to say that we have 'withdrawn' from the discipline. . . . We must, instead . . . acknowledge that it is the discipline . . . that compels us to think" ("'Science Does Not Think,'" 73).

29. Wolfe, "Theory as a Research Program," 46, 47.

30. On this point we might note that Pheng Cheah originally planned to write an essay for this volume on whether there was a linguistic turn. Cheah's thought was that the representation-discursive turn of late twentieth-century theory was not a given (and indeed that it fit awkwardly alongside its more general critique of the human). Among the ideas that might emerge if we were to care less about language, Cheah suggested, was a nondiscursive account of force (as opposed to power). We think it sounds like a great essay and are still looking forward to reading it.

31. Farred, "'Science Does Not Think,'" 73.

32. Frank Kermode's history of his own attempts to insert his thoughts on literary value into what had taken shape as the canon wars can be found at the beginning of *An Appetite for Poetry* (Cambridge: Harvard University Press, 1989). His description reads, in part:

> For quite a long time I had been thinking about the literary canon, its intellectual and institutional status, finding the whole issue to be far more complicated than anybody seemed to have supposed. I presented a brief paper on the subject to the Modern Language Association meeting of 1974, and developed the theme in a lecture of 1978; both are included in *The Art of Telling*. But before that book appeared the topic of canon had quite spontaneously risen to somewhere near the top of the theoretical agenda. A whole issue of *Critical Inquiry*, later published in augmented form as a book, was dedicated to the problem. W. J. T. Mitchell, the editor of the journal, told me he had not planned such an issue, that the contributions had simply arrived on his desk, as if the existence of the topic, and its contentiousness, had mysteriously and simultaneously declared itself everywhere and to everybody. In fact there is no real mystery, for the transfer of attention from works of literature to modes of signification, a transfer required by most modern critical theory, was bound to raise the question of literary value. (2)

33. In addition to Wolfe and Farred, see, for instance, Michael Naas, "'Now Smile': Recent Developments in Jacques Derrida's Work on Photography," *South Atlantic Quarterly* 110.1 (2011): 205–22; Martin Hägglund, "The Arche-Materiality of Time: Deconstruction, Evolution and Speculative Materialism," in Elliott and Attridge, *Theory After 'Theory,'* 265–77.

34. Wolfe, "Theory as a Research Program," 35.

35. Rasch, "Theory after Critical Theory," 58. In Farred's account this is described as thought's movement *through* a discipline ("'Science Does Not Think,'" 73).

36. Rasch, "Theory after Critical Theory," 58, 57.

37. Terada, "The Frailty of the Ontic," 43, 44.

38. It thus may go without saying that the prospect in which theory lives and then dies and then lives again (ad infinitum)—what the subtitle of Elliott and Attridge's introduction calls "theory's nine lives," for instance—doesn't, for us, really alter the picture.

39. Another part of our original thought was that the essays should be relatively shorter. We thought that aiming for briefer intellectual excursions (compared to the relatively standardized length of academic articles of eight thousand to ten thousand words) would allow for more people to participate in the project, to free people up to be more provisional, and to press them a little to trust that some other hands might be able to carry the idea forward. Some of the essays that came back are shorter than others, but even if they had all come back at five thousand words (our original advice), it may be that we were misguided for ever having suggested length limits. Even provisional thoughts sometimes require lots of parts (just as it's true that revolutionary, sea-changing thoughts sometimes get away with too few words). Probably, though, there's still room to think about how our publication conventions push us toward projects that often aspire to air-tightness and that can be easily attached to single authors.

40. It's for this reason that we are grateful to each of our contributors for their willingness to participate in the experiment, and especially to our editor, Courtney Berger, and the readers at Duke University Press, for forwarding a theoretical project that doesn't look (and may often fail to sound) like what we normally value in our theoretical projects.

41. See Macksey and Donato, "The Space Between," xix, xiii.

42. Macksey and Donato, "The Space Between," ix, xii.

43. Macksey, Girard, and Hyppolite, "Concluding Remarks," 319, 320.

PART I *chronologies aside*

chapter 1

Writing the History of Homophobia

Eve Kosofsky Sedgwick

I'd like to begin with a story that has no homosexual content at all. A few weeks ago I was reading Proust—which is pretty much a chronic condition with me—and I got to a particular volume where the narrative about French turn-of-the-century high society happens to be structured around the Dreyfus case. Now, all I really knew about the Dreyfus case was extremely general: I knew it was a political explosion that made Watergate look like a quilting bee and that for about half a decade, as a result of it, the issue of anti-Semitism was the issue, in some respects the most bitter issue ever in French politics and public life. But I decided that it would be worth learning a little more, so I got up and headed for the bookcase and looked up Dreyfus in my 1945 *Encyclopedia Britannica*—and sure enough, there he was, with several pages explaining all the details of the case, all the historical background, all the evidence forged and authentic, all the dramatis personae, all the legal technicalities of his various appeals, all the consequences for the rise and fall of governments. There was only one thing that wasn't mentioned in the *Britannica* article, and that was the small matter that Dreyfus was Jewish and that this probably had some effect on his fate and the importance of his case.

I still don't know what to make of this. It isn't as though the *Britannica* exactly *suppresses* the Jewish dimension of the Dreyfus case: when you look up "anti-Semitism," you find pages about the importance of the Dreyfus case in crystallizing nineteenth-century attitudes toward Jews. But you have to know enough to look up "anti-Semitism"; that is to say, you can learn what's most important about Dreyfus from the *Britannica*, but first you have to know something about Dreyfus that you can't learn by looking up "Dreyfus" in the *Britannica*. The information's there, in a sense, but it's compartmentalized in such a way that you have to already know it in order to learn it.

Okay, here's a more obviously relevant story. Imagine that you're a kid of fourteen or fifteen, you read around a lot, and you've come across a reference somewhere that convinces you that there was some kind of interesting mystery about someone named Oscar Wilde. So, of course, you head for your trusty old *Britannica*. And sure enough, you learn there *was* a scandal about Wilde. The *Britannica* says, "His success as a dramatist had by [1894] gone some way to disabuse hostile critics of the suspicions as regards his personal character which had been excited by the apparent looseness of morals which since his Oxford days it had always pleased him to affect; but to the consternation of his friends, who had ceased to credit the existence of any real moral obliquity, in 1895 came fatal revelations as the result of his bringing a libel action against the Marquis of Queensberry; and at the Old Bailey, in May, Wilde was sentenced to two years imprisonment with hard labour for offenses under the Criminal Law Amendment Act."

Huh? What did Wilde *do*, you ask your fourteen-year-old self. "Looseness of morals," "moral obliquity," "fatal revelations," "offenses under the Criminal Law Amendment Act": if you already know that Wilde's crime was to be gay, then you'll know from these phrases that Wilde's crime was to be gay. If you don't already know it, you certainly aren't going to learn it here. What do you need to look under to learn the truth? Well, I haven't figured that out yet. You might, supposing you already know enough to, look under "homosexuality." But there is no entry for homosexuality. "Homophobia," which was the real reason Wilde went to prison? Don't be silly—there's nothing under "homophobia." Shall we try "lesbian"? No entry for "lesbian." Sex? You can look up sex, but all you'll find is "sexual reproduction," which doesn't include nonreproductive sex and which, in any case, seems, rather remarkably, to be practiced only among the lower animals.

On the other hand, we know that the *Britannica* has not made a systematic policy decision that the word *homosexuality* will never darken its pages. It so happens that if you look up Proust himself, for instance, you learn that homosexuality is one of his characteristic subjects. And, supposing that the treatment of Dreyfus is at all analogous (which it may or may *not* be), it is altogether possible that somewhere else in *Britannica*, if only you could hit on the exactly right word to look it up under, pages and pages of state-of-the-art information (circa 1933) on homosexuality and homophobia are just waiting to reveal themselves to you. But where?

I mention the *Britannica* problem, first because it's an excellent example of the practical difficulties of learning anything about sexual mores from any historical distance—and here the distance is only forty years! But the second reason I mention it is as an *emblem* of the extremely elusive and maddeningly plural ways in which cultures and their various institutions efface and alter sexual meaning. The Britannica—which, after all, is only a single institution, although a large and complicated one—does not have a single strategy for dealing with the subject of homosexuality; its tactics range from apparent candor (in the case of Proust's work), to opaque technicalities ("offense under the Criminal Law Amendment Act"), to euphemism ("suspicions as to his personal character"), to overt condemnation ("moral obliquity"), to a general reluctance to raise the issue where not absolutely forced to (see, for instance, on Whitman), to the blanket denial (see the missing article on "homosexuality"—if you can find it). As with the Dreyfus case too, the even more misleading techniques of displacement, compartmentalization, and false categorization are common in discourse about homosexuality.

The consequences of all this are in a certain sense very simple. The Britannica reader who most urgently needs to know about homosexuality—the young precocious reader, say, who is struggling to make sense of her or his emergent desires and identity—cannot get any of the information that encyclopedias are there to provide. The history, the biology, the sociology, the literature, the multiple and rich biography of homosexuality are all, alike, simply unavailable when needed. That is, the effect of the multiple techniques is singly and simply repressive and homophobic. Or if we are using the Britannica as an emblem, we should say that, at least for Western society of the past two millennia, the many complicated paths by which, as I have said, sexual meaning is falsified, denied, and altered all lead homosexuals to much the same thorny and difficult place.

On the other hand, the multiplicity of the different repressive techniques is itself very consequential, even when it does not change the brute fact of repression. In the Britannica, the effect of all those *different* paths, different codes, for denying or distorting the fact of homosexuality is to make it extraordinarily difficult to translate *back* from the encoded form to the actual truth. Even when we know—as the fourteen-year-old we've imagined does not know—that what we are reading is falsified and encoded, breaking the code in one place does not necessarily get us anywhere with the others. Even once we understand the particular kinds of evasion at work in the Wilde article, we cannot count on using the same decoding techniques for the Sappho article or those again for the Whitman article. And none of these tells us what to think about the missing homosexuality article: what unlikely name to look for it under or whether we're crazy to imagine that it might be in there at all.

I know this is an oblique angle from which to approach the history of homophobia. But then, obliquity—if not "moral" obliquity—is the name of the game here, or one of the names of the game. It is so urgent to use all the *various* means at our command, right now, to reconstitute the effaced history of homophobic meaning, so that we can begin to understand who *we* are and what we can do about changing it. It isn't by accident that I made the emblematic researcher in my little parable not an adult historian but an adolescent whose sense of her or his own sexual and social meaning is rapidly crystallizing in response to whatever appears or doesn't appear in the authoritative books of the culture. And note that I haven't specified whether the nascent sexuality of the adolescent will be gay or straight. It doesn't matter: whichever it is, in a homophobic culture it will be structured in relation to the effacements and misappropriations of homophobia.

But let's assume that that reader, five years later, is you. The sheet I've passed around will give you a more concrete start: it's a *very* selective, *very* idiosyncratic annotated bibliography for those of you who are interested in looking further into this history.[1]

Let me end, also, with a brief list of somewhat more practical applications of the points I've suggested in emblematic form already:

1. You can't study the history of homosexuality without studying the history of homophobia, but the two histories are not the same, and their relation is not consistent. They intertwine as inextricably and as unpredictably as Jewish history with the history of anti-Semitism, or as black history with the history of racism.
2. As I've suggested, you can't study the history of sexuality, either, or of gender, without studying the history of homophobia, but with the same cautions.
3. You can't understand homophobia except through the historical specificity of the institutions through which it is articulated and enforced, but its relation to those institutions is not historically constant. For instance, you cannot trace homophobia without tracing the criminal, civil, or religious law as it concerns homosexuality, but you can never translate directly back from the law to the truth of attitudes or practice, either. The same law, mediated differently through different institutional and ideological systems of enforcement and self-enforcement, for instance, could belong to diametrically different sexual cultures.
4. Because of this, the realities of social stratification and economic and ideological control can never be absent from the historiography of homophobia. The social fractures of class, race, and age, as well as gen-

der, will intersect every issue of sexual preference, and often with a surprisingly definitive force.
5. A corollary: the historiography of homophobia about women and that about men are importantly different projects—though, again, inextricable ones.

The only way I can end is by inviting you into this project—or further into it, for those many of you who have already started to find your way through the tortuous paths of the *Britannica*, and the culture in general, to a more accurate picture of sexual meaning. And of course, wishing you good luck. Let me know if you find out what name the real information is filed under.

Note

1. Unfortunately the text of the bibliography that Sedgwick mentions here has not been located among her papers. The editors have left the original text unaltered and thank Hal Sedgwick and Jonathan Goldberg for making its publication possible.

chapter 2

Late Exercises in Minimal Affirmatives

Anne-Lise François

I

Beside is an interesting preposition . . . because there's nothing very dualistic about it; a number of elements may lie alongside one another, though not an infinity of them.
—Eve Kosofsky Sedgwick, *Touching Feeling*

Le haïku a cette propriété quelque peu fantasmagorique, que l'on s'imagine toujours pouvoir en faire soi-même facilement. [The haiku has this rather phantasmagorical property: that we always suppose we ourselves can write such things easily.]
—Roland Barthes, *L'Empire des signes*

There is room for an amateur to say something about Buddha faces. . . . Anyone who cares about the Lord Buddha can do his face in a few ignorant strokes on sand or blotting paper.
—William Empson, "The Faces of Buddha"

So in his brief 1936 essay "The Faces of Buddha," Empson asserts the adequation of human powers to their otherwise distant object, making or, rather, letting drop the claim with the same complaisance it describes: "anyone," "a few strokes," on whatever happens to be within reach ("paper" or the "sand" at one's feet). The little demanded of the artist, technique, and medium is already Buddha-like in its contented resignation and generous *laissez-aller*, as if the best (kindest) judge of his representations or interpretations were the Buddha himself, whose "face is at once blind and all-seeing ('he knows no more than a Buddha,' they say of a deceived husband in the Far East), so at once sufficient to itself and of universal charity."[1]

Little more than a willingness to put *x* at one's disposal, the undemanding generousness or self-sufficient charity that Empson's remark both describes and models has more recent relatives in the turn away from agonistic critique we see in the late work of figures as different as Barthes and Sedgwick. In this essay I take the "aside" of *Theory Aside* tropologically rather than thematically to designate not the marginalized, minor figures left to the side by theory's more well-known and spectacular controversies but the lateral movement by which in their late work Barthes and Sedgwick set aside the burden of discontented, perfective energies and leave off prying, suspicious efforts to uncover concealed truth. They prefer instead a form of aesthetic engagement that moves laterally, arranging its materials side by side, with something of Empson's offhand casualness.[2]

If this move aside from interpretive struggles in the name of a quieter sense of adequacy seems salutary, I want to use this essay not only to describe these lateral moves but to ask about what it means to read Barthes's and Sedgwick's minimal affirmatives—their vindications of a right to demand little—in the context of today's double discourse of scarce resources and limitless demands. One might well ask whether the lateral move enacted by Barthes and Sedgwick constitutes a true alternative to the forms of critical mastery they decry. By their own admission, the side-stepping they perform does not so much offer a cognitive solution to theoretical impasse as simply change its affective register, according to a movement that closely resembles the suddenly found "rest" (*ataraxia*, freedom from disturbance) that in classical skepticism follows from the skeptic's suspension of judgment. My aim is not to polemicize or challenge an affective mode that abjures polemic, for how can one argue with a summons to take it or leave it? Rather I'd like to raise the question about the place of this accepting, easy mode in a culture (both in the university and beyond) committed to de-skilling labor anywhere it can and to ensuring, at the cost of enormous energy resources, the ever-readiness of cultural goods.

Empson's assertion of easy "doability" occurs in the context of his attempt to work out his sense of the contradictions held together by what he calls the "after-dinner look of many Buddhas, and the rings of fat on the neck"; these contradictions include the power to help in what seems closed in on itself and oblivious to the world and the surprising capacity for sensual satisfaction permitted by an ethic commonly understood as renouncing sensuous desire: "An idea that you must be somehow satisfied as well as mortified before entering repose goes deep into the system, and perhaps into human life. . . . The drooping eyelids of the great creatures are heavy with patience and suffering, and the subtle irony which offends us in their raised eyebrows . . . is in effect an appeal to us to feel, as they do, that it is odd that we let our desires subject us to so much torment in the world. The first thing to say about the Buddha face . . . is that the smile of superiority can mean and be felt to mean simply the power to help."[3]

Quoting from his unpublished manuscript notes ("The normal late Buddha's lips of course are the plump but sharply defined lips of a full and well-organized satisfaction"), Sharon Cameron similarly emphasizes the oddly worldly nature of such achieved repose: "The Buddha visage is enigmatic because, against type, the Buddha has surrendered not desire as such, but rather the pain of its torment. His expression is an antidote to the singular appearances of desire requiring management."[4] As Cameron's paraphrase suggests, the look of mild amusement mixed with regret and surprise at the fuss that Empson finds on the Buddha faces eludes the familiar critique of the pursuit of desire such as that found in Christian asceticism; at stake is not so much desire itself as the aggressiveness of our attempts to secure ourselves from its transience.

If we could distinguish desire from the will to seize (*vouloir saisir*), we might not in the first place have to conceive of it as something requiring "management," sacrifice, or renunciation; such might be the thesis behind the impossible project of Barthes's 1977–78 seminar Le Neutre. There too, drawing on sources found in the parental library, he avails himself of Zen Buddhism and Taoism to articulate an undemanding, nonpunishing ethos of retreat or withdrawal comparable to Empson's—an ethos in which wisdom and laziness alike dictate declining the pursuit of material gain and in which desire is reinflected as an opportunism so passive it seems only to let pass opportunities and recast, however paradoxically, in the image of that which has no image—the watery mirror of Tao that reflects without retaining images and so promises to undo the image-fixing work performed in the mirror of Narcissus. Thus we find under Barthes's early figure of "bienveillance" the same mixture of smiling unconcern and ready (if not actually offered) power to help of Empson's Buddhas: "*Benevolentia* est en retrait sur *Ti voglio bene*, et correspond paradoxalement à son mot à mot: je veux bien ne pas être bloqué par ta demande, ta personne: je ne refuse pas, sans forcément vouloir: position exacte du Neutre, qui n'est pas absence, refus du désir; mais flottement éventuel du désir hors du vouloir-saisir."[5]

In a later session, citing Hipponax's epitaph—"If you are honest and have come from a good place, don't be afraid, sit down and if you like go to sleep"[6]—Barthes defines as the "summum of benevolence" the permission to sleep, here granted by the dead to the living in what is, as he notes, a stunning reversal of the usual law whereby the living are supposed to keep awake for the dead. One of the recurring themes in the seminar is the relinquishing of control over one's image; perhaps just as crucial as the attempt to think desire otherwise than as "a will to seize" is the accompanying renegotiation for release from the demands of the ego-ideal, as if the easiest escape from capture by the narcissistic image were simply to give up the fear of being seized. So under the heading "Sleep, Love, Benevolence," Barthes's notes read, "To sleep: mobilization of trust. Cf. to sleep on both ears [*dormir sur ses deux oreilles*]: on the ear of the other and one's own ≠ to sleep with one ear open. To sleep together [*à deux*]—utopically—implies that the fear of one's image being surprised is abolished; little matter that I be seen while sleeping."[7]

In their emphases on laying to rest not only acquisitive urges but defensive (vigilant, suspicious) powers, Empson and Barthes can also be heard as anticipating the critique—if so mild an intervention can indeed be called a critique—that Sedgwick makes in *Touching Feeling* of our unhappy enchantment with disenchanting, pain-forestalling modes of reading and of our absorption in a struggle, as energetic as it is futile, to avoid being taken unawares by loss and to escape the wound of being read by rather than reading the text's deceptive surface. Throughout the late essays Sedgwick's voice can be heard to proffer an invitation, similar to that of Empson's Buddha faces, to desist from and set aside the torment and terror of being caught out, found in the wrong, humiliated, disappointed, surprised—whether at not having seen enough or at letting be seen too much—precisely the epistemic ordeals and interpretive pitfalls she had so acutely analyzed in *Epistemology of the Closet*. There anticipating her later argument concerning the exclusion of positive affect from paranoid reading, she had shown just how little there is of positive enjoyment in the exercise and pursuit of epistemic privilege, since the latter derive primarily from the disoriented reader's terror of being found wanting in discernment of the always only half-written rules of the game and consequent overidentification with whatever narrative authority appears to "be in the know." Already in this early work, Sedgwick's critical voice addresses the novice reader who experiences herself as credited with knowledge she lacks and taken for something she isn't—like the closeted subject, both on display and not seen at all—and seeks to disabuse her of her overestimation both of the threat of exposure from without and of the efficacy of the disciplinary enforcement of something called "knowledge of the world" as protective cover.[8] Enjoining a kind of suspicion of suspicion itself—a skepticism regarding the good it can do one to have anticipated harm by miming it in advance of its occurrence—Sedgwick's guiding voice in this sense perhaps inevitably competes with the shadowy addresses, the presumption and attribution of knowingness emanating from text to reader.

In later essays collected in *Touching Feeling*, such as "Pedagogy of Buddhism," Sedgwick only makes more explicit her exhaustion at the disabling effects of certain types of academic skepticism simultaneously overly suspicious of anyone's right to speak with assurance and unduly confident in the power of expert or sufficiently vigilant knowledge to secure its object from misinterpretation. Like Empson, she wants to grant permission, to find an alternative to the trap of fetishizing the non-Western object as unknowable by insisting on too great a difference. In their readiness to avail themselves of certain literary works and philosophical traditions (Proust, Zen Buddhism, Taoism, etc.) known to them primarily in vulgarizing, popularizing translation, Barthes and Sedgwick participate in a project of profanation, in Agamben's sense of the term, as returning to common use what had previously been put off limits, a project that necessarily puts them in mimetic relation with the dismantling of pedagogical authority at the core of these traditions ("I have nothing to teach you").[9] Agamben's reminder that contact (*contagione*) is "one of the simplest forms of profanation"—of returning to the profane sphere "that which has been ritually separated"—might productively be juxtaposed alongside Sedgwick's comments on the unsusceptibility of touch to technological amplification, as if contact were not only the means of dissemination and diffusion but also its natural limit.[10]

Yet between the cognitive impasse of "It takes one to know one" of *Epistemology*—later revised in "Paranoid Reading" as "It sets a thief (and, if necessary, becomes one) to catch a thief; it mobilizes guile against suspicion, suspicion against guile"—and the equally circular and hardly reassuring "If you have to ask, you'll never know," by which Sedgwick summarizes the thought that enlightenment has no starting point or development in "Pedagogy in Buddhism," there is only an affective difference, as if the competitive, mimetic energies once mobilized by the promise of an as-yet unattained epistemic foothold or cognitive certainty had simply subsided before a secret to be deciphered immediately (and universally) or never at all.[11] The thought that it requires no special skill and one can't be taught how (to recognize the closet, to understand a koan, to draw the Buddha's face) goes hand in hand and does not contradict the assertion that it takes a certain flare, a lifelong habit, and disposition.

Not surprisingly we find the same conjuncture of seemingly incompatible affects—distance and intimacy, remoteness and availability—in Barthes's writings on haiku and in the figures of *bienveillance*, *délicatesse*, fatigue, and weak retreat, randomly distributed across *Le Neutre*. "Familiarity singularly tinged with aloofness" (a stricter translation would read "familiarity singularly mitigated by the lapsing or falling away of interest [*désintéressement*]) is the phrase Barthes borrows from Suzuki's definition of the Zen concept of *sabi* to describe the neuter as a state of being in love unhooked from the will to seize a partner—a complacency toward desire that neither moves toward seizing it nor exerts itself to deny it.[12] But what is disconcerting and difficult to render accurately is the way this coolness that bears the world no ill will, this spirit of happy accommodation in which critical powers appear to have been put to sleep such that anything goes, complements and cannot be separated from an appetite for minimal variations and an active seeking out of the nuance, the precise and delicate difference. Thus Barthes's remarks on haiku follow the same arc as Empson's remarks on the Buddha faces: an assertion of access, availability, and serviceability, followed by a retreat from and disavowal of crude generalization: "Tout en étant intelligible, le haïku ne veut rien dire, et c'est par cette double condition qu'il semble être offert au sens, d'une façon particulièrement disponible, serviable, à l'instar d'un hôte poli qui vous permet de vous installer largement chez lui, avec vos manies, vos valeurs, vos symboles."[13]

The Orientalist logic at work in Barthes's figure of haiku as a polite host who accommodates all projections and just as quietly disposes of them hardly needs exposing. Indeed if the metaphor invites one to imagine this host as refraining from making a comment on the liberties taken by his guest, the same wordless discretion often becomes the prerogative or incapacity of Barthes's reader before a "writing" that, in Marie Paule Ha's words, "invites, if not a 'no comment,' then at most an admission of its 'justesse,' another trait of the haiku."[14] For a reader of Barthes's (or Empson's or Sedgwick's) relaxed style to stop at the promiscuous indifference of *n'importe* (*quoi, qui; comme tu veux*, as you wish) would be like reading a haiku only once; to belabor the continued sense of exclusion and enigma would be like reading it many times. Barthes calls for reading a haiku twice, not because he wants to strike a balance between the facile and the hermetic, but because the echo makes definitive what might initially have seemed a correctable slightness; the second time, as second time, deprives the haiku of its exceptionality, confirms its ordinariness, while, as the last time, it lets go of the illusion of a correctable obscurity or improvable illumination: "to speak this exquisite language only once would be to attach a meaning to surprise, to effect, to the suddenness of perfection; to speak it many times would postulate that meaning is to be discovered in it, would simulate profundity; between the two, neither singular nor profound, the echo merely draws a line under the nullity of meaning."[15]

Twice and only twice makes an odd unit of its own (with the second instance both confirming the reality of *x* and marking its conclusion), and the figure Barthes uses to describe what this singular echo does—*tirer un trait* (to draw a line)—recalls the acrobatic movement of the haiku's finding its "juste forme" at a single stroke. *Justesse* remains almost untranslatable because the available English equivalents—*exactitude* and *accuracy*—are precisely not *juste*, implying, as they do, something quantifiable, as if all one needed were a more precise measuring stick, whereas *justesse* combines slightness of means (as in having "just" made *x* by the slimmest of margins) with judgment of what is appropriate, a capacity to meet whatever is called for by a given situation. Thus it is impossible to imagine a second or third attempt achieving the just right measure; every first attempt is successful or never at all, since the "juste coup" always just makes it, if only just, in a single stroke. Barthes's haikus, then, offer the possibility of indefinite continuance but not because the present instance is judged lacking and in need of correction from a future reworking.[16]

II

Kafka désirait savoir à quel moment et combien de fois, lorsque huit personnes sont en conversation, il convient de prendre la parole si l'on ne veut pas passer pour silencieux. [Kafka wondered at what moment and how many times, when eight people are seated within the horizon of a conversation, it is appropriate to speak if one does not wish to be considered silent.]
—Maurice Blanchot, *L'Entretien infini*, cited in Barthes, *Le Neutre*

It seemed increasingly clear that Foucault's book was divided against itself in what it wanted from its broad, almost infinitely ramified and subtle critique of the repressive hypothesis. I knew what I wanted from it: some ways of understanding human desire that might be *quite to the side* of prohibition and repression, that might hence be structured quite differently from the heroic, "liberatory," inescapably dualistic righteousness of hunting down and attacking prohibition/repression in all its chameleonic guises.
—Eve Kosofsky Sedgwick, *Touching Feeling* (emphasis added)

If, as our editors claim, theory is susceptible to an oddly moribund vitality, one of its more gripping forms is the positive feedback loop that for Sedgwick haunts the Foucauldian critique of the "repressive hypothesis," as it ironically finds itself identifying ever more pervasive and subtle forms of prohibition, control, and subjugation to power. Thus in the introduction to *Touching Feeling*, Sedgwick recounts how her excitement at the promise of "stepping outside the repressive hypothesis, to forms of thought that would not be structured by questions of prohibition in the first place," subsided in the wake of "Foucault's demonstration of the relentlessly self-propagating, adaptive structure of the repressive hypothesis."[17] For if power does not take the form of an external, censorious agency, it is only because it steals into, shapes, and produces subjectivities in hidden and unlocatable ways, causing the vigilant reader to have to draw an ever wider and always shifting circle inclusive of all the many implied and nonmanifest positive commands (to speak, to enjoy, to eat, to marry, to live) as well as prohibitions not to do x. This protean, assimilative adaptive "inclusivity" goes hand in hand with—and indeed makes possible—what Sedgwick elsewhere calls the "dogged, defensive narrative stiffness of a paranoid temporality . . . in which yesterday can't be allowed to have differed from today and tomorrow must be even more so."[18] That she associates this unceasing redirection of critical energies with compliance to the Oedipal law of generation indicates just how simultaneously productive and implacable it remains.[19]

Barthes's debt to Foucault also appears in *Le Neutre* in his desire to flee a culture that asks him to pursue, lay claim to, and activate desire, and that already anticipates his resistance, rebellion, insurgency.[20] Hence the impossible quest for the nonemphatic "no" or nonsystematic silence—in itself too light, too fleeting to be taken for a committed position or stance. Here again Barthes, like Sedgwick, confronts a theoretical impasse—"the yes/no paradigm"—that becomes the more insoluble the more seriously one takes it, but that the slightest, easiest of gestures can "unplay" or temporarily render inoperative. So, far from "questing," Barthes does no more than lay out in disordered catalogue various types of dodges (*esquives*), side-steps, deviations, retreats or *fuites*, all of them too fugitive to work for long or to be counted on to duplicate their success a second time.

Under the rubric "Réponses à côté" (Answers to the Side) in the 29 April 1978 session, he privileges, as more subtle than silence, verbalized responses that, by "jumping tracks," yield "une très forte impression d'insolite, de lunaire, de non-à-propos énigmatique" and open onto something undetermined. He cites as an example of "a real Neutre, that baffles [*déjoue*] the Yes/No without withdrawing," Mélisande's response to Golaud's interrogation in Maeterlinck's *Pélleas et Mélisande*, a response by which she "answers neither yes nor no, without [this] seeming like an intentional refusal to answer":

> *Golaud:* As-tu aimé Pelléas?
> *Mélisande:* Mais oui; je l'ai aimé. Où est-il?
> *Golaud:* Tu ne me comprends pas?—Tu ne veux pas me comprendre?–Il me semble . . . Eh bien, voici: je te demande si tu l'as aimé d'un amour défendu. . As-tu. . avez-vous été coupables? Dis, dis, oui, oui, oui? . . .
> *Mélisande:* Non, non; nous n'avons pas été coupables.—Pourquoi demandez-vous cela?[21]

To her husband's jealously pressing questions concerning her relations with his brother—"Did you love Pelléas? Have you [the two of you] been guilty?"—Mélisande answers simply, "Yes, I did. No, we haven't been." She does not lie, nor does she refuse to answer; she invents nothing and sends back Golaud's questions as constatives. It is tempting to say that she simply and quietly avails herself of his words to utter her own truth, admitting her love for Pelléas and at once clearing it of guilt. But this would already be to invest with an appropriative will answers that have the force of constatives, no more, no less, of what is already and merely self-evident. The past tense of Golaud's questions, like her answers, adds to the sense of a closed subject, about which there is nothing more to say. But it is the "Where is he?" following on the "Yes, I loved him" that makes for the inconsequence with which she passes to the side of Golaud's implied accusation. Sign of a perfectly good conscience, as in "Yes, she did and she would like to see him, where is he?" or simply of an empty consciousness—of how little he, or anything, is on her mind unless already named and thereby placed before her? With Golaud, figure of the jealous, paranoid reader, we are left to speculate, without being able to eliminate the third possibility of her simply playing dumb all along.

Constrained in the manner of Echo by the preceding syntagm (as, Barthes had previously suggested, all answers inevitably are), Mélisande's replies nevertheless effect a kind of change: a deflation or defusion, a flattening out of what was at stake in Golaud's questioning. Since she does not take on the charge, the bite, the sting of his jealousy, it appears as if she has indeed remained hermeneutically if not sexually innocent, deaf to the hidden "sous-entendu" of his questions, a subtext that would belong not just to Golaud's but to all questions, whatever their literal wording, according to Freud's allegation (cited by Barthes just a few minutes earlier) that all questions are indiscreet and always hide a desire to know what you do in bed and with whom. Barthes introduces the example by describing Golaud as the man of the precise question (Did you sleep with Pelléas?) whose power leans heavily on the precise answer (Yes/No); everyone assumes this is what Golaud wants to know, although he never puts the question directly. Indeed Mélisande's bare answers have the odd effect of retroactively transforming the husband's and master's direct, aggressive interrogation into something blundering, euphemistic, and imprecise; he becomes one who stammers, who can't bring himself to say what he means, while after a slight pause she finds her word without hesitation, released from having to say one way or another by the variously interpretable senses of "love" and "guilt." At least this is how Barthes performs Mélisande in the seminar, interrupting himself after her first "Non, non," to pause and add "on s'attendrait à 'non,' je n'ai pas couché avec Pelléas," so that when (worlds away from Debussy's opera) he delivers her actual line, it's as if he's inserted after her "No, we weren't guilty" the silent parenthesis "whatever we did or didn't do," and the auditorium breaks out in laughter at the achieved double meaning.

The joke rests in part on Barthes's having set up his identification with Mélisande by earlier confiding to his auditors his sense of being cornered, hounded, pegged whenever he is asked to take a position or stance—the same panic that he associates with the mortifying effects of the Name and Image and that lies behind his reticence in explicitly claiming homosexuality as a theme or identity. No one more acutely than D. A. Miller has analyzed the process whereby Barthes's seemingly "phobic" relation to the "act of gay self-nomination" nevertheless accompanies and perhaps in fact propels the multiplication of the traces and inflections of a certain queer disposition.[22] If, following Miller, we can say that Barthes's avoidance of the name means that homosexuality "come[s] to inflect every topic, no matter how remote,"[23] not as an identity to be claimed or owned but as an uncapturable and only just perceptible nuance, equally noteworthy are the surprisingly relaxed confessions that accompany and, as it were, fall to the side of Barthes's habit of dodging "la question" (the French article la indicating not a particular question but the structure and scene of questioning) whose disguised assertiveness denies him "the right not to know"—"the right to an uncertain desire." His suspicion of all questions as structurally indiscreet, whatever their surface content, no doubt inevitably falls prey to the mimetic logic that Sedgwick describes as constitutive of paranoia, since the eventual victim of an obtrusive gaze must in the first place diagnose that gaze as prying. But these meta-entrapments do not seem to particularly bother him, as he "étale"s (spreads, lays out) "par bribes" ("in snatches") his minor neuroses and predilections, much in the manner of the cobbler, evoked at the beginning of the seminar, to whom Aristotle derisively compares the sophists because they, like him, only lay out their wares of all sizes, never bothering to teach one how to make a shoe or sustain an argument: "I don't manufacture a concept of the Neuter; I lay out some Neuters,"[24] Barthes declares, reprising the verb *étaler* that also carries the temporal sense of spreading out across time in discrete stages and suggests the Neuter's double movement of attenuation (flattening) and making available, however lightly, without the possibility of development, or in French, *approfondissement*.

III

A surface is what insists on being looked *at* rather than what we must train ourselves to see *through*.
—Stephen Best and Sharon Marcus, "Surface Reading: An Introduction"

To the extent to which the theory can account only for "near" phenomena, it is a weak theory, little better than a description of the phenomena which it purports to explain.
—Silvan Tomkins, quoted in Sedgwick, *Touching Feeling*

The observance of these customs was only possible with some such form of construction as that furnished by our system of wooden architecture, easily pulled down, easily built up. . . . In the tea-room fugitiveness is suggested in the thatched roof, frailty in the slender pillars, lightness in the bamboo support, apparent carelessness in the use of commonplace materials.
—Kakuzo Okakura, *The Book of Tea*

Il faut tenir pour treize semaines sur l'intenable, ensuite cela s'abolira.
—Barthes, "Introductory Session," in *Le Neutre*

Empson's informal comments on the Buddha faces and their relative accessibility to nonspecialists have gained new resonance following the recent critical turn toward "surface reading" and away from the modes of "symptomatic" reading once de rigueur at the height of Marxist and psychoanalytically informed theory. Thus in their introduction to the 2009 special issue of *Representations* devoted to "surface reading," Stephen Best and Sharon Marcus convincingly assess a certain discontent with and lassitude or exhaustion of suspicion marking our critical moment: a loss of interest in or energy for the critical work of "restoring to the surface the history that the text represses," a disenchantment with disenchantment itself, a weariness that remains, ironically, yet another form of wariness if not of deceptive appearances, then of the good of their demystification and the critical labor involved.²⁵

As the epigraph suggests, Best and Marcus's notion of surface reading plays on the idea of the surface as a figure of availability making no special demands on its viewers. Where an earlier form of adversarial, agonistic ideology critique required "training" the reader to do the heavy work of penetrating, exposing, and wresting the text's otherwise undisclosed secrets, Best and Marcus speak of the "paradoxical space of minimal critical agency," in which critique barely distinguishes itself from "description"—the same term that Silvan Tomkins uses to designate "weak theory." "Describing" or "unthreading" is the Penelope-like task Barthes sets himself to do with each word-figure in Le Neutre: "Within each figure, the matter is neither of explaining nor of defining, but only of describing (in a nonexhaustive manner)."²⁶ In the opening session, he tells his auditors that he "took the Neutral for a walk not along the grid of words but along a network of readings, which is to say, a library." The library was that of his "maison de vacances" or summer house (also the mother's house)—an unchosen inheritance, then, and a figure for what happened to be available, that Barthes presents as coming to him from a "familial elsewhere"; rather than correcting "its huge deficiencies," he says he has only culled from it arbitrarily according to personal taste. The sense of the seminar as a promenade taken in the maison de vacances, in a space and time released of critical vigilance and all claims to systematic comprehensiveness (the leisurely, unhurried verb *promener* hearkening back to Rousseau's *Promenades* from which Barthes has just quoted), identifies Le Neutre and its figures as pastoral, a category that might also encompass surface reading, with its emphasis on lightened work, on the sufficiency of "mere" restatement or reinflection. Barthes's emphasis on survey, like Tomkin's on description and Sedgwick's on laying out, would all thus seem to line up with what Best and Marcus identify as the promise of "digital modes of reading" to "bypass the selectivity and evaluative energy that have been considered the hallmark of good criticism."²⁷

The temptation is thus to designate Barthes's *Neutral*, Sedgwick's "reparative reading," and the other contemporary critical practices that Best and Marcus group under surface reading as a pastoral slide from the georgics of high theory. To do so, however, would be misguided and not just because it would only reintroduce the binary thinking that such figures would only set aside (or walk away from) without opposing, without contesting.²⁸ For if we can compare the ethos of "nondoing" and noncommittal—of leaving one's force in place, without directing or finalizing it—in Le Neutre, and the equally "passive and minimal" performances of "opening around" on which Sedgwick draws in Touching Feeling as part of her project of reframing the role of theory as accompaniment rather than critique, there are also stronger grounds for distinguishing Barthes's and Sedgwick's positions from Best and Marcus's more recent ones.

One difference emerges when we compare Barthes's deliberately nonexhaustive "un-threading," filament by filament, of a particular texture of ideas woven around one term, and computational, data-collecting practices that assume no critical intervention on the part of the collector (whether immediately human or computer-enabled) and that deliberately leave open the specific usages to which such data might eventually be put. When Barthes's relaxed approach is juxtaposed to this newer and far more pointedly impersonal and nonproximate form of reading, it immediately becomes clear how closely attached he remains to notions of both craft and curation, even as he turns away from critical agon. As we have seen, Barthes repeatedly stresses the ease with which one can move from object to object. But it is also the case that he continues to imagine his interest in a particular object, however light and fleeting, as a *particular* interest. His model continues to insist on the finite nonexportability of its engagements, as opposed to surface reading's promise of general applicability and constant availability. The former corresponds to the "anyone can" of the Empsonian sketch, fully completed, and as easily undone, at the time of its execution; the latter to the always merely potential "anyone could with enough time" and to the delegation in the meanwhile of this power to time-saving specialists and machines, by which Max Weber once characterized scientific modernity. Recall his claim that "the increasing intellectualization and rationalization of knowledge do not indicate . . . an increased and general knowledge of the conditions under which one lives. It means something else, namely, that if one wished one could but learn it any time. Hence it means that in principle there are no mysterious, incalculable forces that come into play, but rather that one can, in principle, master all things by calculation."[29] Such a global and totalizing reach, even if and precisely because never realized, contrasts squarely not only with what Jean-Claude Milner calls Barthes's vindication of the right to "shrink objects to finite dimensions" but with the "resistance to amplification" that Sedgwick attributes to touch and the localism of Tomkin's "weak theory."[30]

Indeed a different kind of nonfungibility increasingly emerges over the course of Sedgwick's late work. In the introduction to Touching Feeling, she follows Tomkins in describing the drives (in contrast to affects) as "relatively narrowly constrained in their aims" ("breathing will not satisfy my hunger, nor will sleeping satisfy my need to excrete waste"), time-constrained, and constrained in their range of objects: "Only a tiny subset of gasses satisfy my need to breathe or of liquids my need to drink."[31] At this point she values affects because they have "greater freedom" with respect to time, object, and aim: they can wait; they may take any object; they can find satisfaction in a seemingly limitless range of doings. But in the essay "The Weather in Proust," she appears to value the drives (now called "needs") for precisely these reasons: their limited but nonnegotiable demands mean that they are both satiable and unavailable for Oedipal rivalry and mediation.[32] What for Sedgwick was still a self-evident proposition—that my breathing does not prevent someone else from breathing—has perhaps never been so within the environmental justice movement and is now an increasingly contested claim, given the commodification of the commons and the unequal distribution of water and air that climate change will only exacerbate.

Still I think it worth lingering over the different sense of "enoughness," of something within easy but importantly not permanent and not constant reach, afforded by her rereading of Michael Balint—different, that is, from the dominant sense of "available," "accessible," "reachable," "doable" as defined by the contradiction of permanent precarity and permanent "on-ness" of late industrial capitalism's wired but hungry workers. In a remarkable echo of Barthes's figure of "benevolence" (that which wishes you no harm but is in retreat from desire), Sedgwick, glossing Balint's idea of the "benign transference," writes:

> Neither competitively nor genitally organized, the benign transference does not demand to be gratified by "external action" on the part of its object. Instead, Balint writes, what it requires from its object is a mode of being, specifically the mode of being that characterizes natural elements. It "presupposes an environment that accepts and consents to sustain and carry the patient like the earth or the water sustains and carries a man who entrusts his weight to them. In contrast to ordinary objects, especially to ordinary human objects, no action is expected from these primary objects or substances; yet they must be there and must—tacitly or explicitly—consent to be used, otherwise the patient cannot achieve any change: without water it is impossible to swim, without earth impossible to move on."[33]

Rather than trouble the question of what it means to imagine water as "consenting" to hold, sustain, and carry us, I simply want to juxtapose this passage alongside Barthes's anecdote of a benignly withheld consent. Under the figure "Kairos" ("mesure convenable, juste. Moment convenable, opportun, occasion"; the just, appropriate, fitting measure, the convenient moment, opportune, occasion), he recounts the story of the sage Thales as told by Diogenes Laertius: "'Sa mère l'exhortait à se marier, il lui répondit: "Non, par Zeus, il n'est pas encore temps." Elle l'y invita une nouvelle fois quand il eut pris de l'âge, mais il lui dit: "Il n'est plus temps."' Esquive parfaite du système: le *kairos* lui-même ne fonde pas un système . . . À plus forte raison, l'objet qu'il brouille: aucun système du mariage ou du célibat, même personnel (très difficile d'arriver à cela, et surtout de le faire entendre.)"[34] Thales was never quite unavailable, only the time was never right, as was perhaps the case with the writing of this essay.

Indeed with more time I could have developed a comparison of Sedgwick's "needs" to what many inhabitants of late capitalist industrial societies now experience as their "daily bread": access to the data-storage servers now running all the time at enormous expenditures of energy because, the industry claims, consumers demand immediate access all the time. Whatever their interest in satiable and sated affects, assertions of sufficiency, easiness, and doability of the kind perused in this essay can't but provoke doubt and a fresh round of critical suspicion, especially as they appear to lift the requirement for special training in disciplines already fraught with cultural misapprehensions, at a time when entire foreign-language departments are facing elimination in an academy ever more dominated by English-language pedagogy and when a discourse of scarce resources prevails both within the university and without. The most obvious of these doubts concerns the extent to which Barthes and Sedgwick fetishize, misappropriate, or re-Orientalize the Asian traditions on which they draw for "good objects" when rejecting Western master discourses of strong claims-making and perfective activity. This question, which has received close scrutiny elsewhere in responses to Barthes's earlier writings on Japan, China, and Morocco, might also partially be addressed by Sedgwick's suggestion in "Pedagogy of Buddhism" of how much of the ongoing and long-since condensed relations of mutual if never symmetrical determination and construction is missed by the "dominant scholarly topos" of "adaptation," a topos that, along with its cognates—perversion, debasement, simplification, vulgarization—"implies that an Asian original is adapting or being adapted, for the essentially different habits, sensibilities, Weltanschauung of the West."[35] In her essay, Sedgwick proposes to supplement "adaptation" with "the tautological circuit of "recognition/realization" so as to explain how "the sense of recognition [might] arise from bringing together with its Buddhist original some historically Buddhist idea now naturalized by its continued usage in Western thought."[36] So we might assert, ever so tentatively and ever so lightly, that by the very thinness of his contact with Taoism and Buddhism (as thin as the walls of the Japanese tea ceremony room), Barthes enacts the lightness of touch for which he searches, just as he performs a kind of *frôlement* or "grazing" when he quotes freely, in passing or anecdotally, from popular French translations and Westernized accounts (Suzuki, Kakuzo, Maspero, Grenier), in much the same way he does from Diogenes Laertius, Sextus Empiricus, Hegel, Tolstoy, and others, assuming in his auditors the same degree of familiarity or nonfamiliarity with these texts and the practices of nondogmatic authority they are supposed to represent.[37]

But to fully address this problematic of "inexpert" or "unauthorized" borrowings from wandering—unschooled—teachings from a place called Asia, one would have to contend first with Edward Said's account of Orientalism as the site of the production of expert, specialist, and technocratic knowledges, an account that draws a direct link between the libraries of British colonial administration and the comparative literature departments of today's (or now yesterday's) universities. This brings me to a related concern: the uneasy proximity of a certain qualified emphasis on ease of access and concomitant futility of effort in Empson, Barthes, and Sedgwick, to the seemingly similar emphases on ease, effortlessness, instantaneity, precarity, and unskilled labor defining late capitalism in the electronic age. If these theorists know something of the pleasure of impasse *and* release experienced when the openness or availability of x makes the hard work of decoding or unlocking it neither needed nor helpful, this strange loosening has its dystopian parallel in the contradictory position in which the humanities at accredited universities now find themselves: confronted with a strangely instrumentalized empty formalism, unable to say how they are training students for particular jobs and uncertain as to the worth of degrees that have nevertheless become a near universal requirement, but only because student debt has become a precondition of employment in the increasingly skill-less service economy.

Thus the insouciant versatility of Sedgwick's affects—capable of taking multiple objects and enjoying a freedom of aim, time, and means of discharge—finds its mirror image in Hardt and Negri's Marxian figure of the "free" proletarian whom capital makes "free" of all means of sustaining himself otherwise. *Disponible* is what capital wants labor to be, or so Hardt and Negri suggest, citing Marx on the proletariat's poverty as "the general possibility of material wealth": "When they are separated from the soil and from all other means of production, workers are doubly free: free in the sense that they are not bound in servitude and also free in that they have no encumbrances."[38] Such freedom or *disponibilité* most properly belongs, as recent precarity studies have shown, to the flex workers of late capitalism, who are at the disposal of the market even when employed, always available and always releasable, as ready to be moved or temporarily repositioned as definitively terminated.[39]

Is it enough to say that this ever more rigid demand for flexibility deliberately obscures the other, erotically inflected sense of *disponible* as easygoing and within easy reach that we find in Barthes's writings on haiku or cinemagoing?[40] Among the many definitions of *disponible*, *Le Grand Robert* offers the following: "Qui peut interrompre ses activités pour s'occuper d'autrui; être disponible pour qqn, pour s'occuper de ses enfants. Un père, une mère toujours disponible."[41]

Highlighting the treachery whereby the always available becomes unavailable for absence, this definition demands to be read through Winnicott's concept of the "good enough mother," who knows how to time her absences, to make them neither too long nor too short, so that the infant learns to play—to dream of her return or "to think *about something else*" but not indefinitely.[42] We know from the seminar "Comment Vivre Ensemble," Barthes's interest in "idiorrhythmy" as a figure of permissiveness within retreat, allowing freedom, discretion, and variation in monastic life and skeptical suspense, and perhaps further attention to the musical sense of "rest" or *repos* as a variable pause of discretionary length might support and enhance the weak defense of asystemicity by which Barthes's and Sedgwick's late experiments in sitting down might answer the charges of ideological complacency and naïveté to which they are vulnerable.[43] Thus everything in academic training prepares us to receive the seminar as the "work" of the late Barthes, the anecdotal ramblings of a scholar who has earned his right to be fanciful, to relax, even go to sleep on the job— except that the power to sleep, understood as a capacity for trust, as a relinquishing of the fear of and fantasies about the other's gaze, an abandonment of the narcissistic fear and dream of having one's image captured by the other, emerges in the course of these thirteen weeks as a power, as a gift if not a talent or achievement, and not simply a lapse or checking out.[44] *Disponible* in French also refers to ready cash or capital awaiting reinvestment, but this figure of free-floating nonattachment can easily shade into its opposite of simply not usable, not fit for use of any kind, which may explain why the tropes of "good enough" and "good for nothing" (the epithet to which Barthes aspires after the example of the oak who was spared the ax for being good for nothing) recur closely intertwined in his and, to a less explicit extent, Sedgwick's late work.

Notes

1. Empson, *Argufying*, 574.

2. The more common sense of "stepping aside" as a deferential move to make way for the supposedly more powerful is ironized in an extraordinary sentence from Robert Walser cited by Ben Lerner: "Modestly stepping aside can never be recommended as a continual practice in strong enough terms." This deferential sense continually shadows the other, more irreverent sense I wish to privilege here—that of simply stepping to the side of a problem rather than solving it. See the essay excerpted from Lerner's introduction to Walser's *A Schoolboy's Diary and Other Stories* (NYRB Classics, 2013) here: http://www.newyorker.com/online/blogs/books/2013/09/robert-walser-disappearing-acts.html, accessed 7 October, 2013.

3. Empson, *Argufying*, 573–74.

4. Cameron, *Impersonality*, 9.

5. Barthes, *Le Neutre*, 40–41; "*Benevolentia* doesn't go as far as *Ti voglio bene* yet paradoxically corresponds to its word-for-word translation: I accept not to be blocked by your request, your person: I don't refuse, without necessarily wanting to: exactly the position of the Neutral, which is not absence, refusal of desire, but possible wavering of desire outside of will-to-possess" (*The Neutral*, 15).

6. My translation of Barthes's French (*Le Neutre*, 71).

7. Barthes, *Le Neutre*, 40. *Abolish* is the same verb that Barthes uses in the reflexive form when declaring at the start of the seminar that it will not result in a book but simply disappear. One can take this promised self-abolishment, posthumously belied by the publication of the seminar notes and the seminar itself in MP3, not as a modest concession to the inevitable limits of what one person can achieve or preserve but as the highest ambition for a project that would complete itself after the manner of the painter Apelles, who, by giving up, succeeded in doing what in trying he could only fail to do. In the 27 May 1978 session, Barthes cites Sextus Empiricus's comparison of *ataraxia* to the *kairos* of the painter Apelles, who, "painting a horse and unable to render the lather perfectly, . . . finally in a rage flung at the picture the sponge on which he wiped the paints off his brush, thus succeeding in producing a faithful image of the lather" (174).

8. The long passage from *Epistemology of the Closet* I have in mind reads as follows:

> The inexplicit compact by which novel-readers voluntarily plunge into worlds that strip them, however temporarily, of the painfully acquired cognitive maps of their ordinary lives (awfulness of going to a party without knowing anyone) on condition of an invisibility that promises cognitive exemption and eventual privilege, creates, especially at the beginning of books, a space of high anxiety and dependence. In this space a reader's identification with modes of categorization ascribed to her by a narrator may be almost vindictively eager. Any appeal, for instance, to or beyond "knowledge of the world" depends for its enormous

novelistic force on the anxious surplus of this early overidentification with the novel's organizing eye. . . . The position of a reader in this chain of privilege is fraught with promise and vulnerability. The ostentatious presumption by the narrator that a reader is similarly entitled—rather than, what in truth she necessarily is, disoriented—sets up relations of flattery, threat, and complicity between reader and narrator that may in turn restructure the perception of the conformation originally associated with the "worldly." (97)

9. "Ce n'est jamais un savoir doctrinal qui est mobilisé: je ne sais rien et ne prétends rien savoir du bouddhisme, du taoïsme, de la théologie négative, du scepticisme: ces objets, comme corps doctrinaux, systématiques, historiques, tels qu'on pourrait les trouver dans des histoires de la pensée, des religions—ces objets sont tout à fait absents de mon discours → à la limite: quand je cite du bouddhisme ou du scepticisme, il ne faut pas me croire: je suis hors maîtrise, je n'ai aucune maîtrise" (Barthes, Le Neutre, 97).

10. Agamben, Profanations, 74.

11. Sedgwick, Touching Feeling, 126–27.

12. Le Neutre, 65.

13. Barthes, L'Empire des signes, 89. "While being quite intelligible, the haiku means nothing, and it is by this double condition that it seems open to meaning, in a particularly available, serviceable way—the way of a polite host who lets you make yourself at home with all your preferences, your values, your symbols intact" (Empire of Signs, 69).

14. Ha, Figuring the East, 113.

15. Barthes, Empire of Signs, 76.

16. In his last seminar, La Préparation du Roman, Barthes reprises and somewhat revises these claims about haiku. Beginning with the mystery of something that even across translation appears completely accessible and utterly familiar to him, he again notes his (but not just his, everyone's) desire "d'en faire soi-même," to make some oneself. Under the section "le Temps qu'il fait," he cites Yaha's line "I watch the clouds pass" as indirectly indicating that it is summer, and summer is passing, and one will not get up to say so, something of which one could as well make a novel as a haiku, because structurally this telling of what time it is or what the weather is doing by indirection "has no reason to finish": "The haiku is brief, but not finished, not closed" (67, my translation).

17. Sedgwick, Touching Feeling, 12.

18. Sedgwick, Touching Feeling, 147.

19. Here Sedgwick links "the knowing, anxious, paranoid determination that no horror, however apparently unthinkable, shall ever come to the reader as *new*" (Touching Feeling, 146) to the Oedipal compact by which "it happened to my father's father, it happened to my father, it is happening to me, it will happen to my son, and it will happen to my son's son" (147). As an oblique allusion to the avuncular, her concluding question, "But isn't it a feature of queer possibility—only a contingent feature, but a real one . . . —that our generational relations don't always proceed in this lockstep?," indirectly evokes the story of Thales (discussed below) of whom it was said "that he adopted the son of his sister; and that once being asked why he did not himself become a father, he answered that it was because he was fond of children" (Diogenes Laertius, Lives and Opinions of Eminent Philosophers, I 26, 1:27).

20. See, for example, Barthes's claim that "arrogance" begins "when one forces someone who is not hungry to eat. . . . Mankind having spent millennia (and still now) being hungry, what is 'mythified,' spoken, 'discursivized' is hunger, not its opposite → (in a general way, positive passions [the 'appetites'] are spoken much more than the 'negative' ones, the inappetences)" (The Neutral, 152).

21. Barthes, Le Neutre, 150. "Golaud: Did you love Pelléas? Mélisande: Why yes; yes, I loved him. Where is he? Golaud: Do you not understand me? Don't you want to understand me? I feel . . . What I feel is . . . It's this, tell me this: I ask you whether you loved him with a forbidden love. Did you? Tell me, were you guilty? Tell me, tell me! Yes, yes, yes? Mélisande: No, no, no, we were not guilty . . . Why do you ask me that?" (The Neutral, 112–13).

22. Miller, Bringing Out Roland Barthes, 23.
23. Miller, Bringing Out Roland Barthes, 25.
24. Barthes, The Neutral, 36.
25. Best and Marcus, "Surface Reading," 4.
26. Barthes, The Neutral, 11.
27. Best and Marcus, "Surface Reading," 17. For Jean-Claude Milner, the shift from a "critical intelligence" bent on unmasking hidden secrets to one defined as "seeing what there is to be seen" happens much earlier and is already definitively expressed in structuralism's turn away from Marxism to Saussurean linguistics in the 1960s. In a brief essay that appeared in Le Magazine littéraire in 1993, he calls Barthes the artisan of this "rehabilitation of surfaces" (reprinted in Le Périple Structural: Figures et paradigme [Paris: Éditions du Seuil, 2002], 116, my translation). Submitting to the shattering of the finite and the fragmentary nature of discourse, "the last Barthes" becomes for Milner a "figure all at once pathetic and peaceful" (119).

28. Sedgwick never denies the validity of "paranoid" analyses of the workings of power. Barthes repeatedly returns to the figure of Eurylochus, a disciple of Pyrrho who, pressed for answers from his students, simply dove into the river and swam away (The Neutral, 111).

29. Max Weber, "Science as Vocation," in From Max Weber: Essays in Sociology, translated by H. H. Gerth and C. Wright Mills (New York: Oxford University Press, 1958), 139.

30. Milner, 118, Le Périple Structural, my translation.
31. Sedgwick, Touching Feeling, 18.
32. Sedgwick, The Weather in Proust, 11–12. The passage is worth quoting in full:

> The human need for air is satiable because, like the needs to drink, eat, and excrete, but unlike the libido, it is a biological drive in the strongest sense of the term: unlike sexual desire, for example, its satisfaction is necessary to sustain individual life. And, unlike Oedipally structured sexuality, it is not intrinsically organized around rivalry or mediation. The need to breathe, to eat and drink, to have one's weight supported are nonnegotiable, but being finite and satiable, they are not zero sum: except in extreme situations, one is rarely deprived by the satisfaction of another's need. Balint's interest in existential or survival-implicating functions, which he links to the weather elements—air, water, earth, and fire—is held in common by the pioneers of object-relations psychology. Like Ferenczi and Winnicott, Balint likes to attach friendly language to

such "benign" or satiable object relations—what he also calls "the harmonious mix-up," and Winnicott calls the "holding environment"—the one where, as Winnicott hauntingly points out, it becomes possible for the infant to think about *something else*, something beyond the mother's care.

33. Sedgwick, *The Weather in Proust*, 11.

34. Barthes, *Le Neutre*, 218. "The story is told that, when his mother tried to force him to marry, he replied it was too soon, and when she pressed him again later in life, he replied that it was too late. [For Barthes this represents a] → Perfect dodge or sidestepping of the system: the kairos [sense of timing, of the right or opportune moment] itself doesn't found a system (as it does with the Sophists). Even more so with the object it blurs: [there is] no system of marriage or celibacy, even personal (very difficult to reach that point, and especially to make it understood)" (*The Neutral*, 172).

35. Sedgwick, *Touching Feeling*, 156: "Adaptation emphasizes how an original is being altered, modified, fitted for a different use, maybe even decentered, drawn out of an earlier orbit by the gravitational pull of an alien body."

36. Sedgwick, *Touching Feeling*, 165.

37. For an argument deeply consonant with my own, see Rudolphus Teeuwen's "An Epoch of Rest: Roland Barthes' 'Neutral' and the Utopia of Weariness," *Cultural Critique* 80 (2012): 1–26, in which he contrasts, and ultimately allows the Neutral to undo the contrast between, Seidensticker's expert, authoritative "Confucian" communicative discourse and Barthes's lassitude with methodological rigor.

38. Marx, "Economic Manuscript of 1861–63," quoted in Hardt and Negri, *Empire*, 54. Here Sedgwick's turn toward Balint's "drives/needs" (however troubled and tenuous their distinction from "affects/desires" must remain) might sound a cautionary ecological note to Marx's "freedom" so conceived, for, however "free" of land the dispossessed may be, land, air, and water continue to make nonnegotiable if finite claims on them.

39. For an entry into the extensive bibliography of "precarity studies," see the first footnote to the chapter "After the Good Life, an Impasse" (293n) of Lauren Berlant's *Cruel Optimism* (Durham: Duke University Press, 2011).

40. See Barthes's comments in "Leaving the Movie Theater," on the "availability [disponibilité] (even more than cruising), the inoccupation of bodies" in the movie house defining "modern eroticism" (*The Rustle of Language*, translated by Richard Howard [Oxford: Basil Blackwell, 1986], 346).

41. "Who can interrupt their activities to take care of others; to be available for/to someone, to take care of their children. An always available father, mother." *Le Grand Robert de la langue française*, ed. Alain Rey (Paris: Dictionnaires Le Robert, 2001), volume 2.

42. Agamben's work of discriminating among potentialities might help tease out the ambiguities in the phrase: is "une mère toujours disponible" one who is always actually present and attentive or one who is well-disposed toward interruptions, drifts, self-absentings, asynchronous rhythms? See his *Potentialities: Collected Essays in Philosophy*, translated by Daniel Heller-Roazen (Stanford: Stanford University Press, 1991).

43. See, in particular, Barthes's discussion of *l'idiorrythmie* in the seminar's opening session on 12 January 1977 (*Comment Vivre Ensemble: Simulations Romanesques de Quelques Espaces Quotidiens; Notes de cours et de séminaires au Collège de France, 1976–77* [Paris: Éditions du Seuil, 2002], 36–40). For a fascinating discussion of Barthes's anecdote of the mother

pushing an empty pram while dragging her child by the hand, as it relates to contemporary forms of labor precarity, see Michelle Ty's "Beckett and the Character of the Unchosen," paper presented at the 2013 ACLA in Toronto.

44. "Dormir à deux—utopiquement—implique qu'est abolie la peur de l'image surprise: peu importe que je sois vu en train de dormir" (Barthes, *Le Neutre*, 71).

chapter 3

Comparative Noncontemporaneities:
C. L. R. James and Ernst Bloch

Natalie Melas

The Spaniards, the most advanced Europeans of their day, annexed the island, called it Hispaniola, and took the backward natives under their protection. They introduced Christianity, forced labour in mines, murder, rape, bloodhounds, strange diseases and artificial famine (by the destruction of cultivation to starve the rebellious). These and other requirements of the higher civilisation reduced the native population from an estimated half-a-million, perhaps a million, to 60,000 in 15 years.
—C. L. R. James, *The Black Jacobins*

Marxism is not itself radical like destructive capitalism, not itself omitting like the abstract calculation of the latter; nor is it half enlightening, but wholly departing and surpassing, it is least of all ascetic towards the claims of "nature," this antiquarium of unsolvedness.
—Ernst Bloch, *Heritage of Our Times*

Times change, or at least they move on. A standpoint, or a critique, or a movement that may once have possessed political exigency risks becoming nostalgic, irrelevant, or even reactionary if it loses critical purchase on the present. What is the point, for instance, of invoking anticolonial movements when the present context appears to make them moot, or, put more strongly, when their conditions of possibility no longer seem to obtain and the times seem to call for some other response? And yet if pursuing a critique without taking account of changed conditions risks irrelevance, then uncritically seeking to remain up to date or pursuing timeliness for its own sake risks the sheer triviality of the commodity's shelf life. What is it exactly that the times demand, and what are the implications of acceding to that imagined demand? Such questions and concerns, common enough in these times, index, in part at least, what Reinhardt Koselleck has called "futures past," that is to say, the condition of inhabiting a present that constitutes a future different from the one imagined or projected in a preceding era, a present that thus becomes a vantage point on what he pithily names a "former future."[1] It is a condition that takes a particularly acute form in modernity, an era or historical modality in which the experience of a new temporality—a temporality of progress and chance—makes ever greater demands on the future. The accelerating tempo of this temporality particularly under the pressure of technical transformations, Koselleck suggests, progressively narrows the interval between past and future, or experience and expectation.

Theorists of (mainly) European history have argued for some time now that the substantive interplay (or dialectic) between experience and expectation that constitutes historical development has stalled or somehow been exhausted. François Hartog, for instance, asks whether the interval between experience and expectation Koselleck identifies may not by now have become an impassable rupture, a rupture that exceeds modernity's regimes of historicity, suspends historical time, and opens on to a kind of perpetual present, immobile and ungraspable.[2] This condition one might loosely call "terminal presentism" has also been diagnosed in a range of writings as an effect of the end of history or the triumph of capitalism. Most influentially elaborated in Fredric Jameson's notion of postmodernism some decades ago, the general idea is that this condition obtains when capitalism has extended its reach everywhere, overwhelming the last pockets and vestiges of precapitalist modes of production. In historical or epochal terms, the entire globe, now intimately bound in a single economic system, shares in a single historical modality and therefore inhabits a singular present. This sense of a presentism without exit is only intensified in the current moment under the nearly hegemonic influence of neoliberalism.

I schematize here in order to point to a general consensus that our contemporary condition amounts to a crisis of historicity that gives on to a present whose relation to the past is foreclosed or uncertain and whose investment in the future is dubious, short of catastrophe. This terminal presentism has occasioned attention to different modalities of historical reflection and encounter (memory and trauma, for instance) and increasingly to futurity as well, but less to presentness as such.[3] When it goes unexamined, the present is presumed to constitute a unified field of contemporaneity construed in relation to noncontemporaneity. The standpoint of futures past, that is, of imagining one's own contemporaneity as marking the definitive end of a formerly imagined future, implies a notion of contemporaneity derived from the foreclosure and therefore noncontemporaneity of a former future. Contemporaneity thus takes form as the culmination of a failed teleology; the present is that time in which a certain past definitively no longer obtains. Albeit retroactively, such a vision presumes a particularly linear temporality, one that is no less progressive or developmental for marking the failure of progress instead of its materialization. Paradoxically the gesture of announcing an end to teleology installs at once a rupture with the past and a teleological representation of that past. Moreover determining obsolescence, or consigning something to the proverbial dustbin of history, requires epochal or periodizing limits, and these in turn presume a meaningfully progressive temporal sequence, even when what is consigned to the dustbin is teleology itself, that is, the idea that history is moving toward a particular goal. A kind of developmental logic persists in antiprogressivist accounts of historical time, and the terminal present they adduce, ambivalent or paradoxical though it may be in its form, is strictly bounded in its distinction from its opposite, noncontemporaneity.

David Scott's masterful polemic in *Conscripts of Modernity: The Tragedy of Colonial Enlightenment* offers a subtle example of the limits of such a construction of contemporaneity. Starting from a virtuosic reading of C. L. R. James's 1938 work *The Black Jacobins* (with a special emphasis on selected revisions James made for the 1963 edition) Scott posits the contemporary relation to the anticolonial past in Koselleck's terms. The postcolonial present is a superseded or "elapsed" anticolonial future:

> That future which constituted James's horizon of expectation (the emergence of nation-state sovereignty, the revolutionary transition to socialism) and which *The Black Jacobins* anticipated, we live today as the bleak ruins of our postcolonial present. Our generation looks back, so to put it, through the remains of a present that James and his generation looked forward to (however contentiously) as the open horizon of a possible future; *James's erstwhile future has elapsed in our disappearing present*. But if this is so, if the longing for anticolonial revolution, the longing for the overcoming of the colonial past that shaped James's horizon of expectation in *The Black Jacobins* is not one that we can inhabit today, then it may be part of our task to set it aside and begin another work of reimagining other futures for us to long for, for us to anticipate.[4]

Scott is not particularly concerned with capitalism writ large, nor does he fall strictly into line with the standpoint I have named "terminal presentism," but his argument is fundamentally informed by a Koselleckian framework of futures past. Anticolonial revolution, or the total overcoming of colonialism (through sovereignty and socialism), which was James's expectation and the future upon which he predicated his actions and writings in the late 1930s, is what today, according to Scott, we live "as the bleak ruins of our postcolonial present." James's future, in other words, failed and has become a ruin in the present. It is therefore "an erstwhile future," and our present, this passage suggests, is to a large extent constituted by our sense of the ruination and the elapsing of this particular future.[5]

Over the length of Conscripts of Modernity, Scott argues against what he calls the anticolonial "romance" plot or narrative structure of total revolutionary overcoming. These "stories of salvation and redemption" in which colonialism is an "obstacle to be overcome," he contends, "have lost their salience" in view of the failures of decolonization. Reading between the lines of James's 1963 revisions, which cast Toussaint L'Ouverture as a tragic hero, Scott instead urges us to see our postcolonial moment as a tragic plot, one that renounces the total and teleological overcoming of injustice and loss in favor of contingency, unyielding ambiguity, and paradox. In this tragic schema, the colonial past is precisely not to be overcome and, more darkly, is not overcomable for it is paradoxically and inextricably constitutive of this postcolonial present. On the book's last page Scott writes, "The colonial past may never let go. This is a hard truth."[6]

Two very different relations to the past are adumbrated here: on the one hand, with respect to the colonial past, a sobering, tragic, antiteleological relation and, on the other, with respect to the more recent anticolonial past, a sequential development that renders that past obsolete so that it can be overcome or set aside in order to open a perspective onto a new future. On a purely formal or logical register, there is a marked inconsistency inasmuch as Scott's argument appears to rely upon precisely the progressive temporal scheme he wishes to correct in the reflexive contemporary iterations of the anticolonial position. Admittedly his articulation of the present and its demands as a "problem space" endeavors to avoid ascribing a progressive or developmental logic to temporal sequence. That anticolonialism no longer responds to the current problem space does not, in principle, make it obsolete or anachronistic. But to describe anticolonialism (or sovereignty, or socialism) as a future past does precisely that, not only because the forward progress of modernity's temporality is what drives the logic of futures past but also because, phenomenologically or experientially, futures past determine the present through the historicist negativity of the perception of anachronism or obsolescence. What secures our sense of contemporaneity, on this view, is the certainty that a former future has elapsed. The tragic present Scott enjoins upon us may be contradictory, contingent, and ambiguous, but it is also unified and singular to the extent that it delineates its contemporaneity strictly against the noncontemporaneity of a former aspiration.[7] Contemporaneity negates and supplants noncontemporaneity. This encloses the certainties of the present and leaves unexplored whether or how former futures might impinge upon or intervene into them.

To probe and unsettle this schema I turn to two texts written in the 1930s, Ernst Bloch's *Heritage of Our Times* and C. L. R. James's *The Black Jacobins*, both of which open novel perspectives on noncontemporaneity that challenge the developmentalist orthodoxies of the Marxist historicism within which they operate and acutely respond to the conditions of the times. Bloch provides a thoroughgoing philosophical reflection on noncontemporaneity prompted by the rise of Nazism, and his polyvalent account can be read as an effective rejoinder, or even a kind of corrective to the temporal uniformity of terminal presentism. James's historical account of the Haitian revolution undercuts the stagist temporality underpinning theories of revolution and thereby provides a surprising response to the colonial temporalization of race. In bringing Bloch and James into comparison, I do not aim to measure their positions relative to each other, or to advocate for one standpoint over the other in terms of the strength of the arguments or their special relevance to our times. Instead of setting them up merely as abstract authorities on noncontemporaneity, I set them side by side, enjambed across the colonial divide, as it were, and attempt to read them as discrepant contemporaries. This involves a somewhat oblique approach to what counts as a theoretical text and what forms of thought and writing amount to "theorizing."

Since Johannes Fabian's watershed polemic on how the discipline of anthropology constructs its object, *Time and the Other*, "allochronism" or the "denial of coevalness" has been a central locus of postcolonial critique. Dipesh Chakrabarty, extending the critique to the historicism that informs the discipline of history, poses the problem as follows: "We treat fundamental [Western] thinkers who are dead and gone not only as people belonging to their own times but also as though they were our contemporaries," even as, in formerly colonial contexts, we treat our contemporaries as through they belonged to a bygone era.[8] Both Fabian and Chakrabarty argue for a more polyvalent conception of the present, or contemporaneity within the discursive parameters that constitute the subject and object of knowledge in their academic disciplines. Bloch and James take up, I argue, an allied temporal problematic in the rather different register of a direct engagement in their times, but *as* contemporaries, of each other, of course, but also more uncertainly and non-contemporaneously, of us, or of my own writing here. The idea is to experiment with positing a form of contemporaneity for these texts that is not predicated on the absolute transcendence of time, of the times, that is so often implicitly and reflexively imputed to the usual theoretical authorities. This theoretical gambit might take the form of a question: How might one begin to formulate a contemporaneity that would not be premised on the exclusion of the non-contemporaneous, but that would instead take critical account of non-contemporaneity?

....

Noncontemporaneity (Ungleichzeitigkeit) is a term the German Marxist philosopher Ernst Bloch develops in his *Heritage of Our Times*, first published in 1935.[9] The book is, as Bloch puts in in his preface, "essentially written during the times it examines" but because it is a period of crisis or transition, those times are looked upon from the perspective of the last stages of the old (bourgeois) order's decay when the new (communist) order is discernible, just around the corner. Hence the paradoxical task of retrieving the heritage of the present (of *these* times, as the German title specifies: *Erbschaft Dieser Zeit*), akin, as Bloch tells it, to inspecting the heritable contents of an old aunt's apartment before she is quite dead.[10] Much of the book is highly topical and many of its sections are dated.[11] The section that elaborates the philosophical dimensions of noncontemporaneity, "Non-contemporaneity and Obligation to Its Dialectic," is dated May 1932. It is worth recalling that May 1932 is a pivotal transitional moment in the rise of fascism in Germany. This date falls between Hindenburg's narrow win against Hitler in the presidential election in April 1932 and his appointment of Hitler as chancellor in January 1933, the year during which the Nazis would violently consolidate an absolute hold on power and in which, consequently, Bloch would seek refuge in Switzerland, where *Heritage of Our Times* was first published.

On the cusp of the Third Reich, and against the overwhelming consensus on the left that the irrational, mythical, premodern discourses so deftly maneuvered by fascist ideology were anachronistic, reactionary, and wholly reducible to "the offensive of the ruling class and the elements of its disintegration," Bloch develops the idea of noncontemporaneity to account for the mass appeal of Nazism and argues for the subversive and contradictory capacity underlying these "archaisms" or "anachronisms," and ultimately for their necessity to communist revolution.[12] Noncontemporaneity is first of all a neutral term with respect to temporal value derived from historicist presumptions of progress. By adding a negative prefix to the common adjective *gleichzeitig*, a compound word combining *gleich* (same) with *Zeit* (time; meaning "simultaneous, concurrent, contemporary, synchronous"), Bloch implicitly draws a distinction from other terms he uses, such as *anachronism, backwardness, archaism*, and even *tradition*, all of which inflect the notion of noncoincidence with some kind of value, usually negative. Noncontemporaneity (*Ungleichzeitigkeit*), in contrast, simply marks temporal noncoincidence; it does not indicate whether the lack of simultaneity refers to a holdover from the past or a projection into the future. And this fundamental ambiguity animates the paradox of Bloch's argument for the futurity or utopian content of "unbecome" or unresolved pasts. The two most likely English translations of *ungleichzeitig*, "noncontemporaneous" and "nonsynchronous," while etymologically equivalent to the German, in effect convey quite different connotations, with "contemporaneous" emphasizing a shared historical era or period and "synchronous" pointing to a more abstract or not specifically historical temporal coincidence. Bloch's noncontemporaneity calls into question the historical meaning and political force of temporal coincidence, such that the oscillation between an unspecified temporality and historical punctuality is constantly at play in the word.[13]

Contemporaneity in Bloch's schema is constituted by and corresponds to the most advanced phase of capitalism, what he sometimes calls the "capitalist now." For Bloch, the proletariat embodies most fully "the objectively contemporaneous contradiction of the times" because it is a class that originates with the capitalist mode of production and therefore whose "deprivation [is] born purely of today." Proletarian resistance to the "capitalist now" is contemporaneous and carries no repressed or estranged content out of the past; in Bloch's words, it "complains about no figures and memories."[14] Those classes whose modes of production capitalism sweeps aside, however, such as the peasantry and the petite bourgeoisie, become noncontemporaneous, and their alienation and rage drive them to the reactivation of all manner of figures and memories, from Aryan purity to feudal anticapitalism. An orthodox Marxism might argue that these classes are reactionary, that their historical stage has passed, and that the proletarian vanguard will bring them into genuine contemporaneity. In a deeply heterodox move—heterodox enough that some may argue that, like other aspects of Bloch's philosophy, it is no longer properly Marxist at all[15]—Bloch implicitly but thoroughly contests this unilinear developmentalist model of temporality. He insists that noncontemporaneity is a viable contradiction and thus a potentially vital anticapitalist element, even if it doesn't by itself function as a revolutionary or "driving" force. Key here is the idea that noncontemporaneity names not only a subjective disposition of withdrawal from the present—an inability to keep up—but also, Bloch writes, an "'objective' element' which is distant from and alien to the present; it thus embraces *declining remnants* and above all *an unrefurbished past* which is not yet 'resolved' in capitalist terms."[16] This unresolved or unsubsumed past includes traces or consciousness of all those things that, under capitalism, "have been increasingly destroyed and not been replaced."[17]

For Bloch, noncontemporaneity is neither a negativity to be subsumed by contemporaneity, capitalist or proletarian, nor is it a deficit that must be overcome in order for contemporaneity to return to itself in a higher unity. Instead noncontemporaneity has its own quasi-dialectical force, a positivity that emerges from within the negativity, a turn by which the unresolved past presages or contains in seed-like form a "*still possible future.*" Bloch unfolds the ambiguity central to the very neutrality of the term *noncontemporaneity* in a wonderfully paradoxical phrase, "intentional contents *of a still non-contemporaneous kind,*" where the word "still" acts as the pivot on which noncontemporaneity turns from the unresolved past to possible futures.[18] This brings noncontemporaneity in line with "the subversive utopian element 'of man,' 'of life,' which has not as yet found fulfillment at any time, and which is thus the final goad of every revolution."[19] The crucial point is that Bloch's argument does not culminate in an emancipated or proletarian contemporaneity that cancels out and reabsorbs noncontemporaneity. On the contrary, contemporaneity expands to include noncontemporaneity and thus becomes fundamentally noncoincident. At the end of "Non-contemporaneity and Obligation to Its Dialectic," Bloch proposes a "multi-temporal and multi-spatial dialectic," characterized by "polyrhythmics and counterpoint." The present Bloch urges against the perfect synchrony of capitalism's now is a dynamic point of congregation where pasts riddled with the future meet possible futures partially presaged in the unresolved past.

Bloch's idea of noncontemporaneity displaces linear historical narratives of progress as the sole mechanism for countering capitalism and disturbs the unity of contemporaneity. His point is not to promote the virtue or usefulness of the contents or events of any particular era in the past for the present. Indeed with the withering and often sarcastic rhetoric of the section in which he catalogues the various pasts conjured in his fascist present, he is at pains to locate his analysis outside the bounds of any specific historical object of nostalgia, outside nostalgia altogether. The remnant of any past (not necessarily a revolutionary past or a glorious heyday) could, in principle, become a noncontemporaneous contradiction. The ultimate horizon of Bloch's analysis is not historicism per se but capitalist contemporaneity as an index of the general depropriation and alienation attending the ongoing process of "all people and things becoming a commodity [Ware-Werden aller Menschen und Dinge]," where the overarching temporal form of "becoming-commodity" is implicitly understood as forced synchronization. Consequently an oppositional stance does not have to be in step with history or historical development in order to function as a contradiction. [20]

....

First published in England in 1938, C. L. R. James's *The Black Jacobins: Toussaint Louverture and the San Domingo Revolution* is nearly contemporaneous with Bloch's *Heritage of Our Times*, though there is no indication that either author knew of the other's existence.[21] These two writers appear antithetical in their styles and dispositions, with James's elegantly concise English prose and worldly commitments contrasting with Bloch's complex impressionistic style and affinity for mysticism and utopian thought. Moreover James's deep schooling in European history and literature and in radical philosophy is not matched by any schooling or apparent interest on Bloch's part in African politics or Caribbean history and culture. Bloch peppers the expository part of "Non-contemporaneity and Obligation to Its Dialectic" with references to exotic locales and elements—"Papua," "negro drums," "central Africa," "Mohammedan fanaticism," "jungles," "Indian sects of murderers and Chinese secret societies"—but, with the exception of one provocative aside ("with a non-contemporaneity which becomes extraterritoriality in places"), these are stereotypical metaphors for apparently unregenerate archaisms.[22] *Heritage of Our Times* focuses exclusively on Europe, but while colonialism marks a limit to Bloch's own theorization of noncontemporaneity, that theorization is clearly pertinent to the "denial of coevalness" academic postcolonial critics like Fabian and Chakrabarty identify as part of colonial structures of thought and domination (though these authors make only cursory reference to Bloch). Colonial modernity, with its evolutionary, progressive drive (whether anthropological or historicist), consigns precolonial formations to anachronism, and these formations are part and parcel of all that capitalism destroys and does not replace, to recall Bloch's language. The application of Bloch's theorization of noncontemporaneity to postcolonial epistemological critiques is thus rather straightforward: it would entail examining the equivalence between Bloch's European, precapitalist noncontemporaneity and precolonial formations and evaluating his notion of a polyvalent present in terms of anticolonial and postcolonial contexts.[23] More surprising and less direct is the noncontemporaneity underlying James's contemporary text, The Black Jacobins. The developmentalist presumptions of modernity are certainly at play there, especially in the form of the temporalization of race, but The Black Jacobins is, as it were, a pre-postcolonial text, to put it awkwardly, and is not particularly concerned with coevalness in the context of epistemology and the colonial ordering of knowledge. James, whose thought in the 1930s is radicalized from a nationalist anticolonialism to a revolutionary Trotskyism and from a Caribbean (or Trinidadian) to a pan-African perspective, responds to the intersection of fascism and incipient anticolonial revolts by overwriting the temporalization of race as backwardness with the revolutionary modernity of Haiti's slave revolution. Whereas Bloch's noncontemporaneity locates in anachronisms traces of unresolved pasts, James's noncontemporaneity finds in the Haitian past a precocious, unresolved modernity.

Like Bloch's *Heritage of Our Times*, James's The Black Jacobins is a book of the times and for the times. It's true, of course, that James's text is a history of the revolution that led to Haiti's independence in 1804, but The Black Jacobins approaches that revolution from a profoundly contemporaneous standpoint, which, like Bloch's, is poised on the cusp of anticipated radical change. As James makes explicit in his 1938 preface, the book is quite immediately of its time: "It was in the stillness of a seaside suburb that could be heard most clearly and insistently the booming of Franco's heavy artillery, the rattle of Stalin's firing squads and the fierce shrill turmoil of the revolutionary movement striving for clarity and influence. Such is our age and this book is of it, with something of the fever and the fret. Nor does the writer regret it. The book is the history of a revolution and written under different circumstances it would have been a different but not necessarily a better book."[24]

These final sentences of the preface declare the book to belong to its times and detail some of their defining events: the Spanish Civil War, which broke out in 1936, the same year the Moscow trials began, aimed at purging Stalin's rivals. They are events exactly corresponding with James's research and writing for the book (1936–38), and as such they do not include other, slightly earlier events that were perhaps even more decisive for its powerful and prescient anticolonial argument, notably Mussolini's invasion of Ethiopia (then Abyssinia) in 1935 and the metropolitan resistance movement it inspired, which introduced James to pan-African thought and activism. Given the punctilious exactitude with which James identifies the immediately contemporary age, the last sentence almost surprises with its assertion of contingency. Where one might have expected an argument for necessity, for how the times make this book necessary, James instead underlines the circumstantial force of the times and therefore the book's relativity or convertibility: "Under different circumstances it would have been a different but not necessarily a better book." The most visible trace of the circumstances of the 1930s on the text of The Black Jacobins is the way it treats the Haitian Revolution in tandem not just with the French and the Russian Revolution but, most important, also with the coming anticolonial African uprisings, which indeed the book predicts. James proudly notes this accomplishment throughout the revised 1963 edition, most gleefully perhaps in footnotes where he draws attention to his prescience by reminding the reader of the original time of writing.[25]

The historiography of The Black Jacobins, or perhaps more precisely its disposition with respect to the writing of history, draws from many sources; the French radical historians, starting with Michelet, are one important influence. But by James's own accounting, no single work had a greater impact on him during those years than Trotsky's The History of the Russian Revolution ("And I read that book very hard").[26] What is striking therefore, and has not to my knowledge drawn much commentary, is the extent to which James's account of the slave revolution in San Domingo in the late eighteenth century sidesteps the historical, developmental framework of Trotsky's idea of world revolution and diverges from the theory of combined and uneven development that he famously developed in The History of the Russian Revolution as an alternative to strictly "evolutionist" or stagist theories of revolution in order to account for the Russian Revolution's deviation from the standard model of development. For Trotsky, there is a "historic succession of revolutionary ideas and forms," which he traces from the bourgeois revolution in England in the seventeenth century, which took a religious cast, to the French Revolution in the late eighteenth century, which materialized in the form of democracy, and finally the Russian Revolution, which heralded the direct accession to power of the masses.[27] Each revolution manifests a particular stage of bourgeois society, and together they chart a progressive development of class consciousness. This world-historical development is clear enough in its outlines, but in order to account for how that final stage emerged not from the most advanced capitalist economies but from "backward" Russia, Trotsky advances the idea of combined and uneven development:

> Unevenness, the most general law of the historic process, reveals itself most sharply and complexly in the destiny of the backward countries. Under the whip of external necessity, their backward culture is compelled to make leaps. From the universal law of unevenness thus derives another law which, for the lack of a better name, we may call the law of *combined development*—by which we mean a drawing together of the different stages of the journey, a combining of separate steps, an amalgam of archaic with more contemporary forms. Without this law, to be taken of course in its whole material content, it is impossible to understand the history of Russia, and indeed of any country of the second, third or tenth cultural class.[28]

James remarks on the exceptionally rapid transformation, in the resounding words of his preface, "of slaves, trembling in their hundreds before a single white man, into a people able to organise themselves and defeat the most powerful European nations of the day."[29] But he never analyzes this remarkable and swift development in terms of a "leap," nor does he investigate the nature of the specific "external necessity" that might have propelled the Haitian slaves out of cultural backwardness, beyond the general transformative context of the French Revolution itself. James likewise makes no mention whatsoever of the combination of specific steps in a historical process that might have led to the Haitian Revolution, or of any significant amalgamations of archaic with contemporary forms. Developmentalism of any sort seems nearly absent from *The Black Jacobins* as an explanatory frame, whereas it permeates Trotsky's understanding of revolution. James argues persuasively for how the rebelling slaves, and particularly the exemplary figure of Toussaint, embodied the "concrete realisation of liberty, equality and fraternity" of the French Revolution to the highest degree,[30] but the argument itself is not historical; it does not, that is to say, explain events by reference to developments over time. Moreover, as Cedric Robinson notes, James makes frequent reference to the idea of a "revolutionary class" and to the economic determinations of history underlying Marxist theories of revolution but never elaborates an argument for how slaves could come to function in that class dynamic in the place of the industrial proletariat.[31] For someone who read Trotsky (and Lenin and Marx) intensely and carefully and who had just authored the definitive work on the Third International of that time, these omissions are notable indeed. A full analysis would require careful examination of *The Black Jacobins* in relation to the various publications

James worked on concurrently, *World Revolution, 1917–1936* but also *A History of Negro Revolt* and various pamphlets, articles, and speeches. Here I want to explore only some consequences and ramifications for the peculiar status of noncontemporaneity in *The Black Jacobins*.

James's departure from Trotsky's developmental account of revolution must be understood in the immediate context of the temporalization of race. Colonial modernity construes race as a constitutive measure of noncontemporaneity, to the extent that racial difference is synonymous with backwardness and whiteness with modernity's contemporaneity. This temporal association of race is more consistent even than race's identification with skin pigmentation, as the case of the Irish or the Oriental demonstrate. James is initially interested in the figure of Toussaint as a rebuttal to theories of racial backwardness. He wrote briefly in defense of Toussaint a year prior to leaving Trinidad, in an article entitled "The Intelligence of the Negro," which rebuts an article by a certain Sydney Harland that called into question the intelligence of Toussaint L'Ouverture and reaffirmed ideas about the biological basis of racial hierarchy.[32] In this exchange the figure of Toussaint contributes to and recalls a broad project of black vindicationalism, a discourse that arose in the late nineteenth century in response to the virulent degradations of scientific racism and that often featured Toussaint L'Ouverture as proof of the black man's capacity for sovereignty and for civilizational development.[33] Vindicationalism contests racial inferiority from within the developmentalist logic of civilizational improvement. The point was to dispute the racializing association of blackness with backwardness by vindicating the African's ability to catch up and progress on the temporal scale of modernity. There are traces of a civilizational bias, or what some of James's critics condemn as Eurocentrism and elitism in *The Black Jacobins*: a premium on literacy and civility, offhand references to social or cultural backwardness, and to the stereotypical African "bush." But these largely operate at the level of rhetoric, and even there unevenly, as James often demonstrates an acute and ironic consciousness of their origins in colonial ideology. More important, however, the whole emphasis on a subject's capacity for development and with it the unilinear temporal evolution that gives vindicationalist discourse its conceptual purchase is underplayed, in part because the focus in *The Black Jacobins* has shifted substantially from the exemplary figure of Toussaint to the world-historical implications of the Haitian Revolution in tandem with the French Revolution and also, crucially, as harbinger or, more strongly, a scientifically detectable historical sign of the African emancipation in the near future. The Haitian Revolution in *The Black Jacobins*, in other words, is not marshaled as proof of the black man's capacity for civilizational development; rather it is given as the index of his ontological claim to modernity's multidimensional present at one of its inaugural historical moments (the French Revolution) and of the imminence of his successful revolt against contemporary colonialism. The backwardness vindicationalism sought to contest from within the logic of civilizational development is replaced or overlain in *The Black Jacobins* by a revolutionary simultaneity or contemporaneity that in effect gives on to a noncontemporaneity of the future. Almost uncannily when observed through the lens of Bloch's convertible term, James in effect flips the noncontemporaneity of racial backwardness over to the vanguardist noncontemporaneity of a future revolution. The intersection or even collision of these two responses to racial oppression, vindicationalism and revolution, results in the disruption of a unidirectional temporal order, for the past intrudes into the present as a trace of the future. The Haitian Revolution in James's schema is akin or structurally parallel to the "unresolved" past in Bloch but with the signal difference, as we will see a little further on, that its status is not utopian.

Two features of the Haitian Revolution implicitly place it outside the purview of Trotsky's combined and uneven development: the first is its modernity, or the contemporaneity of its contradiction, in Bloch's terms, and the second is its intrinsic claim on a future, that is to say, the fact (for James this has a quasi-empirical grounding) that its revolutionary purpose must be carried forward in the coming African revolution. In *The Black Jacobins* James is presciently intent on drawing out the modernity of the Haitian slaves in revolt. He argues that, owing to the rupture of the Middle Passage, the slaves were irremediably cut off from precapitalist, African modes of life, even as, owing to the quasi-industrial nature of the division of labor on the sugar plantation, the slaves were, in his words, "closer to a modern proletariat than any group of workers in existence at the time."[34] The slaves are a group, if not definitively a class, whose deprivation, to recall Bloch's characterization of the proletariat, is "born purely of today" and whose revolt therefore emerges from immediate material conditions. James is the first to assert the fundamental modernity of the plantation system, a position that would be developed in a different direction by his student Eric Williams in *Capitalism and Slavery* and later by U.S. anthropologists, political theorists, and cultural critics.[35] His emphasis is overwhelmingly on the revolution as a product of the social and economic conditions of plantation slavery. While James notes the role of Vodou in fomenting the revolution and is aware of the very large proportion of slaves at that time who were African-born, these are not decisive factors in his analysis. Later historians will place far greater weight on them.[36]

But if the Haitian Revolution in James's account is a mass movement emerging from the depredations of the contemporary working conditions of "sugar-factories" and is therefore timely and not backward, it also extends into the future. *The Black Jacobins* downplays the African origins of the Haitian Revolution but powerfully invests in its African future. Parallels between conditions in late eighteenth-century Haiti and contemporary colonialism in Africa (of the 1930s) are woven throughout the text, but *The Black Jacobins* is a historical narrative and not a work of political theory, so James nowhere elaborates an explicit argument for their interconnection. The point strongly implied, however, is that the Haitian Revolution is not an isolated event or a distinct stage in a sequence of revolutionary developments but rather the beginning of anticolonial revolution whose accomplishment lies in the future. The rhetoric of the parallels and analogies between past, present, and future in the text produces a striking telescoping effect, or a kind of translatable contemporaneity across the span of more than a century of historical time. In his discussion of the historic meeting of the Convention in Paris during which slavery was abolished in early 1794, for instance, James recalls the denunciations suffered by the Abbé Grégoire some five years earlier for daring to advocate the much more modest cause of equality for mulattoes and the gradual abolition of slavery and notes, as an aside, "He had been treated as anyone would be treated who for the Union of South Africa to-day proposed merely social and political equality for educated Africans and relief from the slavery of the pass-laws for the rest. Like Grégoire he would be denounced as a Bolshevik and would be lucky to escape lynching."[37] The offhand use of a number of starkly noncontemporaneous terms (*Bolshevism* and *lynching* in a Jacobin context) only underscores on the one hand the persistence of racial discrimination and hence the immediate equivalence between 1780s France and 1930s South Africa (or the United States), even as, on the other hand, the 1794 decree points to the potentially rapid mutability of racial status. In another instance, with reference to the brutal pigmentocratic laws of San Domingo designed to repress the mulattoes, James details a trend that had mulattoes seeking to prove their colored ancestry was Carib and not African in order to circumvent these legal constraints. Noting that these are stories "which we can understand better after Hitlerism than we could have done before," he goes on to comment, "The racial discriminations in Africa today are, as they were in San Domingo, matters of Government policy, enforced by bullets and bayonets, and we have lived to see the rulers of a European nation make the Aryan grandmother as precious for their fellow-countrymen as the Carib ancestor was to the Mulatto. The cause in each case is the same—the justification of plunder by any obvious differentiation from those holding power."[38] The reference to the insights Hitlerism brings from the present of The Black Jacobins provides a fascinating parallel to Bloch. Whereas Nazi revitalization of racial mythologies prompts Bloch to reevaluate the developmental historicism that defines and dismisses anachronism, it makes possible for James the direct comparison of colonialist and fascist racism and thus starkly levels out the steep curve of modernity that would have previously relegated racial categories to its antecedents or its margins and installed a sharp, temporalized dividing line between Europe and the colonies.[39] James's analogies are clear traces of the profound effect of the times, the specific circumstances of the 1930s, on presumptions about the temporalization of race, and though they may present themselves as mere rhetorical devices, their reconfiguration of racial comparison has important theoretical consequences.

Racial discrimination in South Africa (or Germany) during the immediate present of the writing of the The Black Jacobins is comparatively contemporaneous with racial discrimination in San Domingo of the 1780s because, in effect, what is "still non-contemporaneous" about the Haitian Revolution is the near future of the African revolution (or indeed, with Germany also in mind, world revolution). Whereas the remnants of the past in Bloch's noncontemporaneity belong to bygone, premodern eras passed over by the capitalist now, the Haitian Revolution instantiates instead anticolonial *modernity* as an uncompleted past that becomes a kind of relic of or for the immediate future of the coming African revolutions. Unlike Bloch's remnants, then, noncontemporaneity in The Black Jacobins is a relic of modernity, an anachronism, as it were, of the future. One can read this as an inversion of the Koselleckian framework of futures past inasmuch as the Haitian Revolution in James's account stands *not* as a future past but as a precocious future in the past. The chronological sequentiality of epochs is thus distended and destabilized, opening up a "multi-temporal and multi-spatial dialectic," to recall Bloch's formulation. James's untimely or noncontemporaneous modernity differs from the Blochian schema of noncontemporaneity because incompletion no longer signals a properly utopian disposition, if we understand utopia to

Comparative Noncontemporaneities 71

be that which, in Bloch's words "has not as yet found fulfillment at any time."[40] Black emancipation, The Black Jacobins demonstrates, has found fulfillment in modern times. Though imperfect, tenuous, and incomplete, that emancipation radically belongs to the kingdom of this world, to recall Alejo Carpentier's title, and not to a hope lodged outside, before, or beyond it. Bloch's extensive meditation on utopia, in his magnum opus, The Principle of Hope, and beyond, it must be noted, locates traces of utopia throughout this world and indeed constantly troubles conventional distinctions between the utopian and the non-utopian. Nonetheless, as the two sections following "Noncontemporaniety and Obligation to its Dialectic" make clear ("On the Original History of The Third Reich" and "Not Hades, But Heaven On Earth"), the utopian dimension of non-contemporaneity is for him ultimately beholden to a millenarian mysticism. In James' The Black Jacobins, I would argue, a distinctly nonutopian possibility underlies the peculiar copresence of various epochal times in this text that figures Haiti's Revolution not only as a historical precursor for the coming African revolutions but also as a portent and a parallel. James's text certainly implies a sequential development that will lead from the Haitian Revolution to the African revolutions, but that is not the only form of temporality connecting these events or these times. This is the crucial point here. Epochs are not closed in on themselves with absolute limits; instead the historical time of modernity is presented or represented with a multidirectional aspect in which there is a complex interplay between contemporaneity and noncontemporaneity.

Bloch and James offer examples, or better, figures of a contemporaneity that is not won at the expense of the absolute foreclosure of noncontemporaneity and which thus implies a differentiated articulation of historical or epochal time. At issue here is neither the total coevalness of all times, nor the global accomplishment of historical co-presence suggested in the bland triumphalism of end-of-history arguments. Both Bloch and James express this differentiation within a broader developmental or progressivist temporality, but because they believed the revolution (or at least a radical transformation) was just around the corner, they wrote about their present as though it were, or could be, the past and this already unsettles at once the fixity and the unity of contemporaneity. Hence, for both of them in different ways, just because something is out of date or out of step with the present doesn't make it irrelevant or ineffective or annul its capacity to bear on the present. Indeed, despite the catastrophic failure of the expectations that conditioned the writing of these texts in the 1930s, when Bloch and James later revised them and wrote new prefaces, they did not repudiate or disavow their claims or consign them to obsolescence. Even now while no longer topical, these texts are not outdated. They are, I would urge, non-contemporaneous.

Nothing can relieve us from the difficulties of attempting to decipher the demands of our time, but I hope that this exploration of comparative noncontemporaneities suggests at least a certain skepticism about striving for exact correspondences or perfectly timely responses. At the start of this essay I distinguished two forms of unified contemporaneity: the terminal presentism underlying the end-of-history arguments on the one hand and the more layered variegations of Scott's critique of postcolonial theory's outdated investments in anticolonial overcoming on the other. I argued that while Scott urges a tragic modality for the postcolonial present ("the colonial past may never let go"), he also urges us to let go of anticolonial aspirations on the grounds that they index a Koselleckian future past. His extraordinary account of James's 1963 revisions to *The Black Jacobins* suggests that these revisions bring the work up to date with the disappointments of decolonization in the 1960s and by extension bring James into line with our contemporary postcolonial condition. Scott is right to call postcolonial studies to task for unthinkingly reproducing anticolonial positions as though these responded to the urgencies of the present and for neglecting the historical conditions of its own production. But when that critique forecloses the anticolonial past to demarcate a unified contemporaneity, it leaves us with an impoverished present from which a whole realm of potentialities has been dismissed, first among them the enduring and critical noncontemporaneity of *The Black Jacobins* itself.

Notes

I am grateful to Leslie Adelson and Fouad Makki for astute comments on a draft of this essay and most especially to Jason Potts and Daniel Stout for their editorial gusto, their intellectual acuity, and their patience.

1. Koselleck *Futures Past*, 11.
2. Hartog, *Régimes d'historicité*, 28.
3. But see Erber, "Contemporaneity and Its Discontents," which traces a renewed emphasis on "contemporaneity" in discourses around art and also elaborates a trenchant critique of the Eurocentrism underlying Agamben's argument.
4. Scott, *Conscripts of Modernity*, 45, emphasis added.
5. It is worth noting in passing that the figures of ruins and of elapsing potentially signify rather different dispositions with respect to a past, with elapsing marking a clear and decisive break and ruins, on the contrary, suggesting fragmentary persistence and even the uncertain temporal dwelling amid ruins
6. Scott, *Conscripts of Modernity*, 220.

7. In an important critique of Scott's argument, Gary Wilder contests the "restrictive oppositions" between total overcoming and negotiation with colonial modernity and points out the error of rejecting "as outdated the very prospect of colonial emancipation itself rather than the revolutionary and national forms through which it was pursued at a particular historical moment" (Wilder, "Untimely Vision," 102–3). His fine-grained elaboration of Aimé Césaire's postcolonial politics as a counter-example of a history discounted by Scott's scheme provides an essential historical supplement to the more speculative cast of my own emphasis on figures of noncontemporaneity.

8. Chakrabarty, *Provincializing Europe*, 5. Giorgio Agamben in his important meditation on contemporaneity opens with an observation strikingly similar to Chakrabarty's initial observation but neglects Chakrabarty's colonial corollary (*What Is an Apparatus?*, 39).

9. Bloch makes use of the terms as early as *The Spirit of Utopia* (1919), but it finds its fullest philosophical development in *Heritage of Our Times*. For a cogent account, see Durst, "Ernst Bloch's Theory of Nonsimultaneity." Another prominent use of the word is the notion of the "non-contemporaneity of contemporaries" (*Ungleichzeitigkeit des Gleichzeitigen*), with reference to the theory of generational differences in the sociologist Karl Mannheim's pivotal 1923 essay *The Problem of Generations*.

10. Bloch, *Heritage of Our Times*, 4

11. The dating of the sections that comprise the part of *Heritage of Our Times* (roughly half the book) entitled "Non-contemporaneity and Intoxication," of which the theoretical section I treat here is, in Bloch's words, the "orientating center," calls for sustained attention to the play of contemporaneity and noncontemporaneity in Bloch's own text. The sections are not all in chronological order and at least a few sub-subsections were added after the book's original publication. An analysis of the complex topicality of *Heritage of Our Times* would also have to take account of the varied forms this text takes, from brief impressionistic evocations ("Half," "Mustiness"), to journalistic vignettes ("Range and Merriment (1929)" on dance marathons), to outright polemic ("Amusement, co., Horror, Third Reich (September 1930)"). My own limited aim here is to produce an account of the main elements of Bloch's theory of non-contemporaneity, but it is, of necessity, woefully incomplete and reductive in its schematization.

12. Bloch, *Heritage of Our Times*, 110. The argument struck most contemporary commentators, Walter Benjamin among them, as itself peculiarly out of synch with the times and drew quite a bit of criticism. Anson Rabinbach quotes Benjamin's reaction to *Heritage of Our Times* in a private letter: "The serious objection which I have of this book (if not of its author as well) is that it in absolutely no way corresponds to the conditions in which it appears, but rather takes its place inappropriately, like a great lord, who arriving at the scene of an area devastated by an earthquake can find nothing more urgent to do than to spread out the Persian carpets—which by the way are already somewhat moth-eaten—and to display the somewhat tarnished golden and silver vessels, and the already faded brocade and damask garments which his servants had brought" ("Unclaimed Heritage," 5). And the allegory ends thus: "After an earthquake, in a devastated area, nothing remains for the great lord but to distribute the Persian carpets for blankets, to cut the brocade cloth into coats, and to melt down the ornamental vessels" (21). See letter from Walter Benjamin to Alfred Cohn, 6 February 1935, *Walter Benjamin, Briefe*,

vol. 2, edited by Gershom Scholem and Theodor W. Adorno (Frankfurt am Main, 1966), 648, 649. For an account of the orthodox critique of Bloch's *Heritage of Our Times*, see Rabinbach, "Unclaimed Heritage," 20.

13. Bloch sets his "noncontemporaneity" in dialogue with Nietzsche's notion of "untimeliness" or *Unzeitgemässigkeit*. Nietzsche's untimeliness as he develops the idea or stance in the early essays collected in *Untimely Meditations* first of all defies the timeliness contained both in the banality of bourgeois fashion and in the grand teleological certainties of Hegelian philosophies of history, and it does so partly through a critical, comparative consideration of the present from the standpoint of another time, often Greek antiquity. The term carries something of the privilege and originality of the thinker who exceeds the bounds of time, and, famously scribbled on the back of an 1874 photograph of himself ("Friedrich the untimely one"), is a quality the philosopher ascribes to himself. While, like Nietzsche's untimeliness, Bloch's noncontemporaneity registers a critical standpoint with respect to unexamined teleologies, noncontemporaneity is not transhistorical. Nor is it a quality reserved for the exceptional man or the philosopher; instead it applies to entire classes of people, where it refers at once to their historical circumstance relative to the dominant mode of production and to their subjective disposition.

14. Bloch, *Heritage of Our Times*, 113, 111.

15. Jay, *Marxism and Totality*, 174.

16. Bloch, *Heritage of Our Times*, 108, emphasis in original. *Unrefurbished* is perhaps an overly concrete translation here for the German *unaufgearbeitete*, which can mean "unincorporated" or "un-reprocessed." The word *resolved* here, rendering the German *aufgehoben*—the third moment of the dialectic—is perhaps more technically equivalent to *sublated*.

17. Bloch, *Heritage of Our Times*, 109.

18. Bloch, *Heritage of Our Times*, 112, emphasis in original.

19. Bloch, *Heritage of Our Times*, 112.

20. Bloch, *Heritage of Our Times*, 110. It is important briefly to point to the polemical context in which Bloch develops the idea of anticapitalist noncontemporaneity and what has come to be known as the "expressionism debate," in which he engaged with his erstwhile friend Georg Lukács. Begun in the second decade of the twentieth century and intensifying in the 1930s, the debate touched on many questions—modernism versus realism, the status of myth or fantasy and reason, of actuality or concrete reality and utopia, of history and reification—and has been carefully studied. Suffice it to remark here, in the guise of a cautionary pause, that in Lukács's view Bloch's noncontemporaneity, with its sights on utopia, far from resisting becoming-commodity, in fact eases and abets the process by concealing the only genuine source of resistance and revolution that is punctually located in the concrete conditions of history and objective reality. See Durst, "Ernst Bloch's Theory of Nonsimultaneity"; Rabinbach, "Unclaimed Heritage." Several key texts in the debate are collected and analyzed in Jameson, *Aesthetics and Politics*.

21. With James a confirmed Trotskyist until the late 1940s and Bloch a staunch supporter of Stalin, they are unlikely to have agreed on much had their paths intersected in those times, as they well might have during the years they both spent in the United

States in the late 1930s and 1940s. Enzo Traverso comments on the tantalizing affinity between James's American writings and Adorno's and explores some of the ramifications of the "missed rendez-vous" of left intellectuals of the black and the German-Jewish Atlantic (Traverso, L'histoire comme champ de bataille, 241–51)

22. Bloch, Heritage of Our Times, 102. On the other hand, Jennifer Wenzel draws attention to another essay of Bloch's dated, like "Non-contemporaneity and Obligation to its Dialectic" to 1932 that suggests a more critical approach to the analogy between "extraterritorial" primitivism and local German variants (Wenzel, Bulletproof, 192–93).

23. Until quite recently there have been relatively few attempts to bring the insights of Western Marxism and the Frankfurt school to bear on colonial situations. But see Chaudhary, Lloyd, Wenzel, and Wilder for particularly promising interventions.

24. James, The Black Jacobins, xi.

25. Robert Hill's chapter, "In England 1932–38," in Paul Buhle's edited collection C. L. R. James: His Life and Work, 61–80, is an indispensable reference for this period of James's life. James's own account of these years in a 1971 lecture is fascinating and accessible ("How I Wrote The Black Jacobins," reprinted in "Lectures on The Black Jacobins"). Anthony Bogues in Caliban's Freedom cautions against overstating the effect of James's radicalization in England, arguing that his fiction writing and his devotion to cricket in Trinidad had already laid the foundations for an identification with the masses. Finally, Cedric Robinson provides a fine-grained materialist analysis of James's intellectual development in Black Marxism, chapter 10.

26. James, "Lectures on The Black Jacobins," 67.

27. Trotsky, History of the Russian Revolution, 15.

28. Trotsky, History of the Russian Revolution, 5–6.

29. James, The Black Jacobins, ix.

30. James, The Black Jacobins, 265.

31. Robinson, Black Marxism, 275–76.

32. For an account of this exchange, see Bogues, Caliban's Freedom, 20–21; Scott, Conscripts of Modernity, 79–81.

33. See Scott, Conscripts of Modernity, 83–87.

34. James, The Black Jacobins, 86.

35. Scholars of our time working in a postcolonial intellectual framework have emphasized the "silencing" of Haiti's revolutionary or modern past, to cite the title of one of the first works to articulate this position, Michel-Rolph Trouillot's Silencing the Past. In an important analysis of the neglect of Haitian modernity and particularly of its sources and consequences in the immediate region of the Caribbean, Sibylle Fischer develops the concept of the Haitian Revolution as a "disavowed" modernity, emphasizing the stakes of the deliberate repression of the world-historical reach of radical antislavery as an intimate constituent of political and philosophical modernity (Fischer, Modernity Disavowed). Susan Buck-Morss ("Hegel and Haiti") draws out the full implications of Haiti for the rhetoric and politics of modernity and emancipation. James, intent on his times, makes relatively little of this historiographic neglect in and of itself.

36. Recent historians of the Haitian Revolution grant more salience to African survivals and to the local culture as crucial factors in the uprising. See, for instance, Dubois, Avengers of the New World.

37. James, The Black Jacobins, 141.

38. James, *The Black Jacobins*, 41, 43.

39. The parallel between fascist and colonial racism and the exterminatory impulses and campaigns they inspired is also central to Aimé Césaire's polemic in *Discourse on Colonialism*. Michael Rothberg explores this complex conjunction in his *Multidirectional Memory*.

40. Bloch, *Heritage of Our Times*, 112.

chapter 4

On Suicide, and Other Forms of Social Extinguishment

Elizabeth A. Povinelli

I

It is now commonplace to note that the generational shift from Althusser to Foucault marked a conceptual shift from a negative-repressive analytics of liberal power to a positive-productive one. For some scholars, this generational shift is nowhere more clearly marked than in Foucault's first volume of the *History of Sexuality*. Foucault begins his study with the lulling images of the repressive hypothesis: "For a long time, the story goes . . . repression operated as a sentence to disappear, but also an injunction to silence, an affirmation of nonexistence, and, by implication, an admission that there was nothing to say about such things, nothing to see, and nothing to know." But he soothes his readers only to make the inverse argument more dramatic. "The question I would like to pose is not, Why are we repressed? But rather, Why do we say, with so much passion and so much resentment . . . that we are repressed?"[1] And the question is not merely one of sexual repression—overturning commonsense understandings of the history of sexuality has direct ramifications on commonsense understandings of liberal power.[2] The question for Foucault was how to think power outside the domineering image of the repressive state. The answer demanded a shift in the analytics of power from "the old power of death that symbolized sovereign power" to a new power over "the administration of bodies and calculated management of life." Historians of European power must understand that "the ancient right to *take* life or *let* live" had been replaced "by a power to *foster* life or *disallow* it to the point of death."[3] I think that it is fair to say that Foucault's plea has become today's axiom. When it comes to an analysis of contemporary liberal power, critical theory centers *on its capacity to produce and manage life*—to make live and let die—rather than to repress or kill life.

This essay critically reencounters the analytics of power associated with the axiom that liberal power centers on the production and management of life, with a specific focus on how this reencounter might alter the terrain of sexual politics. My purpose is not to challenge this analysis of liberalism, nor to challenge how the internal nature and dynamics of an earlier form of liberal power differs from newer forms of neoliberal power nor how biopolitical discussions have themselves become a new form of the repressive hypothesis vis-à-vis a fixation on the thanatopolitical.[4] Instead this essay examines how the enthrallment of the productive powers seems to have atrophied the capacity of critical theory to consider *the irreducible coincidence of the production and extinguishment of life* in its own political projects and ethical impulses. And how, in doing so, critical theory has been normalized in the political domain where sexuality meets life. It is as if in discovering that biopolitics works not by repressing or killing life but by producing bodies and their pleasures through the management of populations, critical theory relieved itself of the burden of ethical responsibility for the necessary extinguishment of the political futures it, or others, sought. What might the future of critical theory have been if it had distinguished its approach to power from the problem of the repressive forces but nevertheless allowed itself to acknowledge its own acts of altercide and suicide?

This question seems especially pertinent given the number of critical theorists currently exploring what an affirmative form of biopolitical thought might look like—a project with which I would broadly align my own work. To begin sketching an answer, this essay starts with a set of scholars attempting to build an affirmative form of the biopolitical out of the Spinozean philosophical concept of *conatus* (a complex concept translated as *striving to persevere in being*, which defines the essence of all finite modes and which is expressed in affects such as desire). It then moves these attempts through the well-known debate between French and German critical theory about the problems of normative commitment and adjudication in relation to new social projects; namely, on what basis does one decide which of the proliferating alternative social projects should become actual social worlds? I then place this discussion in contemporary liberal debates about sexuality. The purpose of reentering this debate is not to resolve it but rather to note how both sides sidestep the irreducible coincidence of extinguishment and potentiation in every progressive and conservative political project. I end by speculating on how key concepts that developed in the wake of the repressive hypothesis—multiplicity, plasticity, and finitude—continually externalize the problem of extinguishment and its political and ethical demands.

II

Before I even begin, some might object to the way I have set up "Althusser" and "Foucault" as the names we use to mark the emergence of an era in which liberal formations of power are no longer understood as primarily constituted through a complex of repressive forces but as most deeply rooted in their ability to produce forms of life. "Isn't this a rather reductive reading of these thinkers and those you place on either side of these critical theoretical camps?" "Isn't this just the old opposition between Hegelian and Spinozean philosophies distorting the evolving work of complex thinkers?"[5] It is certainly true, these same people might say, that those theorists associated with the repressive hypothesis saw violence as part and parcel of liberal—and colonial—power, and insofar as they did they marked the influence of Hegel on French critical theory. Althusser, Fanon, Bataille: all were part of the generation confronted by Alexandre Kojève's reading of Hegel and its compelling coordination of terror and recognition.[6] In Kojève's account the "absolute liquefaction" that the slave experiences, that makes the slave as such in the battle of recognition, is the necessary condition of self-consciousness.[7] What wonder that someone like Fanon saw an equally horrific subjective self-shattering in the conflagration of violent revolution as necessary for the liberation of the colonized from the colonial order. And it is certainly true that while Foucault would credit the influence of Heidegger, others associated with the turn to the productivity of power, such as Deleuze and Guattari, would cite the persuasive influence of Spinoza on their thinking about the arrangements of contemporary liberal truth and life: truth as immanent to specific arrangements (*agencements*) of life.[8] In the process of shifting influences the great revolutionary confrontation gave way to inner revolutions. Violent liquefactions were replaced by the experimental potentialities of bodies and their pleasures.[9] And as they did so, a certain aspect of the political has receded into a deep and silent background, namely, progressive politics' relation to the extinguishment of social projects and worlds. Foucault would famously turn away from subjective terror and toward subjective experimentation as the basis of social transformation. Freedom from liberal formations of power came from "an exercise of the self on the self by which one attempts to develop and transform oneself, and to attain a certain mode of being."[10]

But a strong case could be made that, in retrospect, the repressive and productive hypotheses of power were hardly as oppositional as they might initially have seemed. Althusser's writings were certainly state focused in the ways Foucault critiqued—and the national coordination of U.S. mayors to remove Occupy sites just as the rhetoric of the 99 percent was taking hold might certainly give us pause before side-stepping the repressive powers that the liberal state always holds in reserve. But the writings of Althusser and Fanon, and earlier, Antonio Gramsci, never represented the repressive terror of state violence as sufficient to the operation of power. They insisted that the repressive powers of the state were integrally dependent on its productive forces. Who can forget Gramsci's account of hegemony, with its rich metaphors of trench warfare; Fanon's account of the colonization of men through the insinuations of racist language; or Althusser's insistence that ideological state apparatuses (and not repressive state apparatuses) produced the subjects that it would then exploit? And Fanon surely thought as deeply about the constitution of subjectivities in the colonial condition as Foucault did in the Western ordering of things.[11] On the other side of the barricade, Foucault returned to the problem of the state in his late thinking, castigating the state phobia of certain domains of the intellectual left because of its alignment with neoliberalism. And Deleuze remained more ambivalent about the complete rejection of the repressive approach to desire than did Foucault.[12] Don't these facts suggest that the sides are closer than they might have initially appeared—that the repressive hypothesis never repressed the field of productivity?

In a series of essays comparing Heidegger's evolving reflections on being, world, and thing and Foucault's on subjectivity, power, and freedom, the philosopher Herbert Dreyfus pivots the confrontation not so much at the level of the negative and positive modalities of power as at the level of each modality's relation to the status of entities and truth. Dreyfus notes that both Heidegger and Foucault came to reject the repressive understanding of world, because it projected into every given world an essential truth independent of the particular arrangements of that world. The repressive understanding, in other words, produces truth as invariable. And it was the status of truth—and its relationship to various metaphysics of substance—rather than repressive or productive powers per se that was at stake for Heidegger and Foucault. For them the question wasn't the repressive or productive nature of liberal or colonial power, à la Gramsci, Althusser, or Fanon, but the status of any and every thing posited as the motive force of subjectivity and history in the first or last instance.

Thus the deep link between Foucault's thoughts about the productivity of liberal power and his thoughts about the constitution of truth: namely, that the language games of power make truth and that the truth of liberal power can be found in its techniques for making live and letting die.¹³ In other words, when it comes to liberal power, productivity is squared: *liberal arrangements produce their own truths about power, and these truths about power center on its capacity to produce and manage life.* Foucault's "flip-flops"—first opposing the critical obsession with the state, then accusing the left of being statephobic—are understandable in this light. Foucault was neither disinterested in the state nor interested only in productive power. His deeper interest was whether there was a center point around which any or all arrangements of force-power revolved, or whether force-power constituted the center point— and thus the shape of the immanent potentialities (or what we might call "otherwises") within a given arrangement. "The state is nothing else but the effect, the profile, the mobile shape of a perpetual statification (*étatisation*) or statifications, in the sense of incessant transactions which modify, or move, or drastically change, or insidiously shift sources of finance, modes of investment, decision-making centers, forms and types of control, relationships between local powers, the central authority, and so on."¹⁴

As much as it might be useful to think about the tautological bind between the claim that truth is an effect of power and the claim that power is an effect of truth, my purpose here is to think something slightly different. Let us say that, no matter how much critical thought abhors a tautology, these two statements capture something crucial about the radical interiority of every social world. In every social world the production of subjects and nonsubjects, bodies and antibodies, pleasures and discomforts, people and populations presuppose an existing regime of background truth and entail this truth through their material reproduction. This indeed could describe Althusser's claim that the social reproduction of capitalism depended on the production of subjects as well as Foucault's contention that subjects are the effect of discursive formations. But insofar as this is true, then to create a new social form, a new alternative social world, the world that is materially (that are the existing subjects and nonsubjects, bodies and antibodies, pleasures and discomforts, people and populations) must be extinguished. In other words, in trying to secure or disturb a world, we extinguish one world in the very act of trying to keep another world in place, to return to this place, or to create new places.

III

Given my emphasis on the irreducible coincidence of the production and extinguishment of life in every political project, Spinoza's philosophical concept of conatus seems a potentially potent tool.[15] Of particular importance for the discussion here are Spinoza's thoughts about the infinite modalities of substance and the ethics of entities. To be sure, when Spinoza naturalized God—the divine—he did not radically *plasticize* truth. Eternal laws of nature remained for Spinoza, and *everything* flowed from these laws. But because of the infinite nature of substance, "everything" is an infinite immanence arising out of every and any finite arrangement of entities (or modes)—a multiplicity of beings and becomings. And each "everything," every *something*, participates in the ethical essence of being. For Spinoza, the essence of any finite mode, including an arrangement (*agencement*), is a striving (conatus) to persevere in being.[16] And insofar as the object of conatus is *perseverare*, the potential end of conatus might be to persevere or not, to be or become or to cease being altogether.

It is not Spinoza's philosophy per se that interests me here, but rather how numerous critical theorists have explored the potentialities of conatus for the political present, especially the legacy of the notion of the biopolitical. Most of these have stressed the productive positivities of conatus. Working through the writings of Deleuze, for instance, Rosie Braidotti has noted the "implicit positivity" of the "notion of desire as conatus."[17] For Deleuze and Guattari, this implicit positivity dwelled not merely in all actual things but also in all potential things—the body with organs and the body-without-organs within every organic arrangement.[18] And in his effort to develop a positive form of biopower, Roberto Esposito has recently linked Spinoza's notion of conatus to his claim in the *Political Treatise* that "every natural thing has as much right from Nature as it has power to exist and to act." Esposito places the emphasis on "the intrinsic modality that life assumes in the expression of its own unrestrainable power to exist" and in doing so brackets what might be a more Nietzschean reading, namely, the relative power that *restrains* the existence and actions of various bioformations in a given field of equally often opposing striving actors (actants).[19] It is as if saving biopower from internal negativity necessitated banishing conatus's potential from the horizon of attention.

The affirmative nature of a biopolitical conatus provides a penumbral shadow over a number of Foucault's interviews about the gay rights movement, held around the same time he was lecturing on the concept of biopower. In these interviews, Foucault rejected the repressive understanding of power that he saw lurking in the political aspiration for gay liberation even as he embraced the political potentialities of gay *freedom*. Gay friendship was the specific outcome of these gay experiments of freedom; they were intense and satisfying relations that refused to conform to the opposing norms of sexual promiscuity and intimate bonding.[20] When pressed how he could say no to gay liberation and yes to gay freedom, Foucault replied that freedom is not the liberation of the gay subject into a "happy human being imbued with a sexuality to which the subject could achieve a complete and satisfying relationship."[21] Freedom is a set of ongoing reflexive practices that the subject undergoes in relation to a given formation of power; freedom is a constant, considered potentiating rather than liberating of difference. Freedom simultaneously confronts power and is power; it confronts the given organization of life, and it is the transformative capacity we exercise to disturb this given organization. Thus was Foucault able to square his interest in the creative innovations and variations of sexual acts and intimacies emerging in the "laboratories of sexual experimentation" in New York and San Francisco, even as he showed little interest in the liberation movement.[22] This striving to potentiate an otherwise within any given social formation has been the focus of much queer theory. The emphasis on freedom as potentiation seems to have built a new corridor for thinking politically after the great, often violent social upheavals of the 1960s. Consequently very little critical theory has focused on repression, negation, extinguishment; consideration of such issues has mainly appeared as sociological material: the murder of Matthew Shepard, the suicide of Tyler Clementi.[23]

There would seem to be notable exceptions—Edelman, Bersani, and others associated with the antisocial critique in queer theory. Judith Halberstam, reviewing the work of Leo Bersani and Lee Edelman, positively notes that the antisocial, negative, and antirelational theory of sexuality "upends our understanding of the interconnectedness of intimacy, romance and sexual contact and replaces it with a harsh but radically realistic recognition of both the selfishness of sex and its destructive power."[24] But it remains unclear whether, or how, their focus on the annihilative forces of sexuality speaks to the ethical dilemma of the politicalization of conatus. How does the centering of the death drive in queer theory and politics confront or figure the other (or the form of the self against which the queer is figured as the truth of the self) as something with equal ethical force—as having legitimately invested conatus?[25]

Before placing critical pressure on this emphasis, let me first note that the positivities of conatus present a number of problems to liberal formations of power. Conventional liberal political science has relied on substantive or procedural grounds to determine which given or potential form of life has more or less claim on existence in any given social collectivity. But conatus asserts that to be, or *potentially to be*, is already to have the claim on the right to existence—the essence of being is the right to strive to exist. No method of liberal adjudication—reflective equilibrium, public reason, or substantive principles like freedom and autonomy—can puncture the simple assertion that if you are or could be, you have the same right to strive to continue to be as anything else. To decide to extinguish another form of life or to passively contribute to its exhaustion cannot be justified on any grounds other than, it seems, the *differential* power of natural things "to exist and to act." It is hardly therefore a wonder that the critical literature focusing on the politics of potentiating has given rise to such a trenchant critique based on the problem of adjudication and justification. Take, for instance, Nancy Fraser's engagement with the debate between Habermas ("the leading exponent of German Critical Theory") and Foucault ("the most political of the French poststructuralists").[26]

At the heart of Fraser's critique of Foucault lay a simple question: What are the justifiable norms that allow him to adjudicate among the riotous proliferation of social life forms, some of which actively seek to annul others? If he had no normative commitment, was he simply observant of actual and potential life as it struggled, often confrontationally, to be and persevere in being a political actor in the directionality of life? If we consider the act of being "passive" (to let them die) as an activity, these observational politics are as implicated in politics as confrontational politics. If each and every actual world and each and every potential world have an equal right to strive to persevere, then on what ethical or political grounds do decisions to extinguish (or let die) one or another world rest? The Habermasian answer is to bracket all but one normative commitment, namely, the commitment to deliberative reason as the basis of public decisions about which forms of life will be enhanced, let die, or actively extinguished.[27] What is Foucault's commitment? What if one striving potentiating meets and opposes another? Can progressive politics avoid this question—and thus the problem of extinguishment? How would the sign *progressive* read if it were understood as always actively maintaining, producing, and *extinguishing* worlds? In its refusal of the repressive hypothesis, how has it avoided the politics of its own practices of extinguishment?

We can question whether Habermas or Fraser avoids the problem of extinguishment. Fraser concludes her rightfully influential essay "From Recognition to Redistribution" by stating her hope to do justice to *all* current struggles against injustice. As others have noted, all current struggles against injustice can become one justice only if the contradictory struggles have been leveled by some ruler or another—a cardinal measure introduced into the ordinal measure. And so, properly speaking, we can only always say, "Do justice to all current struggles against injustice that meet my measure for what injustice consists of." But nevertheless Fraser's point is well taken, even if it could be applied as forcibly to German critical theory as to French. After all, like any politics properly speaking, intentional progressive politics seek to change the actual world because they find this world unjust, wrong, or aesthetically displeasing. They seek to extinguish one form of life with a hope that another will emerge which is less unjust, less wrong, or more to their standards of the right and beautiful. The stakes of this debate rest in part on what constitutes "politics properly speaking" and whether one mode of political action is more or less touched by the problem of extinguishment than another.

Take, for example, the confrontation between the so-called inclusive and transformational wings of contemporary gaylesbianqueer politics. A large part of the progressive gaylesbianqueer rights movement seems to fit squarely within the recognition camp, seeking to do away with the sexually discriminatory institutions of marriage, civil service, immigration, and nationalization through the politics of sexual recognition. Another part argues that the politics of inclusion is not truly political because it does not touch the class, racial, or imperial underpinnings of liberal inclusion. Like Jacques Rancière, this part sees this inclusive gesture as merely a policing tactic rather than a political action.[28] Political action does not merely redistribute forms of life into already existing social categories; it ruptures the given arrangement of social life, thereby transforming the normal distribution of roles, places, and occupations within "the common."[29] To be sure, the "inclusive" wing of the movement often disputes the characterization of their politics as merely inclusive. By incorporating nonheterosexual forms of marriage and intimacy into existing political frameworks, they insist that all frameworks that had previously depended on heterosexual presuppositions are transformed.

Rather than focusing on which of these two wings of the progressive gaylesbianqueer movement is more or less transformative, let us pause on the image of social becoming captured in terms such as *transformation* and *rupture*. Why does neither side in this debate emphasize their desire to extinguish one world as the basis of pulling another world into being? And aren't these forms of extinguishment deeply insinuated in the act and experience of progressive justice rather than merely superficially related to it? *Having experienced the injustice of sexual discrimination, whether personally or as a witness to* others, I seek to extinguish the social world as it is currently constituted so that others do not have to experience its injustice. Here gaylesbiantqueer bashings and killings make their compelling appearance. Isn't it on behalf of all the Matthew Shepards and potential Matthew Shepards that the necessity to extinguish the possibility of such actions becomes vital and urgent? But how, in acting decisively to transform the (produce a) world in which such actions are thinkable, are we engaged in an act of altercide and a suicide?

Take altercide. We can certainly focus on the positivities of freedom, as Foucault did when discussing the ethics of friendship and care of the self that he witnessed among gay men in the 1970s and 1980s. The ongoing reflexive practices that defined for Foucault gay freedom can certainly be seen as the potentiating rather than liberating of difference. But there are other practices of sexual freedom seeking to potentiate a different and perhaps opposing world: the sexual politics of so-called ultraconservative Christians.[30] Not only are members of this public striving to persevere within what they view as a hostile, sexually saturated culture awash with homosexuals and aborted fetuses, but they are striving to potentiate a world in which the intensity of their striving would give way to their version of palliative care, to an easier form of coping. To do this, however, they must rupture and transform the given world. They will not be appeased by appeals to the private nature of religious belief; they are not struggling to be added to the world as another sector of the pluralized public. They are seeking to anchor all possible ways of asking and answering questions about sexuality around a theology of sin, pleasure, and temporality. In this world all psychological, biological, and discursive approaches to sexuality will be anchored in the first and last instance in an understanding of the world that would include the central battle between God and Devil, the resurrection of the body, the abomination of the flesh outside the sacrament of marriage. *Do I want this potential world to become an actual world? Is it a future I want?* However I respond to this question, I either must ignore the "face" of an entity striving to persevere in being—or to become—or characterize that face in all sorts of ways and through all sorts of rhetorical moves: exposing its hypocrisy, demonizing its demons, sneering at its ignorance. And of course neither the "face" nor the entity is simply a human face. It is one aspect of a form of life that extends beyond human sociality and being into an interlocking arrangement of concepts, materials, and institutions. Nor is this face merely in front of us. We are one of the inter-faces of the thing that is presented to us as if it were physically outward and in front of us but is actually complexly already inside of us.

Take suicide. Here I do not mean the suicide in the sense—or at the level—of those who take their lives, such as Tyler Clementi. Rather, I mean how, in the attempt to save them, I extinguish the world that gave sense to "me." After all, if we understand subjectivity as a phenomenon that emerges from within a social order, then this "I" that experienced discrimination is the same "I" that was produced by this discrimination. I may reflect on the injustice of the world and seek to extinguish the world as it is because it is unjust. But as a result, "I" am seeking to extinguish "me" since I am the result of the conditions that made me. The metaphysics of liberation do not uncover these moments, for I must not only extinguish *that* but also *me*. When I extinguish I am making a world in which I no longer make sense, and I am making it without the capacities that I am trying to bestow on the subsequent generation and without certain knowledge of the subsequent world. When I act to lend my effort to undermining what I perceive as an unjust form of life, "I" will no longer be there, and I have no idea what will emerge *there* where none of us are yet.[31] And not simply "I," of course: the entire network that constitutes the social content and relationalities lying at the heart of my claim to be me will have been extinguished. The account that best captures for me the simultaneity and pathos of subjective suicide as a necessary condition of progressive social politics comes from James Baldwin's *Notes of a Native Son*. In the essay that gives the volume its title, Baldwin reflects on the pathos of his father, who "had to prepare the child for the day when the child would be despised" by "creat[ing] in the child ... a stronger antidote to this poison than one had found for oneself."[32] Through recourse to images of poison, amputation, and gangrene, Baldwin conveys not only the subjective conditions of domination but also the existential conditions of social rupture—how bodies and minds can remain at once in the world and out of sequence with the world it is seeking to create or has successfully created. Son looks at son, son at father, mother at daughter, and subsequent generations to antecedent ones with the same painful alienation.

Given that the concept of conatus is coupled to perseverance and thus coupled to the play of social forces that could negate its powers and thus its being, why has so little critical attention been paid to elaborating *the irreducible coincidence of the production and extinguishment of life* in its own political projects and ethical impulses? How are we thinking the productivities of power such that we are precluding the extinguishment of worlds? Or, in the case of the antisocial thesis in queer theory, simply transforming extinguishment into the endless productivity of the otherwise?

IV

Perhaps the most obvious way we preclude any consideration of extinguishment is by conflating the concept of multiplicity and the politics of pluralism. Theories of multiplicity posit that, in any given arrangement, multiple potential otherwises (futures of the other) already exist internal to these arrangements: the multiplicity of the otherwise is in the actual. The question critical theory asks is what releases one or another of these potential otherwises into the actual. For instance, Foucault's focus on subjugated knowledges is not to liberate a repressed thought but to capacitate modes of life, currently all around us but having no explicit force among us, so that they can be.[33] Theories of political pluralism (pluralization), on the other hand, focus on how a set of existing diverse social groups can be related in such a way that they can coexist peacefully side by side. In other words, political pluralism is a governmental technique for managing actually existing difference without harm or annihilation. The plural becomes pluralized, a matter of numerical arrangement and bracketing.

To see what might be at stake in distinguishing theories of multiplicity and the politics of pluralization, let me return to my earlier discussion of contemporary sexual politics. One might have gotten the impression from my discussion that Christians and gaylesbianqueers were distinct social worlds and projects. But as we know many gaylesbianqueers are Christian and share some key ontological beliefs about time, the body, and salvation with other Christians. As Christians, many gays and lesbians believe in sin and the afterlife, the presence of God and the Devil in daily life. The vast majority simply do not believe that homosexuality is a sin.[34] They see their fellow Christians as making a category mistake, as having mistakenly divided up a shared world. Thus internal to Christianity is an actual world of difference—how every given arrangement is a complex arrangement of movement and rest—and multiple potential worlds in which this difference might be rearranged. Pluralization seeks to find a framework within which these actual differences can coexist. Theories of multiplicity ask how one capacitates these potential futures and thus the subjects and nonsubjects, bodies and antibodies, pleasures and discomforts, people and populations that might emerge with them.

The question is how these two approaches have become somewhat fused in current discussions of the productivity of power and an affirmative biopolitics. Have we focused so fully on the concept of freedom as potentiation (vis-à-vis the productive hypothesis) rather than liberation (vis-à-vis the repressive hypothesis) that we have avoided the irreducible coincidence of potentiation and extinguishment—of the object of conatus as the ability or failure to persevere in a given arrangement of forces? If gaylesbiantrans Christians succeed in creating the conditions within which homosexuality is not a sin, they will have succeeded in extinguishing the world in which it is—and with that world all the subjects and nonsubjects, bodies and antibodies, pleasures and discomforts, people and populations that might emerge with them. Can we open our eyes to the implicit positivity of conatus without closing them to the forms of life that will persevere or be extinguished as the condition of another form of life emerging?

Perhaps the avoidance of extinguishment in theories of multiplicity is an artifact of the generational debate between the repressive and productive hypotheses rather than an internal necessity of the theories themselves. After all, while Foucault was critiquing the repressive hypothesis in his *History of Sexuality* through the formations of power (*dispositifs du pouvoir*), Deleuze was attempting to reconceive of desire as a set of arrangements (*agencements du désir*) rather than a category of lack—less the repression of desire than the arrangement of heterogeneous elements.[35] In its emphasis on repression, psychoanalysis kept on the conceptual table the energetics of the process of working-through. Psychic resistance was aggressively obstinate. Subjective transformation was slow, stubborn, and limited, and it often included as its outcome merely a new stance toward a psychic formation rather than the transformation of that formation. There were limits to how many new organs a subject could grow and how many could go missing over the course of a life. Thus, compared with those portraits that foreground "transformation," how much more complete is Baldwin's portrait of his father's experience—and his own—when viewed from a framework that foregrounds the stubborn nature of arrangements of bodies? Why isn't the pathos of figures such as Baldwin's father more often the narrative or theoretical focus of critical theory? Where is the ethical and political thought that is on the side of potentiality and yet has a relation to the limits of plasticity?

One might be tempted to think that the concept of finitude would provide a curative salve to the problem of extinguishment. After all, finitude would seem to encompass extinguishment in the way I am discussing it here: that within the concept of conatus as striving to persevere in being is the concept of a limit to being as existence. And yet even the most subtle and profound thinker of finitude, multiplicity, and relationality, Jean-Luc Nancy, finds a way through the Hegelian and Heideggerian traditions to extinguishment.

In a particularly rich and lucid account, Nancy compares Hegelian and Heideggerian takes on finitude. For Hegel, in negation "finite being goes out of itself and is taken into infinitude," whereas for Heidegger, in death "finitude is an opening to infinitude." For Nancy, death is fundamentally transformed into nondeath as "the final status of being is the opening to the infinite" precisely because the finite is never singular but always a sharing of being—a plurality of being as the basis of being—which is revealed and opened at its limit.[36] Reading this meditation through my previous discussion, the plurality of being constitutes the possibility of an infinity of potential beings. But insofar as the finite becomes an opening to infinity, the necessity to think extinguishment may once again be closed.

Other issues arise as we consider extinguishment in relation to finitude, issues that would necessitate a longer paper and perhaps a different archive. How, for instance, has the conceptual content and dynamic of finitude been determined by a specific kind of being, human beings, and a particular form of life, carbon life? In other words, how has the drama of finitude necessitated a particular drama about a minute segment of the vast forms in which entities are?

....

A kind of postscript. Where does this leave us? How does one foster a political otherwise when to succeed comes at the price of extinguishing another—and the self? Although I cannot answer these questions here, it seems to me two issues would need to be addressed in any attempt to do so. The first is the issue of altercide and characterization. The challenge the concept of conatus presents to critical theory is the radical leveling of modes of being; insofar as a mode of being is, or could be, that mode has as much of a right to strive to persevere as any other. How do we characterize that which we will extinguish? Stripped of the ability to rank being on one or another basis, progressive politics faces the task of potentiating without stereotyping or scapegoating the forms of life it will necessarily extinguish. The second is the issue of suicide and world. If we must extinguish without recourse to a cardinal measure, we must also act even though the world in which our actions would have made maximal sense will be extinguished at the moment of our success, its cardinal measure subsumed by a new world. These seem the deep ethical stakes of a political practice unmoored by the repressive hypothesis but awake to the problem of extinguishment. And these seem to demand a new archive and genre of thought.[37]

Notes

1. Foucault, *The History of Sexuality*, 3–4, 8, 9.
2. "The representation of power has remained under the spell of the monarchy. In political thought and analysis, we still have not cut off the head of the king." (Foucault, *The History of Sexuality*, 89). See also "The Ethics of the Concern for Self as a Practice of Freedom," in *Ethics, Subjectivity and Truth*, edited by Paul Rabinow (New York: New Press, 1990), 281–301, 282, where Foucault assents to the characterization of a shift in his focus on subjectivity and power to care of self as a shift from a focus on games of truth with "coercive practice" to the practices of "self-formation of the subject."
3. Foucault. *The History of Sexuality*, 139–40, 138.
4. For my thoughts about how the formations of power may have shifted in late liberalism, see Elizabeth A. Povinelli, *Economies of Abandonment: Social Belonging and Endurance in Late Liberalism* (Durham: Duke University Press, 2012). For a discussion of the cryptothanatopolitics within contemporary discussions of biopolitics, see Timothy C. Campbell, *Improper Life, Technology and Biopolitics from Heidegger to Agamben* (Minneapolis: University of Minnesota Press, 2011).
5. Althusser's student Pierre Macherey would later describe this confrontation between terror and experimentation as a byproduct of a confrontation between the philosophies of Hegel and Spinoza—and the mistaken belief that the thought of Hegel and of Spinoza were simply opposed rather than constituting a "single unique discourse, in the interior of which their respective positions would be indistinguishable," each marking the internal limit case of the other. Pierre Macherey, *Hegel or Spinoza*, translated by Susan M. Ruddick (Minneapolis: University of Minnesota Press, 2011), 4.
6. Althusser's engagement with Kojève's thinking became clearer after the publication of his early essays on Hegel. See Louis Althusser, *The Spectre of Hegel: Early Writings*, edited by François Matheron, translated by G. M. Goshgarian (London: Verso, 1997).
7. Kojève, "In Place of Introduction," especially 21–22.
8. Deleuze famously called Spinoza the prince of philosophers. See Gilles Deleuze, *Expressionism in Philosophy: Spinoza* (New York: Zone, 1992).
9. David Harvey would argue that this theoretical shift reflected a social shift the organization of capital. See David Harvey, *The Condition of Postmodernity: An Enquiry into the Origins of Cultural Change* (London: Wiley-Blackwell, 1991). See also the BBC documentary *The Century of the Self* (BBC Four, 2002).
10. Fanon, "Concerning Violence," in *The Wretched of the Earth*, 36; Foucault, "The Ethics of the Concern for Self as a Practice of Freedom," in *Ethics*, 282.
11. Fanon, "Concerning Violence," 36.
12. Foucault, "31 January 1979," in *The Birth of Biopolitics*, 75–100; Deleuze, *Foucault*.
13. See, for instance, Nikolas Rose, *The Politics of Life Itself: Biomedicine, Power, and Subjectivity in the Twenty-first Century* (Princeton: Princeton University Press, 2006).
14. Foucault, "31 January 1979," 77.
15. See Christopher Norris, *Spinoza and the Origin of Critical Theory* (London: Basil Blackwell, 1991).
16. Spinoza, *Ethics*, IIIp7, IIIp9.
17. Braidotti, *Transpositions*, 150.
18. See Deleuze, *Foucault*.

19. Esposito, *Bios*, 185–86.
20. Foucault, "Sexual Choice, Sexual Act," in *Ethics, Subjectivity and Truth*, 141–56, 151.
21. Foucault, "The Ethics of the Concern for Self as a Practice of Freedom," 281–301, 283.
22. Foucault, "Sexual Choice, Sexual Act," 151.
23. See, for instance, Lee Edelman, *No Future: Queer Theory and the Death Drive* (Durham: Duke University Press, 2004).
24. Halberstam, "Anti-social Turn in Queer Studies," 140.
25. Heather Love's reflections on the melancholic hold of past forms of sexuality on contemporary gay and lesbian longings would be relevant here. Heather Love, *Feeling Backward: Loss and the Politics of Queer History* (Durham: Duke University Press, 2007).
26. Fraser, *Unruly Practices*, 36.
27. See Jürgen Habermas, *Between Facts and Norms: Contributions to a Discourse Theory of Law and Democracy* (Cambridge, Mass.: MIT Press, 1992); Nancy Fraser. "From Redistribution to Recognition: Dilemmas of Justice in a 'Post-Socialist' Age," *New Left Review* 1.212 (1995): 69–93.
28. See Rancière, *Disagreement*.
29. See Rancière, *Disagreement*.
30. Perhaps the best study of the challenge nonliberal practices of piety pose to critical theory is Saba Mahmood's *Politics of Piety: The Islamic Revival and the Feminist Subject* (Princeton: Princeton University Press, 2005).
31. Patchen Markell, *Bound by Recognition* (Princeton: Princeton University Press, 2003) has attempted to take the necessary indeterminacy of social being as the basis of a politics of acknowledgment.
32. Baldwin, *Notes of a Native Son*, 106.
33. See Foucault, "Society Must Be Defended."
34. See Dawne Moon, *God, Sex, and Politics: Homosexuality and Everyday Theologies* (Chicago: University of Chicago Press, 2004); Melissa M. Wilcox, *Coming out in Christianity: Religion, Identity, and Community* (Bloomington: Indiana University Press, 2003).
35. Deleuze, *Foucault*.
36. Nancy puts the same point slightly differently as well: "Finitude does not mean that we are noninfinite—like small, insignificant beings within a grand, universal, and continuous being—but it means that we are *infinitely* finite, infinitely exposed to our existence as a nonessence, infinitely exposed to the otherness of our own 'being.'" Jean-Luc Nancy, "On Finitude and Sovereignty: A Workshop with Jean-Luc Nancy," lecture presented at Birkbeck Institute for the Humanities, May 2005, http://birkbeck.academia.edu/GilbertLeung/Papers/291788/On_Finitude_and_Sovereignty_A_Workshop_with_Jean-Luc_Nancy. See also Jean Luc-Nancy, *The Birth to Presence* (Stanford: Stanford University Press, 1994).
37. A reader of this essay provided one very interesting direction for this archive of suicide and altercide: the manifesto of radical feminism and queer theory, Monique Wittig's proclamations that "woman" must be abolished and the altercide of "I Hate Straights." Does the manifesto evidence a new stance toward the equal right for that which we extinguish to persevere?

PART II *approaches aside*

chapter 5

What Is Historical Poetics?

Simon Jarvis

Yopie Prins has recently recommended that the study of lyric poetry proceed as a "historical poetics." The rubric concisely collides two familiar desiderata. But what is historical poetics?

Prins's short piece, sensibly, does not attempt to settle the matter by a definition. It does, however, give some indications—albeit sometimes negative or indirect—as to how we might understand the phrase. The essay looks again at Sidney Lanier's attempt at a *Science of English Verse* (1880). Prins does not expect to find there a guide to scansion: "Practical application is not the point of historical poetics." Instead she seeks a stimulus to overlooked questions: "What were the political and philosophical stakes of thinking about prosody? . . . What kinds of knowledge or ways of knowing are implicit in Lanier's claim to 'science'?" These sorts of questions could help us, it is indicated, to displace what Prins considers still to be a dominant set of assumptions in the study of lyric: "A turn to historical poetics is one way to theorize as well as to historicize alternatives to the assumption of voice in lyric reading. Historical poetics could open up a reading of various experiments in prosody and dysprosody, challenging us to think again about poetic practices that now seem obscure, obsolete, even obtuse."[1]

This is as close as the essay comes to a formal statement of the nature of historical poetics, and it is worth considering its terms closely. It is hard to specify what is meant by the phrase "the assumption of voice in lyric reading." A very wide range of claims could be imagined as instances of "the assumption of voice in lyric reading," some defensible, others not. It could refer to a very minimal claim indeed—as, for example, that poems can be, and often have been, read aloud, and that this may be something which it might be good to take into account when we are thinking about them. Or it could refer to a very large claim, as, for example, that the printed text of a poem is only the poor and inadequate bodily vessel of its ideally sonorous soul.

Clearly no essay consisting only of a few pages is going to have the space to discriminate among all these different kinds of claim. The result of the essay's not doing so, however, is that the concept of historical poetics itself must remain unspecified, because the most concrete idea of historical poetics that is given there is that it is going to help us to develop alternatives to this "assumption"—or rather, to this very broad range of quite various assumptions.

Yet perhaps it is clear what is envisaged, even if it is not quite spelt out. What is envisaged, surely, is a practice which might be able to treat the history of poetics as a better initial guide than, say, a theory of rhythm and meter grounded in the latest developments in phonology, to what is at stake in historically changing practices of verse composition, distribution, and reception. Documents from the history of poetics—treatises like Lanier's, evidently, but also letters, reviews, advertisements, printing history—are inevitably saturated with all sorts of cultural idioms which can help us to connect them to the culture of which they are part and in which the people who produced, distributed, and consumed verse texts and performances lived. They may therefore also help us to understand how the minute details, the organization of poetics texts and performances—and not only their paraphrasable content—resonated with larger-scale organizations of thinking and feeling in the societies in which they were made and circulated.

It is worth pausing to note that if the phrase "historical poetics" is not original with Prins (nor with the research group in which Prins participated under this rubric at the Center for Cultural Analysis at Rutgers),[2] this way of understanding it is. The phrase has cropped up fleetingly in a number of contexts before Prins, but there have been few determined efforts to raise it as a standard. The film historian David Bordwell's attempt along these lines would no doubt appear simply formalist to many literary theorists. But what if "formalism" were *already* "historical poetics"? The earliest recorded appeal to the phrase *historical poetics* is one of the most significant: the *Istoricheskaia Poetika* of Aleksandr Veselovsky (1838–1906). The work first appeared as part of a collection of Veselovsky's writings in 1913 and was then reprinted in 1940 and 1989. Veselovsky's education was undertaken in Europe and especially in Germany, where he found it puzzling that, while there were departments of world history and specialists in that subject, there were no departments of world literature and no experts in the topic.[3] "Historical poetics" emerges from Veselovsky's idea of the comparative study of world literature. Igor Shaitanov has summarized its aim in the following fashion: "Historical poetics urges one to concentrate on the word and the text, but, unlike most modern textual approaches, historical poetics historicizes its subject when it engages itself not with the word in the text (after the long-standing practices of new criticism) but with the word in the genre."[4] A recent champion of Veselovsky's, Boris Maslov, defines historical poetics as "the study of the evolution of constitutive forms of creative (ritual, poetic, literary) uses of language." As Maslov has recently pointed out, one striking feature of Veselovsky's approach to world literature was his insistence on what Maslov calls "an astonishingly broad definition of literary history, which he explicitly equates with cultural history (Kulturgeschichte)."[5] Veselovsky rejected the use of aesthetic criteria to separate objects proper to poetics from those outside its purview. In his report back from Berlin as one of those "sent abroad in preparation for professorship," Veselovsky warned that "as long as the historical and everyday aspect remains nothing but an appendix or an accessory, a Beiwerk, of literary enquiry . . . the history of literature will remain as it has been up until now: a bibliographic guide, an aesthetic excursus, a treatise on itinerant stories, or a political sermon. Until then, literary history cannot exist."[6]

Veselovsky's simultaneous demands for exhaustive global knowledge and minute formal specification might lead us to share René Wellek's verdict that "Veselovsky has assigned to scholarship a task which can hardly ever be solved."[7] But Wellek went on to say that "the Russian Formalists, however, have taken up his challenge." This may surprise us, because we are so used to thinking that precisely what the "formalists" left out was history. How could formalists be the inheritors of historical poetics? Shaitanov, however, confirms the connection: "The figure who is conspicuous for his absence in Western reconstructions of Russian theoretical thought is Aleksandr Veselovskii. Without him contemporary literary theory in Russia lacks its source, unity and continuity. No matter how distant the extremes to which Bakhtin and the formalists may have run, they were always aware that they worked within the field which bore the name given to it by Veselovskii—historical poetics."[8]

If we think more closely about what is actually in the work of "the Russian Formalists," Shaitanov's claim that they were always aware that they were already working within the field of historical poetics may not seem so strange after all. Boris Eikhenbaum insisted, "We are not 'formalists,' but rather, if you like, specifiers." He repeated the point on the next page for good measure: "So we are not formalists and do not constitute a 'method.'"[9] Whether one considers Viktor Zhirmunsky's *The Composition of Lyric Poems*, Tynianov's *Archaists and Innovators* (Tynianov's own preferred title would have been *Archaist-Innovators*), or Eikhenbaum's *Melodics of Russian Lyric Verse*, what one has is indeed historical poetics, in the sense of an attention to developing features of verse organization which these scholars themselves take to be intelligible not as a synchronic diagram but only as a historically changing dynamic. Form, says Tynianov, far from being some kind of fixed container for a changing content, the glass into which we pour the wine, owns a dynamic: the *continuous violation of automatism*.[10] It is, in this way, historical at its core. But the Russian poeticians contribute not to a history of the world conducted by means of poetry reading but to a history of how poems get made.

It is at this point that one needs to ask how the "historical poetics" envisaged by Prins would differ from the "neoformalism that . . . Cultural Studies might yet put to good use," proposed by Herbert Tucker in his essay "The Fix of Form" and exemplified in Tucker's own peerless *Epic: Britain's Heroic Muse 1790–1910*.[11] Superficially the two projects share much. Both critics have been especially interested in rhythm and meter; both want to try to get at some thicker sense of why meter matters, how we might specify the cultural and historical and affective significances deployed by metrical repertoires and by particular gestures within those repertoires. But I think there is one (under-articulated) belief in Prins's idea of historical poetics which need not be implied in Tucker's. This belief is that there is no part of poetics which does not stand in need of becoming historical or of being "historicized." The implication, I believe, is that because our ways of reading, writing, hearing, and performing rhythm and meter themselves are historically variable, we may not separate the scansion of verse, for example, from historical inquiry. The implication is that, although Lanier's science of verse can't be our science of verse, it and other documents like it can help us to develop a historically nuanced way of hearing, reading, and scanning the metrical verse of the past.

I am a latecomer and an outsider in this debate among Victorianists as to historical poetics and (cultural) neoformalism. My own interest in the topic has developed out of my work on the German tradition of historical aesthetics from Hegel to Adorno, and especially from Adorno's *Aesthetic Theory*, a work which still remains to be properly read by Anglophone poeticians, whose engagement with Adorno has too often been limited to a short radio talk he once gave about lyric poetry.[12] Two ideas developing from it have been especially important to the way in which I myself should want to formulate any historical poetics: (1) Historicism has not been taken to entail, for example, ethical or political relativism.[13] There is no reason why it should entail aesthetic relativism either. (2) Works of art are records of a historical process of thinking-through-making. The Platonic and then scientific assumption that their artifactual character means that they have nothing to do with cognition and with truth is to be rejected.[14] The (historical) truth-content of works of art is to be sought precisely in their technical organization, which, far from being a transhistorical frame for the work of art, is instead its most intimately historical aspect, that which is most vulnerable to becoming obsolete or to missing its moment.[15]

There is no need to recapitulate here the arguments which I have already made at length elsewhere in support of these positions.[16] I want instead to explore what I take to be an especially critical case in the difficulties faced by historical poetics in its search for larger cultural resonance: the case of the intense delight once afforded by, and now perhaps rarely gleaned from, Alexander Pope's verse technique. What the case study will show, I hope, is not only that verse, with all its continuous series of minute verbal, paralinguistic, and extralinguistic gestures, is itself an essential part of the historical record but that what happens in verse thinking is usually both more and less than what happens in the statements made about it by poets and readers. All is not representation. Gossip, correspondence, manuscripts, printing, editing, reviews, metrical theories: all these represent essential evidence about the historical meaning of verse-thinking. Yet they remain liable to be exceeded or corrected by what happens in that verse-thinking itself.

In fulfilling a commitment to participate in a collection of essays about theory by providing an essay about Pope's versification, I am deliberately aligning myself with a particular conception of theory. With Adorno, I understand critical theory as "the rebellion of experience against empiricism."[17] This essay is offered as exemplifying something of my own conception of a historical poetics, even as I acknowledge that it leaves many of the conceivable tasks of such a poetics unaddressed.

The Poet's Hand

The first page of the manuscript of the second of Pope's Pastorals, "Summer,"[18] places us vividly in front of some of the vital energies and contradictions of Pope's verse art. A reader examining the document in Maynard Mack's collection of Pope's manuscripts will immediately recognize that one striking feature of the manuscript is the extraordinary care which the young poet has taken to make this page look like a printed book. The title matter is, almost to the point of trompe l'oeil, uncannily like the best early eighteenth-century printed letter; the poet has also included an element whose function pertains entirely to printed books: the catchword at the foot of each page. The manuscript has been produced after an extensive course of circulations of the poem among men of taste and potential patrons; it represents the end point of an already very protracted sequence of blottings, cuttings, polishings, and refinements.[19] The calligraphic achievement of producing a near-facsimile of a contemporary printed letter is a strategy with clear advantages, but also with clear risks. It represents the poem as already worthy of that permanence which print affords; it is in this sense already a claim to deserve publication. Yet it might also remind us of a series of possibly even childish wishes in relation to authorship: of a fantasy preoccupation with the matter of print and with the fact of being printed, potentially at the expense of a concern with the underlying matter of the poem itself. Pope's friend, the painter Jonathan Richardson, wrote in his *Essay on the Theory of Painting* that "an Author must Think, but 'tis no matter how he Writes, he has no Care about that, 'tis sufficient if what he writes be legible: A curious Mechanick's hand must be exquisite, but his Thoughts are commonly pretty much at liberty, but a Painter is engaged in both respects."[20] If we credit this schema, Pope's exquisite hand risks turning him from author to artisan.

It is because of this potential ambivalence in readers' responses to this manuscript—and it certainly is a manuscript designed for a readership—that the fact that it retains a visible change becomes so important. In a change Pope wrote into the last line on the second page of the "Summer" manuscript, the river Cam is deprived of its "Laurel Banks," perhaps on the grounds that it did not in reality have any, and is awarded some equally chimerical "winding Vales" instead. What is remarkable is less the change itself than the fact of its appearing on this page at all. The correction, with others like it in the whole body of the manuscript, crucially changes the meaning of the document, in a way which goes far beyond changing the content of one line of verse. It makes it clear that this document too can be mutilated, that even this elaborately worked mimesis of print can be hacked at, cut into, if anything whatever should appear amiss with any of the expressions in it. And with this gesture, the copy at once makes clear where the poet stands. However beautiful a print-like page of manuscript, it is only an instrument. It can and must be made ugly if the poem demands it. By writing this fine page, and by then defacing it, the poet has, in a way, taken and survived a serious risk. He has exposed to a small but critically important public how deeply and perhaps even childishly seduced he is by the literal artifact of printed verse, by the thought of his becoming a printed poet; and he has at the same time conspicuously put away this childish thing, has overcome and sublated it, by proving himself willing to sacrifice it.

What we can glimpse here is not only a document in Pope's relationship to print culture, something which has been very thoroughly and illuminatingly explored in work of the last few decades on Pope.[21] We can, in addition, see in this page something of what we might call—in what I offer as a term of praise—the psychopathology of Pope's verse. Pope's verse concentrates and explores an ambivalence which is central to literate verse-art itself: an ambivalence about those aspects of verse which can seem susceptible of being classified under the heading of "mere" technique. Pope was already completely immersed in English and European verse when, at the age of fifteen, he was provided by his first and crucially important mentor, William Walsh, with what felt enough like a mission for the poet to remember it many years later and report it to Joseph Spence: "[When] about fifteen, I got acquainted with Mr. Walsh. He encouraged me much, and used to tell me that there was one way left of excelling, for though we had had several great poets, we never had any one great poet that was correct—and he desired me to make that my study and aim."[22] It is hard now for us to conceive just how exhilarating this possibility might have seemed to Pope. To write correctly does not here mean to close down the range of expressive possibilities but, rather, to constitute it. It means the opening up of *every* aspect of language to the possibility of a peculiarly prosodic expressiveness, to admit no feature of language which could not now become a source of this specifically prosodic cutting, marking, handling, and working over. Pope greatly extends the repertoire of such possible constraints, not only in those he explicitly mentions in his well-known early letter to Cromwell or in the *Essay on Criticism*—the avoidance of hiatus, of completely monosyllabic lines, of cliché-rhymes, of repetitively placed caesuras, and so on—but also in those he never mentions but observably creates: the avoidance of clusters of piled-up consonants and of excessively marked alliteration, the provision of elaborated patterns of assonance, the domestication of complex polysyllables within the English verse line, and many other such features.[23] Every prohibition creates an expressive possibility because its transgression now bears significance, can be seen as a transgression. What we do when we insist that this significance must always be local mimesis of the semantic content can, in the event, become a drastic abridgement of the repertoire of Pope's prosodic virtuosity.

"Mere Vocals"

Pope's Pastorals focus the question of attitudes to mere technique especially sharply. They show too how persistently the embarrassment about verse virtuosity has embedded itself in critical thinking. The editors of the still standard text of these poems note that "criticism of the Pastorals has tended from the beginning to prize the craftsmanship revealed in their verse and to minimize the worth of their substance. Thus Johnson said that 'To charge these Pastorals with want of invention is to require what was never intended. . . . It is surely sufficient for an author of sixteen . . . to have obtained sufficient power of language and skill in metre to exhibit a series of versification, which had in English poetry no precedent, nor has since had an imitation.' Praise such as this, generous though it is, tends to reduce Pope's achievement to something approaching the level of mere technical virtuosity."[24] Johnson is making an astonishingly large claim for Pope here, but his twentieth-century editors still find it slightly demeaning to him because it concerns technique. Although the "mereness" of "mere" technical virtuosity is a chimera imagined by Pope's editors rather than supplied by Johnson's judgment, it nevertheless provokes their energetic resistance, a resistance which inevitably decants into an entirely unconvincing attempt to show that what we might equally call the mere content of the Pastorals in some way represents some profound and enduring set of human truths. Where Pope's later editors stumble, Johnson is instead right on the money: the Pastorals are remarkable above all for their astonishing virtuosity in versification. But the Twickenham editors' dissatisfaction with "mere" technique has very deep roots. Indeed the period at which Pope himself was securing his position as England's most brilliant poet—the period in which, all contemporaries agreed, unprecedented and unrepeatable advances had been made in verse technique—may well also have been the canonical epoch of the depreciation of verse technique.

Distrust of mere technical virtuosity, of the kind we have just been considering, is everywhere in early eighteenth-century criticism, anecdote, received wisdom, and gossip about verse. The editor of a 1718 text of Samuel Daniel represented his wares as old-fashioned value for money: "If they have not that Turn of Versification," the editor wrote of Daniel and others among the good old poets, "which is the Pride of our modern Attempters, yet they bring us instead of that false Beauty, solid Sense, proper Language, and beautiful Figures."[25] Charles Gildon's Complete Art of Poetry considered this "Smoothness of Versification" to have become a permanent collective technological acquisition: Gildon considered such smoothness as "now so common, that it has swallow'd up all the more substantial Graces of Poetry; and it is as difficult now to find the meanest *Scribbler* of the Times, without this Quality, as to meet in them the *Genius* and *Essence of Poesy*." Gildon strongly censures the scholar Vossius for having considered meter as a defining feature of poetry and argues that Aristotle's definition from mimesis is the product of a politer age and people than the Dutch scholar's.[26] These critical commonplaces, of which the period affords literally hundreds of examples, were swiftly codified in reference works such as Ephraim Chambers's *Cyclopaedia*, whose entry for "Versification" insists that the word "is properly applied to what the poet does more by labour, art, and rule, than by invention, and the genius of furor poeticus. The matter of *versification*, is long and short syllables, and feet composed of them; and its form, the arrangement of them, in correct, and numerous, and harmonious *verses*; but this is no more than what a mere translator may pretend to, and which the Catilinarian war, put in verse, might merit. . . . It is with reason, therefore, that these simple matters are distinguished from the grand poetry, and called by the name *versification*. See POETRY."[27] In all these instances, of course, what is at work is the application of a certain kind of metaphysics to the production of art, a kind of metaphysics which is put into the service of a particular kind of argument about the kinds of work that artists do. The artist's genius is, in the encyclopaedist's diagram, a matter of ideas. Execution is for artisans.

Pope himself attracted more of these sorts of attacks than any other poet in the century. Few even of his enemies tried to claim that he was an unskillful writer of verse. This itself, in the event, made the series of assaults on Pope into a kind of inadvertent advertising in his favor. The more he was assailed by his enemies as a poet of mere sound, of mere virtuosity, the more he came to sound like a poet one really ought to read. A representative instance is provided by William Bond's *The Progress of Dulness*, published under the name "Henry Stanhope":

'Tis true! if finest Notes alone could show,
Tun'd justly high, or regularly low,
That we should Fame to these mere *Vocals* give,
POPE more, than we can offer, should receive.
For, when some gliding *River* is his Theme,
His Lines run smoother, than the smoothest Stream;
Not so, when thro' the Trees fierce *Boreas* blows,
The Period blustring with the Tempest grows.

> But what Fools Periods read, for Periods sake?
> Such Chimes improve not Heads, but make 'em Ach;
> Tho' strict in Cadence on the Numbers rub,
> Their frothy Substance is Whip-Syllabub;
> With most *Seraphic Emptiness* they roll,
> Sound without Sense, and Body without Soul.[28]

Bond finds it hard to decide whether Pope is a sergeant-major or a sweet trolley. The numbers rub along in strict cadence like a military formation, but what is produced is considered mere froth. Even so, it is curious to find one of Pope's *enemies* comparing his versification to a delicious luxury treat. (As a way of dissuading the reader from rushing out to buy Pope's *Dunciad*, this approach has its limitations.) Bond's ambivalence is representative. Johnson believed that there was an element of self-deception in this kind of attitude to the melodiousness of Pope's verse: remarking of Pope that "his poetry has been censured as too uniformly musical, and as glutting the ear with unvaried sweetness," Johnson commented, "I suspect this to be the cant of those who judge by principles rather than perception: and who would even themselves have less pleasure in his works, if he had tried to relieve attention by studied discords, or affected to break his lines and vary his pauses."[29] "Cant," as often in Johnson, carries the sense here of hypocritical disavowal of pleasure.

"Correctness" as Expressive Saturation

It is at this point that I want to turn to Pope's own thinking. Far from being impervious to the kinds of suspicion of technical virtuosity which I have outlined, I want to suggest, Pope himself is likely to have internalized them. We find repeatedly in Pope's writings assaults on mere technical virtuosity, of a kind which are not so far from those leveled at Pope by his opponents. In the course of one of the most extended single statements of his poetics, *An Essay on Criticism*, Pope remarks:

> But most by *Numbers* judge a Poet's Song,
> And *smooth* or *rough*, with them, is *right* or *wrong*;
> In the bright *Muse* tho' thousand *Charms* conspire,
> Her *Voice* is all these tuneful Fools admire,
> Who haunt *Parnassus* but to please their Ear,
> Not mend their Minds; as some to *Church* repair,
> Not for the *Doctrine*, but the *Musick* there.[30]

The passage, of course, does not suggest that smoothness or musicality are not desirable in verse, but rather, in accordance with a venerable logic, that these ornaments are valuable only insofar as they are in the service of something more important still. The lines do not suggest that it is improper to enjoy music in church but that it is culpable to go to church for the sake of music rather than for the sake of doctrine. The music must be in the service of doctrine, just as, so the passage implies, sound must be in the service of sense. The passage is part of the preparation, of course, for the much more celebrated sequence setting out Pope's prescription of prosodic echoing.

I want to set that passage to one side for the moment, however, not only because iconicity has recently been well written about by Tom Jones and Simon Alderson, among others,[31] but because I think it has come so completely to dominate discussion of Pope's versification as to diminish the entire topic. Instead I want to think briefly about the question of the status which we can accord poets' own poetics when we think about their verse practice. Verse always involves at least two kinds of thinking at once: a semantic and syntactical thinking and a metrico-rhythmic kind of thinking. Both these kinds of thinking involve both sound and sense. There are not two kinds of sound involved, one kind doing semantic and syntactical jobs and the other doing metrical and rhythmic ones. Instead there are (at least) two kinds of colliding constraints: the constraint of making sense in English and the constraints selected by the poet's metrical art. Both these sets of pressures are legible and audible in a single line of verse and in its performances, silent or vocalized: stress has a critical role in the intelligibility of spoken English, not merely a prosodic role in the rule-following of metrical verse.

What does all this imply about the reliability of poets' statements about verse art? Making verse involves the collision of a conscious and an unconscious or half-conscious kind of thinking, or, or also, between an explicit and an implicit kind of thinking. But poetics is not itself part of that making. When, and insofar as, the poet does poetics, he or she is thinking explicitly. The poet's poetics is therefore very likely to be a kind of traducing or abridgement of poetic thinking, which betrays it as it legitimates it—which ends, for example, in the unsustainable distinction made by the *Pastorals*' twentieth-century editors between mere "craftsmanship" on the one hand and "substance" on the other. The metaphysics which divides art into art proper and craft has failed: technique is the way art thinks. But in an epoch undergoing the elevation of art into a liberal vocation, this technical thinking becomes a source of intense ambivalence, and becomes therefore the subject of a series of disavowals. Its uncomfortably para-intentional and para-rational thinking must be represented as sheer making, a skill which must heteronomously be subordinated to a directing intention.

This, then, is the obvious convenience of the argument from verbal mimesis. It provides a systematic rationale for this troublingly liminal mode of prosodic thinking; it puts this thinking through technique in its proper, subordinate place. I cannot address here the still controverted question of "sound symbolism" in language;[32] I want only to consider the damage done by organizing the discussion of the prosodic intelligence primarily around this topic. It is worth exploring the possibility, that is, that Pope's poetic of verbal echo does not at all represent the key to the significance of his verse technique but rather an instance of an attempt to contain and explain its worryingly para-rational energies. There is another point of entry available: to consider verse as a process of cutting, marking, and working over language. Pope's verse art, I want to suggest, is continuously preoccupied with ornamentation in this sense. The multiplication of constraints in Pope's verse style is precisely the condition of the possibility of its expressivity. The more constraints, the more expressive resources. What we conceive of only negatively—the notion of "correctness" in verse—is, for Pope, an exhilarating, perhaps even dangerous program of the continual saturation of language with the idioms, experiments, flourishes, and melodies of verse virtuosity.

"Overpowering Pleasure"

It is time to turn to practice. We can indicate what might be involved here by considering some aspects of the melodics of a single passage from that poem by Pope which was perhaps more read and admired throughout Europe than any other in his century and which, by contrast, has, for many readers, become among the most difficult to read and admire today, his *Essay on Man*. Samuel Johnson's judgments on the poem well capture the reasons for both kinds of response: "The vigorous contraction of some thoughts, the luxuriant amplification of others, the incidental illustrations, and sometimes the dignity, sometimes the softness of the verse, enchain philosophy, suspend criticism, and oppress judgment by overpowering pleasure."[33] These remarks testify to a lost world of prosodic experience. Johnson's verse experience is close to Wordsworth's, the experience of a bewitching melody,[34] but it is further, perhaps, from what readers today experience or fail to experience. We may know what Johnson means by "the vigorous contraction of some thoughts," but can we so readily imagine a verse culture in which "amplification" could be qualified as, and could feel, "luxuriant"? Or in which verse melody might produce pleasure sufficiently "overpowering" to "suspend criticism" and "oppress judgment"? Although I have selected the most favorable of Johnson's remarks, their ambivalence is acute. Most of him thinks that it must be a good thing for a poet to produce "overpowering pleasure." When writing of Akenside's *Pleasures of the Imagination*, Johnson was capable of the flat declaration that, "With the philosophical or religious tenets of the author I have nothing to do; my business is with his poetry."[35] But here each word is weighted to bring out the cost of Pope's melody in a way which anticipates Wordsworth's complaints about Pope's black arts; that Pope's verse art "enchains" and "oppresses" suggests that the pleasures of being overpowered by his melody must be at least partly masochistic. And certainly in Johnson's broader judgment, the ambivalence tends toward outright rejection: "Never were penury of knowledge and vulgarity of sentiment so happily disguised."[36]

Many readers today, perhaps, simply and honestly do not understand what is meant by the kind of claim Johnson is making, the claim that Pope's verse melody overpowers and suspends criticism. I want to try to indicate now what kind of thing I think Johnson might have meant, not in the least in the spirit of attempting to *reason* anyone into accepting against his or her will the brilliance of Pope's versification but rather in the hope of opening up an arena of virtuosity which time and poetics have closed. Part of my larger point will be to show how the perversity of Pope's verse virtuosity—a pleasure, that is, in virtuosity for its own sake, just that kind of virtuosity which the poet himself has earlier stigmatized as potentially idolatrous—does not at all echo, illustrate, or reinforce but rather runs counter to some of the main lines of the poem's design.

When in the first Epistle Pope is developing his physico-theological argument about the universal fitness of the creation, he proceeds in part by countenancing possible objections to it. If everything in this world has been so wondrously designed, he imagines a skeptical reader asking, why could it not have been made even better, made, that is, even more advantageously to human beings?

> Why has not Man a microscopic eye?
> For this plain reason, Man is not a Fly.
> Say what the use, were finer optics giv'n,
> T'inspect a mite, not comprehend the heav'n?
> Or touch, if tremblingly alive all o'er,
> To smart and agonize at ev'ry pore?

> Or quick effluvia darting thro' the brain,
> Die of a rose in aromatic pain?
> If nature thunder'd in his op'ning ears,
> And stunn'd him with the music of the spheres,
> How would he wish that Heav'n had left him still
> The whis'pring Zephyr, and the purling rill?
> Who finds not Providence all good and wise,
> Alike in what it gives, and what denies?[37]

When, in his *Essay on Criticism*, Pope introduced a depreciation of lines consisting entirely of monosyllables—"And ten low Words oft creep in one dull Line"[38]—he added a further expressive resource to the arsenal of his verse thinking. Syllabicity, from this point onward, becomes a further marked feature of verse-handling. One may (I have) count the number of entirely monosyllabic lines over entire poems and long stretches of couplet-writing for other poets of this period and find that no poet has so few of them as Pope. At the same time one needs to note that Pope's line is not actually a prohibition on monosyllabics, only on a certain kind of monosyllabic: the relative lack of importance of the words, their "lowness," is not only an issue of diction but also of rhythm, because, as Marina Tarlinskaia's analysis has shown, the semantic weight of monosyllables is a critical factor in determining their stress value.[39] Many English monosyllables, especially monosyllabic prepositions, adjectives, and adverbs, are almost completely metrically ambiguous, and so a line which contains a great many of them is likely to be rhythmically sluggish in that its metrico-rhythmic contour is difficult to decipher. Pope's line of warning is an exemplary creep: Only two of its syllables, *and* and *in*, are certainly unstressed, while the stress value of many others is ambiguous.

My claim for Pope doesn't entail believing that his poems are better than others of the period because they contain fewer monosyllabics. It is rather an attempt to interpret the significance of Pope's having *marked* this previously less attended to feature of the verse segmentation of linguistic material. Monosyllabicity and polysyllabicity henceforth become an expressive resource, as they are here. The opening line performs in this respect a violent yoking of two different kinds of handling. "Why has not Man" is a hemistich typical of many of Pope's opening half-lines. If you try to push too violent an iambic grid down on top of it—"Why *has* not *Man*"—you will not be reading but chanting. If you begin with the stress, "*Why* has not *Man*," you produce a rather ugly scurry or lurch across your two unstressed syllables. The phrase in fact seems to push toward a solution which holds metrical and semantico-syntactic criteria against each other, granting evenly at least a secondary degree of emphasis to each of the first four words in the line: "Why has not Man." The effect is deliberative but also tense because it produces a kind of pile-up of emphasis, a need for release which is then powerfully gratified in the second half of the line: "a microscopic eye." Polysyllables introduce a different kind of melodic opportunity. They are readily legible rhythmically, for the reason that their stress values are less subject to syntactical alterations. They bear their tune inside them as word-stress. Now put this line with its answering pair: "For this plain reason, Man is not a Fly." Here the stress on *plain* is the immediately striking feature, because it falls at a place, the third, which is much less often stressed in Pope than its neighbors, two and four. (The demands of fitting English syntax to Pope's heroic line mean that, on the relatively rare occasions when this position is occupied by a stressed word, it is almost always an adjective. One can in fact construct a kind of miniature lexicon for each of Pope's poems, made exclusively out of the stressed adjectives which appear in this position; such a lexicon gives, for each poem, a kind of epitome of its evaluative substructure.) "For this plain reason," in its marked sequence of emphases, is a kind of rhythmic rhyme to the first hemistich of the previous line: "Why has not Man." But this time there is no polysyllabic release. Instead there is just this blunt sequence of monosyllables: "Man is not a Fly." The couplet is a compressed act of virtuosity, an effect which while we are reading, and following Pope's packed sense, will have gone past us, and which is meant to go past us, well before we can notice it. Yet in another sense we must notice it, even in order to be able to read the poem. Verse reading requires of the human brain a barely credible complexity of attention: we are always and everywhere making language do two jobs at once, to make sense and to hold a tune. For this reason the verse somersault I have just turned into slow motion cannot in fact not be registered, at some level, as we read. These evanescent, these fleeting effects are part of what Johnson called the "overpowering" and Wordsworth the "bewitching" quality of Pope's verse. Their efficacy is dependent on the poet's finding the cognitive target perfectly: too marked, and the poet will seem to be looking over our shoulder, as he does in his Cecilia's Day ode, inviting us to admire the mimetic decorum of his word-painting; too recessive, and the verse will feel what Pope's contemporaries called "harsh." Pope's instrumentations receive their force from being always just out of reach, always on the borders of perceptibility, and hence, evidently, of demonstrability.

What this brings out, I hope, is the dependence of every local effect upon the poet's development and refinement of repertoire. Naturalistic theories of verse aesthetics have a kind of hocus-pocus about them: it sounds as though a story is being told in which these sounds necessarily and magically (or eucharistically, if we remember the origins of the phrase *hocus-pocus* in *hoc est corpus*) have these effects on all rational readers. The relation between poet and reader posited here is not one of natural compulsion, in which the poem "has effects on" readers, but rather of seduction. The poet does things with tunes by being a person who has come to invest, perversely and perhaps irrationally, extremely powerful affects in the wrappings and trimmings of paralanguage. He invites the reader to share this fixation with him: the virtuosically fantasized significances of art-verse prosody entice answeringly virtuosic performances of fantasy from their readers. Reading Pope means developing a peculiar competence in Pope-reading: prosodic gestures, since they have no fixed or natural value, take on a value which we learn to hear through a whole authorship. So (to return to the present passage) the extremely striking line "Or touch, if tremblingly alive all o'er" works its effects largely because of the repertoire behind it. The line's syntax demands emphasis on *all*; without that stress, the line would not sound like spoken English. Only around one in forty times does this place in one of Pope's lines receive a stress. So the metrical mind, which is patiently and silently logging all this as it learns how to read Pope, receives a powerful poke in the sensorium at this point. The adverb *tremblingly* quivers out to us because it is in Pope's verse lexicon a nonce; this is its only outing in his whole verse authorship. And then there is the succession of four I sounds in the three words *tremblingly alive all*. This is a miniature deployment of an instrumentational idiom which Pope exploits and perhaps invents in *The Rape of the Lock*, in the passage in which Belinda sets out on the Thames:

> But now secure the painted Vessel glides,
> The Sun-beams trembling on the floating Tydes,
> While melting Musick steals upon the Sky,
> And soften'd Sounds along the Waters die.[40]

From this point onward in the authorship—but then, from this point onward in English poetry—there is always the possibility of reverting to the set of associations among water, light, and fleetingness established and pinned on to the letter I by this passage. But none of these "effects," which make up what makes this line in some way feel alive, is something that it just does to us or must just do to anyone. They are effects which we can learn to recognize, yet without recognizing that we recognize them.

Let me take one more line, perhaps the zenith of the "overpowering pleasure" which Johnson believed this poem could afford: "Die of a rose in aromatic pain." The whole line is a rhythmic half-rhyme with the line I began with, "Why has not Man a microscopic eye." Each line arranges six monosyllables around a quadrisyllable, and each puts its polysyllable in just the same metrical place in the line. Additionally *aromatic* is itself a half-rhyme with *microscopic*, and *Die* rhymes in answer to *Why*. If you doubt whether Pope could possibly have intended this, I concede that there is doubt and only insist in my turn that it is not certain, in the case of so immedicable a verse-junkie as Pope, that he did not intend it either. The entire sphere of thinking I am trying to open up, the sphere of the prosodic intelligence, is a para-intentional sphere, in which the most interesting and powerful effects are always those just at the edge of the poet's superveningly explicit intelligence. So here the intensely compressed semantic thinking of this line, in which *a rose* is wrested round to become the name of a medical complaint, and in which this is yoked together with the super-Petrarchan oxymoron of *aromatic pain*, by the differential repetition of the cluster *ro*, now stressed, now unstressed, is accompanied and interfered with by a no less compressed achievement of verse thinking.

5

I have deliberately inverted in this account the usual order of exegesis, in which consideration of technique comes only after paraphrase, with the result that the former is made redundantly to confirm and to intensify whatever has happened in the latter. Instead I have tried to begin with what is apparently a question of mere melody and to show how it is already and also a form of thinking. So, to return to our couplet, the tune, which we of course receive at just the same time as the paraphrasable content rather than as its echo, inducts us into the explicit thinking going on here. The reason given is in fact a parody of reason-giving: "Why has not Man a microscopic eye?/ For this plain reason, Man is not a Fly." Translation? Stop asking stupid questions. The tone here is that of an exasperated parent, faced with the child's inexhaustible "Why?" The reader is being invited to put away a childish fantasy, the fantasy that it would be better if human beings had super X-ray vision and ultra-enhanced powers of hearing. But the verse is not inviting us to put away that fantasy at all. The verse is encouraging us to explore it, to relish it, to—as Johnson might say—*luxuriate* in it, just as though the perversity of verse itself, its fixations upon the supposed sheer stuff of paralanguage, its "mere vocals," were also what we were being explicitly invited to grow out of and implicitly invited to develop and ramify. The end of this verse paragraph performs an experience very frequently met with in this poem. A delicious and tempting series of surmises are not merely reported to us but are used to operate upon us, to seduce us, and then the rhetorical question brings us back to the poem's subject-position, its argument: "Who finds not Providence all good and wise / Alike in what it gives, and what denies?" But with a rhetorical question there is always the risk that the reader may give the wrong answer. "Who wants to be a millionaire?" "I do." "Who finds not Providence all good and wise?"

It is here, perhaps, that we can begin to conjecture something of the historical meaning of Pope's unprecedented and unrepeatable mastery of verse melody. Many of its most sublime achievements—"Die of a rose in aromatic pain"; "Dismiss my soul, where no carnation fades"; "The sick'ning stars fade off th'etherial plain"[41]—are offered to us under a kind of crossing-out. They come crossed out because they come as the voice of the possibility we are to delete: the childish wish which needs to learn how partial evil is universal good, the flower-fancier, unable to imagine heaven except as a celestial garden center. The exception, of course, is the last of these lines, which comes at the lowering of the *Dunciad*'s curtain and at that point at which Pope's poem comes out as the serious grand poem of the deletion of the possibility of grandeur. Johnson, as a delighted reader, could measure the powers of Pope's verse melody more candidly than, perhaps, Pope could afford to do himself. His brief remarks capture in a few sentences the deep ambivalence about verse thinking which runs through Pope's whole corpus. What was almost Pope's first literary aspiration, to be the first truly correct English poet, was an infinitely more perilous wish than has been appreciated. It announced the lifelong civil warfare of his verse. Refinement, polish, correctness: these were universally admitted by contemporary readers to be the distinguishing surface of *modern* verse. There is a close, if subterranean connection between the polishing of verse and the polishing of the person proposed by Shaftesbury, those amicable collisions of sociability in which our rust is rubbed off. Yet in Pope's hands, correctness, as we have seen, is by no means a mere privative. It constitutes the means by which, potentially, *every* feature of language and paralanguage becomes a site for the pararational or even for the perverse investment of feeling. Pope's correctness is a survival capsule for poetry, a way in which verse thinking might be able both to have its cake and eat it. It is the apotropaic and propitiatory mimesis of a modernity which the poet hopes at once to delight, to ward off, and to survive. It is a periapt whose image is the manuscript of *Summer*, held out in an immaculate facsimile of print which the poet has nevertheless found it necessary to deface.

None of this provides an exhaustive answer to the question which I have taken for my title. But it does suggest some caveats. The relationship between thinking *about* verse and thinking *in* verse is not necessarily a cooperative one. It may instead be a powerfully antagonistic, repressive, or deceptive one. It is certainly true, as Prins insists, that "the sound of poetry is never heard without mediation."[42] Yet it is equally true that no talk of anything's being "mediated" can be meaningful without positing that there is something to mediate.[43] Historical poetics needs above all to be wary of thinking that it can exit from the painful difficulty of specifying the history of verse technique by filling that space up with representations, with the way in which verse has been talked about, mediated, and distributed. If historical poetics is not to assume the role of a clumsy patron—"one who looks with unconcern on a Man struggling for life in the water and when he has reached ground encumbers him with help"—it needs to keep an ear out for everything in the practice of verse thinking that resists, rather than merely confirming, the available representations of that practice.

Notes

1. Prins, "Historical Poetics, Dysprosody, and the Science of English Verse," 233, 230.
2. Prins, "Historical Poetics, Dysprosody, and the Science of English Verse," 234.
3. Veselovsky, "Envisioning World Literature in 1863," 9.
4. Shaitanov, "Aleksandr Veselovskii's Historical Poetics," 441.
5. Maslov, "The Semantics of *Aoidos* and Related Compounds," 4, 2.
6. Maslov, "The Semantics of *Aoidos* and Related Compounds," 1; Veselovsky, "Envisioning World Literature in 1863," 13.
7. Wellek, 279, quoted in Maslov, "The Semantics of *Aoidos* and Related Compounds," 1.
8. Shaitanov, "Aleksandr Veselovskii's Historical Poetics," 441.
9. Eikhenbaum, "Concerning the Question of the Formalists," 51, 52. I thank David Duff for drawing my attention to the term *specifiers* and for directing me to this source for it.
10. Tynianov, *The Problem of Verse Language*, 47. See also Duff, "Maximal Tensions and Minimal Conditions," 559–61.
11. Tucker, "The Fix of Form"; see also Rudy, "On Cultural Neoformalism, Spasmodic Poetry, and the Victorian Ballad."
12. Adorno, *Noten zur Literatur*, 49–68.
13. Adorno, *Ästhetische Theorie*, 179–205.

14. *Pace* Geuss, "Is Poetry a Form of Knowledge?" See Jarvis, "Bedlam or Parnassus."
15. Adorno, *Ästhetische Theorie*, 74–97.
16. See especially Jarvis, *Adorno*; "Bedlam or Parnassus"; *Wordsworth's Philosophic Song*.
17. Adorno, *Vorlesung zur Einleitung in die Soziologie*, 56.
18. Mack, *The Last and Greatest Art*, 29.
19. A note on the cover leaf explains, "This Copy is that wch past thro ye / hands of Mr Walsh, Mr Congreve, Mr Main- / waring, Dr Garth, Mr Granville, Mr / Southern, Sr H. Sheers, Sr W. Trumbull, / Ld. Halifax, Ld. Wharton, Marq. of Dorchestr., / D. of Bucks. &c." (Mack, *The Last and Greatest Art*, 19).
20. Richardson, *An Essay on the Theory of Painting*, 28.
21. McLaverty, *Pope, Print and Meaning*; Foxon, *Pope and the Early Eighteenth-Century Book Trade*.
22. Spence, *Observations, Anecdotes, and Characters of Books and Men*, 1: 32.
23. Sherburn, *The Correspondence of Alexander Pope*, 1: 105–8; Audra and Williams, *The Poems of Alexander Pope*, 276–84, II. 337–83. Pope later seems to have used the letter as the basis of a fabricated letter he represented as having been sent to the better known William Walsh (Sherburn, *The Correspondence of Alexander Pope*, 1: 22).
24. Audra and Williams, *The Poems of Alexander Pope*, 50; Johnson, *The Lives of the Poets*, 4: 66.
25. Daniel, *The Works of Mr. Samuel Daniel*, ix–x.
26. Gildon, *The Complete Art of Poetry*, 1: 83, 76.
27. Chambers, "Versification," *Cyclopaedia*.
28. Barnard, *Pope*, 92.
29. Johnson, *The Lives of the Poets*, 4: 78–79.
30. Audra and Williams, *The Poems of Alexander Pope*, 276–77.
31. Alderson, "Alexander Pope and the Nature of Language" and "Iconic Forms in English Poetry of the Time of Dryden and Pope"; Jones, "Plato's *Cratylus*, Dionysius of Halicarnassus, and the Correctness of Names in Pope's Homer."
32. See Hinton, Nichols and Ohala, *Sound Symbolism*.
33. Johnson, *The Lives of the Poets*, 4: 77.
34. Wordsworth, "Essay, Supplementary to the Preface," 649.
35. Johnson, *The Lives of the Poets*, 4: 173.
36. Johnson, *The Lives of the Poets*, 4: 76.
37. Mack, *The Poems of Alexander Pope*.
38. Audra and Williams, *The Poems of Alexander Pope*, 278, I. 347.
39. Tarlinskaia, *English Verse*, 63–69.
40. Tillotson, *The Poems of Alexander Pope*, 162, ii. 47–50.
41. Rumbold, *The Dunciad in Four Books*, 326, iv. 418; 356, iv. 636.
42. Prins, "Historical Poetics, Dysprosody, and the Science of English Verse," 229.
43. "The universality of mediation does not confer on us the right to level everything in heaven and earth to mediation. . . . The mediation of immediacy is a determination of reflection, meaningful only in relation to what is set over against it, the immediate" (Adorno, *Negative Dialektik*, 173).

chapter 6

The Biopolitics of Recognition:
Making Female Subjects of Globalization

Pheng Cheah

In the past fifteen years, the concept of recognition has emerged as an important analytical category in critical theory for understanding the normative grounds of social and political struggles in the contemporary world. The resurrection of this dusty Hegelian term, first popularized in the mid-twentieth century by Alexandre Kojève, to the position of discursive hegemony has become so complete that in an exchange published in 2003, Nancy Fraser and Axel Honneth could blithely assert that "'recognition' has become a keyword of our time," that its "salience is now indisputable," especially in contemporary globalization. "Hegel's old figure of 'the struggle for recognition' finds new purchase as a rapidly globalizing capitalism accelerates transcultural contacts, fracturing interpretive schemata, pluralizing value horizons, and politicizing identities and differences."[1] According to this view, the exercise of power is essentially reducible to the conferring or withholding of recognition in social relations, a gesture or action that is registered at the level of experience as an edifying affirmation (in the case of empowerment) or a hurtful diminishment or injurious exclusion (in the case of oppression and coercion).

The normative claims of the recognition paradigm, however, gain an entirely different meaning in view of the ascendancy of the practical discourse of human capital in contemporary global capitalism. Not all proponents of human capital development are of the same political persuasion as the neoliberal economists of the Chicago School who coined and elaborated the concept. As Robert Reich puts it in a recent newspaper article, "Over the long term, the only way to improve the living standards of most Americans is to invest in our people—especially their educations, skills and the communications and transportation systems linking them together and with the rest of the world. In the global economy, the only 'asset' that's unique to any nation—and that determines its living standards—is the people who make it up. Everything else—money, equipment, factories, supplies—moves across global boundaries at the flick of a computer key. . . . Spending on education, infrastructure and basic R&D is fundamentally different from other categories of government spending. These outlays are really investments in the future productivity of our people."[2]

As the most indispensable element of the competitive game of global capitalist accumulation, the development of human capital is constraining and coercive. But the modality of power at work here is fundamentally inclusionary rather than exclusionary because it is intended to improve the lives of the subjects it produces by making them more productive. It operates by positive investment, enhancement, and augmentation rather than by prohibition, repression, or the inducement of feelings of lack or hurt in response to disrespect. It works by a concentration of focus, the intensification of a caring look, a looking after, rather than by disregard or looking away. Most important, this concentrated focus does not operate in the first instance at the level of the *form* of consciousness or experience but in terms of the physical materiality of bodies and populations and the milieu of their subsistence.

This kind of productive power is most clearly seen in the fabrication of various types of female subjects of transnational labor in the current dispensation of global capitalist accumulation. The making of such female subjects illustrates that the apparent feasibility of the recognition model of power (and its popularity in the house of theory) is premised on and sustained by the biopolitics of human capital. Indeed, the account of normativity found in the recognition paradigm, as it has made its way into progressive policies for global human development focusing on women and supporting human rights instruments, ironically consolidates and reinforces the oppressive dynamic of power in contemporary globalization because such policies are necessarily imbricated in the processes and technologies of power that capitalize humanity. A thorough examination of this modality of global power requires that we (1) correct the tenacious misunderstanding of Foucault's account of power as exclusionary repression that is widespread in contemporary theory, and (2) understand precisely how the relation of norms to life in his analytics of biopower diverges sharply from that found in the recognition paradigm.

Versions of Recognition

Because of its ubiquity and plasticity, the recognition paradigm deserves a more thorough reconstruction than I can provide here. Its flexibility lies in its prodigious capacity for being inflected in multiple ways: postcolonial, psychoanalytical, and "poststructuralist." As is well known, the paradigm's philosophical source is Hegel's detranscendentalization of Fichte's theory of the constitution of the self-determining practical subject through a structure of intersubjective interlocution, namely, that an efficacious self-consciousness comes into being only by being determined by a summons from another rational being that is like itself.[3] Axel Honneth has argued that Hegel's philosophy of recognition elaborates a quasi-transcendental normative source for the progressive reordering or transformation of unequal social and political relations that is immanent to the structures of subject formation. Because subjects are formed as distinctive identities in intersubjective relations, the process of individuation that generates the consciousness of a concrete ethical subject necessarily occurs within the context of communicative relations. Hence, an ethical struggle for recognition at various levels of collective life is built into the medium of subject formation, and this provides a normative check on relations of domination and oppression. Consequently, the full development of an individual necessarily involves the ethical imperative that he or she responds to the other's demand for higher forms of recognition. This struggle leads to a world that is more just: it can destroy existing forms of ethical life that are inadequate for affording recognition and cause the progressive development of higher forms of ethical life that can meet these demands for recognition.[4]

Despite their claims of being post-metaphysical and their suspicion of ontology, all contemporary variations of the philosophy of recognition presuppose an ontology of the human subject according to which social and ethical norms have precedence over and constitutively shape the fundamental aspects of individual and social life. This ontology can be reduced to three principles. First, consciousness, or more precisely, its communicational, signifying, and value-forming capacities are accorded primacy in the constitution of human subjects through structures of interlocution. Second, such intersubjective structures give rise to and are in turn informed by norms and values that become institutionalized and organize collective human life. Third, individual subjects are constituted by norms and value patterns in a process of construction, understood as the establishment of modes of meaningful action for a practical subject in specific sociopolitical settings or as the production of the intelligible form that enables the actualization of a corporeal subject.

Accordingly, oppression has an implicit ontological meaning. The norms that constitute sociopolitical subjects can have a coercive and harmful effect on their existence because, by not giving them due recognition, these norms impede subjects from achieving their optimal end. As Nancy Fraser puts it in her formulation of misrecognition as status-subordination and the obstruction of parity of participation:

> If and when [institutionalized patterns of cultural value] constitute actors as peers, capable of participating on a par with one another in social life, then we can speak of *reciprocal recognition* and *status equality*. When, in contrast, institutionalized patterns of cultural value constitute some actors as inferior, excluded, wholly other, or simply invisible, hence as less than full partners in social interaction, then we should speak of *misrecognition* and *status subordination*. . . . [Misrecognition] constitutes an institutionalized relation of *subordination* and a violation of justice. To be misrecognized, accordingly, is not to suffer distorted identity or impaired subjectivity as a result of being depreciated by others. It is rather to be constituted by *institutionalized patterns of cultural value* in ways that prevent one from participating as a peer in social life. . . . [Misrecognition] arises, more precisely, when institutions structure interaction according to cultural norms that impede parity of participation.[5]

The squabbles between the contemporary American and German progeny of the Frankfurt School over whether the aim of recognition is to achieve parity of status or full self-realization and whether the norms causing misrecognition are social or psychological in their mode of operation are beside the point. In both cases, injustice stems from the exclusionary violence of anthropologistic intelligible form, which can issue from social institutions or psychologically damaging interactions between individual subjects. Conversely, a claim for recognition involves the critical revaluation or resignification of this normative form so that it is no longer obstructive. For Fraser, it is to "deinstitutionalize patterns of cultural value that impede parity of participation and to replace them with patterns that foster it."[6] For Honneth, recognition involves establishing principles of rational legitimation for modern institutions that facilitate individual self-realization because they enable subjects to "experience intersubjective recognition" of their personal autonomy as well as "their specific needs and particular capacities."[7]

For present purposes, what is noteworthy is the norm's fundamentally prescriptive character. As a meaningful form, its relation to life and existence is initially one of exteriority. Norms are what human beings collectively prescribe to life to regulate it. They give intelligibility and ethical direction to and shape what is otherwise chaotic and meaningless matter, thereby bringing out and developing the implicit rational end that is immanent to life. Hence, norms and the conditions of intelligibility and normativity that they determine can always be changed by human processes.

In the Frankfurt School version of recognition, the generation and revaluation of norms occur through collective free and rational deliberation. However, recognition can also be understood as a form of hegemonic social control. The transformation of a given order of recognition is then a consequence of political critique, subversion, and contestation. Although it is not a sustained engagement with the philosophy of recognition, Judith Butler's work on violence and power on the international stage is an influential example of this politicized understanding of recognition. Here, Butler seeks to extend the account of subjection she formulated from the operations of the repressive law of heteronormative sexuality into a critique of the violence of Western secular norms in the U.S. War on Terror. The shared human condition of corporeal vulnerability or the precariousness of human life, she suggests, is a normative source for principles of equality. However, this normative source is obscured or blocked out by normativity in the second sense of hegemonic social control. Hegemonic norms articulate the criteria of intelligibility and recognizability that determine what counts as a life that is human and, therefore, one that is worthy of being protected or grieved. These norms function as exclusionary representational frames. They are said to limit the accessibility to the media of those they exclude or to portray them in a negative dehumanizing manner that deprives them of credibility, thereby barring them from admission to and appearance in the public sphere as equal actors and fellow human beings.[8] These representational frames are also deployed at a political level to influence and actively produce the unequal distribution of wealth and a hierarchical, discriminatory ordering of populations that favor and protect some over others from the general human condition of vulnerability.[9]

Butler's use of the term *recognition* should be understood in at least two senses. First, it is a normative process of hegemonic control through the "production" of human life or, more precisely, the articulation of epistemic conditions that determine what is intelligible and recognizable as human life, that leads to violence to peoples who are considered as having lives that are not worth protecting in contemporary warfare or from disaster and famine.[10] But this normative process of epistemic production by which the West defines itself is said to generate its own subversions in a mechanical manner that is predictably similar to the way that Butler saw heterosexual gender norms as generating their own subversion: the iteration of the norm across time in its significative expression sets off the return of the constitutive ghostly outside according to a schema adapted from Julia Kristeva's account of the constitution of society through the abjection of impure others.[11] The return of the abjected other then undermines the norms of recognition, putting into question the criteria that determine what counts as a life. Second, this subversion then points to a fuller sense of recognition because it redefines the parameters of intelligibility and recognizability of human life in order to include those human others who were previously excluded.

We see here the same exteriority of norms to life that we saw in the Frankfurt School version of recognition. Although Butler suggests that "the 'being' of life is itself constituted through selective means . . . [and] we cannot refer to this 'being' outside of the operations of power," the norm is an intelligible form that is analytically prior to the life that it shapes because her account of geopolitical violence is resolutely part of a philosophy of the intersubjective constitution of consciousness.[12] "If a life is produced according to the norms by which life is recognized," she writes, "this implies neither that everything about a life is produced according to such norms nor that we must reject the idea that there is a remainder of 'life'—suspended and spectral—that limns and haunts every normative instance of life. Production is partial and is, indeed, perpetually haunted by its ontologically uncertain double. Indeed, every normative instance is shadowed by its own failure."[13] The suggestion that life exceeds norms and renders them unstable, thereby causing a transformation in the criteria of recognition in the direction of greater universality, is premised on the analytical separability of norms from the lives that they frame. The fitting of life to an intelligible form that precedes and presides over it means that there can always be an inadequacy or lack of fit, that the fitting is forced and the norm coercively constrains and stifles life. This opens the way for an unquestioned universal humanism that is naïve in the simplicity and anguished sentimentality of its endorsement of human rights. Butler figures the struggle of human life against the norm as the cry of a vulnerable voice: "The task at hand is to establish modes of public seeing and hearing that might well respond to the cry of the human within the sphere of appearance."[14] "The recognition of shared precariousness introduces strong normative commitments of equality and invites a more robust universalizing of rights that seeks to address basic human needs for food, shelter, and other conditions for persisting and flourishing."[15] Here Butler is in unison with her not-so distant Frankfurt School cousin from the recognition family. Honneth had likewise argued that a critical theory of society that goes beyond all given forms of social organization must "express the unmet demands of humanity at large."[16]

Not Recognizing Human Capital: Productive Inclusionary Power and the Feminization of Labor

The fundamental axiom of the recognition paradigm is the intersubjective constitution of subjects through the internalization of social norms. As a form of disempowerment, recognition/nonrecognition operates through exclusionary mechanisms of intelligible, that is, psychical, intellectual, or imaginary form. When Fraser and Honneth explain oppression in terms of institutionalized patterns of cultural value that exclude actors from participation in public life or the experience or feeling of injury when one's capacities are not recognized, and when Butler suggests that violence is caused by norms that exclude certain populations by determining what is human, what is at stake is precisely the oppressive power of intelligible form. Norms operate oppressively in the following manner. First, nonrecognition is the withholding of intelligible form. Second, when recognition is regarded as a form of hegemonic control, norms create hierarchical differentiations that discriminate against and exclude certain groups. Third, these norms are primarily negative in character. They express the prohibition or disapprobation of a hegemonic force, an intentional withholding of regard that diminishes the worth and capacities of the targeted subjects. Simply put, the recognition model of power in all its versions is an example of the juridico-discursive representation of power that Foucault regarded as having been displaced with the rise of industrial capitalism. For although lip service is paid to power's productive character when norms are said to produce or constitute their targeted subjects (in Butler's case), they are productive only in a highly limited sense. First, they make subjects that are deficient beings, beings excluded from care or the fostering of capacities on the basis of a lack. Second, power operates not at the level of life's physical forces but at the epistemic level of intelligible representational forms. Such forms enable the recognition of living beings only by constraining them. In Butler's words, "Life has to be intelligible *as a life*, has to conform to certain conceptions of what life is, in order to become recognizable. So just as norms of recognizability prepare the way for recognition, so schemas of intelligibility condition and produce norms of recognizability."[17] Simply put, a Foucauldian account of productive power is hollowed out, and a notion of power as prohibitive and repressive is surreptitiously smuggled back to fill this empty form. This approach is representative of a popular misinterpretation of Foucault.

The more important question, however, is whether the recognition model of power leads to a fundamental misrecognition of how power operates in contemporary global capitalism. Unlike sovereign and colonial power, which functioned through physical violence, the obscuring of voices by ideology or discourse, or the withholding of regard through ideational mechanisms, global capitalism primarily operates by recognizing subjects, according them regard so that their interests as subjects of corporeal needs can be incorporated into the very fabric of the global system of accumulation, where their capacities can be augmented and cultivated as human capital. The examples of the recognition paradigm I have discussed are united in their mesmerizing focus on the cultural dimension of globality. For them, the ethico-political significance of globality is that it extends the coercive operation of norms into a global field that exceeds the borders of nations. Hence, Fraser and Honneth suggest that the injustices of global capitalism ought to be analyzed in terms of recognition because globalization intensifies transcultural contact, and the resulting fracturing of interpretive schemata and pluralization of value horizons has caused a worldwide resurgence of the politics of recognition. For Butler, the exemplary case of global politics is neo-imperial warfare, which, she argues, is stimulated and justified by the dissemination of representations of other cultures and religions in the global media.

Unfortunately, the warm ethical scene of intersubjective recognition as a solution to global injustice ironically mirrors the operations of global capitalism at the level of high theory. It is often suggested that the U.S. preemptive War on Terror in the aftermath of September 11 is a revival of the imperial-colonial form of power, especially given the widespread deployment of Orientalist images about Islamic fundamentalism. In this regard, the War on Terror has been an unexpected boon for some quarters of critical theory because it seemed to confirm the continuing relevance of the discursive-linguistic turn, which, being incapable of analyzing economic issues, was quick to justify this incapability through dismissive charges of economic reductionism. However, a more fundamental question about the War on Terror should be: What are the material conditions of this ability to wage war in the first place? The form of power that sustains the exercise of U.S. imperial sovereignty is not repressive. It is the power of commerce and economic productivity within a global financial system of credit that funds the capability of the United States to exercise its military campaign of shock and awe followed by occupation.[18] More important, this financial power rests on and in turn feeds back into a web of political instrumentalities for the cultivation of human capital that now extends throughout the globe and continues its productive work in countries in the postcolonial South without much critical attention in high theory.

The cultivation of human capital is a dynamic within the international division of labor that characterizes the current dispensation of global capitalism. As major OECD countries achieved postindustrial status, there was a massive transfer of industrial production and lower value-adding services to countries in Asia and Latin America. Labor-intensive production processes were outsourced to developing countries with lower labor costs through foreign direct investment and international subcontracting, while research and development and technical and managerial control remained in the North. This new international division of labor is sustained by the feminization of labor at various levels of the global economy, that is, the production of various interrelated types of female subjects of globalization: educated middle-class white-collar women in professional occupations, female factory workers in export-oriented industries and newly established industrial zones, and various forms of transnational female labor in low-status "feminized" occupations such as domestic helpers, workers in restaurants and hotels, entertainers, and sex workers.[19] As Jayati Ghosh puts it, "The Asian export boom was fueled by the productive contributions of Asian women: in the form of paid labour in export-related activities and in services, through the remittances made by migrant women workers, and through the vast amounts of unpaid labour of women as liberalization and government fiscal contraction transferred many areas to public provision of goods and services to households (and thereby to women within households)."[20]

The case of sex workers in Thailand illustrates how the different modalities of feminized labor are intimately connected. The rapid industrialization of the capital city of Bangkok at the expense of rural regions, such as northern Thailand, leads to the migration of young women to the city in search of work to alleviate rural poverty. Failure to find adequate income from non-sex work such as factory or service work increases the supply of potential sex workers.[21] The promotion of Thailand as a destination for international (sex) tourism opens up avenues for transnational migration for sex work, trafficked or consensual.[22]

These different forms of feminized labor occupy a transnational space where women are bought and sold as different kinds of labor within the global economy. They are human capital in a colloquial sense: commodities in a circuit of transnational exchange that profits many parties. But they are also human capital in the meaning of economic discourse: important resources of a country that can be profitably developed because they are amenable to potentially endless education and augmentation by either governmental planning or individual initiative. The doctrine of enhancing economic growth in globalization by cultivating human capital is widely institutionalized. Countries receiving foreign investment in export-oriented industries and labor-exporting countries justify the feminization of labor in terms of their beneficial contribution to economic and social development. For example, labor migration provides fruitful employment when the home country cannot absorb its own labor, and it enhances the capabilities of the migrant worker by vocational training or on-the-job training while overseas. Foreign exchange remittances and their conversion into fixed capital and the enhancement of the worker's abilities so that she can gain better employment or initiate small business enterprises on her repatriation increase the home country's resources. Thus, international bodies concerned with global economic development and developing nation-states in the South have promoted labor migration as a mechanism for developing the human capital of the migrant and also as a means of improving the welfare of her immediate family and, more generally, her source country.[23]

As examples of human capital development, the formation of such female subjects of globalization occurs according to a dynamic that is fundamentally inclusionary. Hence, the most progressive universalistic discourses of economic and social development such as that of the United Nations constantly emphasize the importance of developing human capital. A 2007 publication of the UN Economic and Social Commission for Asia and the Pacific (ESCAP), entitled *Perspectives on Gender and Migration* stresses that in formulating migration policies, "governments are encouraged to pursue co-development strategies in which source and destination countries cooperate to promote cross-border communication and investment, the development of human capital, the efficient transfer of remittances and return migration. Migration policies should benefit countries of origin and destination, and, in particular, migrants themselves."[24] Indeed, UN discourse regards globalization as highly advantageous for improving the situation of women because it brings about the greatest degree of inclusion. The shift from "women and development" to "gender and globalization" acknowledges globalization's inclusionary character. The former was concerned with the exclusion of women from development as a result of gender inequality.[25] In contradistinction, the latter emphasizes the positive agency of globalization on the conditions of women's lives. Globalization may have reinforced existing gender inequality by extending the traditional sexual division of labor to new locations and forms of work. But it has increased employment opportunities for women, alleviated poverty through labor migration, created new associations, and strengthened networks of mutual support for women and improved their access to health care, microcredit, and information.[26]

Such female subjects cast doubt on the pertinence of both the recognition paradigm and a Marxist theory of ideology for analyzing the politics of contemporary globalization for two reasons. First, with the exception of those who are trafficked, these subjects participate willingly in globalization processes through the exercise of their rational will. Second, even if they are oppressed or exploited, they want to be included by and in globalization because it creates conditions that encourage their voluntary servitude. In her seminal study of young rural women who migrate to Bangkok as sex workers, Pasuk Phongpaichit argues that they are not hapless victims who are blind to their true interests and needs: "It is not some sort of helpless dependent status which ends them up in the business of selling their bodies. Rather it is the responsibilities which they themselves feel."[27] They see themselves as full earning members of the household and are considered so because their remittances help to bolster the family's agrarian economy. They do not seek to escape family life but are helping to support the family and to improve its position in village society. Indeed, family members often serve as agents for recruitment, and some villages have developed a vested interest in the business.

Such female subjects of globalization are fabricated by a systematic form of subjectification that produces rational consent. This rational will-formation cannot be explained in terms of ideological mystification or the imposition of exclusionary norms that withhold recognition. First, the fact that they are incorporated into the global system of needs through willing consent distinguishes them from the proletariat. For Marx, the proletariat is a revolutionary class who will destroy the entire class structure and redeem humanity from its alienation because it is "a class of civil society which is not a class of civil society," a class produced by civil society only in its exclusion from it.[28] It does not and cannot belong to civil society because it is barred from participation in civil society and sharing its benefits. In contradistinction, globalization does not exclude these female subjects and make them accept this exclusion through ideological mystification. It includes them through their rational acquiescence. Second, although Orientalism and patriarchal discourse are undoubtedly at work in the portrayal of these female subjects as docile, submissive labor or as objects for sexual exploitation who, being not-quite human, do not need to be recognized as rights-bearing subjects, we cannot assume that these projected norms are ideologically internalized in the process of subjectification. These women are far from duped and see themselves as being enabled by their rational decision to become sex workers. Similarly, what drives the emigration of foreign domestic workers is not only their ideological constitution as good wives, daughters, mothers, or sisters but, more crucially, the crafting of their interests as subjects of needs by government policies. Their oppression and subjectification occur not by silencing them but by incorporating their needs and interests in the fabric of global capitalism. Whatever the role of ideology in making the wills of these women migrants, they also go with the firm desire to improve their lives because this is how their needs and interests have been shaped by governmental action. As a UN report on world population notes, "the large majority of migrant women are involved in voluntary migration. Although women's propensity to migrate is significantly influenced by their family and marital status, research shows that women are key actors in this process and often play a key role in migration decisions. Migration often provides women with an opportunity to engage in waged employment and thereby increases their ability, through remittances, to improve the welfare of the family remaining in the country of origin."[29]

Phongpaichit suggests that we must look to political-economic forces to understand how the material interests and needs of women sex workers qua rational actors are shaped:

> It is within an economic system structured in this particular way that the actions of the migrant girls must be understood. They were not fleeing from a family background or rural society which oppressed women in conventional ways. Rather, they were engaging in an entrepreneurial move designed to sustain the family units of a rural economy which was coming under increasing pressure. They did so because their accustomed position in that rural society allocated them a considerable responsibility for earning income to maintain the family. The returns available in this particular business, rather than in any other business accessible to an unskilled and uneducated person, had a powerful effect on their choices. Our survey clearly showed that the girls felt they were making a perfectly rational decision within the context of their particular social and economic structure, and they could not escape from it. The migration is thus an intrinsic part of Thailand's economic orientation.[30]

Read against the grain of Phongpaichit's Marxist vocabulary of the determination of individual choice by socioeconomic relations, this emphasis on political-economic forces indicates that what is shaped is not just the minds of these female subjects of globalization but, more important, the physicality of their bodies and the material surroundings in which they subsist as members of a population. The consent to participate in globalizing processes is generated by changes at this level and not psychical coercion or ideological mystification. Indeed, the development of the population braids together state policy in many areas (such as mortality and fertility, environmental issues that can affect the price of food, import-export ratios) that do not have an immediately obvious impact on the psychical lives of individuals but have an unseen impact on their physical existence. The rational will of such subjects is the product-effect of a complex form of physical causality that Foucault analyzed under the concept of biopower.

It is commonplace to say that biopolitical technologies deploy knowledge and discourse. But what the popular misinterpretation of Foucault has always evaded and covered over is the *physical* character of the causality of discourse and knowledge in producing subjects. Instead, discourse is seen as constituting subjects at the level of form. As we have seen, in Butler's attempt to splice a pseudo-Foucauldian notion of productive power to recognition as coercion, power constitutes subjects through constricting and repressive norms. This process of constitution is precisely a formation, a *formal* causality that works at the epistemic level of how a living subject becomes recognizable through an intelligible form. The process is described as one of materialization only insofar as materialization is understood as the actualization of what is merely potential through an intelligible form. Hence, power is directed at consciousness and its various faculties. It operates in processes of thought, appearance, and experience in the phenomenological sense. More precisely, these forms are internalized by individual or collective subjects who are thereby formed as subjects who are constitutively lacking, in terms of both their experience of themselves and how they appear to others.

We can call this a formal understanding of power, where power is deployed through forms. It dovetails neatly with a philosophy of the intersubjective constitution of consciousness and is also compatible with Marxist theories of ideology. Simply put, ideology is a type of power that works at the level of consciousness to naturalize the restrictions or fetters that particularistic capitalist social forms or relations of production place on the universal satisfaction of human needs. Even when ideology is defined in terms of hegemony (Gramsci) or as material practice (Althusser), it is always understood as the materialization of *ideas* through the practices of individual subjects that are ideologically constituted within specific institutional contexts, for example, subjects who act according to religious beliefs or patriarchal norms.[31] The materialization of ideology deepens the alienation of the subject of consciousness from his or her truly human needs. Thus, in formal accounts of power, politics invariably takes the shape of a critique of processes of subject formation. Where such accounts are Marxist, the critique of subject formation leads to an attempt to transform the social forms that gave rise to such subjects.

The female subjects of globalization discussed earlier show, however, that the reach of processes of subjectification is so deep and extensive that they do not primarily operate at the level of form and consciousness. They are directed at the physical aspects of life and not at the psyche of individual or collective subjects such that the psyche itself is an effect of power's physical effectivity. It is especially important that we come to terms with power's physical dimension because we now live in a postsocialist age. We cannot adequately explain the tenaciousness of global capitalism or hope to resist it if we cling to the dogma that oppression primarily operates through forms of consciousness and that we can overcome oppression by changing the *form* of the subject and its corresponding social formation. Indeed, such a focus can distract us from the more fundamental operations of power that ought to be the target of critical attention and political intervention. As I will suggest, the optimal solution proposed by the recognition paradigm—recognition of the most inclusive and universal kind—is part of the operation of power.

Let us reread Foucault with fresh eyes to see how he formulated the idea of biopower to account for power's fundamentally physical dimension. This was always implied by the use of the term *technology* to characterize biopolitics since it suggests that knowledge is a direct efficient causal force. Biopower or the power over life, as distinguished from the repressive power of the sovereign over his territory, is concerned with the maximization of a state's forces (calculated in terms of its resources and possibilities). It involves the enhancement and regulatory control of the forces, aptitudes, and capacities of the living human being either as an individual body (discipline) or as a biological species divided into populations (government). Biopower is philosophically incompatible with any philosophy of the intersubjective constitution of consciousness because biopolitical production does not occur at the level of ideational form and its impact on consciousness, or even by delineating the form and contours of a corporeal subjectivity. Rather, the production occurs at the level of the physics and material logistics of bodies and biological existence within a natural milieu. Foucault emphasizes that whereas law works in the imaginary because its prohibitive character involves imagining things that can and must not be done, technologies of security and government "work within reality, by getting the components of reality to work in relation to each other, thanks to and through a series of analyses and specific arrangements."[32] The political domain is part of the domain of physics and nature because it concerns "the interplay of reality with itself."[33]

The popular misinterpretation of Foucault ignores Foucault's argument that the character of power has changed because of a historical change in its target, from citizen-subjects to the population as a living species. With the rise of technologies of security and government, the sharp distinction between the physical operations of biopolitics and modalities of power that work at the level of the formation of consciousness and the psyche becomes undeniable. More precisely, the governmental arm of biopower is irreconcilable with the recognition paradigm in at least two ways. First, government's fundamental premise is that its object, the population, is something that is not entirely amenable to its rational control. This distinguishes government not only from sovereignty but the total control of the body that characterizes discipline. By definition, a living mass such as a population cannot be rendered docile and completely useful. It cannot be controlled in the same way as individual bodies because it is subject to larger biological processes that are characterized by chance and randomness. Indeed, even if total control was possible, to render the population docile is to eradicate what made life attractive as a potentially limitless resource to power in the first place: life's natural unpredictability. Consequently, government seeks only to regulate its object, to achieve a state of equilibrium or regularity by predicting the probability of random events that can occur in a living mass and by compensating for its effects. As Foucault puts it, regulation involves "a technology which aims to establish a sort of homeostasis . . . by achieving an overall equilibrium that protects the security of the whole from internal dangers. . . . [A] technology of security; . . . a reassuring or regulatory technology."[34] Biopower is therefore inseparable from a fundamental rethinking of the physical-biological dimension of human existence as something that power must respect because power must function within this element. Accordingly, power is a type of physical action. The biological nature of human beings refers to the *interface* between the natural-biological processes of the human species and the geographical milieu of its existence that can affect these biological forces. These forces can be optimized toward specific, limited ends through regulatory technologies that work within nature insofar as it shapes the milieu of our existence.

Second, the productive regulation of the natural-biological dimension of human existence presupposes a relation between norm and material reality entirely different from the shaping of the *meaning* of human life by intelligible forms or constraining social norms. In Foucault's view, power does not seek to constrain (the natural reality of) human life but instead lets it develop or unfold in an optimal way. Although the power to make live can optimize life, there is a limit to its reach. Technologies of government can plan the material milieu in which the population lives and so shape the population. But they are unable to completely penetrate the biological processes of the population and its environment because these processes are subject to the contingency and accidentality of the temporal and the uncertain. Their *regulatory* function indicates that the technical organization of life and the political tendency toward systematization is based on the presupposition of power's impotence, its inability to eliminate the aleatory.

We should note in passing that before Butler imposed her account of subjection onto global politics, her attempt to reconcile a philosophy of recognition with a Foucauldian account of power was already conceptually misguided. Her characterization of subjection as the "internalization" of a hegemonic norm through incorporation, understood as the inscription of the body's surface by signifying processes to generate a psychical interiority, is incompatible with Foucault's account of the biopolitical formation of subjects in several respects.[35] First, she understands the process of normalization as involving prohibition and therefore views norms in analogy with and as an extension and even a constitutive iteration of repressive law in daily practices. Second, by limiting the productivity of power to processes of signification at the *surface* of the body, performances or stylizations that delineate its meaningful, intelligible form, she obscures the *physical* nature of biopolitical production and confuses it with the phenomenological topoi of embodiment and internalization, which are linked to a psychoanalytical argument about the productive nature of prohibition.[36] These psychoanalytical and phenomenological themes are alien to Foucault's thought. The understanding of the functioning of social norms in terms of internalization treats the norm as something like a law in that it possesses a prohibitive power that forms a psychical interiority.

In contradistinction, Foucault emphasized that biopower intervenes at a material level that precedes and cannot be reduced to the psychical form of subjects. The targets of regulation can be phenomena that have an important effect on the population through calculation, analysis, and reflection even though they "seem far removed from the population itself and its immediate behavior, fecundity, and desire to reproduce."[37] He also rigorously distinguished the process of normation found in disciplinary techniques from the process of normalization found in security mechanisms such as those dealing with disease and mortality. In normation, a norm functions prescriptively to distinguish between the normal and abnormal through behavioral training. In normalization, however, the norm is not something that precedes and is imposed on material reality but is instead something that emerges as a response to life. It is generated from complex negotiations with material reality in which distributions of normality are plotted and unfavorable distributions are brought in line with favorable distributions, thereby giving rise to the norm as an end result:

> We have then a system that is . . . exactly the opposite of the one we have seen with the disciplines. In the disciplines one started from a norm, and it was in relation to the training carried out with reference to the norm that the normal could be distinguished from the abnormal. Here, instead, we have a plotting of the normal and the abnormal, of different curves of normality, and the operation of normalization consists in establishing an interplay between these different distributions of normality and [in] acting to bring the most unfavorable in line with the more favorable. So we have here something that starts from the normal and makes use of certain distributions considered to be . . . more normal than others, or at any rate more favorable than the others. These distributions will serve as the norm. The norm is an interplay of differential normalities. . . . So, . . . what is involved here is no longer normation, but rather normalization in the strict sense.[38]

As a response to living nature, norms have to respect nature so as to better regulate and optimize the forces of a living species. This respect for nature is initially the regulatory enhancement of the forces of a population and subsequently, with the rise of liberal governmentality, the encouragement of the free play of human interests.

The greatest shortcoming of understanding global oppression through the recognition paradigm is that it can propose only utopian solutions that are based on the changing of social norms. Such solutions are merely lists of ideal desiderata for just human beings, whether justice is understood in terms of reason or feeling and affect. Such ideals supposedly have persuasive force for similarly just rational or feeling human beings. There is very little attempt to identify effective mechanisms in the contaminated world created by globalization to achieve these goals other than utopian appeals to rational human decency or ethical sentiment to recognize and protect universal human rights.

A biopolitical analysis of subject formation shows us that oppression can occur not only because of a lack of recognition or a particularistic mode of recognition but precisely through the most universal form of recognition. Therein lies its prodigious capacity and strength. For biopower shapes desire not by prohibition and censorship but by encouraging the spontaneous production of the collective interest by the play of desire. In Foucault's words, "The problem is how they can say yes; it is how to say yes to this desire. The problem is not therefore the limit of concupiscence or the limit of self-esteem in the sense of love of oneself, but concerns rather everything that stimulates and encourages this self-esteem, this desire, so that it can produce its necessary beneficial effects."[39] This is precisely the scene of recognition where a subject is empowered because its claims to be recognized are acknowledged. But this is emphatically not the scene of intersubjectivity as the quasi-transcendental source of ethical normative force celebrated by the contemporary Frankfurt School. It is instead the site of governmental intervention in and manipulative regulation of the natural processes that constitute the population.

Indeed, for Foucault, these technologies create the universal subject of humanity with all its physical and intellectual capacities and its claims for its rights to be recognized. Biopolitical technologies are accompanied by the rise of corresponding domains of knowledge and the various accounts of subject formation articulated in philosophical discourse are thematic figures that reflect the subject produced by these technologies. Accordingly, "man, as he is thought and defined by the so-called human sciences of the nineteenth century, and as he is reflected in nineteenth century humanism," Foucault suggests, "is nothing other than a figure of population."[40] This does not mean that humanity as the bearer of rights is a mere ideological fiction that is opposed to concrete man, as the early Marx claimed. Foucault's point is that the concrete human being as the material subject of capacities, needs, and interests is crafted by technologies of power. Hence, he notes the irony that the struggle against power in the nineteenth century took the form of an affirmation of the rights of man as a concrete living being when these rights were the juridical codification of the capacities of life produced by biopolitical technologies.

> Against this power that was still new in the nineteenth century, the forces that resisted relied for support on the very thing it invested, that is, on life and man as a living being. . . . What was demanded and what served as an objective was life, understood as the basic needs, man's concrete essence, the realization of his potential, a plenitude of the possible. . . . What we have seen has been a very real process of struggle; life as a political object was in a sense taken at face value and turned back against the system that was bent on controlling it. It was life more than the law that became the issue of political struggles, even if the latter were formulated through affirmations concerning rights. The "right" to life, to one's body, to health, to happiness, to the satisfaction of needs, and beyond all the oppressions or "alienations," the "right" to rediscover what one is and all that one can be, this "right" . . . was the political response to all these new procedures of power.[41]

These technologies are the material conditions that enable any ethical claim for recognition. The recognition of humanity and the protection of fundamental human rights occur at a subsequent level, once the subject of humanity has been produced in this biopolitical field. Hence, the historical emergence of human rights and the universal human subject that asks for its rights to be recognized are always already inscribed within and circumscribed by the web of technologies that facilitated the rise of capitalism and sustain it today.

Recognition as the Effect of Biopower, Biopower as a Response to Life

I have suggested that in the case of the production of transnational female labor as human capital, power primarily works by productive incorporation rather than by prohibition and repression through force or ideology. We have to understand incorporation in two senses: first, the bodily aptitudes and needs and interests of these women subjects are crafted by biopolitical technologies; second, they are crafted in such a way that they belong to the global capitalist system of means and ends in their very constitution as subjects. These processes of incorporation are gestures of inclusion. They render the recognition paradigm problematic because these oppressed subjects want to be invested more and not less by technologies of power. They want more and not less governmental intervention in their lives. Power is here a silently affirmative process of physical investment that makes them as subjects with capacities and needs that they then regard as being worthy of recognition. In the reflective gesture of demanding recognition, the subject willingly says *yes* to and affirms this initial investment. It asks to be invested with more power because this can improve its life. In other words, recognition is not a limit to power but is a negotiation with power generated by a given state of power, a sharing or partaking of processes of power that are already in operation and that have already invested the subject of recognition at the most material level of its being.

In contradistinction, if we understand power in terms of a prohibition that forms the psyche, then power is essentially the withholding of recognition or a deficient, injurious form of recognition. A theory of subjectification based on the internalization of coercive norms cannot account for the making of postcolonial female subjects by biopolitical technologies that shape physical needs and rational interests through processes of normalization that secure physical, geographical, and environmental conditions most favorable to the enhancement of the population. The focus on the law's prohibition and its performative subversion renders invisible the pervasive operations of biopower in various physical domains and obscures the need for the laborious negotiation with governmental technologies that impinge on every facet of the daily lives of these subjects such as directives concerning unemployment, the development of international tourism, and the export of migrant labor as a means for increasing foreign exchange reserves. An ethical critique aimed at making sovereign power ashamed of its oppressiveness is seductive for intellectuals because it makes us feel that we are doing something. But it is of limited effectiveness. For what is at stake is not the question of good and evil but a calculation of forces and interests that seeks to maximize them in all subjects so as to render everyone healthy and viable. An obsession with prohibition leads to a myopic and moralistic focus on contesting the exceptional decisions of sovereign-imperial power at the expense of tracking the complex functioning of the many unexceptional quotidian forms of power that make us what we are.

The different forms of recognition in global capitalism—what Honneth would call the "recognition order" of contemporary globalization—are so many effects of power that try to mitigate or alleviate its undesirable consequences. The governmental apparatuses forming female subjects of globalization have achieved modular status and sustain contemporary postcolonial projects of economic development especially for rapidly industrializing East and Southeast Asian countries with strong developmental states. Although they are governed by an inclusionary dynamic, they also have oppressive and exclusionary effects. In contemporary globalization, the deployment of biopolitical technologies has intensified to the point that they have broken out of the grasp of the territorial state and can render state sovereignty problematic. In the striated world of global capitalism, developing human capital is accompanied by the demand for less government and the rise of neoliberalism in the North but has oppressive consequences for the citizens of poorer postcolonial states desperately trying to climb up the hierarchy of the new international division of labor. The resources for augmenting the human capital of women workers are not universally available to all countries. In principle, poorer postcolonial countries also wish to cultivate their populations and enhance their bodily aptitudes. But since attracting inflows of capital is the best way to increase a country's forces, they also have to suspend care for some parts of their population and, indeed, have to sacrifice their welfare. In the name of development, there is greater governmental control where states acquiesce to harsh labor conditions for local factory workers and actively promote the exportation of migrant workers who are vulnerable to abuse in host countries because they are not part of the population there. While these sacrificial practices are exclusionary, they have to be situated within a larger dynamic of inclusion. They are not the resurrection of repressive colonial power but are part of the postcolonial biopolitics of human capital.

The revitalization of recognition as a paradigm for global justice should be understood within this larger field of the biopolitical development of human capital. The latter sustains the former as its condition of possibility but at the same time makes its ideal goals ultimately unachievable. With the decline of socialism as a genuine alternative, the only way forward is for countries to play the competitive game of developing human capital and the recognition of human rights within the framework of global capitalist accumulation. The different women subjects that are incorporated by this game are the different types of female labor specified in UN documents as the various categories of women workers who are especially vulnerable and whose contributions and rights deserve to be universally recognized and protected. But as the following example from a UN ESCAP document on women and globalization makes clear, the main reason they should be recognized and protected is because "human capacity building" is crucial if one wishes to increase the comparative advantage of a country's economy by moving to higher value-added manufacturing and the tertiary sector and knowledge-based enterprises:

> The rapid changes in job-market requirements and needed skills increase the emphasis on training and life-long learning to raise workers' employability and improve access to employment. Countries need to continually invest in skills and knowledge-development and the training of their workforce in light of these changes, including advances in technology and work organization. The risks are higher for the vulnerable groups and reduce their opportunities and incentives for training. To progress to higher levels of value-added employment (and thus towards higher incomes at the individual and aggregate levels), the population and workforce of the country must steadily improve their knowledge and skills for contributing effectively to the changing job market requirements. Human resources development or human capital formation are essential for sustaining a productive work force. Importantly, as policy attends to the development of both human and social capital, there are two elements that deserve special attention: making new information technologies available to wider segments of the population and building productive assets, especially for the poor men and women at the household level.[42]

These highly desirable goals are part of an elaborate transnational recognition order that joins NGOs, workers' groups, civil society groups, and international organizations, subregional bodies, and state governments. In the case of migrant labor, source countries should recognize their workers as resources and seek to train them and protect their rights. If a host country recognizes the source country's right to economic development, it should recognize the rights of migrant workers and permit them to transfer benefits and pensions back to the source country. In turn, migrant workers should recognize their source country as their home and send back money because the source country is their permanent home in which they can fully develop themselves as human capital. In transnational NGO policy talk, consultation and cooperation are synonyms for recognition. But the fact that this elaborate recognition order falls under the sign of a mere "ought" or "should" (as Hegel would have said) indicates that the base on which it rests—human capital—is always marked by unevenness. For capital is always a matter of difference and not equality, always a more or less, a matter of magnitude and relation. The development of human capital always takes place within an unequal field of resources and competition. As we have seen, some countries need to subcontract this task through labor exportation. Hence, a dynamic that is in principle inclusionary will always have exclusion-effects. Subsequently, these exclusion-effects can be symbolically coded and explained in terms of the withholding of recognition or the imposition of particularistic norms of recognition. In turn, recognition can be proposed as a way of alleviating these exclusion-effects. But even the fullest form of recognition can only provisionally alleviate these exclusion-effects because this inequality is structural to the processes of developing human capital, which creates human subjects with the power for recognition.

The biopolitical basis of the recognition order of the UN and transnational NGOs renders it inherently aporetic: we cannot not want to be part of this system of creating useful human beings even if this makes us susceptible to being used. This is because it is only within this field that we are concretely endowed with whatever concrete capacities and, therefore, needs and rights we have that subsequently become recognizable and enforceable within a juridical discourse. Without an analysis of this biopolitical basis, we cannot come to terms with the tenaciousness of global capitalism and the difficulty of resisting it. Resistance is nevertheless possible because biopolitical technologies have to "respect" and negotiate with what is natural to the life of the population in order to create human capital. Consequently, there is always something radically uncertain and explosive about life that challenges biopower's grip. The radically disruptive place of chance is structural to the regulatory power of norms. But such disruptiveness is not the unruliness of the behavior of individual subjects that in some way exceed and are external to norms because they have been excluded by these norms. The destabilization issues instead from life as the shifting ground for all biopolitical norms, from that which is internal to a norm as its irreducible physical material structure.

There is nothing vulnerable or precarious about life because it is not merely an effect of biopower but a disruptive force that is always implicated in biopower as its basis. We can call this force "power of life" in order to distinguish it from "power over life." Where there is life, there is no human subject, no human, no subject, and power creates the human subject as a response to life, to regulate and even to provisionally arrest life. Since life is unpredictable and has no inherent meaning, its enhancement as a resource requires that we regulate it by giving it ends. However, these ends also cannot be against life since that would extinguish the very resourcefulness of life that attracted power to it. But this resourcefulness, being impenetrable to human reason, can never be a source for the articulation of normative ideals that are embodied in and actualized by a universal or global subject of progressive transformation, such as humanity, the proletariat, the multitude, and other equivalent phenomena. However, as the moving ground that sustains global capitalism, it gives rise to strategies and techniques for resistance at many levels that can lead to different, less oppressive modes of subjectification.

Notes

A longer version of this chapter, "The Biopolitics of Recognition: Making Female Subjects of Globalization," appeared in *boundary 2* 40.2 (2013): 81–112.

1. Fraser and Honneth, *Redistribution or Recognition?*, 1.
2. Robert Reich, "Sensible Budget Invests in Our Future," *San Francisco Chronicle*, 6 February 2011.
3. For Fichte's argument that the practical subject comes into being in response to a summons (*Aufforderung*) from another rational being, see J. G. Fichte, *Foundations of Natural Right According to the Principles of the Wissenschaftslehre*, edited by Frederick Neuhouser, translated by Michael Baur (Cambridge: Cambridge University Press, 2000), §3: 29–39. The intersubjective constitution of subjectivity means that we are necessarily social beings. See also Dieter Henrich, "Fichte's Original Insight," translated by David R. Lachterman, *Contemporary German Philosophy* 1 (1982): 15–53. For the theory reader, the standard text on Hegel's concept of recognition is the pages on the lord and bondsman in the section on self-consciousness in G. W. F. Hegel, *Phenomenology of Spirit*, translated by A. V. Miller (Oxford: Oxford University Press, 1977), §§ 178–96, 111–19. In fact, the motif of recognition occurs throughout Hegel's philosophy of spirit and functions differently at various levels of spirit.
4. Axel Honneth develops this perspective from a reading of Hegel's Jena writings. See Axel Honneth, *The Struggle for Recognition: The Moral Grammar of Social Conflicts*, translated by Joel Anderson (Cambridge, UK: Polity Press, 1995).
5. Nancy Fraser, "Social Justice in the Age of Identity Politics: Redistribution, Recognition, and Participation," in Fraser and Honneth, *Redistribution or Recognition?*, 29, emphases in the original.
6. Fraser, "Social Justice in the Age of Identity Politics," 30.
7. Axel Honneth, "Redistribution as Recognition: A Response to Nancy Fraser," in Fraser and Honneth, *Redistribution or Recognition?*, 189.
8. See Butler, *Precarious Life*, xviii, xx–xxi.
9. See Butler, *Frames of War*, 28.
10. Butler, *Frames of War*, 7, 31.
11. See Butler, *Precarious Life*, 91; *Frames of War*, 3–4, 7, 12.
12. Butler, *Frames of War*, 1.
13. Butler, *Frames of War*, 7.
14. Butler, *Precarious Life*, 147.
15. Butler, *Frames of War*, 29.
16. Axel Honneth, "The Point of Recognition," in Fraser and Honneth, *Redistribution or Recognition?*, 244.

17. Butler, *Frames of War*, 7.

18. For a lucid discussion of the economic basis of the U.S. war on terror, see Giovanni Arrighi, *Adam Smith in Beijing: Lineages of the Twenty-first Century* (London: Verso, 2007).

19. I have discussed the feminization of labor in *Inhuman Conditions: On Cosmopolitanism and Human Rights* (Cambridge: Harvard University Press, 2006), ch. 6.

20. Ghosh, *Impact of Globalization on Women*, 21.

21. For a fuller discussion of the economic conditions that stimulate the supply and demand for internal migration of women for sex work and the link between sex work and the economic rationality of development in Thailand, see Pasuk Phongpaichit, *From Peasant Girls to Bangkok Masseuses*, Women, Work and Development, No. 2 (Geneva: International Labour Office, 1982).

22. For a discussion of the transnational traffic of migrant sex workers from and to Thailand, see Pasuk Phongpaichit, Sungsidh Piriyarangsan, and Nualnoi Treerat, *Guns, Girls, Gambling, Ganja: Thailand's Illegal Economy and Public Policy* (Chiang Mai, Thailand: Silkworm Books, 1998), chs. 8–9.

23. Punpuing, "Female Migration in Thailand," 22: "Migration often permits an individual to improve his/her economic status and the society to distribute human resources. Human capital is transferred from areas of surplus labour and low wages to areas where labour is scarce and wages are high."

24. *Perspectives on Gender and Migration: From the Regional Seminar on Strengthening the Capacity of National Machineries for Gender Equality to Shape Migration Policies and Protect Migrant Women, Bangkok, 22–24 November 2006*. Bangkok, Thailand: United Nations Economic and Social Commission for Asia and the Pacific, 2007, 2. The Report of the UN Secretary General on International Migration and Development of 1 July 2003, also discusses the link between international migration and economic and social development. See www.iom.int/jahia/webdav/shared/shared/mainsite/policy_and_research/un/58/A_58_98_en.pdf,intro., para. 2.

25. See United Nations Development Program, section on women's empowerment, http://www.undp.org/women/.

26. See the United Nations Economic and Social Commission for Asia and the Pacific (UN ESCAP) paper on "Women and Globalization," www.unescap.org/sdd/publications/gender/Pub_globalization.pdf.

27. Phongpaichit, *From Peasant Girls to Bangkok Masseuses*, 68.

28. Marx, "Contribution to the Critique of Hegel's Philosophy of Right," 256.

29. United Nations Commission on Population and Development, *Concise Report on World Population Monitoring. 1997: International Migration and Development*, www.actrav.itcilo.org/actrav-english/telearn/global/ilo/seura/migwod2.htm, para. 58.

30. Phongpaichit, *From Peasant Girls to Bangkok Masseuses*, 74–75.

31. On the materiality of ideology, see Louis Althusser, "Ideology and Ideological State Apparatus," in *Lenin and Philosophy and Other Essays*, translated by Ben Brewster (New York: Monthly Review Press, 2001), 112–15.

32. Michel Foucault, *Security, Territory, Population: Lectures at the Collège de France 1977–78*, 47.

33. Foucault, *Security, Territory, Population*, 47.

34. Michel Foucault, "'Society Must Be Defended,'" 249.

35. See Butler, *Gender Trouble*, 135.

36. See Butler, *The Psychic Life of Power*, 19.

37. Foucault, *Security, Territory, Population*, 72.
38. Foucault, *Security, Territory, Population*, 63.
39. Foucault, *Security, Territory, Population*, 73.
40. Foucault, *Security, Territory, Population*, 79.
41. Foucault, *The History of Sexuality*, 144–45.
42. UN ESCAP, "Women and Globalization," www.unescap.org/sdd/publications/gender/Pub_globalization.pdf.

chapter 7

Before Racial Construction

Irene Tucker

On the evening of 11 June 1963, just hours after ordering the Alabama National Guard to accompany two African American students onto the campus of the University of Alabama in fulfillment of a recent district court desegregation order, President John F. Kennedy spoke on national television: "If an American, because his skin is dark, cannot eat lunch in a restaurant open to the public, if he cannot send his children to the best public school available, if he cannot vote for the public officials who represent him, if, in short, he cannot enjoy the full and free life which all of us want, then who among us would be content to have the color of his skin changed and stand in his place?"[1]

Kennedy's speech, which *Ebony* magazine called "the most important document about the Negro ever delivered by an American President,"[2] and which was delivered only hours before the assassination of the civil rights activist Medgar Evers, is noteworthy for the deliberateness with which it details the various realms of public accommodation Kennedy meant to bring under legal challenge. (The legislation he introduced several weeks later, which sought to abolish formally the laws of Jim Crow, eventually became the Civil Rights Act of 1964.)[3] But Kennedy's address is equally remarkable, I want to suggest, for the test of equality—and, implicitly, the model of race—it offers. Racial discrimination counts as an injustice because membership in any given race is arbitrary: to distribute resources or assign meaning or value on the basis of qualities that are themselves without meaning is thus to transmute a particularly American promise of freedom into something like the capriciousness of fate. Racial discrimination is not, in this sense, merely an obvious slight against America's purported equality. It is rather a more intricate perversion. For if America is the country in which anyone can be anything, it seems particularly egregious to set up barriers on the basis of something—for example, "dark skin[ned]"—which anyone might have been.

With its emphasis on the arbitrariness of the association between the mark that identifies a particular race (an American's "dark skin") and the qualities and values assigned to that mark (the compulsion to eat lunch at this counter and not another) Kennedy's rhetoric doubtless brings to mind a certain moment in critical theory as well: the "linguistic turn" of structuralism and poststructuralism. I want to suggest that virtually all critical analyses of race *as a category* continue to mark out their analytical fields and to conceive of their political interventions from within a logic predicated upon a relation between an arbitrary signifier and that which it signifies—that is, from within a logic that is fundamentally linguistic.[4] In critical race studies this commitment to arbitrary signification goes by the name of "racial construction." In its most basic rendering, such a view instructs us that for all their apparent obviousness and self-evidence, racial categories do not really exist; they are (merely) constructed, which is to say without sound basis in biology. Writing in the opening essay in what is inarguably the locus classicus of the literature of race-as-sign, Henry Louis Gates's 1985 *"Race," Writing and Difference*, Anthony Appiah reminds his readers of the biologists' case for race's illusoriness: "Apart from the visible morphological categories of skin, hair and bone by which we are inclined to assign people to the broadest racial categories—black, white, yellow—there are few genetic characteristics to be found in the population of England that are not found in similar proportions in Zaire or in China, and few too (though more) which are found in Zaire but not in similar proportions in China or in England."[5]

In our current moment the claim for race's biological insubstantiality and the resulting critique that notes the arbitrariness of the racial sign are so familiar as to require no further argument. But if demonstrating race's insubstantiality no longer counts as a big revelation—indeed no longer counts as much of a revelation at all—this racial linguisticism nonetheless lives on in the many histories of race that document the multiple (and hence arbitrary) meanings cultures have assigned to racial signification. We are repeatedly presented with histories by which blackness came to be associated with, say, primitivism or spiritual authenticity or violence so that we may discover the contingency of such associations. If the relation between the racial sign and the various meanings attributed to it can be shown to have a history, this account implies, then surely it could have had—or might have in the future—a different history

In what follows I pursue a different sort of historicization. Rather than taking the signs of racial difference as given, and then tracing the variety of meanings race has had, I historicize the signs of racial difference themselves. What does an earlier history suggest about why we are so interested in reading skin as the sign of race in the first place? If, in the face of our knowing better, we still find ourselves perceiving racial differences with an instantaneousness that feels precritical, perhaps we ought to consider the possibility that the production of the experience of immediate and self-evident knowing—more specifically the rendering people instantly and immediately legible—is what race is *doing*. The immediacy of our perception of race is what makes skin-centered race of its historical moment. Such immediacy is the salient quality of modern race, not a symptom that we have forgotten race's history or that we have become uncritically acculturated.

I start by asking why, in the final quarter of the eighteenth century, *skin* suddenly came to be privileged as the primary sign of racial difference. During his lifetime and throughout much of the nineteenth century, Kant was recognized as being the first thinker to isolate and privilege skin color as the primary marker of racial difference, as well as to theorize such a privileging. Darwin, for one, lists Kant within the still familiar catalogue of natural historians—Linnaeus, Buffon, and Blumenbach are some of the others—whose accounts of human difference influenced his own theory of race in *The Descent of Man*.[6] The current tendency to read Kant primarily through his theorization of the aesthetic in his *Critique of Judgment* has resulted in his writing on race being overlooked entirely, or, when read, considered in isolation from the body of his more well-known work. Instead I want to return to the case Kant makes for privileging skin as the marker of race in his 1788 essay, "On the Use of Teleological Principles in Philosophy." That essay, which introduces a conception of race as a quality that is at once essential and unchanging, marks a striking departure from older, "humoral" conceptions of human variety that understood skin color to be the consequence of a complex interaction of forces both within bodies and between bodies and their surrounding environments. In marking its distance from a humoral model that emphasized changeability, Kant's essay belongs to a moment in the eighteenth century in which notions of health and sickness and of human variety, long thought to be intimately intertwined, pulled apart. This bifurcation was the result of the radical reconception known as modern "anatomical" medicine. Sometimes called "Paris medicine," in recognition of its embrace of the egalitarian spirit of the age of democratic revolutions, this model of medicine was premised on the principles that human bodies are fundamentally like one another and that disease is located within organs in the interiors of bodies, inaccessible to direct observation by doctors and patients alike. By establishing the likeness of bodies as a function of their internal similarity, modern anatomical medicine effected a dramatic change in the idea of skin: skin went from being the porous boundary connecting bodies and environments to a boundary that concealed the defining likeness of one body with every other.

But I am not simply suggesting that, in the closing decades of the eighteenth century, race comes to be legible in the skin because skin's function and significance are in flux and thus vulnerable to redefinition. The case I want to make is, rather, a positive one: that instantaneously legible skin-based race comes into being as a structure for resolving the incoherences that followed from anatomical medicine's effort to make scientifically verifiable a fundamental likeness of bodies that was localized deep in the body's interior, beyond straightforward observation. Rather than being the consequence of historical transition and instability, then, race turns out to represent a drive *toward* stability. It is precisely this stabilizing function that helps account for race's peculiar staying power, helps account for why it is that we find ourselves noticing race even when we know we should know better. Historians have long puzzled over why the complex of discourses known as the Enlightenment that ventured the revolutionary claim that all humans are by their very nature equal took place in the same era in which differences in skin color came to be understood as indelible evidence of essential differences in human capacity.[7] The context of anatomical medicine allows us to see that the coincidence of universalism and embodied and inalterable racial difference was the consequence not of the Enlightenment's failure to live up to its professed ideals but rather of the conflict of two not entirely compatible sets of political and intellectual commitments: first, to universal likeness and the political equality that was understood to follow axiomatically from that likeness, and, second, to an instantiation of that likeness that promised to turn it into something that might be proved by science. This second commitment, to making universal equality something that might be observed empirically rather than asserted as a political principle or taken as an article of faith, operates to undermine the first. The specificity of the bodies understood to instantiate universal likeness works against the likeness these bodies were meant to show. In accounting for what would seem, on first glance, the historical paradox of the Enlightenment invention of race, the history of race discernible in the encounter of anatomical medicine and Kant's critical philosophy also traces the movement from less to more familiar models. In this story, race begins as a register of human likeness; it becomes the mark of difference we now understand it to be only in the wake of the move to make that likeness visible.

Beyond Humors: Distinguishing Race and Medicine

Viewed solely as a moment in the history of medicine, anatomical medicine, premised on the notion that human bodies are fundamentally like one another, marks a fundamental break with the humoral model of the body that preceded it. For the purposes of our discussion, two aspects of the earlier humoral paradigm are salient. First, each humoral body was understood to be unique, characterized by its own particular mixture of humors: blood, phlegm, black bile, and yellow bile. What counted as sickness differed from body to body, different states of disequilibrium of each body's particular balance. Second, humoral bodies were understood to have an essentially porous relation to their environments, which meant that each person's balance of humors was created in relation to and could be disrupted by the particular mix of wetness, dryness, heat, and cold in the immediate surroundings. Skin functioned as the porous boundary between forces within a given humoral body and the environmental forces outside it, which meant that skin color was understood to be affected by things like the amount of sunlight in a given locale and was expected to change as an individual's environment changed. Skin color was just one register among many of human variety; temperament was likewise understood to be the effect of the interaction of bodily humors and climatic forces. So although bodies were essentially particular and changeable, they tended to manifest similarities to other bodies that shared their environment. Health and sickness, on the one hand, and human variety, on the other, are by this account different aspects of a single system.

In this regard, the same paradigm shift that marked anatomical medicine's break from humoral medicine also established, for the first time, the discursive independence of issues of health and sickness and issues of human difference. Even as it sought to establish the autonomy of the body from its environment—and, relatedly, bodies' fundamental likeness to one another—as well as the autonomy of medical knowledge from what we might broadly characterize as anthropological knowledge, anatomical medicine remained shadowed by its relation to questions of human variety and race.

Anatomical medicine understands all bodies to be operating by way of identical mechanisms. Disease is located on organs buried deep within the bodies, and while those organs aren't directly observable by either patients or their doctors, the fact that all bodies are presumed to be alike offers a new, indirect method for diagnosis: the autopsy. Rather than correlating symptoms with the condition of internal organs they couldn't see, physicians diagnosed by comparing a patient's symptoms to the state of the internal organs drawn of other people's dead bodies—bodies these physicians would have seen autopsied in the course of their medical training. In this regard, the "standardized" body is not an actual, observable material body at all, but an idea, the presumption of the likeness of a particular patient's diseased but inaccessible internal organs and the internal organs of the dead, autopsied body of someone else by which diagnoses can be made. Because the humoral model of the body had understood sickness to entail the interaction of bodies and their environments, patients were as likely as physicians to discern the causal steps by which balanced humors became imbalanced, to diagnose the ailment, and to act to bring about a cure. By contrast, in anatomical medicine, because the pathology of disease is not directly observable but must draw upon knowledge gained elsewhere—that is, the autopsies that were a central part of the newly codified anatomical physician's education—doctors are in a position to know things about their patients' bodies the patients themselves cannot know.

The same structure of standardness that lends exclusive authority to the physician also has built within it a fundamental incoherence. On the one hand, anatomical medicine's power to diagnose is predicated upon the presumption that the sick body of a patient and the autopsied dead body are fundamentally like one another. But the comparability of the sick body and the dead body depends upon excluding analytically the progression of the disease, the process by which the sick patient comes to be dead. For the physician, or anyone else, to have a sense of the progression from sick to dead, the state of the sick body and the state of the dead body must of necessity be *different* from one another.[8] To the degree to which the process of a disease's progression—the process of dying—must be excluded, so too must the possibility of intervening to bring about a cure, of affecting the body from the outside. Anatomical physicians' authority to treat what ails a given patient thus stands in significant tension with their power to diagnose. Doctors assert the exclusive authority of their knowledge to figure out what is wrong with a patient only at the price of losing the ground from which they might claim to be able to do something about it.

At the very same late eighteenth-century moment in which anatomical medicine's founding physicians were making the case for the likeness of human bodies and developing the complex of practices necessary for diagnosing and treating those like bodies, Kant laid out the terms of his revolutionary new "critical philosophy." Committed, like anatomical medicine, to the lawfulness and regularity of the natural world and the subjects who would apprehend that world, Kant generated a methodology for knowing this lawfully ordered world that, by the close of his life, he would discover to be plagued by many of the same incoherences that dogged anatomical medicine. According to the critical philosophy, we know something exists because we can have thoughts about it. The reverse is true as well: the fact that subjects can have thoughts about a real, ongoing, and necessarily interconnected world stands as evidence of the existence of those subjects.[9] For Kant, such mutuality of constitution of necessity has a temporal element as well. While skeptics like Hume worried that we can have no way of being certain that the images we perceive exist beyond the moments we perceive them—and in that sense no way of knowing whether they exist outside our heads, our fantasies—for Kant, establishing the realness of both the world and the subjects who know that world depends upon establishing the persistence of both through time. But the problem, for Kant, is this: although our many perceptual encounters occur successively, the simple fact that we must see one image before we see another tells us nothing about the temporal state of the perceived items in and of themselves. Here is where the mutually constituting relation of subjects and the object world Kant terms the "transcendental deduction" is crucial. Imagine, for a moment, a book on a shelf. Although we cannot, strictly speaking, experience the spine, the front and back covers, and the inside pages of that book at the same time, we nonetheless know the spine, covers, and pages to be part of the image we have of the book. They are all essential—in Kantian terms, "necessary" or "lawful"—qualities of the book. How do we come to know this about books? We know because we experience a book's spine, covers, and pages successively, as we pull the book off the shelf and turn it over in our hands. And how do we synthesize these successive experiences of disparate elements into the unitary thing we know as a book? We do it because we experience ourselves as persisting over time. It is our persistence as subjects that enables us to knit together the different elements, to know, even if we can't quite experience, that they are all parts of the same thing. Our same persistence as subjects allows us to experience the covers and spines and pages of many books over time and to understand those elements to be part of what makes a book a book, even as we understand the water stains or yellowed edges we encounter on some to be contingent, nonnecessary qualities. And how do we experience our own persistence as subjects though time? We know we persist because we are able to experience the unchanging and essential qualities of the book.

But while a sense of our own persistence is a necessary condition for our understanding of the book as an object, it is not sufficient. For in order for us to see a book, we not only need to understand the back cover and the inside pages as part of the same object despite the fact they can be perceived only successively; we also need to know that other images we perceive as part of the same succession—the bookshelf itself, say—ought not to be synthesized along with our images of the cover and pages. We include some images we experience successively and exclude others because we have an idea of a book. In order for us to have such an idea, we need a concept of time itself, and that concept needs to be "mind-independent"—that is, existing outside the sort of mutually constituting relations of sequentiality that link our experience of our own duration as subjects to our experience of the duration of the synthesized book. Such a notion of time allows us to understand the various elements of a book as not simply sequentially apprehensible images but as images that constitute a book because they are caused or intended, which is to say, organized according to an idea. It is this quality of being caused or intended that allows us to distinguish between the kind of thing we are seeing when we see a book's cover and the kind of thing we are seeing when we see a water stain on that cover.

Structuring the existence of both subjects and the noumenal world on the ground of temporal persistence—sameness over time—means relegating the idea of change over time to the contingent. Kant's system requires, in other words, that we treat all versions of change like the water stain: as something that can happen to an object in the world rather than a fundamental quality of that object. This is true even when, as with the process of dying, the change in question is inevitable (and in that sense as much a defining quality of the subject or object as its dimensions or rationality). That the process of moving from being sick to being dead poses as great a theoretical challenge to Kant's critical philosophy as it does for the emergent discipline of anatomical medicine becomes poignantly apparent in the late-career work *The Conflict of the Faculties*, whose final essay begins as an attempt to theorize the proper relation between the disciplines of philosophy and medicine but almost immediately morphs into something like a lamentation upon the philosopher's own slow death. Subtitled *On the Power of the Mind to Master Its Morbid Feelings by Sheer Resolution*, Kant's essay is structured as a letter to Professor Cristoph Wilhelm Hufeland of the University of Jena in response to Hufeland's recently published *Macrobiotics, Or the Art of Prolonging Human Life*. In taking aim against regimen, Kant positions himself as a critic of the humoral bodily paradigm, for which the category of the regimen was crucial, and whose founding premise, we recall, was that individual patients had full access to the forces in their bodies governing their states of health or sickness. As Kant explains, for Hufeland, the development of "the art of prolonging human life" is predicated on the presumption that the degree to which an individual enjoys his or her life is a reliable gauge of that individual's health, such that he or she might fulfill their two most ardent desires at once: "to have a long life and to enjoy good health during it."[10]

> [A man] can *feel* well (to judge by his comfortable feeling of vitality), but he can never *know* that he is healthy. The cause of natural death is always illness, whether one feels it or not. There are many people of whom one can say, without really wanting to ridicule them, that they are always *sickly* but can never be *sick*. Their regimen consists in constantly deviating from and returning to their way of life, and by this they manage to get on well and live a long, if not a robust life. I have outlived a good many of my friends or acquaintance who boasted of perfect health and lived by an orderly regimen adopted once and for all, while the seed of death (illness) lay in them unnoticed, ready to develop. They felt healthy and did not know they were ill; for while the cause of natural death is always illness, *causality* cannot be felt. It requires understanding, whose judgment can err. . . . Hence if he does not feel ill, he is entitled to express his well-being only by saying that he is *apparently* in good health. So a long life, considered in retrospect, can testify only to the health one *has enjoyed*, and the art of a regimen will have to prove its skill or science primarily in the art of *prolonging* life (not enjoying it). (181)[11]

Kant objects to Hufeland from within what is clearly an anatomical paradigm: a patient's sense of her own health as she experiences it can only be apparent, felt rather than known.[12] This disarticulation of knowing from feeling means that knowledge of one's actual state of health is always only retrospective: "A long life, *considered in retrospect*, can testify only to the health one has enjoyed." The advent of the autopsy provided anatomical medicine and the anatomizing doctor with a means of knowing and a point of "retrospection" from which the patient was barred. Hence Kant's emphasis on *enjoyment*, a word whose experiential focus suggests that even a retrospect taken at the last possible moment could still testify only to one's *feelings*.[13]

A moment later Kant takes up the challenge of the legibility of changing bodies in a way that is more intimate and which at the same time slides repeatedly back and forth between offering a narration of his own experience and an account of an unspecified "patient." Kant recalls the effects of his contracting "catarrh accompanied by distress in the head." "The result of it," he remembers, "was that I felt disorganized—or at least weakened and dulled—in my intellectual work; and since this ailment has attached itself to the natural weaknesses of my old age, it will end only with life itself." Now describing the patient, Kant details the decline:

> This pathological condition of the patient, which accompanies and impedes his thinking, in so far as thinking is holding firmly onto a concept (of the unity of ideas connected in his consciousness) produces the feeling of a spasmic state in his organ of thought (his brain). This feeling, as of a burden, does not really weaken his thought and reflection itself, or his memory of preceding thought; but when he is setting forth his thoughts . . . the very need to guard against distractions which would interrupt the firm coherence of ideas **in their temporal sequence** produces an involuntary spasmic condition of the brain, which takes the form of an inability to maintain unity of consciousness in his ideas, **as one takes the place of the preceding one**. In every discourse I first prepare (the reader or the audience) for what I intend to say by indicating, in prospect, my destination, and, in retrospect, the starting point of my argument (without these two points of reference a discourse has no consistency). And the result of this pathological condition is that when the time comes for me to connect the two, I must suddenly ask my audience (or myself, silently): now where was I? where did I start from? This is a defect, not so much of the mind or of the memory alone, as rather of *presence of mind* (in connecting ideas)—that is, an involuntary *distraction*. (207, boldface added)

But it is Kant's notion that the coherence of ideas across time might be figured as an oscillation between subject and object—as a shifting from what subjects do to the ideas they think about—that offers him, at least temporarily, a way around the difficulty of thinking about things that change lawfully. Kant seems here almost to present the same descriptions twice, first as a set of symptoms plaguing an unknown "patient" and then, again, as an account of his own symptoms. I say Kant *almost* seems to do this because he actually offers no explanation at all of the relation governing the two sets of descriptions, simply passing from one to the other without remark. Inasmuch as the two points of view are articulated in terms of a rhetoric of pathology, the passage's compositional ambiguations effectively invite us as readers to engage in something like medical diagnosis: Are "brain spasms" and "distraction" different names for a single condition? What would be the sort of evidence by which one might make such a judgment?

Here thought itself fails to remain unchanging—the very thought whose constancy ensures the constancy of both the world and the subject inhabiting and seeking to know it. Kant presents this collapse of thinking under the pressure of a failure of self-consistency, in both third- and first-person variations, and as a lack of coherence of temporal sequence. While the consistency that at once announces and constitutes thought is initially described in temporal terms, as the capacity to "indicate, in prospect, my destination, and, in retrospect, the starting point of my argument," it is also present, at least by negation, as a seamless oscillation between subject and object. To think coherently from one point of one's argument to the next necessarily involves the capacity to treat one's just completed thought as the object of one's further contemplation. We are thus presented with an exemplification of Kant's critical method and its undoing. Here the subject's thoughts start off by being figured not just as sensations but also as independent objects in the world insofar as they are past. The speaker articulates an itinerary, the map of a movement between a starting point and a destination. But because what needs to be represented is the subject's experience of his change over time, not simply his plotting of the then and the yet-to-be, subject and object collapse into one another.

Kant's unacknowledged oscillation between first- and third-person, between diagnosed object and dying subject, not only announces his borrowing of the diagnostic methods of anatomical medicine in order to transform what is changing and hence illegible into a set of lawful relations; it also reveals what he gains by *not* specifying the precise relation between the incoherent philosopher and the patient plagued with brain spasm. Not specifying allows Kant to posit the fundamental interchangeability of the patient with the philosopher. This interchangeability, in turn, rescues Kant's critical philosophy since it points to the fact that the perspective from which lawfulness is discerned is neither the spasmodic patient's nor the philosopher's. That is, not specifying demonstrates that the irreconcilability between Kant's critical philosophy and the knowledge of lawfully changing objects cannot be recognized from within critical philosophy itself. It can be rendered discernible only by way of the sort of rhetorical performance offered here. By choosing the structure of the anatomical body as the framework within which to make apparent the lawfully rational mind's incapacity to account for its own decline, Kant suggests that we can come to understand what it is that critical philosophy cannot teach us insofar as our thinking minds must depend upon the continued life of the bodies we inhabit.

The formal structure that this passage calls into being allows readers to recognize the temporally dilated likeness of patient and philosopher in an instant precisely because, as readers, we occupy a register ontologically distinct from that of either Kant or the possibly imaginary patient he describes. And it is precisely this formal structure Kant draws upon in "On the Use of Teleological Principles in Philosophy" when he defines race as the essential quality of human likeness made instantaneously legible in the skin. As readers we can see this move as an effort to materialize the formal, rhetorical structure that allows him to see instantaneously the fundamental likeness of dying (in process) bodies. This move converts such seeing from an idea, a point of view to be voluntarily occupied, into a thing in the world and positions his skin-centered model of race as a departure from the prevailing humoralism (here represented in the writing of the South Sea voyager Georg Forster). Kant decries forms of humoralism like Forster's that offer a world of what Kant calls "natural description": a world characterized by the multiple and discrete comings-into-being of qualities that need not reproduce themselves. Such descriptions are inadequate, from Kant's perspective, because they fail to offer evidence of a singular, unitary humanity or the coherent natural world that would allow the individual subjects of that world to recognize their own continuity of self: phlegmatic individuals are the products of the cool, damp north, while the sanguine hail from warm and moist equatorial regions, and so on. Rather than remaining constant through time, both the world and the subject that occupy this humorally conceived world change as their relation to one another is altered. Because Forster's natural description posits as many causes as there are combinations of climatic conditions and individual bodies, Kant argues that such a view does not allow us to read the continuity of the subject and object worlds back from the conditions of that world at any given moment. In a world in which bodies change with their environment, we can know only what we are present to witness at any given moment.

The skin-based model of race Kant proposes matters as an alternative because it stands as evidence of a world legible by way of "natural history." Such a world is one in which a subject need not be present at the moment of generation to witness the specific causal sequences that brought the relations of the world into being, because prior causes are discernible in the present relations of the world. Kant seizes upon what he understands to be an inconsistency in the evidence for humoralism so as to propose an alternative account of the relations bodied forth by skin color. In his view Forster's sudden jump from the olive-skinned Arabs of North Africa to the "blackest Negroes in Senegal" undermines his claim that color can be reliably correlated to the gradual changes in climate. The fact that an individual's skin color is as likely to resemble that of his or her parents as that of other inhabitants of the same area suggests that the fitness of human beings to their motherlands cannot coexist with their dispersion over the face of the earth. If Forster's humoral model of human variety posits a Providence with the wisdom to make an individual's body fit for his or her environment, Kant asks why that same Providence is too short-sighted to anticipate the possibility of "a second transplanting." For Kant, the noncorrelation of skin color to place is evidence not of Providence's failure of vision but instead of Forster's analytical failure: skin color stands as evidence not for an individual's fitness for a particular environment but for the universal human fitness for *all climates*, a fitness that is made manifest by the sheer variety of environments to which the various skin colors demonstrate that humans have migrated at some point in the past. In this way the variety of skin colors manifests the common human potential to be various, a common capacity for change—now complete—that is legible in an instant.

In Kant's telling, then, skin color, that outward manifestation of internal "seeds," common to all and observable by none, instantiates the fundamental and universal likeness of humans, a likeness expressive of the freedom to be anywhere. And surely, for all the remoteness of Kant's talk of seeds, there is a descriptive canniness about the insight that what we're seeing when we register the color of individuals' skins as a significant fact about them is their resemblance to one another. But if a reading of Kant's most straightforward statement about the topic would seem to resolve the paradox of the Enlightenment invention of modern race by insisting upon the consilience of the two projects, the very need for race to secure the recognition of human equality posited by Kant's critical philosophy—to secure, not merely to indicate—suggests that the frameworks for knowing subjects are not entirely in accord with one another. I have been arguing that a broadened understanding of what ought to be included in Kant's "writing on race" offers a reading of this discord; once we attend to his efforts to grapple with the emergent discourse of anatomical medicine and that discourse's notion of the standardized body, we see that the logic of the Kantian Enlightenment demands not simply that we come to understand how to know likeness but that we come to know that likeness in an instant. Such instantaneous knowing, we have seen, underwrites the likeness of humans and their bodies by excluding from its purview the inevitable change those bodies undergo, the processes of aging and dying. So while the skin-based notion of race Kant invents

Before Racial Construction 155

operates to fulfill the Enlightenment's central aspiration to universal likeness, the anatomical medicine that allows us to parse the logic of race's utility offers us another way of understanding this aspiration. Viewed within the context of anatomical medicine's standardized body, the (raced) Enlightenment subjects are those whose epistemological and political equality are made to stand as proof of their power to live forever. Equality turns out to be the aspiration to immortality, a flight from the vulnerability that comes less of the qualities associated with inhabiting a particular time and place than of the tragedy of finitude itself.

In tracing back modern, skin-based race to its moment of theorization, we find, to our surprise, a race without racism. But if such a discovery would seem, on the face of it, sufficient reason to return Kant's formulation to the historical obscurity from which we have only just now rescued it, I want to suggest that we might pause and take more than a moment to reflect before we do so. In his *What Was African American Literature?*, Kenneth Warren laments that for all the theoretical sophistication and historical nuance that has characterized recent studies of race, racism has remained woefully underanalyzed, taken as a given: "The 'discovery' made again and again by recent scholarship is that despite news to the contrary 'racism' still exists."[14] Insofar as Kant's Enlightenment interrogation of the relations between philosophy and anatomical medicine returns us to a race without racism, such an analysis affords us an opportunity not to ignore the harms of various racisms but to consider their mechanisms and motivations by not simply presuming their operation. If the defining instantaneity of race turns out to announce a universal aspiration to a likeness that would allow us to escape the privation of our finitude as individual subjects, then we can also glimpse the ways in which the institutional structures of instantaneity—the police snapshot, the glance of an airport security officer—might operate to constitute, rather than merely to reflect, racism's privations. And in this regard, it becomes possible to read the Kennedy speech with which I began afresh, not as an account of the contingency of the circumscriptions of particularity but as a way through those circumscriptions, a catalogue of dilations of a lifetime by which we discover our common aspiration to lives lived full and various.

Notes

1. Reprinted in *Ebony Magazine*, September 1963, 233.
2. *Ebony*, 233.
3. Abel, *Signs of the Times*, 288.

4. While I have offered my methodology as a salutary corrective to a predominant discourse of racial construction, I would be the first to admit that over the past decade and a half, there has been a great outpouring of important scholarship that circumvents this constructionist model altogether. I am thinking, just to take a few prominent recent examples, of writing ranging from Saidhiya Hartman's and Jacqueline Goldsby's work on lynching, Brent Edwards's work on black cosmopolitanism and, more recently, jazz performativity, to Elizabeth McHenry's work on nineteenth-century African American literary societies. Such scholarship understands its task not to be discovering what race means, or the processes by which it refers, or the sorts of qualities it purports to name or describe, but rather dedicates itself to offering accounts of how individuals and populations designated as members of a particular race come to envision the possibilities and limitations for acting in the world. And certainly such positivism, in declining to accord race a stability or descriptive force beyond its immediate context, could be said to count as a theory of race: race is nothing more—or less—than the ways people use, recognize, or impose the term at any given moment.

Generally speaking, I conceive of my work as a supplement to rather than a commentary on this body of scholarship. Yet it is a supplementarity of a very specific order. Even the complexity of describing such positivism—by what principle are the uses, recognitions, impositions to be brought in relation to one another?—hints at the ways in which pragmatist historicizations of race, taken to their logical conclusion, offer discrete thick cultural descriptions in place of something like a history of race. Stated plainly, the discontinuity of such formations is hardly anodyne, as the controversy surrounding Kenneth Warren's brilliant and provocative *What Was African-American Literature?* (Cambridge: Harvard University Press, 2011) surely attests. For Warren, "African-American literature" was but is no more. The "collective enterprise we now know as African American or black literature . . . gained coherence as an undertaking in the social world defined by the system of Jim Crow segregation," and insofar as such a literature was produced by "black writers [who] knew that their work would in all likelihood be evaluated instrumentally, in terms of whether or not it could be added to the arsenal of arguments, achievements and propositions needed to attack the justifications for, and counteract the effects of, Jim Crow," such a literature can be said to have ended with the formal dismantling of legal segregation that was the triumph of the civil rights movement. The resistance to Warren's declaration that African American literature comes in and out of existence in the space of just over half a century bespeaks both the analytical and political downsides of an embrace of such historicism: it is difficult to see how the refusal to engage race as a category beyond its immediate discursive or institutional context can help but foreclose the possibility of seeing how a given history of racially designated individuals and populations extends, interrupts, or supplements previous or coincident treatments, leaving us instead with a kind of opacity of historical immanence.

5. Appiah, "The Uncompleted Argument," 21–22.

6. Darwin, "On the Races of Man."

7. As George Frederickson puts it, "What makes Western racism so autonomous and conspicuous in world history has been that it developed in a context that presumed human equality of some kind." Or consider the perplexity with which Nancy Stepan opens her intellectual history of "scientific racism," in her 1982 *The Idea of Race in Science*: "A fundamental question about the history of racism in the first half of the nineteenth

century is why it was that, just as the battle against slavery was being won by abolitionists, the war against racism in European thought was being lost." Stepan, looking away from the eighteenth century toward the nineteenth, doesn't so much explain the turn from Enlightenment universalism to the multiple-origin stories of scientific racism as she redescribes it as a failure of ideological conviction; the rise of European racism bespeaks the fleetingness of the abolitionist ideals. Frederickson, for his part, identifies a dialectic by which racial hierarchies are introduced as an intellectual structure for making sense of inequalities that begin needing explanation only once equality is the presumptive norm. See George M. Frederickson, *Racism: A Short History* (Princeton: Princeton University Press, 2002), 11; Nancy Leys Stepan, *The Idea of Race in Science: Great Britain 1800–1960* (New Haven: Macmillan, 1982), 1.

8. In their jointly authored essay, "Anatomie," John Locke and Thomas Sydenham object to autopsies precisely on the grounds of challenge posed by the temporal progression of disease—the changefulness of bodies—to the diagnostic authority of the standardized body. How are physicians to know that the lesions they discover on an organ as a result of an autopsy are the *causes* of death and not death's *effects*? John Locke and Thomas Sydenham, "Anatomie," reprinted in full in Kenneth Dewhurst, "Locke and Sydenham on the Teaching of Anatomy," *Medical History* 2 (1958): 1–12.

9. My discussion throughout this section is indebted to Jay F. Rosenberg's lucid and incisive *Accessing Kant: A Relaxed Introduction to the Critique of Pure Reason* (Oxford: Oxford University Press, 2005), as well as Ernst Cassirer's *Kant's Life and Thought* (New Haven: Yale University Press, 1981).

10. Kant, *The Conflict of the Faculties*, 179. Subsequent pages are cited parenthetically.

11. In his only other extended writing devoted solely to the relationship between medicine and philosophy, *De Medicina Corporis, quae Philosophorum est* (On Philosophers' Medicine of the Body), a lecture delivered at the Rektoratsrede in either October 1786 or October 1788, Kant elaborates a position somewhat closer to Hufeland's than the one he offers in the final essay of the *Conflict*. In this earlier essay he outlines a mutually supplementary relation between medicine's and philosophy's respective capacities to control the state of the body: while the art of medicine should not be practiced "mechanically" upon humans in the way that veterinary medicine is practiced on domestic cattle, but instead ought to enlist the powers of the human mind in helping to mend the body, there is a danger in assuming, as Hufeland seems to in the notion of regimen that Kant criticizes in the opening passages of the *Conflict*, that medicine and philosophy act upon the body in the same manner or at the same time, or that they are mutually apprehensible modes. Here is Kant: "Since we want to act advisedly toward our end, and since the doctor and the philosopher obviously take different views of the nature of things and act accordingly, I think it is most important that neither of them crosses over the limits of his competence; seized with a certain meddlesomeness, the philosopher would seem to wish to play the doctor, and the doctor the philosopher. There is no doubt as to what constitutes their respective limits: the doctor is qualified to treat the disordered mind by measures applied to the body; the philosopher, to treat the body through the influence of the mind." Immanuel Kant, "On the Philosophers' Medicine of the Body," translated by Mary J. Gregor, in *Kant's Latin Writings: Translations, Commentaries and Notes*, edited and translated by Lewis White Beck in collaboration with Mary J. Gregor, Ralf Meerbote, and John Reuscher (New York: Peter Lang, 1986), 230. In her introduction to this essay,

Mary J. Gregor makes the case for Kant's detailed knowledge of and interest in contemporary medical debates.

12. A number of critics and historians have noted Kant's abiding interest in medicine, as well as his sustained engagement with a number of the era's most prominent physicians. Marshall Brown details Kant's close intellectual and personal friendship with Markus Herz, focusing in particular on the way Herz's category of a "pathological soul" influenced Kant during the conceptualization of *The Critique of Pure Reason*. See Marshall Brown, "From the Transcendental to the Supernatural: Kant and the Doctors," *Bucknell Review* 39.2 (1996): 151–69. Susan Meld Shell offers the testimony of Kant's friend and contemporary R. B. Jachmann regarding Kant's obsession with his health on the way to making the case that Kant's version of philosophical self-awareness is fundamentally predicated upon the humans' existence as "a community of bodies": "Perhaps no man who ever lived paid a more exact attention to his body and everything that affected it." In Shell's account, the "recalcitrance of bodies," both others' and one's own, offers the grounds for establishing the necessity of mutual relations of substances that, in Kant's view, "allow us to distinguish between knowledge and fantasy." Susan Meld Shell, *The Embodiment of Reason: Kant on Spirit, Generation, Community* (Chicago: University of Chicago Press, 1996), 2, 3, and see especially the introduction and ch. 10, "Kant's Hypochondria: A Phenomenology of Spirit."

13. While the sense of inaccess to the inner workings of one's body was particularly acute during the decades in which the humoral paradigm was in the process of being actively supplanted by an anatomical logic, I want to make clear that the forms of illegibility I am describing are not merely the consequence of the shift in paradigms but are the consequence of an ongoing dynamic within the theory (and practice) of anatomical medicine itself. Consider an essay by the physician Abigail Zuger entitled "Healthy Right up to the Day You're Not," published in the *New York Times* on 30 September 2008:

> It is as fragile and elusive as a soap bubble, as protean as a Lava lamp. It is as hard to define as love or happiness, and even harder to trap and keep.
>
> This is your health we're talking about, the intangible that you probably think people like me can help you achieve and maintain. Why do we all persist in treating health like a bankable asset? Is it the solidity of our flesh and bone? The lab reports that look like bank statements? Either way, the operant fiction is that with diligent adherence to expert advice, pretty much anyone can sock away a nice little stash of health for the future.

14. Warren, *What Was African American Literature?* 85.

chapter 8

Archive Favor:
African American Literature
before and after Theory

Jordan Alexander Stein

Bibliography is a technical branch of literary analysis, variously concerned with describing the characteristics of manuscripts and printed books, with assessing the formal and historical relations between them, with studying the transmission of printed works, and with editing authoritative editions.[1] A long-standing mode of literary study, bibliography was nonetheless influenced by developments in literary theory during the twentieth century. By the 1980s high-profile bibliographic scholars including Jerome McGann, D. F. McKenzie, and D. C. Greetham critically engaged the challenges of poststructuralism, steering the former field's concerns beyond those of authorial intention and toward a more expansive notion of what counts as a text.[2] Despite such cross-pollinations with literary theory—and despite the fact that no serious bibliographer could at present imagine that the empirical work of cataloguing or editing is not also interpretive work—literary studies as practiced by English departments in the United States (and to a lesser extent in the United Kingdom and Canada) has for more than three generations maintained a studied ignorance of bibliography in favor of the kind of abstract interpretations otherwise afforded by literary theory and criticism.

Few areas of literary study epitomize the tensions between its bibliographic and theoretical modes as powerfully as has the study of African American literature. To be sure, some of this exemplarity is a matter of timing. The origins of African American literary studies are conventionally traced to the 1960s, when the momentum of the Civil Rights and Black Arts movements brought unprecedented attention to literary productions by (and, to a lesser extent, for and about) African Americans. By the early 1970s student protests for ethnic studies and history classes on college campuses culminated in a Ford Foundation initiative that sponsored the formation of several black studies programs nationally and created a model for many others.[3] Such programs collaborated broadly with existing humanities disciplines, including English departments. Yet, as I have suggested, the prevailing method among English departments at the time emphasized the interpretation of texts over the more empirical practices of recovering them. As the 1970s and 1980s wore on, the priority of interpretation within English departments led to both an incorporation of literary theory into teaching and scholarship and a continued deprioritization of more empirical methods, including not only bibliography but genealogical authentication and archival research more generally. While some scholars were recovering African American texts, many were discounting the very methods of textual recovery.[4]

As the present essay will demonstrate, this discrepancy is more rhetorical than actual, and all along bibliographic scholarship quietly served as the basis for the production of texts and editions that students and scholars would need to produce interpretations. But inasmuch as the unavailability of editions before the 1980s often tautologically reinforced the exclusion of African American texts from serious study, it becomes clear that African American literary studies was institutionalized within English departments during a moment in the twentieth century when the disconnection between objects of study and the methods of studying them was especially stark. Due to the vicissitudes of its institutional history, African American literary studies opens a particularly clear window onto the problem of methodological disconnection as it reverberates across English more generally.

Taking African American literary studies as its case study, the present essay demonstrates that by avowing favor for one critical mode over another, literary scholars misrecognize the sufficient aspects of their research processes for necessary ones. In fact many of the most successful African Americanists of this first academic generation—including now distinguished scholars like William L. Andrews, Houston Baker, Hazel Carby, Frances Smith Foster, and my chief example, Henry Louis Gates Jr.—bridged the interpretive concerns favored by English departments with the archival investigations required by African American texts, generating interpretations alongside editions. As a result the field that came to be known as African American literary studies was forged from bibliographic and theoretical research simultaneously. This methodological pluralism epitomized by the architects of African American literary studies has had considerable success in redefining what scholars talk about when they talk about American literature writ large. Yet in spite of its remarkable successes, this pragmatic combination of interpretation and bibliography has rarely been recognized as a methodology at all.

This essay explores the counterfactual possibility that bibliographic techniques and interpretive formulations were never in contradiction with one other, leading to the speculative conclusion that an emphasis on methodology might have enabled African American literary studies to critique the canon debates of the 1990s rather than simply galvanize them. The ultimate aim of this essay is diagnostic, and my main point is not to offer a critique of canonization or any particular method so much as to redescribe what literary studies has already accomplished but has not come to realize. I contend that those of us who work in African Americanist (and indeed Americanist) literary studies are, methodologically speaking, somewhere altogether different than we may think, due to the ways that certain professional idioms, detailed below, have encouraged a faulty analysis of the forces animating this field's propulsion.

I. *The Priority of Interpretation*

The year 1986 was not the first time that bibliographers and literary critics disagreed. But that year witnessed one of the most significant challenges to close textual analysis ever issued, when D. F. McKenzie's 1985 Panizzi lectures at Oxford University were published as *Bibliography and the Sociology of Texts*. In the opening lecture McKenzie revisited the famous New Critical essay "The Intentional Fallacy" by William K. Wimsatt and Monroe C. Beardsley, specifically challenging its proposition that "the design or intention of the author is neither available nor desirable as a standard for judging the success of a work of literary art."[5] Wimsatt and Beardsley argued that one might instead concentrate on the effects of the words of a poem rather than guess about its author's aims, and by 1986 a caricatured version of their view—often summarized as "formalism"—had become the bête noire of deconstruction (which nevertheless generally concentrated more on poetic effects than on authorial intentions). Yet by comparison to that of deconstruction, McKenzie's challenge to formalism was seismic. His first lecture demonstrated that Wimsatt and Beardsley's epigraph, taken from William Congreve's *The Way of the World*, contained a misquotation in its first line. McKenzie's version of the line, "He owns, with Toil, he wrought the following Scenes," follows precisely on Congreve's authorized edition of the play from 1710, while Wimsatt and Beardsley's version, "He owns with toil he wrote the following scenes," is an accurate copy of the text that appears in George H. Nettleton and Arthur E. Case's anthology *British Dramatists from Dryden to Shelley* (1939).[6] The misquotation, in other words, is Nettleton and

Case's, which Wimsatt and Beardsley merely reproduced. But in drawing attention to this textual error—"wrote" for "wrought" and the elision of a pair of bracketing commas—McKenzie demonstrated that close textual analysis was only as good as the text it was analyzing. The bibliographer's challenge to the literary critics was that even formalists needed to pay attention to the material conditions of textual production.

This challenge went largely unmet. Though McKenzie's work was widely influential in the field of critical bibliography and is now considered foundational to most versions of book history (Bibliography and the Sociology of Texts was translated into French by no less influential a scholar than Roger Chartier), his point about textual analysis fell on largely deaf ears among literary scholars, who were busy debating the nature of interpretation. Contemporary with the publication of McKenzie's volume in 1986, the MLA journal Profession devoted an issue to "the value of theory in English studies," organizing a set of contributions around the question of whether a focus on critical methodology was a hindrance to the study of literature qua literature. The same year, PMLA devoted forums to evaluating the merits of different styles of interpretation, including psychoanalytic and reader-response criticism. A guest column in PMLA appraised the journal's anonymous review policy (in effect only since 1980) of "assessing the value of submitted work solely on the basis of what's on the page."[7] And the essays that otherwise populate the journal overwhelmingly attend to recognizably canonical works of literature, with unselfconscious use of aesthetic terms like *genre*, *style*, *metrics*, and *the sublime*. To be sure, PMLA in 1986 also published essays that would later appear in agenda-setting books of the late 1980s and early 1990s, such as Joseph Boone on marriage and form and Amy Kaplan on the social construction of realism. But the transition that such essays can (in retrospect) be taken to represent, from aesthetic concerns to historical and cultural ones, was everywhere framed as a shift in interpretation. The task of literary scholarship was to interpret literary texts, not, as McKenzie argued, to interpret material texts. Almost no essays devoted to bibliographic studies appear in any prominent literary studies journals in the mid- to late 1980s, and the rare ones that do—such as a piece by John Southerland in *Critical Inquiry*—were largely critical of McKenzie's methodology.[8]

If there is a single reason why this was the case, it is probably that bibliographic scholarship was widely dismissed among literary scholars as unfashionable work.[9] Indeed whether one or one's teachers were formalists or deconstructivists, feminists or historicists, the leading literary scholars of the 1980s were overwhelmingly trained as critics, whose priority was literary interpretation. In the terms of Gerald Graff's authoritative history of the profession, critics represented "a common cause of diverse groups who sought an alternative to the research model that would close the yawning gap between investigators and generalists," and they had emerged as early in the professional study of literature as 1915 (though their heyday would be in the 1930s and after).[10] What critics had in common was not a commitment to form or politics or aesthetics but rather a strong rejection of the horizon of professional possibilities delimited by the then-standard-issue textbook for graduate studies in English, André Morize's *Problems and Methods of Literary History* (1922), with its detailed focus on preparing editions, establishing a critical bibliography, investigating and interpreting sources, and solving problems of authentication and attribution.[11] The rise of criticism coincided with the priority of interpretation, and both were shaped by a reaction to bibliographic studies and therefore happened at the latter's expense.

The rejection of bibliography in favor of criticism did not mean, however, that there were no bibliographic projects taking place in the 1980s. In fact there were more than ever. Formerly, in the 1950s and 1960s, the production of scholarly editions of collected writings had often been the work of historians, including notable works of use to literary scholars such as Philip Foner's five-volume edition of *The Life and Writings of Frederick Douglass*, published between 1949 and 1952, and Yale University's massive (and still incomplete) edition of *Benjamin Franklin's Papers*, begun in 1959. Slowly historians ceded this work to literary scholars, and in 1976 the MLA established the Committee on Scholarly Editions, which lent its imprimatur to the collected writings of many more indisputably literary figures.[12] By the time *Bibliography and the Sociology of Texts* appeared in 1986, for example, a well-known partnership between Northwestern University and the Newberry Library had brought out nine of the fifteen volumes of *The Writings of Herman Melville* that would be completed in 2009, and Ohio State's *Centenary Edition of the Works of Nathaniel Hawthorne* had published fifteen volumes of the twenty-three that would be completed in 1996—all of which are MLA-approved editions. Methodologically conservative, such editions were organized around a single author's collected works and typically established composite texts that approached as nearly as possible the author's final intentions, according to what was by then known as the Greg-Bowers method of textual criticism.[13] The in-progress status of these major feats of bibliographic scholarship clarifies that the reason PMLA might not have published any essays regarding such scholarship in the mid-1980s is not that it had ceased to be practiced, as it was in fact more squarely within the purview of literary scholarship than ever before. The issue is one of omission rather than absence, and the reason bibliographic scholarship was omitted from the likes of PMLA is that such scholarship was not—and for a generation had not been—particularly valued labor in English departments.

Indeed by 1986, if any kind of labor was valued beside criticism, it was associated not with the establishment of composite texts but with the reprinting of "recovered" texts. The profession-shifting project of canon expansion then under way required new materials for study, especially in the form of textbooks. Between 1986 and 1992 Rutgers University Press reprinted eighteen volumes of stories, novels, and poetry under the auspices of the American Women Writers Series. Oxford University Press created several more modest series during the same time, focusing variously on early modern and early American women's writings. And the era's most ambitious recovery project appeared in 1988, when Oxford University Press, in partnership with the Schomburg Center for Research in Black Culture (a research branch of the New York Public Library), released forty volumes in the African American Women Writers Series, significantly multiplying the number of texts in print authored by nineteenth-century black women.

While the reprinting of recovered texts might have enabled bibliographic scholarship to reassert its position within the hierarchy of scholarly work, the material conditions of reprinting ironically disenabled that possibility because these and similar reprint series differed from traditionally bibliographic editions in three important ways. First, while they were always prefaced by a critical essay or introduction, the texts themselves were often facsimiles of earlier editions, with little textual editing aside from the silent correction of obvious printer's errors. Second, their importance was conceived in terms of the accessibility of individual volumes rather than an author's collected work or final intention. Third, they were initially published in paperback, suitable for (and marketed to) classroom use. In other words, reprint editions, unlike more properly bibliographic projects, were designed to create texts for the express purpose of using them in the enterprise of literary interpretation. The critical practice of literary interpretation was so naturalized as the main labor of literary studies by the 1980s that the success of recovery projects was judged in terms of the body of interpretive criticism that could be built on any given recovered text—and the sometime failure of this critical literature to materialize led at least one prominent scholar of women authors ultimately to argue against the venture.[14] Well into the 1990s, canon debates remained mired in the question of whether newly recovered texts were "any good," long after the availability of the material texts upon which recovery had been launched.[15]

From the vantage of McKenzie's challenge to formalism, the most striking thing about canon debates is how their commitment to the primacy of interpretation in literary studies led to blindness about the material conditions of textual production that enabled interpretation in the first place. That is, from the perspective of these debates, the name of the game was how to read the book in your hand; much less often was it asked how a particular book got into anyone's hand. When this latter question was asked, it was treated as an interpretive question—a question about gender or power, for instance, or a question of how cultures or nations come to value objects, and not a question about the palpable practices of printing and publishing that materially produce the objects we call books. This blindness, moreover, stems not just from the ubiquity of interpretation in literary studies but also from the sense (fueled in the 1980s and 1990s by a widespread philosophical relativism) that there could be different interpretations but no meaningful alternative to interpretation itself.[16] McKenzie's challenge to formalism had been that one cannot ask questions of interpretation apart from questions of materiality. That is, he claimed that the project he called "the sociology of texts" required multiple methods to interpret different parts of a material text. In an era of proliferating theories, expanding canons, and shifts in interpretation, there was surprisingly little room in literary studies to imagine the existence of multiple methods.

II. The Rhetoric of Either/Or

In a milieu that valued literary interpretation to the exclusion of other modes of literary analysis, texts by and about African Americans presented a problem inasmuch as, before the 1980s, they had largely been collected for content.[17] African American books, the logic ran, represented African American experience, and thus their value was rarely considered in specifically literary terms. Indeed, as early as the late nineteenth century, archives of African American materials were established outside the academy, often with political motives, by bibliophiles and collectors like Arthur Schomburg in Harlem (who bestowed his collection to the New York Public Library), Charles H. Wright in Detroit (who founded the Museum of African American History), and Charles L. Blockson in Philadelphia (whose collection is now part of the Temple University Libraries). The fact that these projects were developed in the context of learned institutions but by philanthropists and collectors rather than by professors makes them of a piece with similar rare book collections, including the Folger Shakespeare Library, the Huntington Library, and the American Antiquarian Society. At all these institutions, cataloguing and accession—the activities preceding bibliography and interpretation alike—were also undertaken by librarians rather than professors. In the case of African American materials, some of the most comprehensive cataloguing in the twentieth century was done by Dorothy Porter (later Dorothy Porter Wesley), a librarian at Howard University, between the 1930s and early 1970s. Likewise the holdings of Afro-Americana at the Library Company of Philadelphia and the Historical Society of Pennsylvania were curated and catalogued by Phil Lapsansky beginning in 1971, and a vast collection of African American periodicals was assembled by James P. Danky, a librarian at the Wisconsin Historical Society, beginning in the mid-1970s.[18] Furthermore many reprint editions of African American texts in the 1960s were published by trade presses rather than university presses, including a series on Arno Press, a now defunct subsidiary of the *New York Times*.

As reprint editions became the province of English professors and university presses by the mid-1980s, however, the perceived value of the African American texts they reproduced shifted in relation to the norms of English study. As Leon Jackson elegantly summarizes, "Beginning in the 1980s, a cohort of scholars, including Robert Stepto, Houston Baker, Barbara Johnson, and Gates himself, initiated a critical paradigm shift that moved emphasis from content to form; from functionalism to aestheticism; from mimesis to reflexivity; and from historicism to theory."[19] One can see this shift had taken effect by the mid-1990s when William Andrews, by then an accomplished textual scholar, could argue that "the best way to bring back into print an ignored or neglected book by a writer of color is not to propose a full-bore textual edition of it. The audience for such a book is not likely to want or need all the textual apparatus."[20] Though Andrews could not know who or what the audience for a book will be, his statement suggests that the intended readership for recovered texts is undergraduate students, or perhaps amateur readers—but, in either case, an audience in pursuit of the kind of meaning that comes from interpretation rather than from a more empirical kind of scholarship. Such an assumption is possible only in a world where African American texts had become subject to the kinds of interpretation prevalent in literary studies.

But if the study of African American texts was secured in part by making those texts available for interpretation, it is nevertheless the case that an equally common move in the scholarship of the 1980s is to insist on the value of interpretation as such. And it is as a result of this second move that much necessary bibliographic work was rhetorically dismissed even as it was being gainfully developed. That dismissal arguably appears nowhere with as much rhetorical finesse as in Gates's influential 1988 monograph, The Signifying Monkey: "After several active years of work applying literary theory to African and Afro-American literatures, I realized that what had early on seemed to me to be the fulfillment of my project as a would-be theorist of black literature was, in fact, only a moment in a progression. The challenge of my project, if not exactly to invent a black theory, was to locate and identify how the 'black tradition' had theorized about itself."[21]

As Gates goes on to explain, his attempts to theorize about his archive reveal that this archive is in turn structured by a theory of citation, adaptation, and "signifying." Though his introduction makes clear that its interpretation or theory is generated by the archive, it is nevertheless touted as a theory. In this way The Signifying Monkey collapses the relationship between an object of interpretation and an interpretation, but, rhetorically at least, this collapse gives priority to the latter, de-emphasizing texts in favor of the abstract categories into which they can be collected. The recursion of these critical moves is moreover avowed as an aspect of method in The Signifying Monkey. The book, Gates writes, attempts "to identify a theory of criticism that is inscribed within the black vernacular tradition and that in turn informs the shape of the Afro-American literary tradition."[22] The Signifying Monkey clearly (and very productively) connects theory with archive, interpretation with bibliography, despite the fact that it repeatedly describes this connection as a recursion rather than a symbiosis.

By emphasizing the theoretical character of his archive, Gates gives rhetorical priority to recovery for the sake of interpretation rather than recovery for the sake of recovery. From the perspective of something like McKenzie's work, it would be difficult not to infer some defensiveness from the ways that The Signifying Monkey makes its metacritical claims. McKenzie's work had allowed for the possibility that the study of material texts would require multiple different methods. But Gates goes to the archives and discovers a range of texts whose aims look very much like the high theoretical aims of literary criticism in the 1980s. One method seems like more than enough.

The example of Gates's work is worth dilating upon at some length because, across much of his career, Gates has insisted on the sufficiency of a single method, even as that method has changed. For present purposes, the most important thing about the claims The Signifying Monkey makes about interpretation is the extent to which Gates's later work reversed them. In a short 2001 essay, Gates argued that bibliographic research may be "unglamorous, but it is indispensable."[23] The apologetic tone of this statement belies the fact that by the turn of the millennium Gates had served as general editor of the Oxford-Schomburg African American Women Writers Series, *The Norton Anthology of African American Literature*, and the republication of Zora Neale Hurston's works. His contributions to such indispensible projects have, in other words, been as glamorous as anyone's. And while one might attribute some modesty to Gates's self-positioning, the idea that bibliographic research is unglamorous resonates with a longer explanation he gave ten years earlier: "We all talk about the glories of literary theory, and I've certainly been a vocal advocate of these techniques. But, to me, the really exciting work is that of textual editing and historical restoration: when we bring these back from the great grave yard of archival dispersion, and make them available through scholarly editions."[24] Explaining the need for bibliographic scholarship, Gates opposes it to literary theory, contrasting the general value of the latter with a more idiosyncratic value for the former, signaled rhetorically by the move from "we" to "me." At other moments Gates deploys such dichotomous thinking to produce real clarity, as when, in a well-known 1991 diagnosis of the culture wars, he argues that different "levels of criticism often get mixed up," leading to disjointed readers' reports "that say things like: 'Not only does so-and-so's paper perpetuate a logic internal to the existing racist, patriarchal order, but footnote 17 gives page numbers to a different edition than is listed in the bibliography.'"[25] At still other moments Gates betrays a certain impatience in binary terms, such as at the 2003 *Critical Inquiry* symposium, where he was reported to have paraphrased a student's question, "What did the theory revolution do to liberate the colonial subject?," and answered it by saying, "I must have missed that part."[26] In both the theoretical exuberance of *The Signifying Monkey* and the "unglamorous" archival plodding of these later essays and interviews, Gates consistently if implicitly positions the methodology of African American literary studies as though it were capable of operating in a single mode: recovery or theory, interpretation or bibliography.

Despite its debts and contributions to both interpretive and bibliographic modes of scholarship, Gates's work evinces an especially clear case of the either/or logic that opposes these modes to one another, as it has eventuated in one of the most significant theorists of African American literature making his claims at the expense of archival projects, and one of the most influential editors of African American literature doing his work at the expense of theory. Recognizing that these two figures are the same person leaves us with a professional tension that seems far less personal and far more structural. Indeed, we might go so far as to speculate that if Gates had not made these contradictory claims, then someone else would have had to. I am arguing, then, that such either/or thinking is ultimately less a hallmark of Gates's own scholarship than a symptom of the professional logic within which he has worked, for the rhetorical opposition between theory and bibliography was, as we have seen, normalized within the profession in the 1980s. African American studies has clearly made significant use of both interpretation and bibliography to generate momentous disciplinary advances in a short space of time. And yet these advances have been announced as either/or when they have necessarily been both/and.

III. Against Exemplarity

There is no question that the reprinting of African American texts and the interpretive work performed on them by prominent critics such as Gates shaped the canon debates of the 1980s. As I have suggested throughout this essay, however, the reprint editions and interpretations of literary texts were a means of participating in the canon debates rather than a means of challenging the terms of those debates. Recovered African American literary texts participated in the canon debates in two ways simultaneously. First, on what can broadly be called aesthetic grounds, recovered texts were read in order to be interpreted, and the ability to sustain literary interpretation meant that a particular African American text could become an exemplary work of literature. Second, on what can broadly be called political grounds, recovered texts were estimated *as* African American texts, auditioning for a place in a canon that was being decried for its racial and gendered elitism. In both cases the question of which texts to add to the canon was often anxiously parlayed into a logic of scarcity, such that inclusion of one book would entail the exclusion of another, with both aesthetic and political consequences. In this context the course syllabus became a volatile site for political and professional debates that extended far beyond any individual classroom. The contradictions of a debate that equivocated unevenly between the representational logic of a survey course and the representational logic of a democratic polity has been detailed by John Guillory's literary sociology of the canon debates.[27] More recently scholars working within the field of African American literary studies have backdated similar contradictions between aesthetic and political representation to founding moments of the field.[28] If the canon debates thus turned on an equivocal but pervasive notion of exemplarity, the claim I wish to advance in this final section is that this exemplarity is of a piece with the either/or thinking that so privileged interpretation above other methods, not coincidentally at the same historical juncture.

The most expedient way to demonstrate this point is to consider exemplarity in relation to the kinds of methods that fortify either/or thinking. Canon debates focused disproportionately on teaching over other aspects of what literary scholars do. Perhaps one reason they did so is that teaching literature is synecdochal. In literary studies classrooms, single texts are taught as representative of genres, single authors become representative of populations, and single passages, closely read, become representative of longer works that can't be discussed comprehensively in class. Literary studies pedagogy depends on exemplary and representative reading. By contrast, literary research methods often require comparatively vast amounts of data aggregation. To choose an example at hand, a text like *The Signifying Monkey* is clearly the product of this kind of wide reading, and its theoretical claims have their purchase as a result of the book's aggregations. But if literary research is in this sense absorptive, drawing lots of evidence into its ken, the writing of literary criticism is often much more porous, in a way that more closely aligns with teaching. Put simply, literary scholars are expected to read much more than they write about. In a succinct account of the ways that the sheer size of literary evidence turns critics into editors, Leah Price rightly observes, "It would be impossible for me to reproduce verbatim all eight volumes of *Clarissa* as evidence for what this chapter argues."[29] Thus the signature method of literary studies—across multiple theoretical developments—has been close reading, the selection of a representative passage. Theoretical claims that critics make about genres or periods or nations work in a broad register precisely to balance a superabundance of literary evidence that can be amassed for any given genre, period, or nation. Literary research and writing require the juggling of claims and evidence at wildly different scales. Yet due to a certain paucity of vocabulary, this juggling act is often shorthanded as "reading."

I have described a complicity among an either/or thinking about method, a priority of interpretation as the method of literary studies, and a concern for exemplary texts and passages as the objects to be interpreted. Taken together, the complicity of these propositions generates a prescriptive account of what a literary scholar would do with a book: read and interpret it on the basis of particular passages. This prescription does very little to account for where books come from, or even what books are. (The widespread idea among literary scholars that books are made by authors will surely come as some surprise to a bookbinder.[30]) I have also argued that such a prescription was implicitly challenged by African American literary studies, for the fairly elemental reason that this field could not take for granted the existence of books to interpret, requiring instead the unfashionable bibliographic and archival labors of identifying, locating, and cataloguing African American materials. On balance, however, these acts of bibliographic labor and recovery factored into the canon debates far less than did the objects they recovered. Yet the inattention to these bibliographic labors was not just a kind of oversight. I am arguing that the logic of exemplarity that animated the canon wars and that drove the desire to get some African American texts onto course syllabi was structured in terms that entailed a neglect of the bibliographer's interest in material texts. Canon debates necessarily did little to honor the multiple methods behind African American literary studies, and African American literature was instead recognized—even, as we have seen, by its practitioners—as a content category, not a hybrid methodology.

Now, fifteen years after the canon debates have cooled, and twenty-five years after the publication of *Bibliography and the Sociology of Texts*, some literary scholars are beginning to embrace the methodological pluralism that joins interpretation and bibliography. For example, Meredith L. McGill has demonstrated that book history illuminates the contingencies of the category of the literary in a way that complies with theoretical aims of deconstruction.[31] Matthew P. Brown has argued for a greater affinity between cultural studies and book history than has been acknowledged by either field.[32] And Lara Langer Cohen and I have pushed for deeper engagement between book historians generally and African American archives specifically, in the hopes that such engagements will challenge the platitudes of each field.[33]

Yet if the methodological pluralism of this more recent work is finding a professional foothold, that is not precisely because it is doing something new. Bridging the materialist concerns of critical bibliography with the interpretive possibilities afforded by literary theory, all of this work in fact does what I have been arguing that African American literary studies has done all along. Rather what is new about this work is the open acknowledgment it makes of the different methods it tries to bring together. We have already seen that in the heyday of literary criticism interpretation was the favored method for literary scholarship, though this favoritism was avowed rhetorically with as much if not more consistency than it was evidenced practically. In such a context, recent claims made on behalf of methodological cross-pollination should be seen as radical interventions indeed.

Arguably this language of pluralism is slowly taking hold due to a broader and keenly felt disciplinary crisis that has left people reaching out for new genres for classifying experience.[34] If, as we have seen, in 1986 *Profession* devoted an issue to worrying the question of whether a focus on critical methodology was a hindrance to the study of literature qua literature, in 2011 the MLA *Newsletter* was instead concerned with the seemingly precarious future of the humanities itself. In those pages MLA president Russell A. Berman issued a succinct statement arguing for expanded language learning and "universal bilingualism," digital scholarship alongside print, and significant restructuring of graduate education and multiple career paths for humanities PhDs.[35] There was hardly a trace of either/or thinking on display. Berman's statement is one of many at the present time that calls upon scholars to prepare for a future in which the humanities will require broad interdisciplinary collaborations and diverse new skills.[36] Yet my argument has been that such promises of an applied methodological pluralism leave the future of the humanities looking like nothing so much as its past.

As this essay has demonstrated through the example of African American literary studies—and more specifically through the methodological tensions between bibliography and interpretation epitomized by this field—multiple disciplinary methods stand behind any number of practical contexts and ordinary activities of literary studies, from assigning a textbook on up. To be absolutely clear, I do not mean to suggest that literary interpretation should yield to bibliographic analysis. Rather, these have been productive categories for the present essay because of the extremely different ways each mode has fared in popularity and estimation during their long careers within literary studies. What interests me is emphatically not one critical mode or another but the ways that different modes work together, the ways that different methods can be practiced, and especially the challenges that come with accounting for and narrating the work of literary studies in plural terms. Though critical bibliography and African American literary studies have taken up different methodological modes with greater facility than has the version of literary studies that emphasizes interpretation at the expense of other methods, none of these fields finally solves these problems. Moreover, my point is that there is not a single solution, nor a master theory, nor a next big thing because there has in fact *never* been a single method or agenda or future for the study of English. The rhetoric of either/or choices and single methods obscures this fact. As we begin to abandon this pernicious language of oneness, we might invite a concept of disciplinary wholeness.[37] This latter concept gestures toward a name for the fact that no scholar is or could become an interdisciplinary research project unto herself, but instead each might pursue the modes of research that she wishes, while learning from scholars working in cognate modes. No act of literary interpretation is possible without the bibliographic labors that produce books, and few books would need to exist without the various practices of reading, teaching, and learning that they occasion. Scenes of such reciprocity constitute the history of our discipline. And as we consider the future of English and of the humanities, we would do well also to learn from its past.

Notes

For helpful readings, comments, and conversation, I thank Robert Chang, Lara Cohen, Leon Jackson, Justine Murison, Janet Neary, and Joe Rezek. Thanks also to Jason Potts and Dan Stout for editorial what-what, and Ben Beck for timely research assistance.

1. Bowers, *Textual and Literary Criticism*, vii–viii.
2. McGann, *A Critique of Modern Textual Criticism*; McKenzie, *Bibliography and the Sociology of Texts*; Greetham, "[Textual] Criticism and Deconstruction."
3. Rooks, *White Money / Black Power*.
4. For the purposes of this essay, I use *theory* to refer to an abstract principle or school of thinking, and *method* to refer to a more practical application. In this usage, New Criticism, poststructuralism, and book history would be examples of theories, while close reading, rhetorical analysis, and descriptive bibliography would be examples of methods. I use *mode* as a middle term, to designate a critical orientation that is not aligned with a single school or indicative of a single process, as in the case of interpretation or bibliography.
5. Wimsatt and Beardsley, "The Intentional Fallacy," 468.
6. McKenzie, *Bibliography and the Sociology of Texts*, 18–28.
7. Jehlen and Quilligan, "Guest Column," 771.
8. Sutherland, "Publishing History."
9. Ironically poststructuralism is now subject to a similar dismissal. For a trenchant reading of the phenomenon by which critical methods are appraised as fashions, see David E. Wellbery's foreword to Friedrich A. Kittler, *Discourse Networks 1800/1900*, translated by Michael Metteer, with Chris Cullens (Stanford: Stanford University Press, 1990).
10. Graff, *Professing Literature*, 121.
11. Graff, *Professing Literature*, 137–38.
12. For a history of the Center for Editions of American Authors, with attention to the editorial practices conducted under its auspices, see G. Thomas Tanselle, "Greg's Theory of Copy-text and the Editing of American Literature," *Studies in Bibliography* 28 (1975): 167–229.
13. Walter Greg, "The Rationale of Copy-text," *Studies in Bibliography* 3 (1950–51): 19–36; Fredson Bowers, *Bibliography and Textual Criticism* (Oxford: Clarendon Press, 1964). Greg's position was critiqued by G. Thomas Tanselle, "The Editor's Problem of Final Authorial Intention," *Studies in Bibliography* 29 (1976): 167–211, and by Steven Mailloux, "Textual Scholarship and 'Author's Final Intentions,'" in *Interpretive Conventions: The*

Reader in the Study of American Fiction (Ithaca: Cornell University Press, 1982), 93–125. Both Tanselle and Maillloux problematize the idea of intention while retaining the centrality of the author (or author-function) to textual editing. For an alternative exploration of the consequences of the Greg-Bowers methods for literary interpretation, I am indebted to Joseph Rezek, "Transatlantic Revision and American Literary History: The Case of Washington Irving," unpublished essay.

14. Poovey, "Recovering Ellen Pickering."

15. For key critiques of the "any good" debate, see Jane P. Tompkins, *Sensational Designs: The Cultural Work of American Fiction 1790–1860* (New York: Oxford University Press, 1985), 186–201; Susan Gillman, *Blood Talk: American Race Melodrama and the Culture of the Occult* (Chicago: University of Chicago Press, 2003), 200–206.

16. A major exception to this claim is Jonathan Culler's essay "Beyond Interpretation: The Prospects of Contemporary Criticism," *Comparative Literature* 28.3 (1976): 244–56. Yet Culler's significant assertion that "there are many tasks that confront criticism, many things we need to advance our understanding of literature, but one thing we do not need is more interpretations of literary works" (245) seems to have largely fallen flat. For instance, Gerald Graff's review of Culler's *The Pursuit of Signs* (into which "Beyond Interpretation" was collected as an introductory essay) favorably situates Culler's argument in relation to popular debates about literary value but fails to engage the question of interpretation at all (Graff, "Culler and Deconstruction," *London Review of Books* 3.16 [1981]: 7–8).

17. Though, as Leon Jackson has argued, "inasmuch as they chose to collect books for obtrusively politicized and instrumental ends, early African American bibliophiles differed significantly from their white compatriots, for whom collecting, while not devoid of cultural politics, functioned more typically to showcase luxury, exoticism, rarity, and prestige" ("The Talking Book and the Talking Book Historian," 289).

18. All three are also scholars responsible for major bibliographies still in use. See Dorothy Porter, *The Negro in the United States: A Selected Bibliography* (Washington, D.C.: Library of Congress, 1970); Philip Lapsansky, *Afro-Americana, 1553–1906: A Catalog of the Holdings of the Library Company of Philadelphia and the Historical Society of Pennsylvania* (Boston: G. K. Hall, 1973); James P. Danky, *African-American Newspapers and Periodicals: A National Bibliography* (Cambridge: Harvard University Press, 1998).

19. Jackson, "The Talking Book and the Talking Book Historian," 255–56.

20. Andrews, "Editing 'Minority' Texts," 50.

21. Gates, *The Signifying Monkey*, ix.

22. Gates, *The Signifying Monkey*, xix.

23. Gates, "African American Studies in the 21st Century," 3.

24. Rowell, "An Interview with Henry Louis Gates, Jr.," 448.

25. Gates, "Goodbye, Columbus?," 717.

26. Mitchell, "Medium Theory," 327.

27. Guillory, *Cultural Capital*.

28. See Kenneth W. Warren, *What Was African American Literature?* (Cambridge: Harvard University Press, 2011). For very different readings of the politics of this moment, see also Henry Louis Gates Jr., *Loose Canons: Notes on the Culture Wars* (New York: Oxford University Press, 1992), especially 87–104; Robert F. Reid-Pharr, *Once You Go Black: Choice, Desire, and the Black American Intellectual* (New York: New York University Press, 2007); Rod-

erick A. Ferguson, *The Reorder of Things: The University and Its Pedagogies of Minority Difference* (Minneapolis: University of Minnesota Press, 2012).

29. Price, *The Anthology and the Rise of the Novel*, 13.

30. See Peter Stallybrass, "'Little Jobs': Broadsides and the Printing Revolution," in *Agent of Change: Print Cultures Studies after Elizabeth L. Eisenstein*, ed. Sabrina Alcorn Baron, Eric N. Lundquist, and Eleanor F. Shevlin (Amherst: University of Massachusetts Press, 2007), 315–41.

31. McGill, *American Literature and the Culture of Reprinting*, 6.

32. Brown, "Book History, Sexy Knowledge, and the Challenge of the New Boredom."

33. Cohen and Stein, *Early African American Print Culture*.

34. See Lauren Berlant, *Cruel Optimism* (Durham: Duke University Press, 2011).

35. Berman, "An Agenda for the Future."

36. See, for example, Cathy N. Davidson, *Now You See It: How the Science of Attention Will Transform the Way We Live, Work, and Learn* (New York: Viking, 2011).

37. Here I'm borrowing the terms of Danielle S. Allen's analysis of democracy in *Talking to Strangers*.

chapter 9

What Cinema Wasn't:
Animating Film Theory's Double Blind Spot

Karen Beckman

The Double Blind Spot

The plot of Alfred Hitchcock's 1938 film, *The Lady Vanishes*, is driven by two questions. First, after Miss Froy (who turns out to be a British spy) disappears, the audience is left to wonder where she is; the second and perhaps more interesting question arises from the fact that after Miss Froy's disappearance, all but one of the characters who had been with her seem to believe that she never existed in the first place. The lady's vanishing thus has a retroactive force: by disappearing, she seems to erase her previous existence. The dual nature of the absence at the heart of this film offers a useful analogy for the "missing" line of thought I discuss in this essay: the recently perceived absence of animation within the discourse of film theory by film and media scholars and the historical neglect of less recent work that has tried to draw film and media scholars' attention to this oversight.

On the one hand, scholars within the field of cinema and media studies have begun actively and productively to highlight this absence. Tom Gunning does exactly this in his 2007 essay, "Moving Away from the Index: Cinema and the Impression of Reality." He asks, "Is it not somewhat strange that photographic theories of the cinema have had such a hold on film theory that much of film theory must immediately add the caveat that they do not apply to animated film? Given that as a technical innovation cinema was first understood as 'animated pictures' and that computer-generated animation techniques are now omnipresent in most feature films, shouldn't this lacuna disturb us?" Later in the same essay, he adds that the marginalization of animation is "one of the great scandals of film theory."[1] Yet on the other hand, we cannot draw attention to this state of neglect, as Gunning does, without simultaneously if inadvertently rendering invisible, or at least "marginal," the body of work that already exists at the intersection of film theory and animation, work largely written by scholars within the adjacent (and at times overlapping) fields of animation studies, film production, and fine arts. As with Miss Froy, recognizing something as suppressed, marginalized, or disappeared has a way of canceling the forms of recognition that may have been happening all along. Recognizing our neglect of animation, as Gunning does, also means neglecting those earlier scholars who were doing what they could to engage it as an object of study.

This second-level occlusion, not of animation but of its critics, the people who were attempting to develop a language for grappling with this visual form, has produced intense frustration in at least some of those scholars working within a film theoretical paradigm on the concept of animation. No one has articulated this feeling more explicitly than Alan Cholodenko, whose two edited volumes and many articles on the intersection of film theory and animation highlight the need both for animation studies scholars to pay more attention to film theory and for film theorists to pay more attention to animation since 1991. In "Animation: Film and Media Studies' 'Blindspot,'" Cholodenko specifically invokes an interaction with Gunning about Cholodenko's contributions to film theory at a conference: "Tom congratulated me for not being bitter about the non–taking up of *The Illusion of Life* in Film Studies in the 14 years that had passed since its publication! I thought about Tom's comments later—who wouldn't?!"[2] Although Gunning's reported comments clearly recognize in a public forum the significance of *The Illusion of Life*'s intervention, they also solidify the volume's "non–taking up" by the field as a fait accompli.

Leading voices within the field of cinema studies, most notably Vivian Sobchack and the late Miriam Hansen, as well as scholars less exclusively aligned with cinema and media studies such as Esther Leslie and Thomas Lamarre, have also written extensively about film theory *and* animation, but they, unlike Cholodenko, have not always made the separation or overlap of the two fields the primary issue in their scholarship. Consequently although this work models an alternative approach within cinema studies, one that takes animation seriously, it has not necessarily catalyzed a fieldwide conversation about the extent to which and the reasons why the cinema studies' theoretical discourse, "film theory," has worked to exclude animation from its purview.[3] Although one could argue that Gunning is overstating the case when he describes the field's shameful neglect of animation, it is true that, until recently, it has rarely been taken up by cinema studies scholars, and for a long time the contributions of Sobchack and Hansen in this area also did not have the kind of impact that they should have had on the field's primary concerns.

Documentary and experimental film offer interesting counterexamples here. David Bordwell and Kristin Thompson clump all three "outsiders" to mainstream cinema—documentary, experimental, and animated film—into a single chapter in their influential textbook, *Film Art: An Introduction*; here the factor they share is that they each embody an alternative to a dominant idea of what cinema is. Chapter 5 begins, "Some of the most basic types of films line up as distinct alternatives. We commonly distinguish documentary from fiction, experimental films from mainstream fare, and animation from live-action filmmaking."[4] There are a couple of issues worth noting here. Within the textbook's paradigm, all three categories are clearly relegated to the margins of the "art of film" and are defined for students entering the field primarily by their difference from live-action fiction film. Yet of these "outsiders," animation, often regarded as a childish film form and lacking either documentary's political and historical credentials or experimental film's association with high-brow categories like the avant-garde, has until recently received the least scholarly attention. Of course not everyone will agree that it would be advantageous for animation to get more attention from film theorists or to play a more central role in the field of cinema and media studies; there may be certain benefits to being left "aside" by Theory. In striking contrast to Cholodenko, some animators and animation scholars manifest something more like relief in response to film theorists' neglect of their field. Steve Reinke, for instance, humorously notes that while "documentary scholarship seems as if it will be forever mired in 'fundamental' questions," the stakes, "luckily, perhaps . . . seem lower for animation scholarship."[5]

In this essay I explore some of the intellectual and institutional conditions that have fostered this (often mutual) history of neglect of which scholars in both fields—cinema studies and animation studies—have become increasingly conscious. What are some of the reasons why the contemporary moment has fostered a growing interest in a blind spot that, though it has been previously highlighted by scholars like Cholodenko, has still been largely ignored? What would be the philosophical and historical stakes of adjusting our pedagogical and intellectual frames for thinking about animation and film theory together? Where, that is, do we go from here? As a first step, we need to understand better the reasons why scholars in cinema studies have resisted engaging animation either as an object of study in its own right or as a useful lens through which to consider those other forms that have found an easier home under the umbrella category of cinema. This seems particularly important to do at a moment when many film scholars express a sense of uncertainty about whether that "cinema's" distinction from animation can be maintained within a digital context, where the use of compositing and the frequent absence of continuous shooting threaten to jeopardize some of the central traits we associate with a cinema that defines itself in opposition to animation.

Structural Blocks

PROFESSIONAL ORGANIZATIONS AND JOURNALS

Conversation between animation studies and cinema and media studies has in part been structurally inhibited by the history of professional organizations, conferences, publications, and departmental affiliations. The Society of Cinema and Media Studies (SCMS) was founded in 1959 as the Society of Cinematologists. Its own print journal, *Cinema Journal*, dates back to 1961 and has an international membership of over three thousand scholars. Only in 2010 did the Society of Cinema and Media Studies Board (the evolving title of this organization reflects the broadening nature of its interests) approve the formation of the Animated Media Scholarly Interest Group under the leadership of Suzanne Buchan, an initiative that reflects today's changing climate.[6] By contrast, the Society of Animation Studies (SAS) was founded much more recently, in 1987, and its online peer-reviewed journal, *Animation Studies*, began in 2006. These historical differences play themselves out across the two organizations' relationship to the discourse of film theory. The SCMS emerged on the brink of contemporary film theory's eruption into the field of film studies. Film theory, apparatus theory and feminist film theory in particular, strongly shaped the trajectory of the field throughout the 1980s, focusing attention on questions of ideology, identification, and the politics of representation. Earlier models of film study, such as film appreciation and biographical approaches, gradually fell out of favor. One of the effects of the "theoretical turn" within film studies was to establish this area of study as rigorous, politically charged, and philosophically inflected, and animation may well have seemed at odds with the agenda of establishing film studies as serious.

By contrast, SAS was founded at the moment when even some of film theory's most energetic voices were expressing doubts about its ongoing utility, at least in its ossified form. It is also a much smaller organization, with membership numbering around 220. Though the society has a newsletter, it is available only to members, and so it has a relatively small readership that is already sufficiently interested in animation to join the society. While Cholodenko, along with other SAS members, has consistently implored the organization's members to engage film studies and its more theoretical discourse, conversations in SAS have tended to remain more focused on practice, and this difference in discursive approaches has perhaps limited the exchange between the two organizations and exacerbated the gap between their key terms: *cinema* and *animation*.

The divisions between these groups aren't absolute, of course, and it is worth taking a peek at where and when the distinctions blur. An online search for the word *animation* in all the issues of *Cinema Journal* and its predecessor, the *Journal of the Society of Cinematologists*, for example, called up 190 citations. Although 169 of these are listed under the generic headings of either "reviews" or "back matter," and though not a single one of these articles has the word *animation* in the title (one had *cartoon*!), reading through the essays renders visible how thoroughly important thinking about animation and movement as central components of cinema was to the journal's (and the field's) early pioneers, even though this preoccupation would soon fade from view. We see traces of this emphasis in Gerald Noxon's 1962 article, "Cinema and Cubism," in which he discusses how cinema's montage of time is spatialized, how naïve film scholars' sense of film realism is, and how important it is to think about film's relation to painting and sculpture if we are to understand cinema's dimensionality. We might also consult Noxon's exploration of cinema narrative's relation to cave painting, Robert Gessner's charting of the grammar of various types of film movement, or John Tibbetts's review of Ralph Stephenson's *The Art of Animation* and Richard Schickel's *The Disney Version*, in which he already bemoans the neglect of Stephenson's "concise little book."[7]

Indeed as *Cinema Journal* replaces its predecessor, reflecting the rapid expansion of the field after 1968 and the concurrent rise of contemporary film theory, "movement" as a topic of primary interest seems to move into the margins of the field, in spite of its prominence in the early days of film studies, perhaps, ironically, because it seems more aesthetic than political a subject.[8]

Cholodenko has systematically resisted this separation. Addressing both SCMS and SAS members, as I have already mentioned, he has called for a greater engagement with film theory and for an understanding of animation as a term that encompasses *all* cinema, but not all SAS members agree. Paul Wells, for example, resists Cholodenko's sense that animation can encompass all film, suggesting instead that "animation is a modernist form, with a proven distinctive language, imbued with an ideologically and metaphysically charged agenda."[9] Like Wells, Buchan also insists upon attention to the specificity of particular forms of animation, yet both of these scholars move relatively easily between the realms of cinema studies and animation studies. For

Buchan, this capacity to address both audiences has been enabled in part through her founding of the journal *Animation* in 2006. While she expresses some resistance to a certain totalizing mode of (and perhaps in some senses a cliché of) film theory, her critical position aligns her with an increasingly large number of cinema and media studies scholars who have rejected universalizing theories of film and spectatorship in favor of more nuanced and historically contingent approaches. In the introduction to her edited collection, *Animated "Worlds,"* for example, Buchan suggests that many of the collected essays "align to the relatively recent 'turn' in film studies, a shift away from 'Grand Theory' that should apply to all films, and increasingly toward 'piecemeal' approaches that concentrate on individual films."[10]

These internal divisions exist within both animation studies and cinema and media studies, and often they become the catalyst for some of the most interesting film theoretical conversations about what the priorities and concerns of these two overlapping realms of study are. In cinema and media studies, for example, there is no consensus among its members (there never has been and nor should there be) on what constitutes "film theory," what its relation to film is, and even—to invoke the specter of André Bazin—what "cinema" itself is, was, and might yet be. The incorporation of television and then music videos, video games, the Internet, and other forms of digitally based moving image culture has resulted in a proliferation of the field's primary objects. It is in this context that an increasing number of scholars have begun to wonder how animation could ever have disappeared from view in the first place, and how cinema and media studies' various theoretical discourses are enabled or challenged by refocusing our attention on the complicated term and the multiple modes of image-making it encompasses.

ANTHOLOGIES AND MONOLOGUES

Though the institutional division of animation and cinema as distinct realms has clearly begun to shift, in part perhaps because of the developments in the field reflected in the name change in 2002 from the Society of Cinema Studies to the more inclusive Society of Cinema and Media Studies, other factors have also helped to sustain the separation.[11] We might look first to the institution of the film theory reader, a heavy tome that provides the skeleton for many introductory and advanced film theory classes. The table of contents of the anthologies from which many of us teach makes quite clear what role animation currently plays in most classroom conversations about film theory: none! Neither Leo Braudy and Marshall Cohen's *Film Theory and Criticism* nor Robert Stam and Toby Miller's *Film and Theory: An An-*

thology includes a single essay devoted to the topic of animation. A new anthology by Timothy Corrigan, Patricia White, and Meta Majaz, *Critical Visions in Film Theory*, suggests, however, and in a couple of different ways, that the existing and perhaps ossified paradigms for teaching film theory are under transition. First, this volume includes a "wide range of alternative tables of contents," reflecting the fact that as the media landscape changes, teachers need constantly to reevaluate the intellectual "architecture" within which we analyze these changes in order to allow new questions, objects, and intersections to come to the fore. This recent anthology also includes three essays that explicitly address animation, further suggesting that the now rather predictable rubrics organizing such anthologies are changing not in parallel with but *because of* the evolving nature of the objects under discussion, objects that need new vocabularies for critical analysis, as well, at times, as new organizing rubrics.[12] Though "realism," for example, is unlikely to disappear as a topic of concern for film theorists, *Critical Vision's* inclusion of Alexander Galloway's discussion of video game realism as an action-based and affective rather than purely visual experience pushes existing theories in challenging new directions. Similarly as digital cinema's production process draws attention to issues surrounding composited images, a wide variety of animated films offer useful historical precedents for us to draw on as we try to understand the nature of cinema's aesthetic and technological evolution. And once we start considering animation, the extent to which film theory has neglected movement as a primary concern becomes far easier to grasp.

Ideally the introduction of animation as a primary topic of concern for the discourse of film theory will not simply add new material to existing anthologies (although it will do this too). It should also help to catalyze full-scale conceptual reorganizations of material in order to render visible affinities, texts, questions, and problems that, without animation, we might never have seen. Let me give an example of how viewing film theory through the lens of animation might alter texts or figures that we thought we knew well. David Rodowick describes Stanley Cavell's *The World Viewed*, first published in 1971, as "the last great work of classical film theory" (along with Siegfried Kracauer's *Theory of Film*).[13] Yet alongside this description, we might note the lingering openness and afterlife of this "bookend" text. *The World Viewed* was first reissued in 1974, and then again in 1979, this time in the form of an enlarged edition that included an additional seventy pages under the subtitle *More of the World Viewed*. Much of the supplemental material in the 1979 edition addresses the otherwise largely repressed question of animation's relation to film (or "movies," to use Cavell's term). My thoughts on the question of why, for Cavell, cartoons are not movies, whether other forms of animation that exceed the realm of the cartoon would challenge the distinctions he establishes, and what is at stake in his resistance to the inclusion of cartoons must be postponed for another time, although these are the kinds of questions that I think are important for us to consider in the contemporary moment. I do, however, want to note the fact that this enlarged edition actually reproduces only one side of a conversation, both parts of which had been published five years earlier in the *Georgia Review* (Winter 1974). Though Cavell acknowledges that he is responding to an essay by Alexander Sesonske, which he does quote at length, the republication of Cavell's response turns a dialogue about movies and cartoons into a monologue, and leaves aside some of the emphases and disagreements that, at least for Sesonske, are central. Cavell first says of Sesonske's response, "Each of these remarks is the negation or parody of something I claim for the experience of movies" and then adds, "There is this asymmetry between his position and mine: He does not have to show that cartoons *are* movies because he has no theory which his taste contradicts. He can simply say, 'the two are not that different.' Whereas I do, apparently, have to show that cartoons are *not* movies, or anyway show that the differences between them are as decisive as my emphasis on reality implies." Cavell goes on to complain, "And of course I cannot show this, in the sense of prove it—any more than I can show that a robot is not a creature or that a human is not a mouse or a dog or a duck. . . . To affect someone's conviction that cartoons are movies, all I could do would be to provide some reflections on cartoons."[14]

Sesonske's response emerges as an essay without a theory, a parody that negates Cavell's own proper theory of what constitutes a movie and that is impossible to rebut because something like "conviction" or belief lies at the heart of the disagreement. Yet these summaries of Sesonske's key points do not quite do his essay justice, not least because Cavell's summary occludes one of Sesonske's central questions, which is a question that has returned as primary to the field in the context of the digital turn, the questions of "what difference motion and editing make to the image," as well as "whether a *succession* of automatic world projections is or must be itself a world projection." Sesonske notes the importance of considering the star status of a character like Mickey Mouse and the fact that so many cartoons are still made up of a succession of photographed images, and raises as a serious question rather than as a parody why, at least for some viewers, cartoons may provide a world "with the same immediacy and conviction, the same sense of moving through its space, the same feeling of intimate acquaintance with its inhabitants."[15]

That Sesonske's disagreement with Cavell over cartoons is articulated through the language of feeling positions him as an interesting early contributor to the conversation about animation's affective landscape, which has recently been advanced by scholars like Judith Halberstam in *The Queer Art of Failure* and Sianne Ngai in *Ugly Feelings*. But perhaps Sesonske's most clearly articulated resistance to Cavell's theory of movies in *The World Viewed* occurs around the very idea of "the world" or "reality as a whole," both of which are taken for granted in Cavell as they are in Dudley Andrew's more recent contribution to a similar conversation. (This resistance might also, if indirectly, be linked to the social and political dimensions of Halberstam's and Ngai's theories of animation.) Sesonske asks, "For what is 'the world' that Cavell says photographs, and therefore movies, are of?" and continues, "It is not clear. 'Reality as a whole?' But what does that imply?" He then goes on to offer a series of examples that illustrate the fabricated nature of the world of the movies, the use of special effects, and the extent to which the temporality of the projected world is also "a matter of choice and not necessity."[16] These are not parodies but serious questions that demonstrate, among other things, the extent to which earlier conversations about the relationship between animation and live-action cinema provide an important historical context for the discussions in which we are now engaged about digital cinema and its relation to analog cinema.

Sesonske's final paragraph may be the most perplexing and suggestive moment in the entire essay, and it too prefigures both Halberstam and Ngai in its suggestion of a politics derived from taking animation seriously as a world projection. Sesonske concludes, "I have deliberately said nothing about that important strand of *The World Viewed* which centers on the concept of modernism, even though I am confident that it is here that our deepest disagreement lies. But the issues there only arise subsequent to those I have discussed—besides my own belief is that they are not issues concerning the ontology of film, but rather the pathology of the times."[17]

FILM THEORY, FILM HISTORY, AND THE PERSISTENCE OF MODERNISM

While Sesonske only gestures toward modernism's role in his disagreements with Cavell in a rather cryptic way, modernism persists as a central feature of Dudley Andrew's recently articulated sense of "what cinema is." Andrew positions what he calls Bazin's "aesthetic of discovery" "at the antipodes of a cinema of manipulation, including most animation and pure digital creation."[18] This exclusion of most animation from modernist cinema's "aesthetic of discovery" certainly has some element of nostalgia for a predigital cinema, but I want to suggest that we might also regard it as the kind of provocative statement capable of animating our conversations about how we think about and through different and evolving forms of moving images. After all, Andrew's exclusion of animation from his specifically modern sense of "cinema" is not total. Of the filmmaker Jia Zhang-ke, for example, he writes:

> Jia Zhang-ke is ready to deploy animation, but always in the service of cinema, not trying to exceed it. The young characters of The World, imprisoned in the theme park where they work behind the scenes, escape by funneling their hopes into the cell phones they continually consult. In a daring move, Jia Zhang-ke inflates the brief text messages they send one another into brilliantly colored wide-screen animation sequences.... These extraordinary animated sequences seem to celebrate and contribute to the intoxicating freedom of the digital, and yet, like the theme park that gives the film its title, they are circumscribed by the human and social drama which they interrupt like holes in cheese. Jia Zhang-ke is, it turns out, a modernist, devoted to the kind of discovery that the neorealists made their mission.[19]

In the contemporary moment of rapid transitions in both media practice and theory, this passage provokes a number of important questions: What does it mean for Andrew to describe animation's position as being "in the service of cinema"? What is at stake in Andrew's insistence on modernist cinema's maintaining the upper hand? What would other, less hierarchical relations between cinema and animation look like? Where do we find them? What sense of "cinema" do they present, and what models of thinking, looking, feeling, and relating to the world do these alternatives to modernist cinema make available? Are there problems with assuming that we can align modernist cinema with "the human" on the one hand, and both "the intoxicating freedom of the digital" and "the theme park" with the animated sequences of this film on the other? Is there room, for example, for understanding something like a humanist animation within the scene Andrew describes, and if not, why not? What is at stake in investments on either side of the responses to this question?

The development of Andrew's thinking about cinema and animation emerges, as it does in Bazin's writing, through close attention to individual films and through a deep investment in a particular "cinematic ethos,"[20] something that is not universally available in all cinematic experiences. For Andrew, this ethos involves an "attitude," modeled by Bazin, "of curiosity, spontaneity, and responsiveness to a reality conceived of as indefinitely enigmatic and worthy of our care." This ethos in part depends upon a movie's "composition occur[ing] right there and then [on set, before the camera], not later on at the computer."[21] Yet by rather polemically excluding animation from the "cinematic ethos," Andrew at least provokes conversation about what exactly is meant by "animation" here; he makes us ponder what an animation-specific ethos might look like, and what is at stake—historically, aesthetically, and politically—in resisting or agreeing with the asserted claims.

Andrew's is not the only recent argument for a noninclusive sense of cinema. David Rodowick, for example, describes Deleuze's cinematic movement-image in it purest form as "rare" and elusive and explores how the ethical stance of Deleuze's books on cinema produces this rarity.[22] While the absence of extended critical discussion about specific animated films in either of these books might seem to render Deleuze irrelevant to the conversation about animation's place in film theory, adopting this position ignores both the potential interest of thinking about animated time, space, and movement through Deleuze and the way animation inflects Deleuze's (and Guattari's) thought outside the context of the cinema books, as, for example, when the Pink Panther paints his way into a discussion of the concepts of the rhizome and "becoming world" in A Thousand Plateaus.[23]

Andrew's recent resistance to animation as cinema, like Rodowick's emphasis on the rarity of certain Deleuzian cinematic phenomena, both occur within the context of a moment when digitization, at least for some, seems to render such divisions obsolete by absorbing all cinema into animation as the dominant category. Lev Manovich describes, for example, a cinematic process of evolution that fundamentally shifts what he perceives as "the opposition between the styles of animation and cinema" that "defined the culture of the moving image in the twentieth century." He continues, "Born from animation, cinema pushed animation to its periphery, only in the end to become one particular case of animation."[24] Cholodenko rightly critiques Manovich's mode of narrating the relationship between film and animation for its presentism, writing, "It is not the case that only recently, with the advent of digital animation, film became animation. It has *never not* been animation." Cholodenko adds, "Cinema was never not a 'particular case of animation,' and Film Studies never not a particular case of animation studies."[25] Yet in the end, though Cholodenko usefully highlights cinema's relation to animation as long and persistent, in contrast to Manovich's "fort-da" narrative, both Cholodenko and Manovich, while making useful polemic interventions, ultimately risk foreclosing, perhaps prematurely, the potentially productive tension between these two terms.[26]

What these conversations demonstrate is that these challenges within the realm of film theory are inextricably bound to the work of film history. In order to respond to the questions that are arising out of the discussions of animation's place in film theory and cinema, we need to consider which terms and lines of argument need to be jettisoned or revised, as well as which texts need to be dug out of the archives, translated, or recontextualized in relation to the specific film experiences that provoked their initial articulation. Consciousness of this interrelation between film theory and film history has been shaping cinema and media studies for at least twenty-five years under the banner of "the film historical turn" (although for some scholars, it has always been present).[27] Without going into the various and important questions that this "turn" has raised in relation to the status of theory and theorizing within the field, I want only to register the fact that this process of making the boundary between film history and film theory more porous has been one of the important structural shifts that has made animation more visible to scholars who work primarily within the realm designated as "theory." The expanded conversation that addresses both historical and theoretical texts promises to stretch film theory through an increased awareness of animation history, which is how much of the non-production-oriented writing about animation might be categorized. This shift will also, I suspect, render visible the theoretical arguments embedded within these texts formerly designated as "history."[28]

LANGUAGE AND LOCATION

At this point I want to return briefly to Bazin in order to highlight at least two further issues pertinent to the discussion of animation's place in film theory. Although Bazin's writing about live-action modernist cinema is often invoked to support the distinction between cinema and animation, it is useful to remember that he wrote on multiple occasions about different types of animation, including that of Walt Disney, whom he describes as "the most important person in cinema after Charlie Chaplin" and "one of the great magicians of cinema."[29] These characterizations suggest that Bazin's particular sense of a "cinematic ethos" was developed not in ignorance or through neglect of animation but in active conversation with it. Our own understanding of Bazin could be enhanced by following this approach.[30]

I note Bazin's perhaps surprising celebration of animation, and of Disney animation at that (!), not to argue for an unlimited sense of what cinema is and was but rather to draw attention to two related issues. What Bazin's celebration of Disney and of animation draw our attention to is, first, that Bazin's writing on animation, much of it not translated into English, has circulated far less in the English-speaking world than the essays that have been translated into English. The same must be said of the theoretical studies of Bazin's writing on animation that have appeared in French, most notably Hervé Joubert-Laurencin's *La Lettre Volante: Quatre essays sur le cinéma d'animation* (1997). One might add that if translated essay anthologies like the two volumes of Bazin's *What Is Cinema?* craft distinct personas of "theorists" through the active suppression of writing that does not fit that caricature, survey anthologies of film theory only further this already oversimplified version of a theorist's thinking, largely for a pedagogical convenience that should not go unquestioned.[31] (No one knows this problem better than Laura Mulvey as a result of the phenomenal impact of her 1975 essay, "Visual Pleasure and Narrative Cinema.") In the case of Bazin, the landscape is beginning to change, in large part because of the pioneering and collaborative efforts of Andrew, both through his work with the Bazin archive and through the publication of his recent volume, coedited with Joubert-Laurencin, *Opening Bazin: Postwar Film Theory and Its Afterlife* (2011). But this is only one example of the many theorists of film whose work has perhaps been distorted by selective and motivated reading, translation, and anthologization.

While corrective interventions like the recent Bazin volume are important, they also serve to highlight broader questions about the politics of translation that are anything but simple. English-language PhD programs in cinema studies tend to emphasize foreign-language learning less, for example, than the adjacent field of art history, in which scholars tend to work on more geographically and linguistically circumscribed regions.[32] Film theory's dependence on translation illuminates some of the ethical conundrums facing those of us participating in "global" and theoretical fields of study trying to pay untranslated texts more attention: Which linguistic discourses get privileged as more likely to be theoretical than others? (French, for example, has an obvious advantage over theoretical material written in languages less fundamentally aligned with Theory.) Who will do the work of translation, and who will evaluate the accuracy of conceptually difficult translations, especially if translation continues to rank lower in academic promotion rituals than other forms of scholarly labor? "Destination" conferences now increasingly attempt to foster better exchange between English-speaking scholars and the rest of the world, but such conferences always raise complex economic, social, and environmental questions: Who will visit whom? Which locations are (in)capable of hosting three thousand film scholars? Who can('t) afford to go? The specter of a global SCMS Skype conference looms somewhere on the horizon, and with it other pertinent questions about the advantages and disadvantages of various forms of disembodied but relatively cheap and accessible intellectual exchange (writing, the conference call, Skype).[33] Although these issues often appear to be mere logistical concerns of professional organizations, it is crucial to note that decisions around these kinds of questions impact the intellectual trajectory of the field and its subfields. In the case of animation theory, two important interventions could immediately be made: First, if English-speaking scholars paid more attention to film theoretical writing in Japanese, animation would emerge as a key area of concern; second, by returning to the untranslated essays in French journals like *Cahiers du cinema*, whose contributions have come to define major concerns of film theory, it would become clear that many postwar French filmmakers and critics were forging their ideas about cinema—what it was and how it was changing—through a consideration of animation as much as of live-action cinema.

The question of language and access is relevant to film theory's partial neglect of animation beyond the realm of national and tribal linguistic divisions, extending also into the challenges of discipline-specific languages. Once we recognize that animators work with a wide variety of media, including drawing, sculpture, collage, painting, photography, and puppetry, it becomes immediately clear that the term *animation* invokes an overwhelming number of long and complex histories of art making, each with medium-specific terminology and theoretical debates of its own. One advantage of art history's relatively recent interest in the field of cinema and media studies, fueled in part by contemporary artists' ever more intense and multifaceted engagement with the history of the moving image, is the growth of productive intradisciplinary spaces to support the cultivation of the analytic language(s) we need to help our conversations develop. Collaborations between cinema and media studies departments and fine arts departments (which often house animators!) can similarly help to support the growth of this discussion about what constitutes a moving image, the variety of ways in which motion is created by filmmakers, and what issues arise out of this variety of approaches.

Yuriko Furuhata's recent work offers just one example of how generative and necessary a multifaceted approach—aware of issues of translation, cultural and genre prejudices, and so on—can be for addressing field "oversights" and elisions. She begins an essay from 2008 thus: "Has Japan ever produced a body of critical writings that deserves to be called 'theory'? The fields of Japanese film studies and film studies in general have been beset by a presumption that goes back to the inaugural work of Noël Burch, who famously claimed that 'the very notion of theory is alien to Japan; it is considered a property of Europe and the West.' This tenet has been questioned in the past, yet its ghost lingers on."[34] The richness of this methodological approach for the question of animation's role in film theory, along with the parallel importance of the existence of appropriate publishing venues, becomes clear in a more recent article by Furuhata (published in *Animation*) that builds on her earlier questions. Here she not only draws our attention to Sergei Eisenstein's writing on Disney but goes on to situate those writings in relation to the work of two Japanese film theorists, Imamura Taihei and Hanada Kiyoteru:

> The heritage of the Eisensteinian conception of plasticity of the image informs much contemporary writings on the animated image, from discussions of cel animation to theorizations of digital morphing. While it is necessary and indeed important to approach plasticity in animation at the level of the image itself, situating this question of plasticity more broadly would open up certain theoretical and political possibilities. Drawing on the insights of two leftist Japanese film theorists' work on Disney animation written in the 1940s and 1950s, this article proposes extending the discussion of cel animation's relation to plasticity beyond the phenomenological *perception* of the image to the material process of *producing* the image. In order to assist this reorientation, I will turn to the work of Japanese theorists Imamura Taihei (1911–1986) and Hanada Kiyoteru (1909–1974).[35]

Furuhata's approach is particularly useful for the conversation about the relationship between cinema and media studies and animation studies in that even as it addresses an overlooked body of theoretical writing on animation, it does not start from a defensive position but rather uses her interdisciplinary skills to help other scholars understand why the overlooked material she writes about matters.

As we go forward, it seems crucial that we not forget the importance of what Paul Wells describes as "the written and recorded work of animators themselves,"[36] for animation studies, more than any other area of moving-image studies (except perhaps experimental film studies, with which it has a lot in common), has existed in large part because of the commitment of practicing animators who have taken time out of their demanding and labor-intensive production schedules to write about what they do, albeit in a genre that often falls outside the categories of theory and history that have often given cinema and media studies its formal structure. Animation now risks being regarded as an exciting and unexplored virgin terrain for film theorists eager to animate, as my title suggests, what many consider to be a half-dead discourse from the past, an area ready to be taken over by scholars who have access to supposedly "more sophisticated" modes of analysis.[37] I believe that film scholars can and do bring important skills and questions to the already existing conversation about animation. Yet in the midst of this excitement, we would do well to remember not only the imperialist habit of oversimplifying the inhabitants of much-desired and conquered terrain but also the history of film theory, in which some of the very best essays of every variety, from Vertov and Eisenstein to Laura Mulvey, Fernando Solanas, and Octavio Getino, were written by practitioners. Rather than imagining film theory bringing a philosophical language to animation, which might describe the approach that Cholodenko has been attempting, we might find more productive starting points in the polyvalence of existing, if dispersed, conversations that include essays by critics in languages other than English, writing by practitioners in which theoretical insights might be embedded but not foregrounded, and writing by scholars within the field of animation studies that has largely been neglected by scholars who identify instead with the field of cinema and media studies. An exchange among these voices would be most productive if the historical blind spots of film theory were acknowledged at the outset, and if participants held open the possibility that animation in its various guises might offer a form, or forms, of philosophical thinking yet to be explored, forms that at least some of us—myself included—have yet to understand.

Notes

1. Gunning, "Moving Away from the Index," 34, 38. Gunning later expands this discussion of animation's neglect by film theory to the neglect of "movement." See Gunning, "The Discovery of Virtual Movement."

2. My own title deliberately invokes Cholodenko's here. See Cholodenko, "Animation: Film and Media Studies' 'Blindspot,'" accessed 5 May 2011, http://gertie.animationstudies.org/files/newsletter_archive/v0120_2007_iss1.pdf. This text, written as a specific address to members of the Society of Cinema and Media Studies, is available only to

members of the Society of Animation Studies. See also Cholodenko, *The Illusion of Life* and *The Illusion of Life II*. Cholodenko's other essays are listed at University of Sydney, accessed 5 May 2011, http://sydney.edu.au/arts/art_history_film/staff/acholodenko.shtml.

3. See, for example, Hansen, "Of Mice and Ducks"; Leslie, *Hollywood Flatlands*; Sobchack, "Final Fantasies" and Meta-Morphing; Lamarre, *The Anime Machine*, especially xiii–xxx. For a fuller discussion of other scholars who have written about animation within the context of film studies and cultural studies, such as Eric Smoodin, Dana Polan, and Donald Crafton, see my introduction to *Animating Film Theory*.

4. Bordwell and Thompson, *Film Art*, 128.

5. Reinke, "The World Is a Cartoon," 9. In spite of this celebration of animation's "luck," Reinke's own coedited volume with Chris Gehman, *The Sharpest Point*, has played a pivotal role in bridging the divides across the disparate fields to which animation is centrally important. In my own experience of wandering into the terrain of animation studies, quite unaware of how much I had been missing, I have been repeatedly struck by the generosity of many animators and animation studies scholars who have helped me to orient myself in the field, and am grateful to all of them, including Cholodenko, Maureen Furniss, Ruth Lingford, Joshua Mosley, Jayne Pilling, Annabelle Honness Roe, Sheila Sofian, and Tess Takahashi, for both their recommendations and their critiques.

6. The society changed its title to incorporate the term *media* in 2002.

7. Noxon, "Pictorial Origins of Cinema Narrative"; Gessner, "Some Notes on Cinematic Movements"; Tibbetts, review, 32.

8. For an extended discussion of cinema and the politics of movement, see Beckman, *Crash*.

9. Wells, "Battlefields for the Undead," 9.

10. Buchan, *Animated "Worlds,"* viii.

11. Cholodenko also notes the importance of this name shift. See Cholodenko, "Animation," 25.

12. The three essays that explicitly address the question of animation in relation to film theory are: Paul Wells, "Notes towards a Theory of Animation"; Lev Manovich, "What Is Digital Cinema?"; Alexander R. Galloway, "Origins of the First-Person Shooter" in *Gaming*.

13. Rodowick, *Virtual Life of Film*, 79.

14. Cavell, *The World Viewed*, 168–69.

15. Sesonske, "The World Viewed," 563.

16. Sesonske, "The World Viewed," 565, 566.

17. Sesonske, "The World Viewed," 570.

18. Andrew, *What Cinema Is!*, 42. As I have already mentioned, some scholars (such as Wells) would like to consider animation a modernist medium, so this attempt to distinguish the two arenas by invoking a modernist lens can be found on both sides of the divide.

19. Andrew, *What Cinema Is!*, 59–60.

20. Andrew, *What Cinema Is!*, 94.

21. Andrew, *What Cinema Is!*, 94, 51.

22. Rodowick, "The World, Time," 108–9.

23. Deleuze and Guattari, *A Thousand Plateaus*, 36. "The Pink Panther imitates nothing, it reproduces nothing, it paints the world its color, pink on pink; this is its becoming world, carried out in such a way that it becomes imperceptible itself, asignifying, makes its own rupture, its own line of flight, follows its own 'aparallel evolution' through to the end" (1).

24. Manovich, *Language*, 298, 302.

25. Cholodenko, "(The) Death (of) the Animator, or: The Felicity of Felix, part 1," 36.

26. Sigmund Freud's discussion of the fort-da narrative can be found in Freud, *Beyond*.

27. For an in-depth series of discussions about the relationship between theory and practice since the so-called historical turn in cinema and media studies, see the "In Focus" issue dedicated to this topic in *Cinema Journal*, "Film History, or a Baedeker Guide to the Historical Turn" (2004), edited by Sumiko Higashi. The dossier includes an essay from the animation scholar Donald Crafton, who specifically aligns collaborative research practices with the approach of people working in the sphere of animation: "Animation aficionados, in particular, do not hesitate to reach out to others in the field" ("Collaborative Research, Doc?," 139).

28. To note only a few key texts, we might recall the important work of Donald Crafton, Giannalberto Bendazzi, John Canemaker, Cecile Starr, and Dominique Willoughby.

29. Bazin, "Fantasia"; Bazin, "Pinocchio."

30. For an interesting article about Bazin and animation, one that emphasizes Bazin's interest in animated abstraction and his critiques rather than celebrations of Disney, see Grant Weidenfeld's "Bazin on the Margins of the Seventh Art," in Andrew and Joubert-Laurencin, *Opening Bazin*.

31. For Joubert-Laurencin's discussion (in French!) of the privileging of the "baziniste" view of Bazin's writing, see Joubert-Laurencin, *La Lettre Volante*, 20. Andrew highlights the two problems I have mentioned regarding the limited circulation of Bazin's work: "Not enough of it is available; that which is available has been neglected, as Hervé Joubert-Laurencin points out in the preface, in favor of the clichés he terms 'bazinism'" (Andrew and Joubert-Laurencin, *Opening Bazin*, xviii).

32. This is not true in the emerging "contemporary" field of art history, which resembles cinema studies more closely in its "global" reach and the consequent English-language-based paradigm.

33. The neglect of Cholodenko's Australian-based scholarship suggests that the question is as much geographic as linguistic, as does the fact that his animation panel was unable to run at SCMS because his two fellow Australian presenters did not make it to the conference. The economics of academic mobility also clearly play an important and underdiscussed role in this question of who gets to speak to whom, and where, as the heated debates about travel costs to the 2009 SCMS conference made clear. The conference was supposed to be held in Tokyo (but was canceled due to the H1N1 virus). The society's Translation and Publication Committee, founded in 1988, does important work in highlighting and circulating in translation previously overlooked, important texts. See the SCMS website: http://www.cmstudies.org/?page=comm_translation&hhSearchTerms=.

34. Furuhata, "Returning to Actuality," 345.

35. Furuhata, "Rethinking Plasticity," 26.
36. Wells, "Battlefields for the Undead."
37. Although Thomas Lamarre's book on anime is excellent, there are traces of this more reductive approach to existing work on animation in his preface, as when he notes, "Analysis is relegated to re-presenting anime narratives, almost in the manner of book reports or movie reviews" (*The Anime Machine*, x).

PART III *figures aside*

chapter 10

Hyperbolic Discounting and Intertemporal Bargaining

William Flesch

I stopped and bought us coffee from a new place, before we went back to the HQ. American coffee, to Corwi's disgust.
"I thought you liked it *aj Tyrko*," she said, sniffing it.
"I do, but even more than I like it *aj Tyrko*, I don't care."
—China Miéville, *The City & the City*

This Ignorant Present

I wouldn't have to pay it back for three years! What are the odds of that much time happening?
—Homer Simpson

I would like to draw attention to George Ainslie's work on the prevalence of hyperbolic discounting of the future in mental life. The idea is very deep, and Ainslie's work is a major point of reference in behavioral economics and in studies of motivation and bargaining. I think it is also highly relevant to the dynamics of literary experience. Ainslie is a behavioral economist and psychiatrist, and now the head of psychiatry at a Veterans Administration medical center in Coatesville, Pennsylvania. His specialty there is addiction, which presents a special and vivid case of his general depiction of the ubiquitous dynamics of internal psychic conflict which hyperbolic discounting describes and predicts.

It is both surprising and not surprising that Ainslie's work should not yet be much known among literary theorists, even those most interested in philosophical psychology, that is, among those who were on the Derridean or Lacanian side of the debate between philosophical literary criticism and new historicist or, roughly, Foucauldian criticism. It is surprising because Ainslie has profound things to say from a perspective that is consistent with (and that sometimes draws from) both psychoanalytic theory and other forms of subtle philosophical thinking; it is not surprising because the psychoanalytic and philosophical tradition in which he writes tends to be the tradition deprecated by continentally minded literary theorists. The philosophical context for Ainslie's ideas is most prominently developed in analytic philosophy, especially decision theory (a sort of solitaire version of game theory); the Freudian background from which he draws is that developed by ego psychologists and by philosophers who have thought about the psyche in the terms offered by ego psychology's account of competition and struggle between the ego, which is not master in its own house, and other agencies in the mind.[1] One place of overlap between Ainslie and the continentally minded, though, is an interest in Melanie Klein. But mainly I think Ainslie hasn't come to the notice of literary theory because of an understandable suspicion of the usually reductive and cheerless explanatory systems based on economics and on experimental psychology. I think that in recent years such suspicion has become somewhat less justified, despite the generally disappointing and simplistic application of evolutionary psychology by the so-called Literary Darwinists.[2] Ainslie's work, on the other hand, is as challenging, important, exciting, provocative, powerful, and far-reaching as anything you'll find in literary theory over the past two decades.

Ainslie understood and named a central experimental and experiential phenomenon and considerably refined its description; then he developed an elegant and far-reaching account of the psychic dynamics that this phenomenon implied. *Hyperbolic discounting*, as Ainslie named it, had been noticed as a possibility before him, but it was Ainslie who saw its continuity and ubiquity in mental life, in all voluntary acts, whether in pigeons or in humans, whether large-scale or small. And it was Ainslie who came up with the idea of *intertemporal bargaining* to describe how organisms (from pigeons to humans) handle the conflicts to which hyperbolic discounting gives rise.

Hyperbolic discounting is a familiar enough experience. Most people, offered (scenario A) a choice between $100 today and $110 a week from today would take the $100 today. There's nothing strange about this, on any theory of choice. The smaller sum is what in *The Maltese Falcon* the charming Caspar Gutman calls "actual money, genuine coin of the realm, sir. With a dollar of this you can buy more than with ten dollars of talk."[3] Even if the future money is guaranteed to be forthcoming, its present value always represents *some* discount of its future value (which is to say, money now is always worth more than money later, because waiting means forgoing what you could do with it for a while; that's why it makes sense to take less money now, and why we expect interest on money whose buying power we forgo for a while). The surprising thing, or what should be surprising, is that the same people, offered (scenario B) a choice between $100 fifty-two weeks from today and $110 fifty-three weeks from today, will choose the $110. This may appear intuitively obvious, but to rational choice economists it seems strange. It seems strange because even people who realize that fifty-two weeks from today scenario B will look the same as scenario A now—people who realize that fifty-two weeks from today they will have to wait another week for $110 even though, had they chosen differently, they would get the money just then—even those people will choose to bind themselves to waiting an extra week a year hence. They know that they are making a choice for themselves, for the selves they will be in fifty-two weeks, that they (the selves they will be) would not make in fifty-two weeks. They are choosing differently from the way they know their future selves would choose, differently from the choice they would make right now. But they—we—do so anyhow.

In scenario A the lesser but more immediate reward trumps the greater but more distant reward (to a measurable extent: no one would choose $100 today over $1,000,000 next week.) But in scenario B, at a certain distance the greater but more distant reward trumps the lesser but less distant reward, even if the temporal difference between the two remains constant (in this case, one week). This says something significant about the relation of our desire to time. Desire does not treat time consistently, even after factoring in how immediate its objects are. We scale time inconsistently. Later time, the time fifty-two weeks from today, say, looks pretty uniform to us (the later, the more uniform), but in the short run sooner is hyperbolically overpreferred to later.

Where does the switch in our apprehension of future time take place? William Hazlitt—yes, that William Hazlitt—wrote an understudied philosophical *Essay on the Principle of Human Action* which argues that we have no more relation to our future selves than we do to other people. We choose therefore for sufficiently future selves as we would advise others to choose in the present. It's always easier to give than to take our own advice, to give it to ourselves as well as others.[4] We give our more remote future selves advice and resolve to take it: I *will* quit smoking on New Year's Day! But we're conspicuously bad at taking our own advice in the present if that advice goes counter to our immediate desires.

So when does a future self become another person? Hazlitt finesses this question, but we can start offering an experimental or statistical answer that will vary as the rewards and the time frames vary. What happens if people are given the choice between $100 four weeks from now and $110 five weeks from now? How about one week versus two weeks? Two days versus nine days? What would you do? Most people, at some point, will switch their preferences, and we could say that point marks the moment when their present relation to future time or a future self changes. But since the stakes matter, it can't be the case that there's a single transitional point: to each choice or desire corresponds a crossover point in the future,[5] which implies—to put it in Hazlitt's and Ainslie's terms—that there are multiple future selves arrayed at multiple distances and diverging in multiple curves from the trajectory our present self is on at the moment.

Ainslie's term *hyperbolic discounting* describes a curve in our relation to future goods that shows how much we discount the value of those goods over time. Rational choosers (look at the policies of financial institutions) should discount exponentially, not hyperbolically. This means that if you discount the value of a future good for a fixed interval before you get that good—say, in intervals of a year—then you should be able (all other things being equal) to value that good a year before you receive it, two years before you receive it, and so forth, on a consistent and uniform basis. As Ainslie observes about the shortcomings of utility theory:[6] "Few utility theorists question the assumption that people discount future utility the way banks do: by subtracting a constant proportion of the utility there would be at any given delay for every additional unit of delay. If a new car delivered today would be worth $10,000 to me and my discount 'rate' is 20% a year, then the prospect of guaranteed delivery today of the same car would have been worth $8,000 to me a year ago, $6,400 two years ago, and so on (disregarding inflation, which merely subtracts another fixed percentage per unit of time)."[7]

This rational way of discounting future utility follows what's called an exponential discount curve. Such a curve could never allow for the switch in preference that we have noted. (Credit card companies and other high-interest lenders make a living on people's willingness to pay ruinous interest later for immediate gratification, even if we know we'll regret our choice.) The increase in value over any fixed time interval will always be the same percentage. If $110 in fifty-three weeks is worth more to you than $100 in fifty-two and you are discounting according to an exponential curve, it can't be the case that such a curve could show you preferring $100 in *any* week over $110 a week later. For such a thing to happen, the curve describing the choice you'd make at any given time has to be highly concave; that is, it has to flex very steeply, more steeply than an exponential curve when the time frame is short, while being somewhat flatter than an exponential curve as the time frame becomes long.

The simplest curve that demonstrates this flexibility is a hyperbolic curve, hence Ainslie's term *hyperbolic discounting*. Much experimental work has shown that hyperbolic discounting is the basic empirical way we evaluate rewards presented over different time periods. We are apt to choose closer rather than more distant rewards, even if the total sum of all the rewards that we'll get is lower (as it wouldn't be under an exponential curve). We'd rather have a cigarette right now than not to have smoked at all today, which is why it's hard to quit smoking, though as we light up we promise ourselves that tomorrow we're not going to smoke, because we'd (now) rather be smoke-free tomorrow, even at the expense of suffering through a nic-fit that we know is small potatoes; yet we prefer not to suffer through it now. This inconsistency in preference cannot be explained on the model of rational choice.

Now the most interesting philosophical accounts of decision theory are particularly focused on this question of preferences among preferences, or second-order (and higher order) preferences. I want to smoke, but I don't want to want to smoke. Or (in holy anorexia, perhaps, or in other ascetic practices),[8] I may want to eat, and even want to want to eat while also wanting not to give in to the desire to eat which I am cultivating. If I don't want to eat, I'm not really being ascetic. So I want to resist a desire rather than (as with quitting smoking) not have it, and I thus display a third-order preference. Psychoanalytically minded critics will see the same dynamic at work in the eroticization of one's own repression, as in the case of Britomart, the knight of chastity, in Spenser's *Faerie Queene* (or even in Milton's "sweet reluctant amorous delay"). Or consider the adolescent Stephen Dedalus, who, mortifying himself, makes sure that "his eyes shunned every encounter with the eyes of women. From time to time also he balked them by a sudden effort of the will, as by lifting them suddenly in the middle of an unfinished sentence and closing the book." Leaving aside the cultivation of sexual interest that gives value to suppressing it by shunning the eyes of women, notice simply that the effort of will here is self-ratifying. The mortification would mean nothing unless it *were* mortification.

Preferences among preferences have been used by various philosophers as a way of trying to describe what commitments in our conflicted psyches make us who we really are. Harry Frankfurt and J. David Velleman, for example, see our most deeply held commitments as either indicative of who we are or as providing us a way to create ourselves by interpreting ourselves as having those commitments.[9] It's not that I really *am* a nonsmoker (or a thin man trying to get out of a fat body). It's that I am the kind of person who wants to be a nonsmoker.[10]

Ainslie's way of thinking about this is to see us as having many different and conflicting preferences at every minute of our life (to allude to Flannery O'Connor's Misfit). Because of hyperbolic discounting, short-term preferences for immediate but finally smaller rewards will occlude or divert us from longer-term preferences (*preferred* preferences) for larger and ultimately more satisfying or life-affirming or life-enhancing rewards. As in Wordsworth's boat-stealing scene, our short-term preferences are like the ridge that blocks from our view the higher mountain behind it. We take the $100 today even though we *know* it makes more sense to take the $110 next week. Likewise, Ainslie's exposition can be helpful in understanding the kind of literary *work* that Wordsworth is doing and describing here, work which requires preferring more difficult preferences. Nearer memories are the ones we can call to mind most easily, even if more difficult, distant memories are ultimately more rewarding or important. Intending to remember them, but putting off that labor, as Wordsworth (and even more so Proust do) is intending a future act of memory; intending one day to write those memories is intending a future act of writing (whence the Narrator's always balked, always reaffirmed "desir de me mettre à travail"), where doing so is remembering harder the things that can be blocked by more trivial recent memories. This is the Proustian or Wordsworthian analogue to Freudian repression: putting off remembering what matters.[11]

Ainslie's discovery of the ubiquity of hyperbolic discounting leads to a radically different and far more provocative question than the standard question about why we act in self-subverting ways.[12] If hyperbolic discounting is ubiquitous and a nearly invariable practice (which much empirical work has shown it to be), the real question becomes, not why we don't maximize our own longer-term interests, but how we ever *do*. How can people quit smoking? How is impulse control possible at all?

This question is not restricted to rational humans (using what Kahneman calls slow and deliberate or System 2 thinking) nor even to intelligent mammals:[13] Ainslie began by showing the fascinating strategies that pigeons used for impulse control. Those strategies involve what he calls intertemporal bargaining.

The idea of intertemporal bargaining is highly applicable to our naïve (our deepest) experiences of narrative and may be illustrated by those experiences. Let me give an example of the kind of intertemporal conflict in an audience's narrative wishing as a way of showing the series of attractive but intertemporally conflicting bargains that the story offers. (I'll give others below.) Such a series, I want to say, largely determines the narrative arc ("the Fichtean curve," as John Gardner called it, or Freytag's triangle) of any competent suspense story. So: we want Hansel to figure out a way to get the children back to the house as soon as the stepmother puts them in danger. And he does! He drops the stones and they defeat her in round one. Our desire is gratified, for now. Then, in round two, he attempts a similar strategy, with the breadcrumbs. But now even children will expect but not want this strategy to work (though the less sophisticated ones may think they do); at least we may feel ambivalent about its working, since we also want an exciting story (that's why we asked for our elders to read it to us to begin with), and the repetition of the strategy would soon become tedious. Now we want the strategy to fail, though we may not see how it will fail until the storyteller cleverly provides the birds to eat the breadcrumbs. Our interest in the story and our interest in the safety of the children have diverged. Round one goes to clever Hansel, but also to the clever story, which is gratifying. Round two pits Hansel *against* the clever story. (He's clever enough to drop the breadcrumbs, but we'd be disappointed in the cleverness of the story if this cleverness succeeded a second time.) So we find ourselves wanting the stepmother to succeed in her intermediate aims. We're not rooting for her, of course, but we are rooting for some medium-term coincidence between her schemes and the story's events. (And it is clever of her, and of the story, to set the branch knocking against the tree so that the children will think the adults are chopping wood not far away.) Our long-term desire is, of course, for Hansel and Gretel to be safe, but our medium-term desire is for them to be endangered. We can indulge that medium-term desire because they seem safe enough for the moment. When the *real* danger begins, when the black, indomitable oven (as Pynchon will call it in *Gravity's Rainbow*) looms before them, our now immediate desire for their safety will overwhelm our earlier desire to see them endangered. The chicken bone is a strategy that seems to work, at least in the short run, to keep them safe, and we want it to keep working (for a while, anyhow). And what about earlier, when they find the witch's gingerbread house? Do we want the hungry children to eat or not? The witch looms nearby (at least to anyone who recognizes the house as bait), but the children are starving. We want them to eat, but cautiously. How cautiously? Well, not too cautiously actually: we also want excitement, and if they just nibble at a shingle or two and get away we'll feel disappointed. The point is that at every moment until the end, we are ambivalent about what we want to happen next, ambivalent between safety and the jeopardy that makes narrative interesting and in fact makes it a pleasure.

This comports with and can help illustrate Ainslie's basic argument about intrapsychic intertemporal bargaining. How does intertemporal bargaining work? Let me try, in the next few paragraphs, to give a basic sense of Ainslie's argument.

I have many competing desires. I comprise or am inhabited by many different agents that want different things, all of whom I am which (to alter a phrase of Bill Arp's that P. G. Wodehouse loved). These agents may be discriminated from each other very accurately by looking at their differing temporal horizons, that is, at the different temporal horizons of their desires. They all seek rewards that I (as a congeries or an experiencer of my congeriate self) will experience as a sum over my lifetime. These different agents compete with one another to get me to act in such a way as to suit their respective individual and temporally individuated ends. But they don't compete only or mainly in a Hobbesian way; rather they make alliances of various sorts between themselves, and those alliances can alter the temporal ranges of the rewards in view of which I act.

How can such alliances across time frames be made, if short-term desires always trump long-term goals? How could the long term ever intervene in the present? What cards, if any, do my longer term desires hold? Let me quote and comment on a couple of contiguous paragraphs from Ainslie's conclusion to *Breakdown of Will*,[14] his fairly recent book-length exposition of his ideas, in order to explain how he maps the multiple alliances and temporal ranges involved in any action. (In the first of these paragraphs, Ainslie refers to "the familiar bargaining game, repeated prisoner's dilemma." If it's not familiar to you, read this footnote.[15])

> Processes that pay off quickly tend to be temporarily preferred to richer but slower-paying processes, a phenomenon that can't be changed by insight per se. However, when people come to look at their current choices as predictors of what they will choose in the future, a logic much like that in the familiar bargaining game, repeated prisoner's dilemma, should recruit additional incentive to choose the richer processes. This mechanism predicts all the major properties that have been ascribed to both the power and freedom of the will.[16]

Ainslie's argument is that if you can get yourself to look at a current choice as a predictor of what you will choose in the future, you can form a near-term desire—not for *that* future so much as for an immediate auspicious prediction of the future. My wish not to be a smoker tomorrow helps me not to smoke today *if* I can take refraining today as a predictor of what I will do tomorrow; such a prediction offers an *immediate* reward, namely that of having a more reliable assurance that I won't smoke tomorrow. That assurance is self-ratifying, since I have the immediate gratification of a *warrant* that I won't smoke tomorrow. (This is like the warrant each prisoner can give the other by not defecting in repeated prisoner's dilemmas.) Not smoking today allows me, right now, to think of myself as a nonsmoker and not only as a person who happens not to be smoking just this minute. It has, as I am about to quote Ainslie, "more value as a precedent than as an event in itself." Indeed this precedential value is probably of some importance to "Hansel and Gretel" as well. The fact that I want them safe in round one (the dropped stones) can reassure me that I really do want them safe in the long run, even when I *don't* want the breadcrumbs to work in round two because I am *also* interested in seeing them endangered. (This kind of reassurance matters because the ambivalence I am noticing in "Hansel and Gretel" is not trivial; it may be, as I can sometimes recall from my own childhood, excruciatingly guilt-inducing for very young children.) Ainslie's account of intertemporal bargaining is like a repeated prisoner's dilemma in the way that a commitment to playing a certain way helps maximize overall reward, but only if that commitment is reliable. I would like to add my own view that even in one-shot prisoner's dilemma, the near-term reward of wishful thinking can help us believe that such wishful thinking is ratified by its evidence that the other prisoner will also engage in such wishful thinking, so that we can solve prisoner's dilemma using Ainslie's theory even in its more standard, one-shot intersubjective form.

The mechanisms that can establish such alliances between shorter and longer term interests, short- and long-term selves, may have some surprising, even baleful consequences, which Ainslie summarizes in the paragraph that directly follows the one I have quoted:

> Further examination of this mechanism reveals how the will is apt to create its own distortion of objective valuation. Four predictions fit commonly observed motivational patterns: A choice may become more valuable as a precedent than as an event in itself, making people legalistic; signs that predict lapses tend to become self-confirming, leading to failures of will so intractable that they seem like symptoms of disease; there will be motivation not to recognize lapses, which creates an underworld much like the Freudian unconscious; and distinct boundaries will recruit motivation better than subtle boundaries, which impairs the ability of will-based strategies to exploit emotional rewards.[17]

Notice how well this fits Stephen Dedalus's disciplinary self-control: his willpower or "sudden effort of will" (as Joyce puts it) is the name of the resultant of alliances, conflicts, and bargains among his different desires: to look at a possible erotic object, to read and to know what the longer term process of reading can teach, to sustain his own purity of intention despite these other desires, to practice self-mortification here and now, to use that practice as a sign of his own long-term capacity for asceticism, to use the difficulty of the practice as a sign that it *is* asceticism, to draw strong but counterproductive boundaries (e.g., by shutting the book from which he is learning). And the outcome of Stephen's ascetic practice certainly includes rigidity and self-deception, at the very least in the motivation not to recognize the lapses that his highly sexualized avoidance of thinking sexually constitute. Purity of heart is to will many things at once but to imagine that you're willing only one, as Kierkegaard all but says.

The Future in the Instant

The power of film [is] to materialize and to satisfy (hence to dematerialize and to thwart) human wishes that escape the satisfaction of the world as it stands; as perhaps it will ever, or can ever, in fact stand. Whose wishes, a character's, or the viewers? We would, I think, like to say both. [It may depend on] the capacity to stake identity upon the power of wishing, upon the capacity and purity of one's imagination and desire.
—Stanley Cavell, "What Becomes of Things on Film"[18]

Let's say—uncontroversially—that literature and rhetoric work, like all interesting statements, by eliciting and then satisfying a desire. This holds in literature at scales from the smallest to the largest, from Hamlet's doggerel rhymes to the plot of *Hamlet* to the resolution and completion of our sense and his own sense of his character, of his person. Interest is a desire to know more. To interest people in what you have to say is to make them want you to say more, and then to give them what they want to know.

We can isolate one aspect of this rhythm—awakening and slaking a desire—by focusing on the fictional aspects of literature. By fiction I am stipulating something roughly consistent with Roman Jakobson's (to name a theorist who himself receives less attention than he might) account of poetic language: any statement openly meant to elicit interest without offering particular reference to or information about the world outside of the fiction. This definition of fiction would cover phenomena ranging from riddles to mysteries, from couplets to epics. In fiction, from the perspective we're taking, form merges seamlessly into content. As works get longer, the balance between form and content shifts, of course: the riddle or couplet is focused on the completion of form by content; the mystery or epic is focused on the delivery of content through form. But let's focus on their reciprocity, on what they have in common. Our focus on fiction can bring that out, since nonfictional discourse may claim interest on the basis of the real world it describes or purports to describe, but fictional discourse must always contain within itself both the question and the answer, the desire and its satisfaction (even and especially if the maintenance of the desire is the satisfaction), and the relation between these two moments is in fiction necessarily internal and so formal.

There are two different ways that Ainslie's approach can help us to understand the phenomenon of literary or fictional experience in general and narrative engrossment and anxiety in particular. In the first place, we can begin to see the extent to which our desire in narrative, as in couplets, is inconsistent at different time levels. We want to wait for a rhyme; we want to cease waiting. And then: We want to be frightened and we want to be safe. We want the protagonist to be balked and blocked, and we want her to get what she wants. We want the hero to give in to a lovely and harmless enough temptation, and we want him to resist it. We want these things both for the characters and for ourselves. Any decent story will orchestrate the different themes of our narrative desire; and so will any decent poem. For a vivid crossover example of the latter, consider the last stanza of George Herbert's poem "Home":

> Come dearest Lord, passe not this holy season,
> My flesh and bones and joynts do pray:
> And ev'n my verse, when by the ryme and reason
> The word is, *Stay*, sayes ever, *Come*.

We want the rhyme, but a longer term desire makes us want the prayer and the meaning. To afford that, the last line gives us the rhyme, a bit too early, satisfies a desire sooner than we quite want. (We want the desire as well: Ainslie has a lot to say about the management of appetite, which you could call a desire for a desire: a longer term desire not to "maximize satiation" but to "optimize longing.")[19] The rhyme may come too soon, but it does offer that satisfaction, by way of the human universal that consists in tropological or schematic arousals and satisfactions; these may include rhyme but will also include other forms of partial or full repetition. In the present case we get the rhetorical scheme called *epanalepsis*, whereby the stanza begins and ends with the same word. (So too does the poem.) And that concluding word *does* rhyme as well, with the poem's title. All of this shows the counterpoint established and juggled between more and less immediate satisfactions.[20] And *reason* as well as rhyme says that the word is *Stay*, but Herbert nevertheless prefers to say *Come*, that is, to defer satisfaction, since that sustains the second-order desire to remain in the salutary state of desiring God's coming rather than the less salutary state of being satisfied.

If intertemporal bargaining allows for alliances between desires of different scales, competently organized narratives will organize and offer such an orchestration of alliances to its audience. We'll feel desires large and small, longer and shorter term, and get some set of them satisfied in ways that make for a through-line within the narrative, one that appeals to a more and more stable array of our preferences among our preferences. (You can see how this can make narrative an effective tool for moralizing or propaganda.) We want Cordelia and Lear to survive, but we want the depth and seriousness of Shakespeare's *King Lear* over that of Nahum Tate, who gives us what we think we want. We want to flee these depths, but as the existence of tragedy shows, we want the depths as well. Shakespearean comedy and romance require the possibility of tragedy to make us feel that we haven't somehow simply preferred the easier, shallower choice.

This sort of desire for what is dark, conflicting as it does with a desire for a happy ending, is one of the ways that hard-boiled noir detective fiction and tragedy overlap. My epigraph from China Miéville's *The City & the City* is a particularly good example of the conflicting preferences we and the noir antihero share.[21] The detective's choice can't quite be rendered coherently on a scale of preferences, but we know what it means. It means noir. The noir detective is typically broken and defeated but unbroken and undefeated. We want him (or her) to be both, to care even though he doesn't care (about some things, like justice), and not to care even though he cares about other things (like coffee or smoking). It's not just that we want him to care even though he doesn't; we want him not to care *so* that he can care even though he doesn't. And of course, in touches like Miéville's, we want him to prefer tough-guy coffee *so* that he can be tougher still by being indifferent to the fact that he prefers it.

Just considering this on the level of the most engrossing, plot-driven stories, we can see how these conflicting preferences lead to a second feature of our relation to narratives: the sense we have of bargaining with them. Ainslie thinks narratives are interesting insofar as we gamble on what will happen;

the fact that it's a real gamble militates against immediate satisfaction. We can't just hyperbolically short-circuit events as we could if we were engaged in the pure wish-fulfillment of daydreaming. Daydreaming is like cheating at solitaire; attending to a narrative means that we don't control the cards we're dealt. When we daydream, we just stoke our fantasies with bite-size hunks of narrative cotton candy, of no substance or staying power.[22] "I suppose you think, Emily, that a little pudding today is better than much tomorrow," says Trollope's Colonel Osborne to Emily Trevelyan (unwittingly describing himself). Trollope offers much pudding by consistently, maddeningly withholding the little that we could all too easily whip up for ourselves. Instead of following our own fantasized inclinations, we gamble on what characters we cannot control will do; we gamble (I'll add) on what the fictionist will do. (Surely, *surely* Dickens agrees that Little Nell can't die, right?)

I think that Ainslie's idea of intertemporal bargaining suggests another and complementary relation that we have with narrative (and with jokes and riddles): a more general idea of what I would call noncausal bargaining. Noncausal bargaining is part of our intertemporal experience of wishing different and inconsistent things to occur in a narrative. The tell-tale compression of the pages still before us (as Austen puts it at the end of *Northanger Abbey*) will often make our wishful and inefficacious bargaining for the various results that we want all the more urgent, since the tale the compression of the pages tells is of the abridgement of the amount of time remaining to juggle or counterpoint our conflicting wishes. Think of the naïve (hence deep) relation we have to narrative when we reluctantly accept some dreadful incident. (Little Nell *does* die, and Snape kills Dumbledore!) We find ourselves demanding some guarantee of restitution for this, at the least something like what Addison called poetic justice. (The common misconstrual of poetic justice as revenge just shows that this is one bargain we may, perforce, accept: Hamlet is poisoned, but he does finally and completely unmask Claudius.) That experience of noncausal bargaining, I've already suggested, is part of our solution of one-shot prisoner's dilemmas, by which wishful thinking about what the other prisoner will do entitles us not only to wish but to think that the other prisoner is wishfully thinking about what we will do. Our own noncausal wishing presents itself as a kind of act of bargaining with the other prisoner. I think that this kind of noncausal bargaining is an internal feature of the experience of narrative, moment to moment and chapter to chapter (we want Glencora to go off with Burgo Fitzgerald, and yet we are glad to accept the bargain Trollope offers us by which she marries Plantagenet Palliser), but it's also part of our emotional and sensory experience of wishfulness, of our own mental body English, when attending to a narrative.

We accept and expect, and we have *the right to expect* (just as we have the right to expect the other prisoner not to defect if we don't): Accepting some narrative events, even painful ones, while also feeling that we have the right to expect other narrative events, is what makes narrative narrative. For any loss we accept (Bambi's mother, Dumbledore, Glencora in the last Palliser novel, Hamlet), we have a right to expect some gain. That makes the narrative loss feel like something we consent to, in return for narrative gain later. We cannot actually affect what happens in a fiction, but we already do affect it in advance by virtue of being representative of the audience the fiction must appeal to. (Dr. Johnson's notorious outrage at the death of Cordelia and his declaration in favor of the general suffrage that preferred Tate's version, in which she survives, to Shakespeare's, is an example of how one may feel that the author has not lived up to his side of the bargain.) If, like me, you think the idea of *identification* is an empty or a weak one when applied to our relation to fictional characters,[23] or if you at least would like a more robust idea of what identification could possibly mean and how it could possibly work, the idea of noncausal bargaining may help. As an audience for a fiction, we are placed in the interesting position of having the right and the ability to demand that at least some wishes (but inevitably not all) should come true in a fiction (if they all came true, it would be daydreaming), just as in our own lives we are able to demand that some, but not all, of our inconsistent desires should be satisfied. The experience in both cases is one of noncausal, that is to say purely wishful bargaining, and the reward in both cases occurs when such noncausal bargaining yields a pleasure-giving outcome.[24]

Noncausal bargaining is an actual and incessant mental activity, the actual and incessant way that we engage with the world, with others, including our future selves. Attending to fiction is just as active and can run just as deeply in our mental life.

Let me give one last example—the version of the prisoner's dilemma called Newcomb's problem. Here's how it works: Imagine a Martian anthropologist with an unparalleled ability to read individual human character and psychology, able to predict what someone will do in the following situation. She gives you two boxes: one is transparent and contains $10,000; the other is opaque and contains *either* $1,000,000 or nothing at all. You know her reputation as a heretofore perfect predictor of what people in your position, who also know her reputation, will do. (She's done this thousands of times before and has never been wrong.) That position is this: you can throw the $10,000 into an incinerator; if she predicts you will do this, and so evince your trust that she will have predicted that you will do this, she will have put $1,000,000 into the opaque box. If she thinks you'll pocket the $10,000, she will have put nothing into the opaque box. She leaves you with the two boxes and ready access to the incinerator. She doesn't even check what you'll do. You are now faced with a choice: keep both boxes or incinerate the $10,000.

If you're tempted to incinerate the $10,000 (as I am), you are engaged in the kind of noncausal bargaining I have in mind. You'd attempt to affect her prediction of what you would do by doing what you wanted her to predict you'd do; since she's so good at predicting, you would have a right to that expectation. I suggest that our relation to fictionists is like the Newcomb chooser's relation to the Martian: We wish and will outcomes already inscribed in the story, with the same passion, the same emotional engagement, the same demand that someone you cannot force to keep a bargain should nevertheless keep it, as we do in real life. Well, it is real life: someone else is presenting us the fiction. And we engage with it as we engage with all those entities we interact with, in our incessantly intersubjective experience, intersubjective to the core, as Ainslie has shown, even when we are most solitary.[25]

Notes

1. Decision theory is a still hotly contested field. A good, polemical introduction to it is Richard Jeffrey's *The Logic of Decision*. More or less analytic philosophers who put Freudian ideas to good use in ways relevant to my project include Richard Moran in *Authority and Estrangement: An Essay on Self-Knowledge* (Princeton: Princeton University Press, 2001); Herbert Fingarette in *Self-Deception*, 2nd ed. (Berkeley: University of California Press, 2000); J. David Velleman in *Self to Self*; and the well-known work of Richard Wollheim and Jonathan Lear. Charles Brenner's *Psychoanalytic Technique and Psychic Conflict* (New York: International Universities Press, 1976) offers a bracing alternative perspective on issues that have concerned psychoanalytically minded literary critics and theorists.

2. The most assiduous cheerleader for Literary Darwinism, and pretty much its intellectual leader, is Joseph Carroll, who keeps track of the field (and pretty much single-handedly drafted the Wikipedia entry on the subject). See, recently, *Reading Human Nature: Literary Darwinism in Theory and Practice* (Albany: State University of New York Press, 2011). Leading lights include Brian Boyd, *On the Origin of Stories: Evolution, Cognition, and Fiction* (Cambridge: Harvard University Press, 2009), and Jonathan Gottschall, *The Story-Telling Animal: How Stories Make Us Human* (Boston: Houghton Mifflin Harcourt, 2012). I criticize the general point of view taken by Carroll, Boyd, and Gottschall in *Comeuppance: Altruistic Punishment, Costly Signaling, and Other Biological Components of Fiction* (Cambridge: Harvard University Press, 2008) and in a review of Boyd in *American Book Review* (September–October 2009). My most basic argument with Literary Darwinism is with

its claims that fiction-making is an adaptation, that is to say something selected for by evolution, as opposed to a byproduct, something that might arise and display its own dynamism within the context of other social adaptations. You can get a decent sense of Literary Darwinism from Brian Boyd, Joseph Carroll, and Jonathan Gottschall, *Evolution and Literary Studies: A Reader* (New York: Columbia University Press, 2010). I disagree with the more polemical arguments in that book, though *Comeuppance* is excerpted in it. Literary Darwinism is often lumped together with approaches to literature from a cognitive, sometimes neuroscientific point of view. Although there is much to be skeptical of in that approach, it doesn't, on the whole, assume that literature and art are adaptations and therefore is more open to the idea that literature and art give interesting evidence about how capacities more central to survival might have evolved. Literary Darwinism tends to be culturally conservative; cognitive neuroscience, at least in some of its manifestations, is friendly to all kinds of cultural criticism. Thus Lisa Zunshine, in her edited collection, *Introduction to Cognitive Cultural Studies* (Baltimore: Johns Hopkins University Press, 2010), cites Raymond Williams as a formative influence, as do several of her contributors. Zunshine is openly hostile to Literary Darwinism. (I reviewed that collection in *Symploke* 18.1–2 [2010]: 327–32.) Theorists of cognition of course see the brain as having evolved to do certain things, so they are in no way against Darwinian explanation, but their ideas of explanation tend to be less naïve than that of Literary Darwinists. Blakey Vermuele, in particular, is fascinated by Darwinian accounts of how fiction may work in relation to a theory of mind, and her subtle and sensitive work is generally admired in both camps. See, most recently, *Why Do We Care about Literary Characters?* (Baltimore: Johns Hopkins University Press, 2010). Essentially, it will be seen, I admire Darwinian thinking that isn't philosophically naïve, that is, that doesn't imagine that science has displaced philosophy. Ainslie belongs to the party of the sophisticates.

3. Dashiell Hammett, *The Maltese Falcon* (New York: Vintage, 1992), 174.

4. On being able to evaluate other people's situations in a more clear-sighted way than our own, see Kahneman, *Thinking Fast and Slow*.

5. That crossover is mathematical: it's when a hyperbolic discounting curve between the present and a future value crosses the exponential discounting curve in which value is discounted by a constant percentage over a fixed time interval. Exponential curves can never cross each other (unless you add constants, which Ainslie has shown to be irrelevant in the cases he's considering), but hyperbolic curves cross exponential curves, and that's where our preferences change.

6. First analyzed by way of exponential discounting by Paul Samuelson in "A Note on Measurement of Utility."

7. George Ainslie, *Breakdown of Will* (New York: Cambridge University Press), 2001, p. 28.

8. For a series of accounts of anorexia as a paradoxical ascetic practice, see Rudolph M. Bell's *Holy Anorexia* (Chicago: University of Chicago Press), 1985. It's not obvious that Bell would accept my interpretation. Nietzsche in *The Genealogy of Morals* is making what I take to be a consistent claim about asceticism as a demonstration of the will's power, which requires the overcoming of a therefore also desired resistance within the will. For examples of the kind of self-temptation that I mean, see Kafka's *Hunger Artist*, where the fact that the Hunger Artist wasn't an ascetic at all but just never found any food that he liked is presented as a crowning irony, and Fitzgerald's "Babylon Revisited," whose ex-

alcoholic main character has one drink a day to show that he can resist it. Miltonic asceticism which leads both to Eve's failure to resist and the Son's successful resistance is summed up in Milton's famous misrecollection of book II of Spenser's *Faerie Queene*: "Assuredly we bring not innocence into the world, we bring impurity much rather; that which purifies us is trial, and trial is by what is contrary. That virtue therefore which is but a youngling in the contemplation of evil, and knows not the utmost that vice promises to her followers, and rejects it, is but a blank virtue, not a pure; her whiteness is but an excremental whiteness. Which was the reason why our sage and serious poet Spenser, whom I dare be known to think a better teacher than Scotus or Aquinas, describing true temperance under the person of Guion, brings him in with his palmer through the cave of Mammon, and the bower of earthly bliss, that he might see and know, and yet abstain." If you don't feel the temptation that vice promises, you don't count as truly virtuous, so you will want to feel that temptation in order for your rejection to be meaningful. This is what Milton praises Guyon for doing, though in Spenser Guyon's journey to the Cave of Mammon is presented as simply a mistake.

9. See previous citations of Velleman and Jeffrey, as well as Frankfurt, *The Importance of What We Care About*; Hirschman, "Against Parsimony."

10. Velleman is explicitly psychoanalytic in his commitments. In a somewhat more continental context, Herbert Fingarette makes and develops similar points in his analysis of self-deception, which inevitably bespeaks self-conflict, an analysis he bolsters with readings of Sartre, Freud, and Kierkegaard.

11. Cf. Stanley Cavell: "Sometimes I sense that to put real confidence in my memory I have to get to the end of all rememberings. That seems to say that I forgo remembering. And now that strikes me as an accurate description of what it is to have confidence in one's memory." *The Claim of Reason* (New York: Oxford University Press), 349.

12. I should add that Ainslie offers some evolutionary speculations about the reason for the ubiquity of hyperbolic discounting. I am not sure I agree with them, and I would certainly contribute some of my own, but it's not necessary to go into this question here. I'll just suggest that hyperbolic discounting seems an inevitable phenomenon in a biological system in which costly signaling or the handicap principle is a dominant determinant of interaction among organisms. See my *Comeuppance* and, for relevant biological background, Amotz Zahavi and Avishag Zahavi, *The Handicap Principle: A Missing Piece of Darwin's Puzzle* (New York: Oxford University Press 1997); Geoffrey Miller, *The Mating Mind: How Sexual Choice Shaped the Evolution of Human Nature* (New York: Doubleday, 2000). Hyperbolic discounting is costly in the relevant sense.

13. See Kahneman, *Thinking Fast and Slow*.

14. The title is a conceptual pun. Ainslie's subject is what's been traditionally called weakness of the will (i.e., our will breaks down), but he explains that weakness by breaking down or decomposing a univocal conception of will into its components, the way you would break down a vector into its components.

15. Let me offer a brief account of prisoner's dilemma. You and a partner, both arrested on a fairly minor charge, are interrogated separately about a major crime you have committed but that the police can't prove. You are each presented the following deal, knowing that the other is also being presented with the same deal and may be taking it even now: you can either confess or not confess to the major crime. There are four possible outcomes, since the outcome of each choice will depend on whether your partner confesses.

A. You choose to confess:
> 1) If you confess to the major crime and your partner doesn't, you'll go free and your partner will get twenty years in jail.
>
> 2) If you both confess, you'll each get five years in jail.

B. You choose not to confess:
> 3) If you don't confess and your partner doesn't, you'll get a year in jail (as will your partner).
>
> 4) If you don't confess and your partner *does*, you'll get the twenty years in jail (and your partner will go free).

So, considering what your partner will do, it is evident that a selfish rationalist should confess, since of the two scenarios in which your partner doesn't confess, (1) is a better outcome for you than (3), and since of the two scenarios in which your partner does confess, (2) is a better outcome than (4). Of course you know your partner is facing the same decision, so your partner is all the more likely to confess, which adds pressure on you to confess.

Now if you both could trust each other *not* to confess, the two of you would do a lot better (outcome 3) than if you both followed the counsels of rational despair and did confess (outcome 2). If you and your partner could communicate, and if you could commit yourselves to a binding agreement, the two of you would agree not to confess. But how could you communicate? And how could such an agreement be made binding?

Repeated prisoner's dilemma answers that question. Let's say both of you know that the two of you will find yourself in this position many times. Then it's very easy to choose (3) rather than confessing, because if you choose to confess in some iteration of the situation, your partner will certainly choose to confess the next time, in order to avoid being fooled twice and going to jail for *another* twenty years instead of the five years that is her greatest risk if she confesses. So not confessing now also allows your partner to infer you won't confess next time: it's in that sense that Ainslie is describing "current choices as predictors of what they will do in the future, a logic much like that in . . . repeated prisoner's dilemma."

16. Ainslie, *Breakdown of Will*, 198–99.

17. Ainslie, *Breakdown of Will*, 199.

18. Reprinted in Stanley Cavell, *Cavell on Film*, ed. William Rothman (Albany, NY: SUNY Press, 2004), 1–9, 6.

19. Ainslie, *Breakdown of Will*, 192. The similarity here with the Lacanian account of desire should be obvious, but the differences probably matter more. Ainslie is interested in the intertemporal conflicts among desires, not in the idea that desire itself is structured in an impossible way. As a lumper by temperament, not a splitter, I would like to say that in many cases Ainslie's account will be consistent with Lacan's, so you can see Ainslie, if you like, as sometimes offering a useful supplement to Lacan, or vice versa. But Ainslie is interested in the strategies of intertemporal bargaining, not in the sheer phenomenology or psychology of the impossibility of desire.

20. These ideas may be compared with Freud's analysis of a joke as an unexpected economy, a satisfaction that comes gratefully quicker than we bargained for.

21. This overlap is the subject of Robert Warshow's great 1953 essay, "The Gangster as Tragic Hero," in *The Immediate Experience* (Cambridge: Harvard University Press, 2002), 97–103.

22. For an essential account of the paradoxical insipidity of daydreaming, see T. C. Schelling, "The Mind as a Consuming Organ," in *Choice and Consequence* (Cambridge: Harvard University Press, 1985), 328–46.

23. See my *Comeuppance*, 12–21.

24. It's worth reading the pages where Ainslie distinguishes between pleasure and reward. I don't need to take account of that difference in this sketch, but I will say that his distinction is not unlike the distinction Burke offers between pleasure and delight in his analysis of the sublime.

25. Ainslie discusses Newcomb's problem on pp. 134–39, and in his somewhat earlier and more technical exposition of intertemporal bargaining in his *Picoeconomics: The Strategic Interaction of Successive Motivational States within the Person* (New York: Cambridge University Press, 1992), 203. There, reviewing Max Weber's discussion of how, as a diagnostic practice, Calvinists might assiduously exercise their will to do good even though they are supposedly already predestined to salvation or damnation, Ainslie argues against causal decision theorists (as they are called: they always take both the opaque box and the $10,000 because nothing they do can affect what the Martian has done) that "doing good for its diagnostic value may not invalidate that diagnostic value." Likewise, I think, wishing that Tiny Tim will survive has some prognostic value, and so we're glad to be worried because worrying makes us wish it, and we're glad to wish it just for that prognostic value. I give a slightly more expansive argument for the relevance of Newcomb's problem to narrative in "Narrative and Noncausal Bargaining," *Novel: A Forum on Fiction* 45.1 (2012): 6–9.

chapter 11

The Primacy of Sensation:
Psychophysics, Phenomenology, Whitehead

Mark B. N. Hansen

By means of sensation I am able to grasp, on the fringe of my own personal life and acts, a life of given consciousness from which these latter emerge, the life of my eyes, hands and ears, which are so many natural selves. Each time I experience a sensation, I feel that it concerns not my own being, the one for which I am responsible and for which I make decisions, but another self which has already sided with the world, which is already open to certain of its aspects and synchronized with them. . . . I experience the sensation as a modality of a general existence, one already destined for a physical world and which runs through me without my being the cause of it.
—Maurice Merleau-Ponty, *The Phenomenology of Perception*

Never has Merleau-Ponty's defense of the autonomy of sensation, its overabundance in relation to any ensuing perception, been more pressing than today, a time in which we find ourselves increasingly immersed in flows of information that fundamentally evade our perceptual grasp. In a world saturated with embedded microcomputational sensors and increasingly driven by massive-scale data gathering and analysis, our human capacity for perception has become increasingly attenuated in its power not just to present our experience to ourselves but to participate in any consequential way in that experience. I propose to use this opportunity for untimely theoretical archaeology to develop an account of sensation, what I shall call "worldly sensibility." In what follows, I attempt to position worldly sensibility as an alternative to a certain phenomenological understanding of subjectivity that has been primarily interested in how the raw material of sensation is developed into the higher-order compound that is our perceived experience. In contrast to this tradition, I treat worldly sensibility as a source of subjectivity—or more precisely, of "superjectivity"—that does not emanate from a substantial subject.

While I argue that this worldly source of subjectivity becomes prominent in the context of twenty-first-century media, I locate a certain anticipation of our contemporary moment in the research project of nineteenth-century psychophysicists like Gustav Fechner and Ernst Mach. Twenty-first-century media and nineteenth-century psychophysics present two distinct forms of sensation—two distinct conceptions of worldly sensibility—as something that lies outside human experience narrowly considered. Psychophysics focuses on sensations that we have—as humans—but that don't rise to the level of perceptual consciousness, and it develops an experimental method that aims to give units to these subperceptual sensations and thereby make them perceivable by us. Twenty-first-century media, with its focus on animating the environment with the aid of microsensors, smartphones, data gathering, and so on, opens a resolutely nonhuman realm of sensing, a direct sensing or sensibility on the part of the world itself.

What accounts for the resonance between these two framings of sensibility is their dependence on media—inscription devices, chronophotography, biometric and environmental sensors—to convert sensation into human experience. In this respect, what is at issue in both—despite a difference of focus—is the operation of an "objective" worldly sensibility that lies outside perceptual consciousness even if it typically involves bodily processes alongside environmental ones. In what follows, I seek to excavate the commonalities between these two framings with the ultimate aim of positioning twenty-first-century media as the legacy of nineteenth-century psychophysics.

But not only of psychophysics. For what such an excavation will afford is a broader context on twenty-first-century media and specifically a way to move back "behind" orthodox phenomenology in order to recuperate a notion of "asubjective" subjectivity that was already being developed in the work of Alfred North Whitehead, whose speculative ontology presented a critique of the limits of perceptual experience. As will become clear, fully appreciating Whitehead's usefulness in our effort to theorize experience in the twenty-first century will require expanding his ideas beyond some of the subjectivizing priorities even he could not avoid maintaining. But throughout the essay my aim is to show how the insights of the philosophical understanding that underwrote the psychophysical project help ground a critique of phenomenology and a critical expansion of Whitehead's own work on perception. In so doing, these philosophical insights of psychophysics pave the way for recovering crucial resources with which to theorize worldly sensibility and the environmental agency of twenty-first-century media, and more precisely, the capacity of such media to impact worldly sensibility *prior to* and *as a condition for* impacting human perceptual experience.

"Objective" Sensations

As it is typically presented, Whitehead's philosophy is understood to hearken back to the British empiricist tradition and to develop—on the basis of a critical retort to Humean skepticism and a constructive appropriation of Lockean sensationalism—an expanded model of perception rooted in the lineages of causal efficacy that stand behind and, in a sense, give body to any act of sense perception. Without in any way putting the correctness of this presentation in question (Whitehead spends much time discussing both Hume and Locke), I want to open a different, less orthodox genealogy of Whitehead's thinking that shifts focus to the role sensation plays in an expanded, environmental conceptualization of the event. This historical contextualization of Whitehead will help us tap the unrealized potential of his metaphysics for addressing the experiential challenges posed by twenty-first-century media.

This genealogy will focus on nineteenth-century psychophysics and its defining effort to measure sensation via the experimental artifact of the "just noticeable difference." Developed by the father of psychophysics, the German scientist Gustav Fechner, the just noticeable difference designates the minimal increase in stimulation necessary to produce a sensory difference. At stake in the psychophysical project, then, was the attempt to address sensation and sensibility independently from their subsumption into higher-order compounds. Psychophysics thus helps articulate an alternative to the post-Kantian path in philosophy which in one form or another—whether one looks to phenomenology (at least in its orthodox formations) or to logical positivism—champions the integration of sensation into higher-order forms of experience and/or linguistic or conceptual analysis. What Whitehead's account of sensation and the psychophysical project share is their sense that our sensational lives are not identical with our perceptual ones: that what we perceive is only part of sensation.

There is, however, a crucial difference between the *speculative* project of Whitehead's *Process and Reality* and the *experimental* project of psychophysics. For where Whitehead criticizes the limits of sense perception in the service of an expanded account of perception, the psychophysical project employs an actual experimental apparatus—what the historian of science Henning Schmidgen calls a "cyborg assemblage"[1]—in order to gain access to sensory dimensions of experience that are otherwise wholly inaccessible to humans. This experimental access to sensation beyond perception will prove crucial in my radicalization of Whitehead's own expansion of perception, for in the context of twenty-first-century media—which operate on sensibility prior to their having any direct impact on human sense perception—it is precisely this experimental supplement that matters. This supplement allows sensibility, insofar as it precedes higher-order integrations, to be part of experience even though it does not form part of what phenomenology thematizes as the "lived" or "Being-in-the-world." In this respect, something that has long been considered a limitation—that the psychophysical approach treats sensations in ways that they are never in fact lived—has in the end turned out to be one of its principal assets.

Twenty-first-century media has helped bring into relief the purchase of the psychophysical model and its guiding ambition. Developed against a panpsychic metaphysical vision,[2] Fechner's 1860 formalization of psychophysics as an experimental research platform focuses on isolating sensation from its inclusiveness within complex confounds of experience. This basic fact cannot be emphasized forcefully enough: what psychophysics inaugurates is a view that grants significance to all sensations, no matter how minute, *in* and *for* themselves. This philosophically inspired practice insists on the necessity for experimental, technical mediation in order to access the domain of subperceptual (bodily *and* worldly) sensibility. Fechner's approach ultimately yields a vision, backed by an experimental protocol, of sensation as itself "objective," as part of, and indeed the very fundament of, the physical world. In this respect, Fechner's insistence that sensation be treated at the level of physical stimuli amounts to an unprecedented approach to the very "Being" of sensation.

Where phenomenology and logical positivism both subsume the atomicity of sensation into higher-order integrations, psychophysical experimentation demonstrates how sensations are meaningful outside of higher-order *perceptual* or *existential* integrations. Far from diminishing experience (as it is alleged to do), the psychophysical exploration of atomic sensations turns out to be the strength of its experimental method; specifically it allows for the exploration of the very microtexture of sensory experience *in itself*, which is to say independently from just this kind of higher-order integration.[3]

Fechner's commitment to an objective view of sensations requires that he develop a form for their measurement: "To measure space we need the substance of the yardstick that occupies this space. In the same way something of a physical nature that underlies the psychic process is necessary for psychic units. Since, however, the psychophysical processes which form the immediate basis of a psychic quantity are not open to direct observation, we must substitute for the yardstick the stimulus, which in outer psychophysics gives rise to the psychic quantity and with which it grows and decreases in a regular manner."[4] Fechner's effort to formalize sensation leads him to postulate what is now known as Fechner's law: that the intensity of a sensation is logarithmically related to the magnitude of its stimulus. For my purposes, the details of Fechner's formalization are less crucial than his fundamental commitment to exteriorize sensation.[5] By establishing a *functional* relationship between sensations, which cannot be directly observed, and stimuli, which not only can be observed *but can be exactly measured*, Fechner opens access to something that has been hitherto simply inaccessible. But he also—and more portentously—shifts the site of the sensory event from the purely psychological (what he calls "inner psychophysics") to the physical. It is at this point that his experimental work rejoins his metaphysical vision, for what guides both—in one case from the microlevel of individual sensations or increments of sensation; in the other from the macrolevel of universal consciousness—is the effort to flatten the ontological divide between mind and nature.[6] Indeed what better "proof" can there be of the fundamental oneness of the mental and the physical than a general scientific procedure for measuring *all* sensation in terms of observable and quantifiable increments of stimulus?

At the same time as it defined the field of psychophysics circa 1860, this formalization also inaugurated a lineage that would stretch—via Ernst Mach, William James, and Bertrand Russell—to Whitehead himself. Consider, for starters, the view Mach expresses in *The Science of Mechanics* of 1883: "Properly speaking the world is not composed of 'things' . . . but of colors, tones, pressures, spaces, times, in short what we ordinarily call individual sensations."[7] In his effort to capture the specificity of Mach's claim here, David Skrbina differentiates it both from Berkeleyian idealism and from previous pansensist views: contra Berkeley, *there is no observing mind involved*, and, contra earlier pansensists, things are not just capable of sensing but *are in themselves sensations*.[8] Together these specifications underscore Mach's commitment to a view of sensations as "objective," meaning independent of a substantial ego or subject; for Mach, the philosopher Andy Hamilton concludes, "the 'given' . . . was not to be construed as given to someone. 'Experience' was essentially subjectless."[9]

A similar view appears in Russell's 1915 article, "The Ultimate Constituents of Matter," which outlines a position that accords primary reality to data of sensation, understood—as was the case with Mach—as objective or, in Russell's words, "extra mental." Russell develops his position by refuting two "errors" that he feels have obscured the discussion of matter:

The first of these is the error that what we see, or perceive through any of our other senses, is subjective; the second is the belief that what is physical must be persistent. Whatever physics may regard as the ultimate constituents of matter, it always supposes these constituents to be indestructible. Since the immediate data of sense are not indestructible but in a state of perpetual flux, it is argued that these data themselves cannot be among the ultimate constituents of matter. I believe this to be a sheer mistake. The persistent particles of mathematical physics I regard as logical constructions, symbolic fictions enabling us to express compendiously very complicated assemblages of facts; and, on the other hand, I believe that the actual data in sensation, the immediate objects of sight or touch or hearing, are extra-mental, purely physical, and among the ultimate constituents of matter.[10]

Though Russell gave up this position in favor of "neutral monism"—the doctrine that sensation belongs to both mind and matter or, more precisely, that sensations belong "equally to psychology and to physics" and thus "are subject to both kinds of [causal] laws"[11]—his 1915 claim about sensation is valuable here insofar as it produces perhaps the strongest statement of a nonsubjectivist monism of sensation. Far from being the property of mental experience added onto physical objects, sensations simply are the primary physical objects composing matter. As such, they range along a continuum from a purely physical pole at one extreme to a mental pole at the other.

This nonsubjective view of sensation developed through the thinking of Fechner, Mach, and Russell levels the hierarchy by which consciousness and perception are ennobled at the expense of sensibility. Along with mathematical calculations, technically based experimentation allows access to the sensible facts that, for Fechner and Mach no less than for Russell and Whitehead, constitute the origin point of knowledge but remain inaccessible to direct perception. In a passage that could easily have been excerpted from *Process and Reality*, Mach writes that "all calculations, constructions, etc. are only intermediary means to approach step by step . . . this evidence [Anschaulichkeit] that perception is not able to attain directly."[12] Experimental procedures—the very basis for Fechner's atomic targeting of sensations—mediate the plenitude of sensibility for a form of perception that is incapable of accessing sensation itself directly. The broader perspective furnished by this psychophysical lineage correlates an "objective" account of sensibility with a demotion of consciousness and perception. In this way, it points toward our contemporary situation—one in which we must rely ever increasingly on media to afford us *indirect* access to the causal efficacy of our own activity.[13]

If we can take Whitehead's work on sensation as a culmination of this experimental tradition, we can start to fill in one answer to Steven Shaviro's provocative recent question: "What if Whitehead, instead of Heidegger, had set the agenda for postmodern thought?"[14] It is my gambit that we can productively extend the scope of Shaviro's thought experiment by opposing to Heidegger not just Whitehead himself but the entire experimental tradition of psychophysical research on sensation that stands behind his project. Doing so allows us to accomplish two things in particular. First, we can develop the resources necessary to expand Whitehead's own reform of perception in the direction of a concept of "nonperceptual sensibility." Second, we can use this concept of "nonperceptual sensibility" to dispense with the residual anthropocentrism that continues to haunt Heidegger's effort to ontologize the agent of Being and that surfaces, for example, in his analysis of hearing. In his effort to establish the ontological primacy of the broad hermeneutic context over individual sound sensations, Heidegger clearly adopts human meaning, replete with the sensory restrictions it involves, as its unquestioned and unquestionable basis.[15] And it is precisely this move, I want to suggest, that strips the psychophysical tradition of its most radical promise: the capacity to access sensations *beyond* the hermeneutic forms given them by human activity. By broadening Shaviro's philosophical fantasy to encompass the entire experimental tradition, and by questioning the residual anthropocentrism of Heidegger's confident defense of hermeneutics against psychophysics, we add another philosophical question to Shaviro's list:[16] can the agency of atomic sensations indeed be "felt" by humans, at least as they have been conceptualized in the Western philosophical tradition?

Whitehead's work makes it possible to ask this question. For where Heidegger seeks to embed individual sensations within larger hermeneutic complexes rooted in human capacities, Whitehead furnishes a metaphysical analysis of universal solidarity that endorses—and explains—Mach's and Russell's insistence on sensations without a subject. Yet in order to bring out this radical potential of Whitehead's expansion of the psychophysical imperative, we will need to repudiate the lingering privilege he himself continues to accord human perception. For while we may feel that the cyborg assemblages of the nineteenth-century psychophysical laboratory or of today's microcomputational sensors and passive-sensing devices irreducibly separate our experience from direct or natural perception, the advent of smart environments, passive sensing, and massive-scale data gathering and predictive analytics in fact affords contemporary consciousness powerful artifactual access to its own otherwise opaque underlying background—its causal efficacy. Thus although we know our experience only indirectly—by way of technical mediation—we also gain a "pharmacological" compensation for what might otherwise seem like a demotion of consciousness in our ability to know it more fully, with a far greater degree of granularity.[17]

Sensations without Subjects

Insofar as Whitehead's ontology extends sensibility to all entities, and not simply to higher-order ones capable of sense perception, it furnishes the basis for conceptualizing a situation in which technical modes of sensing and data gathering replace human consciousness as the primary "presentational" agency involved in any perception, a situation in which a process of "machinic reference" is only later "fed-forward" into human consciousness. On Whitehead's ontology, that is, computational sensing lies on a continuum with living sensing, thus providing us with a framework for exploring how "machinic reference" lies at the heart of contemporary experience. What makes Whitehead's ontology so valuable is the way his approach to sensation effectively inverts the trajectory that led, historically, to its subsumption into perception. For Whitehead, sensibility (in contradistinction to sense perception) is independent of human mental activity insofar as it is embodied in concrete actuality. Extending the psychophysical tradition's insight into the objectivity of sensation, Whitehead attributes sensibility to every actuality, no matter how primitive or "physical." His cosmology thus situates worldly sensibility at a more primitive level than the standard phenomenological account which accords human bodies the role of perceiving sensory qualities of the world.

It is precisely for this reason that Whitehead's cosmology helps us conceptualize twenty-first-century media, for if it is the case that today's media impact the sensible confound prior to and independently of human sense perception, a fundamentally nonanthropocentric and properly machinic approach to sensibility is required: simply put, we must find ways of accessing worldly sensibility that do not channel it exclusively through the higher-order perceptual capabilities characteristic of human life. Developing such means of access calls for a radicalization of Whitehead's own expansion of the Western philosophical doctrine of sense perception; on such a radicalized view, generalized sensibility lies at the heart of causal efficacy and operates independently of and prior to its perception.

That we must expand Whitehead's account attests less to any shortcoming of his philosophy than to the concrete demands posed by a media environment that Whitehead couldn't have envisioned in 1929. The microtemporal and subperceptual operation of twenty-first-century media accordingly necessitates a more extreme excavation and reassembly of sensation and perception. For example, where Whitehead could assume that perceptual and sensory experience was the prerogative of humans and other highly complex sentient beings, the increasing off-loading of sensibility onto the environment has fundamentally altered the rationale for such an assumption; more precisely, it has put into question the legitimacy of using human sensation—with its distinct timeframe and scope—as a benchmark to determine what counts as sensory. This fact, made effectively inescapable by twenty-first-century media, licenses us to expand further Whitehead's own expansion of perception, and specifically to discover, beneath his broadened concept of perception (i.e., "perception in the mode of causal efficacy"), the operation of a "nonperceptual sensibility." Precisely because it is not indexed to the perceptual ratios of the human, this worldly sensibility manages to capture the continuously morphing overlap of sensibilities of varying scales and degrees of complexity.

Far from relegating phenomenology to philosophical backwaters, the pressing, current demand for a concept of worldly sensibility makes phenomenology—or at least certain radicalizations of its project—essential. Eugen Fink's "de-presencing" and Merleau-Ponty's "reversibility," in particular, help concretize something that remains elusive in Whitehead's account: the power of the settled world to perpetuate itself. In Fink's protracted work with Husserl, de-presencing (*Entgegenwärtigung*) designates a primordial worldly temporalization—a passing out of presence—that is requisite for all temporal phenomena to occur.[18] In a complementary way, Merleau-Ponty's notion of reversibility designates the imbrication of sensing with the sensed and points toward a primordial sensibility that comes before distinctions of self and other, subject and object, activity and passivity, and so on.[19] The importance of developments like Fink's and Merleau-Ponty's is to extend the phenomenological project beyond its standard, Cartesian articulation, according to which experience is channeled through a substantial thinking or sensing subject. Liberated from its subjective bias, phenomenology not only resonates with Whitehead's goal to reform the subjective principle of modern philosophy but actually makes a crucial contribution to expanding Whitehead's work. De-presencing and reversibility help us to appreciate that the production of new actualities takes place through the operation of a material domain of sensation—nonperceptual sensibility—that has no necessary connection or relation to any narrowly subjective process. What the radicalization of both Whitehead and the phenomenological project offer, then, is the possibility of providing an alternative, "asubjective" basis for theorizing experience.[20]

Getting there, though, will require expanding on and pushing past some of the limits in the philosophical foundation Whitehead's ontology provides. In *Symbolism* and in *Process and Reality*, Whitehead indicts the narrowness of philosophy's traditional account of perception and seeks to introduce a broader account of perception in terms of two distinct yet normally correlated "pure" modes of perception: perception in the mode of presentational immediacy and perception in the mode of causal efficacy. If the former is a synonym for "sense perception" as it has been understood from Descartes onward, the latter is a novel concept that designates some inchoate capacity of sensing entities to perceive the causal basis for their experiences. As examples, Whitehead names the experience of perceiving that one sees with one's eyes or touches with one's hands.

Its significance notwithstanding, Whitehead's theorization of this supplementary mode of perception introduces a source of ambiguity that attests to the privilege he continues to accord human perception in his account of sensibility. Thus perception in the mode of causal efficacy seems to designate *both* the vague self-referential experience of the causal efficacy beneath sense perception—what Whitehead calls the "witness" of the body—*and the actual causal interchange* between a perceiver and the environment that cannot be limited to a most proximal "causal" source but rather encompasses the entire plethora of actualities comprising the deep causal and sensory background of any perception. If Whitehead manages to dissolve this productive ambiguity when (in *Adventures of Ideas*) he later rechristens perception in the mode of causal efficacy "nonsensuous perception," he does so only at the cost of compromising the (potential) radicality of his reform of perception.[21] For by specifying that nonsensuous perception coincides with the *just-past of present sense perception*—with what happened one-half second in its past—Whitehead severely constrains the scope of "perception in the mode of causal efficacy." He effectively subordinates his own expanded conception of perception to a primordial moment of sense perception, whose presencing it serves to support. Far from encompassing the "vector character" by which perception stretches to encompass all the occasions that led up to it,[22] nonsensuous perception designates only what lies in the most immediate background of a sense perception.

Accordingly when Whitehead rechristens perception in the mode of causal efficacy "nonsensuous perception," he does more than simply shorten the name of his concept; he effectively imposes a restricted model of sensation—the model of human perception with all of its attendant sensory limitations—*as the general basis for determining what constitutes sensation.* To the extent that it collapses the expanded perspective on perception offered by Whitehead in *Process and Reality* back into the narrow mode he started out seeking to reform, this imposition is incongruous and indeed a bit odd. In the end, we can, I think, conclude that, far from extending it to encompass the plethora of actualities informing its operation, Whitehead effectively subordinates his own expansion of perception to the once again privileged mode of human sense perception, now replete with a notion of its constitutive retentionality.

Tracking all of the causal processes informing any act of perception leads us to a very different conclusion. Far from a retrenching around human sense perception, attention to a plurality of processes instead facilitates the discovery of a multiscaled, heterogeneous, and potential texture of sensibility that recalls William James's conception of sensational immediacy as "everything . . . all at once whatever different things it is at once at all."[23] This texture of sensibility comprises nonperceptual sensibility understood as an alternate, radicalized development of Whitehead's reform of perception. Unlike Whitehead's nonsensuous perception, nonperceptual sensibility refers sensation not exclusively to the operation of human sense perception but rather to a worldly sensibility that comes before any such delimited, integrated operation. It is a sensibility that is potential in the sense that it characterizes the relationality—what we might call the "total prehensiveness"—operative at any given moment of the world's continuous self-actualization; only subsequently, and at higher orders of complexity, does it go on to inform concrete sensory events.

Insofar as it extends Whitehead's reform of perception by uncovering its neutral (nonanthropocentric) basis in worldly sensibility, nonperceptual sensibility advances Whitehead's aim of purging philosophy of its "own initial excess of subjectivity."[24] More specifically it builds upon and in a sense culminates the radicalization of Whitehead's revision of subjectivity as a form of non subject-centered superjectivity. As Judith Jones argues in her book *Intensity*, the orthodox account of Whitehead's ontology has tended to trivialize the role of already established entities as purely inert or passive data awaiting some future interaction or concrescence in order to be revivified. This division of the world into "actualities-in-attainment" and "attained actualities," Jones argues, belies a more fundamental operation—contrast—that generates intensity as a nonsubstantial, "asubjective" power. On Jones's account, intensity is more primordial than the division of the subject (formed entities) and superject (entities in formation). As such, intensity designates a source for subjectivity that inheres in the potentiality of the settled world rather than in the subjective aim animating any particular concrescence. As she puts it, "The agency of contrast is the subject, the subject is the agency of contrast. To be a subject is to be a provoked instance of the agency of contrast and that is all it is."[25]

What Jones is seeking to theorize here is a form of subjectivity that is not dependent on or restricted to subjective unification or synthesis but that stems directly from the causal power of the settled world—what Whitehead calls "real potentiality."[26] In my terminology, it would be a non subject-centered form of subjectivity that is inherent in worldly sensibility. This is why I would view nonperceptual sensibility as the culmination of Jones's radicalization of Whitehead's category of subjective intensity: nonperceptual sensibility designates a primitive level of sensibility that is "objective" because it belongs to the relationality of the settled world and that, for this same reason, precedes any and all sensory experience that remains polarized in relation to a unified subjective process.

Insofar as it designates just such a primitive and "objective" level of sensation, nonperceptual sensibility generalizes the insight of nineteenth-century psychophysics in a way that addresses the challenges posed by twenty-first-century media. Specifically, nonperceptual sensibility furnishes the means to address media at a preperceptual and nonanthropocentric level—at a level where media might be said to impact worldly sensibility directly, without being channeled through any delimited subjective unification. Access to nonperceptual sensibility, like access to the objective sensations targeted by psychophysics, remains dependent on experimental procedures—cyborg assemblages—whose operationality exceeds the bounds of human perceptual faculties. What these procedures or assemblages render manifest—or perceptible—is the fact of media's "always-already-having-acted-ness," for if media impacts experience first and foremost through its direct modulation of worldly sensibility, its impact will have been felt long before it is translated, via the operation of feed-forward, into the domain of perception.[27]

Worldly Sensibility and World Appearance

As an alternative to Whitehead's overtly Platonizing account of eternal objects, worldly sensibility not only avoids privileging the restricted process of concrescence but manages to integrate the process as one element in a broader and continuous intensification of the settled world's potentiality. In this picture, far from forming a separate process primarily responsible for the universe's creativity, concrescence assumes a more modest role as part of a larger operation of ongoing sensibility that is only *as a whole* generative of creativity.

Rethought in this way, what Whitehead's speculative empiricism brings to the table is an account of subjectivity—and thus a source of worldly self-sensing, of generalized sensibility—that does not have to be possessed by a subject separate from or transcendent to the world. Indeed by excavating how worldly sensibility continuously gives rise to novelty, and thereby to its own renewal, Whitehead's account of process opens up a source for subjectivity that would no longer need to be a function of a narrow subjective unification. That is why Whitehead is able—at least on the reading I propose—to encompass subjective unification within a broader model of process. From my angle, the crucial element of his account is its capacity to explain how actualities-in-attainment are catalyzed by the real potentiality of attained actualities (or superjects) and then add themselves to this potentiality in an unending cosmic dance.

Conceptualized in relation to Whitehead's larger account of process, where both concrescences and superjects wield subjective power, Merleau-Ponty's account of reversibility between sensing and the sensible furnishes a concept of subjectivity without subject. Specifically, reversibility accords subjectivity—the power of sensing—to every entity in the world. Merleau-Ponty's reversibility thus frees up superjectal subjectivity to become the power of worldly sensibility. On his account, not only would every actual occasion become "on the basis of its sensibility to its past actual world that it incorporates within it,"[28] but it would become *because of the power of the sensibility of all past actualities now operating as superjects and acting, as it were, within it*. In a more general understanding, this means that the power of superjectal subjectivity is autonomous from and broader than its operation within concrescence. It designates nothing less than the capacity for the world to sense itself, to be the primordial sensibility from which all else springs.

In preserving the distance between sensing and sensed, Merleau-Ponty's conception of the *écart* parallels Whitehead's distinction of concrescence and superject. In both cases, a structure of oscillation or reversibility is crucial for the power of sensibility. And in both cases, what fills in the space of the écart is temporalization, conceptualized not as a product of constitution (as on Husserl's account of time-consciousness) but as a power of worldly metamorphosis. Rather than requiring some transcendence of a subject over the world, the temporalization that informs this reversibility is a worldly temporalization: the power of worldly sensibility to act through its own agency and to enhance its own potentiality. Conceptualized in this way, temporalization shares much with Fink's de-presencing (Entgegenwärtigung), which I have elsewhere positioned as a worldly temporalization underlying and giving rise to the retentions and protentions that structure phenomenal experience.[29] Yet Merleau-Ponty's perspective adds a much needed concreteness to this crucial concept. As the operation through which worldly sensibility self-proliferates, reversibility encompasses a plethora of degrees of sensitivity that inform subjective processes of vastly differing force.

As a specification of superjectal subjectivity, reversibility thus opens onto a sensibility that is informed by the causal efficacy of the world itself in all its variety. Reversibility can accordingly be understood as the general texture of worldly sensibility. It characterizes the human relation with the flesh of the world *in the same way* as it does any other relation: as concrete productions of worldly temporalization, of sensibility's self-proliferation. For that reason, and notwithstanding its special status, the human bodymind with its distinct perceptual capacities is rooted in worldly sensibility just as much as is every other entity in the universe. If the human bodymind has unique capacities to perceive the "withness of the body," which is to say the causal efficacy underlying presentational immediacy, these capacities are themselves rooted in a further reversibility involving a broader scope of causal efficacy. Encompassing all of the vectors of causal efficacy that inform the entire arc of experience culminating in such "withness," this broader scope of causal efficacy is precisely what composes the materiality of worldly sensibility. Precisely to the extent that it exceeds the grasp of the body's withness and that it moves transversally across a plethora of divergent levels of operationality, this expanded causal efficacy becomes accessible only with the aid of digital devices and other twenty-first-century media technologies.

With this observation, we can bring together two crucial components of the foregoing analysis: the "objectivity" of sensation central to the psychophysical tradition and the capacity for "subjectivity" central to the phenomenological tradition. In the concept of nonperceptual sensation that I have sought to develop on the basis of Whitehead's philosophy as well as in the concept of worldly sensibility that emerges from a radicalization of Merleau-Ponty's effort to develop a monism of the flesh, we find the resources necessary to treat sensations as elements of the world, even when they are experienced (or "lived") by perceivers (or consciousnesses). To do so, we must generalize subjectivity to any entity that is capable of reversibility, that is produced from other-sensibility, and that generates further worldly sensibility on the basis of its own operation.

It is just this combination that will allow us to fathom how the proliferation of objective sensation accompanying the advent of mobile media and ubiquitous computing comprises both an intensification of our properly human sensibility and an expansion of the domain of worldly sensibility from which it arises. With the unprecedented capacities of our digital devices and sensors to gather information about behavior and about the environment, we possess new artifactual "organs" for excavating the extraperceptual dimensions of experience, our own as well as that of other entities. In order to tap the potential of these new organs for impacting the way we experience and the way we theorize our experience, we must begin by making sensation and sensibility once again central. For it is only on the basis of and through our primitive and preperceptual sensory contact with the world—a contact that is necessarily mediated by twenty-first-century media—that the world can appear to us. Far from being a product of some minimal transcendental distance, the world's appearance is the strict correlate of our immanence within its sensible texture. With Merleau-Ponty, we can thus affirm that "sensibility only makes the world appear because it is already on the side of the world."[30]

Notes

1. Henning Schmidgen, lecture at the Mellon Sawyer Seminar on Phenomenology between Minds and Media, Duke University, 19 May 2012; see Schmidgen, "The Donders Machine: Matter, Signs, and Time in a Physiological Experiment, ca. 1865," *Configurations* 13 (2005): 211–56.

2. Behind Fechner's focused targeting of the minimum unit of sensation stands his bluntly panpsychic vision of the universe as a "superhuman consciousness" (to cite the words of his admirer, and Whitehead's precursor, William James). In works such as *Nanna, or on the Soul-Life of Plants* and *On the Soul-Question*, Fechner develops a conception of the world as composed of a hierarchy of minds, ranging from lesser minds (plants) to greater (superhuman or collective) minds. Fechner's conception is rooted in a concept of continuity that informs his work on plants—regarding plants, he writes, "There are as many individuals as there are leaves on the tree, nay, there are in fact as many as there are cells"—just as much as it does his vision of Earth as an "angel" that supports all life" (quoted in Skrbina, *Panpsychism and the West*, 124–25). For an argument that Fechner's experimental work should be viewed through his metaphysical panpsychist vision, see Michael Heidelberger, *Nature from Within: Gustav Theodor Fechner and His Psychophysical Worldview*, translated by C. Klohr (Pittsburgh: University of Pittsburgh Press, 2004), part 3.

3. Elsewhere I have developed this experimental capacity in terms of the technical distribution of experience and have argued specifically that contemporary biometric

and environmental sensors—to the extent they furnish data of sensibility that "artifactually" presentify the causal basis of experience—comprise a promising surrogate for what Whitehead terms "symbolic reference," the distinctly human capacity for synthesizing sense perception with its causal basis. See Mark B. N. Hansen, "Medien des 21. Jahrhunderts, technisches Empfinden und unsere originäre Umweltbedingung," in *Die technologische Bedingung: Beiträge zur Beschreibung der technischen Welt*, edited by E. Hörl (Berlin: Suhrkamp, 2011), 364–408. I address these questions at length in my forthcoming book on Whitehead and media, *Feed Forward: The Future of 21st Century Media* (Chicago: University of Chicago Press, 2015). In this respect, the forms of passive sensing that surround us today are simply descendents, albeit vastly more complex ones, from the experimental set-ups that produced the psychophysical breakthrough.

4. Fechner, *Elements of Psychophysics*, 48.

5. In formulating this law Fechner performs a formalization of Weber's empirical demonstration that a difference between two stimuli is always perceived as equal—produces the same increment of sensation—if its ratio to the stimuli remains the same, regardless of how the absolute size changes. Fechner sought to articulate a general measure for sensibility, rooted in the technique of determining quanta of sensation via the discernment of "just noticeable differences" in magnitudes of stimuli. "In principle," he explains, "our measure of sensation will consist of dividing every sensation into equal divisions (that is, equal increments), which serve to build it up from zero. The number of equal divisions we conceive as determined, like inches on a yardstick, by the number of corresponding variable stimulus increments that are capable of bringing about identical sensation increments" (Fechner, *Elements of Psychophysics*, 48).

6. In his own appropriation of Fechner's notion of "superhuman consciousness," William James captures the unifying vision behind the psychophysical project. For James, as for Fechner, this universal consciousness must be understood not as a single, neo-Spinozist substance but as the pinnacle of the host of overlapping yet differentiated levels of mind inhabiting the universe. Writing in *A Pluralist Universe*, his assault on the resurgent motif of the "absolute" in philosophy, James summarizes his interest in Fechner by pinpointing both the autonomy of every level of being and their compounding in ever more complex individuals up to the most complex of all, universal consciousness:

> Abstractly set down, [Fechner's] most important conclusion for my purpose in these lectures is that the constitution of the world is identical throughout. In ourselves, visual consciousness goes with our eyes, tactile consciousness with our skin. But although neither skin nor eye knows aught of the sensations of the other, they come together and figure in some sort of relation and combination in the more inclusive consciousness which each of us names his *self*. Quite similarly, then, says Fechner, we must suppose that my consciousness of myself and yours of yourself, although in their immediacy they keep separate and know nothing of each other, are yet known and used together in a higher consciousness, that of the human race, say, into which they enter as constituent parts. Similarly, the whole human and animal kingdoms come together as

> conditions of a consciousness of still wider scope. This combines in the soul of the earth with the consciousness of the vegetable kingdom, which in turn contributes its share of experience to that of the whole solar system, and so on from synthesis to synthesis and height to height, till an absolutely universal consciousness is reached. (William James, A Pluralistic Universe [Lincoln: University of Nebraska Press, 1996], 155–56)

7. Ernst Mach, cited in Skrbina, Panpsychism and the West, 130.

8. Skrbina, Panpsychism and the West, 130.

9. Hamilton, "Ernst Mach and the Elimination of Subjectivity," 117–18.

10. Russell, "The Ultimate Constituents of Matter," 225.

11. Bertrand Russell, The Analysis of Mind, cited in Skrbina, Panpsychism and the West, 178.

12. Mach, cited in Xavier Verley, "Ernst Mach, un physicien philosophe," in Chromaticon II: Annuaire de la philosophie en procès, edited by M. Weber and P. Basile (Louvain, Belgium: Presses universitaires de Louvain, 2006), 113.

13. This philosophical perspective on the psychophysical project allows us to appreciate the significance of the sensory richness of the mind as it was enumerated by Fechner's followers. Thought in relation to Mach's claim about the nontrivial and nonsubstitutable work performed by calculations and technical set-ups, what might appear to be crassly empirical experimentations (e.g., Külpe and Tichener's enumeration of 44,435 discrete sensations) take on a profound significance. Specifically they illustrate the microphysical, subphenomenal scale of experimentally localized sensations: the majority of these 44,435 separate sensory elements are experienced, if they can be said to be experienced at all, at levels well below the thresholds of human perceptual experience and phenomenological integration.

14. Shaviro, Without Criteria, ix.

15. In this context, it is not incidental that Heidegger's target, in his discussion of hearing and hearkening in Being and Time, was the psychophysical approach to the perception of sound:

> It is on the basis of this potentiality for hearing, which is existentially primary, that anything like hearkening [Horchen] becomes possible. Hearkening is phenomenally still more primordial than what is defined "in the first instance" as "hearing" in psychology—the sensing of tones and the perception of sounds. Hearkening too has the kind of Being of the hearing which understands. What we "first" hear is never noises or complexes of sounds, but the creaking waggon, the motor-cycle. We hear the column on the march, the north wind, the woodpecker tapping, the fire crackling. It requires a very artificial and complicated frame of mind to "hear" a "pure noise." The fact that motor-cycles and waggons are what we proximally hear is the phenomenal evidence that in every case Dasein, as Being-in-the-world, already dwells alongside what is ready-to-hand within-the-world; it certainly does not dwell proximally alongside "sensations"; nor would it first have to give shape to the swirl of sensations to provide the springboard from which the subject leaps off and finally arrives at a "world." Dasein, as essentially understanding, is proximally alongside what is understood. (Being and Time, 207)

16. Shaviro enumerates eight questions: of beginnings; of the history of philosophy; of metaphysics; of language; of style; of technology; of representation; and of subjectivity. See Shaviro, *Without Criteria*, ix–xiii.

17. As I characterize it in my forthcoming book, *Feed Forward: The Future of 21st Century Media*, chapter 1, this compensation is "pharmacological" in the sense that it increases our embodied contact with worldly sensibility at the very moment of diminishing our direct perceptual access to it.

18. See Fink, "Vergegenwärtigung und Bild." *Studien zur Phänomenologie, 1930–1939* (The Hague: Nijoff, 1966).

19. See Merleau-Ponty, *The Visible and the Invisible* (Evanston: Northwestern University Press, 1970).

20. I borrow the term *asubjective* from the Czech phenomenologist Jan Patocka, who develops an "asubjective phenomenology of manifestation" that jettisons Husserl's egological phenomenology of constitution in favor of an account of worldly manifestation. On this account, the world manifests itself to beings capable of receiving its manifestations, and when it does so, it is not providing a partial and "unfulfilled" aspect of an object but the object itself in its mode of manifestation, which is to say in its Being. See Patocka, *Qu'est-ce que la Phenomenologie* (Paris: Jérôme Millon, 2002).

21. *Adventures of Ideas* (New York: The Free Press, 1967, originally published 1933), 180–181.

22. In *Process and Reality*, Whitehead writes that "the vector character . . . transfers the cause into the effect. It is a *feeling from* the cause which acquires the subjectivity of the new effect without loss of its original subjectivity in the cause" (237–38). This combination of novel subjectivity and preservation of background is exemplified in the "passage from lower to higher grades of actual occasions": "The transmitted datum acquires sensa enhanced in relevance or even changed in character by the passage from the low-grade external world into the intimacy of the human body. The datum transmitted from the stone becomes the touch-feeling in the hand, but *it preserves the vector character of its origin* from the stone. The touch-feeling in the hand with this vector origin from the stone is transmitted to the percipient in the brain. Thus the final perception is the perception of the stone through the touch in the hand. In this perception the stone is vague and faintly relevant in comparison with the hand. But, however dim, it is there" (119–20, emphasis added).

23. William James, *A Pluralistic Universe* (Rockville, Md.: Arc Manor, 2008), 110.

24. "Philosophy is the self-correction by consciousness of its own initial excess of subjectivity. Each actual occasion contributes to the circumstances of its origin additional formative elements deepening its own peculiar individuality. Consciousness is only the last and greatest of such elements by which the selective character of the individual obscures the external totality from which it originates and which it embodies. An actual individual, of such higher grade, has truck with the totality of things by reason of its sheer actuality; but it has attained its individual depth of being by a selective emphasis limited to its own purposes. The task of philosophy is to recover the totality obscured by selection" (Whitehead, *Process and Reality*, 15).

25. Jones, *Intensity*, 130.

26. That is why she can argue that "the analysis of causal interaction is primarily concerned with intensity and only secondarily with other formal considerations as to the entity as subject-superject" (Jones, *Intensity*, 21).

27. In his deployment of Whitehead's ontology to develop a "nonanthropocentric" account of media, the sound theorist Steve Goodman concurs with this analysis insofar as he situates media at the level of what Whitehead, in an effort to theorize the fundamental solidarity of the universe, calls the "vibratory continuum"; this move wrests media from its capture by human modes of experience and embeds it in the operation of worldly sensibility: "If we subtract human perception," Goodman claims, "everything moves. Anything static is so only at the level of perceptibility. At the molecular or quantum level, everything is in motion, is vibrating. . . . All entities are potential media that can feel or whose vibrations can be felt by other entities" (*Sonic Warfare*, 83). At this level of primordial vibrations, media directly mediate sensibility understood as the "objective" element of the world's continuous reproduction independently of and prior to its solidification into higher-order subjective processes. Accordingly it is only subsequent to this initial modulation of the sensory confound that media can be said to influence sensations proper.

28. Hamrick and van der Veken, *Nature and Logos*, 217.

29. See Mark B. N. Hansen, "Ubiquitous Sensation: Toward an Atmospheric, Collective, and Microtemporal Model of Media," in *Throughout: Art and Culture Emerging with Ubiquitous Computing*, edited by U. Ekman (Cambridge, Mass.: MIT Press, 2012), 63–88.

30. In Renaud Barbaras's paraphrase in "Les Trois Sens de la Chair," 21.

chapter 12

Reading the Social:
Erving Goffman and Sexuality Studies

Heather Love

In his reflection on the genealogy and impact of Gayle Rubin's 1984 essay "Thinking Sex," Steven Epstein argues that the essay was "anointed as a classic because of how it took the insights of empirical studies of sexuality—particularly, historically informed ethnography—and drew out their intellectual and political implications in a way that facilitated an astonishingly interdisciplinary engagement."[1] Rubin's essay is grounded in empirical studies of sexuality, particularly in the postwar field of deviance studies and in the interactionist tradition exemplified by John Gagnon and William Simon. The influence of the deviance paradigm in particular is legible in the aspect of the essay that has been most influential in queer studies: Rubin's formulation of a "radical politics of sexuality" that focuses on the shared condition of sexual stigma.[2] Rubin's attention to the practices and experience of miscellaneous sexual subcultures recalls the urban ecology of Chicago school sociologists and of social problem research more broadly. In her graphic representation of the sex hierarchy as a "charmed circle" representing "Good, Normal, Natural, Blessed Sexuality" surrounded by the "outer limits" of "Bad, Abnormal, Unnatural, Damned Sexuality," Rubin fuses an empirical approach borrowed from deviance studies with a now more familiar theory of social marginality, derived from the work of Foucault (and in turn from his teacher Georges Canguilhem's scholarship on the history of the "normal and the pathological"), which focuses on the immanence of power and its relation to processes of subjectification. According to Epstein, Rubin's fusing of these two traditions is responsible for the near hegemony in queer studies of a model of politics that is based on a coalition of nonnormative and stigmatized subjects: the revenge of those occupying the outer limits on those soaking up material and cultural resources inside the charmed circle.

By emphasizing Rubin's inheritance of these social science traditions, Epstein points to aspects of "Thinking Sex" that tend to get passed over by queer scholars in the humanities: a focus on particular communities; the role of urban space in the organization of sexual life; institutions; social mechanisms of stigmatization; and attention to social practice and ritual. Epstein's emphasis on Rubin's empirical approach fits within a tradition of social science critiques of contemporary queer studies for overemphasizing discourse and representation at the expense of practices, material conditions, and institutions. A truly miscellaneous collection of theorists, cultural critics, poets, novelists, psychoanalysts, and activists have been claimed as precursors for queer studies, from Frantz Fanon to Adrienne Rich, from Monique Wittig to Guy Hoquenghem, from Audre Lorde to Jacques Lacan, from Jean Genet to Cherríe Moraga, from Radclyffe Hall to Gilles Deleuze, from Melanie Klein to Emanuel Levinas, from Simone de Beauvoir to Oscar Wilde, from Gloria Anzaldúa to Harry Hay. Despite the expansiveness of this genealogy, and ongoing growth and transformation in the field, the pioneering work of postwar historians, anthropologists, and sociologists such as Simon and Gagnon, Mary McIntosh, Kenneth Plummer, Jeffrey Weeks, and Jeffrey Escoffier has still received inadequate attention in accounts of the origins of the field. Queer theory is, in Sharon Marcus's words, for everyone[3]—but since the dominant, humanistic branch of the field has defined itself in opposition to empiricism and objectivity, the contributions of empirical research on sexuality to the founding of queer studies continue to be overlooked.

Rubin has pointed repeatedly to the intellectual and political costs of this omission.[4] Among those contemporary scholars—most of them in the social sciences—who do acknowledge the significance of postwar historical, sociological, and anthropological research on sexuality, they credit this work with several key paradigm shifts: the move from seeing sexuality within a pathological, medical, and individual model to seeing it as collective and social; the recognition of variety in the social organization of sexuality, which resulted in a "moral leveling" that emphasized the existence rather than the judgment or reform of practices; drawing a link between sexual stigma and other forms of social stratification; and generating the earliest theories of the social construction of sexuality. Perhaps most important, these scholars suggest that the social world itself is neglected in queer humanities scholarship. In a controversial article Escoffier writes, "Queer theory . . . focuses too exclusively on the discursive aspects of knowledge or power and not enough on political and economic domination or the historical-social structures of repression. Ironically, our age demonstrates an awe-inspiring sophistication about cultural representations but is otherwise marked by a grave underestimation—perhaps even ignorance—of the social."[5] Escoffier originally wrote these words in 1990 in OUT/LOOK, during the year that we now associate with the birth of queer theory. More than thirty years later one might still point to the preponderance of cultural analysis in queer studies, although there are arguably more job and research opportunities for social scientists in sexuality studies now than before. While acknowledging the ongoing significance of Escoffier's critique, Rubin's work makes clear that the humanities and social science approaches are not opposed to each other or even distinguishable from each other in all cases.

The merger in "Thinking Sex" of the deviance studies tradition with Foucauldian discourse analysis points us back to a moment in the early 1960s when these two traditions converge: in the antipsychiatry movement, in the critique of institutions, and in attention to the construction and experience of deviance.[6] With its focus on the variegated and potentially universal category of the social outsider or underdog, research in deviance studies gives us a model of social exclusion that resurfaces in key moments in the history of sexuality studies. This model of shared marginality and collective stigma appears in the urban ecology of Chicago school sociologists and of social problem research more broadly; it is explicitly invoked in postwar social science collections like *Sexual Deviance* (1968) by Gagnon and Simon; it underwrites Rubin's development of a protoqueer model of collectivity in "Thinking Sex"; Michael Warner's attempt to fuse an emergent queer studies with social science research in his important collection *Fear of a Queer Planet* posits a community of deviants in revolt against the "regimes of the normal";[7] and it informs Cathy J. Cohen's 1997 critique of the false universalism of queer studies. Cohen calls for a renewal of queer politics that makes good on its promise of nonidentitarian antinormativity and that focuses on how power structures the sexual field; this essay, entitled "Punks, Bulldaggers, and Welfare Queens," might be understood as a call for queer studies to return to its roots in deviance studies.[8]

Deviance studies and social problem research attended not to major axes of identity (race, class, and gender) but to the fate and stratagems of particular, marked figures—figures like the marijuana user, the stutterer, the jazz musician, the juvenile delinquent, and the former mental patient—or, in Cohen's terms, "punks, bulldaggers, and welfare queens." Thinking through queer studies as the long history of deviance studies can help to reframe the contributions of Foucault, allowing us to see his work in the context of the postwar antipsychiatry movement and the critique of institutions; it can also help us make new sense of his focus on highly particular figures such as the masturbating child, the hysterical woman, the pervert, and the Malthusian couple. Stigma and deviance may indeed seem like outmoded concepts in the contemporary moment of, on the one hand, widespread but uneven gay assimilation and acceptance and, on the other hand, sweeping critiques by queer scholars of homonormativity. By focusing on the microdynamics of social marginalization, it is possible to be more specific about the processes of normalization that shape contemporary gay and lesbian life. In queer polemics about assimilation, we tend to forget the ongoing stigmatization of gender and sexual outsiders. Deviance studies' focus on highly particular figures can help us to make sense of this uneven landscape and to revitalize models of collectivity based on shared marginality—the original promise of queer.

This essay attempts to open the contemporary field of queer studies to a longer tradition of deviance studies and empirical social science more broadly. The divide between the humanities and the social sciences has not always been as strong as it now is. The meteoric rise of queer theory in the early 1990s suggests a stark opposition between a glamorous, elite, and institutionally powerful queer studies and a populist, grounded, and noninstitutional social scientific form of sexuality studies. But these forms of scholarship, institutional locations, and professional, social, and activist networks have also been overlapping. My goal is to make visible one such area of overlap by looking at the influence of the postwar sociologist Erving Goffman on the field of sexuality studies. Goffman may seem an unlikely choice as a precursor for sexuality studies (his work on gender identity and performance is better known); however, he has exerted a powerful if often unremarked influence on the field. Goffman wrote only occasionally about sexuality; he treated nonnormative sexuality as merely one example of the kinds of disadvantaged traits that are stigmatized; and with his notorious stance of detachment, his reflections on the reproduction of social life and social hierarchy are out of synch with the radical politics of most contemporary work in the field. Still, his links to sexuality studies can be identified in his key interests—stigma, institutions, performance, agency, and power—and in his influence on foundational texts in the field such as Esther Newton's *Mother Camp* and Laud Humphrey's *Tearoom Trade*. Goffman's account of the presentation of self and of the social determinants of selfhood also resonates with later, foundational texts like Judith Butler's *Gender Trouble*. In addition, Goffman's own late work on gender—discussed much more rarely than his early scholarship—is corrosive to the notion of human sovereignty; it resonates with anti-identitarian, posthuman, and object-oriented queer and transgender scholarship of the past decade.[9]

Goffman frustrates any clear distinction between a "hard" empiricism and a self-enclosed textuality. His reading practice cuts across the division between the social sciences and the humanities; while its ultimate aim is the description of the social world, it can hardly be called empiricist in any traditional sense. Trained at Chicago, Goffman took an early detour from traditional social scientific method. His dissertation, planned as an ethnography of rural Shetland Islanders, got sidetracked as he began hanging around the hotel observing the workplace relations in the restaurant. (His wry analyses of these interactions formed the basis for his work in *The Presentation of Self in Everyday Life*.) Throughout his career Goffman combined such observations of everyday life—the bread and butter of postwar microsociology—with "research" drawn from a fictional and literary archive. In formulating his account of the social interaction, Goffman drew on a remarkably miscellaneous collection of source materials, including novels, memoirs, biographies, case histories, newspaper clippings, and fabricated anecdotes. While this practice has undermined his authority for many sociologists, it has not yet made him a hero for literary scholars, since he does not respect the literary qualities of texts but instead mines them for insights into the dynamics of human interaction. Goffman ignores the distinction between text and world, enlisting literature as well as other narrative and fictional forms in the service of describing social dynamics and their reinscription of hierarchy. He attends to the microdynamics of scenes, whatever their provenance; he analyzes scenes from "real life" with the slow, careful attention of a close reader; and he reads literature for its representation of social dynamics and hierarchies, without attending to many of the formal and ideological questions native to literary studies. In this sense he provides an example for critics today in search of a method that is empirical without being positivist, attentive to questions of mediation without losing track of the world, self-reflexive without turning in on itself entirely.[10]

Furthermore I want to suggest that Goffman offers a methodological model that is useful for queer studies because of its refusal to speculate about the psychological roots of human behavior. With little time for motivation or the unconscious, Goffman analyzes visible behavior, treating social interaction as a set of moves in a game.[11] His emphasis on visible behavior is characteristic of postwar microsociology, a field that he helped to found. Microanalytic researchers in the postwar period were influenced by behaviorism, but they refused the laboratory model and positivism, drawing instead on European traditions of naturalistic observation in the field.[12] Their methods included a painstaking observation of visible behavior; an ecological approach that focuses on situations and scenes, not individual actors and their motives; an account of behavior, pattern, and scene rather than individuality, subjectivity, or motivation; a focus on description rather than judgment or prescription. Goffman combined this ethological approach with that of deviance studies, characterized by its attention to the effects of social positioning and to the fate of particular social outsiders. Through this combination of microanalysis and deviance studies, Goffman offers a highly specific account of dynamics of hierarchy and exclusion, and he "thins out" this account through his rigorous avoidance of psychological profiling.

I return to Goffman and trace his underacknowledged influence on sexuality studies in order to challenge the impasse between a primarily textual queer studies and the social science tradition in sexuality studies. Goffman's way of reading the social world makes visible historic and conceptual links between the humanities and social sciences that have been obscured by the institutional formation of queer studies. Placing his work in the frame of postwar microsociology and interaction studies suggests the way that research in that field resonates with the antipsychology of contemporary queer studies. I begin by considering the refusal of Goffman's influence in Butler's early work on gender performativity; I then turn to consider an instance of Goffman's engagement with deviance studies in his 1963 book, Stigma: On the Management of Spoiled Identity; finally, I consider the explicit claiming of Goffman as a precursor in the foundational (but hardly canonical) work of Laud Humphreys. Throughout I suggest that Goffman's minimalist view of the subject can make the resources of deviance studies newly available for queer analysis.

....

The fact that Goffman's influence on sexuality studies has rarely been discussed can be understood as a sign of the amnesia about the social science roots of the field.[13] One key site for this erasure is in the lack of attention to Goffman's account of the presentation of self in Butler's account of gender performativity.[14] Butler addresses that legacy to a limited extent in an article that was later revised and incorporated into Gender Trouble, "Performative Acts and Gender Constitution: An Essay in Phenomenology and Feminist Theory" (1988). Published in Theater Journal, this essay engages traditions of performance from theater studies and the social sciences, fields that Butler increasingly downplayed as she developed a discursive theory of performativity. The essay is multidisciplinary in its approach to gender, drawing on, as Butler writes, "theatrical, anthropological, and philosophical discourses, but mainly phenomenology."[15] Butler's explicit aim in the piece is to differentiate her account of gender performativity from related accounts developed in these disciplines, particularly the phenomenological doctrine of constitution and anthropological notions of ritual and performance in everyday life. Despite the critical and distancing focus of the essay, Butler deploys metaphors of theatricality much more freely than elsewhere in her work, as in the following gloss on the concept of an act: "The act that one does, the act that one performs, is, in a sense, an act that has been going on before one arrived on the scene. Hence, gender is an act which has been rehearsed, much as a script survives the particular actors who make use of it, but which requires individual actors in order to be actualized and reproduced as reality once again."[16]

Butler's discussion of Goffman is confined to a single reference. Goffman is held up as a representative of the pitfalls of the concept of theatricality and the expressive account of gender that follows from it. Butler argues that gender should not be "understood as a *role* which either expresses or disguises an interior 'self'"; instead gender "constructs the social fiction of its own psychological interiority."[17] *The Presentation of Self in Everyday Life* is adduced as an example of such a limited and limiting account of theatricality. According to Butler's reading, Goffman's account of social life depends on a stable, interior self that acts in and on the world; such a view underestimates the power of norms, particularly of linguistic norms, and aggrandizes individual agency. Butler writes, "As opposed to a view such as Erving Goffman's which posits a self which assumes and exchanges various 'roles' within the complex social expectations of the 'game' of modern life, I am suggesting that this self is not only irretrievably 'outside,' constituted in social discourse, but that the ascription of interiority is itself a publically regulated and sanctioned form of essence fabrication." Butler argues that Goffman assumes a preexisting gendered self that takes up and discards social roles at will; at the same time, by subscribing, through this notion of the self, to the stabilization of gender, Goffman implicitly participates in "a social policy of gender regulation and control."[18] By missing the radical potential of gender performativity as distinguished from the performance of gender, Goffman contributes to the perpetuation of the status quo.[19]

While reiterating a long-standing critique of the conservatism of Goffman's steely-eyed view of the stability of the social order, Butler at the same time seriously underestimates the complexity of Goffman's account of individual agency. His view of the self is far from being substantial in this sense but is rather thoroughly constituted in and by social interaction. The evisceration of the self as an expressive or authentic core is not only a repeated argument in Goffman's writing. It also formed the basis for an important feature of his methodology, as he makes clear in the introduction to the 1967 collection *Interaction Ritual*:

> I assume the proper study of interaction is not the individual and his psychology, but rather the syntactical relations among the acts of different persons mutually present to one another. None the less, since it is individual actors who contribute the ultimate materials, it will always be reasonable to ask what general properties they must have if this sort of contribution is to be expected of them. What minimal model of the actor is needed if we are to wind him up, stick him in amongst his fellows, and have an orderly traffic in behavior emerge? What minimal model is required if the student is to anticipate the lines along which an individual, qua interactant, can be effective or break down? That is what these papers are about. A psychology is necessarily involved, but one stripped and cramped to suit the sociological study of conversation, track meets, banquets, jury trials, and street loitering.
>
> Not, then, men and their moments. Rather moments and their men.[20]

Goffman, far from "ascribing interiority," as Butler argues, summarily distances psychological accounts of the subject; while he does see individuals as implicated in social games, by prioritizing the rules of those games ("syntactical relations") rather than the desires of those who play them, he undermines rather than amplifies individual agency. Goffman strikes a note of resignation as he explains that since actors "contribute materials" to social situations, some minimal notion of the self is needed in order to account for interactions. The "self," for Goffman, is a methodological necessity, more like a game piece, counter, or stick figure than a fleshed-out psychological self. By identifying the goal of such specification as an "orderly traffic in behavior," he makes clear that one of the key social frames for the behavior of these actors is the context of his own interpretive study of them. This extreme self-reflexivity, as well as a willingness to "strike the set" and dispense with any interpretive frame, runs throughout Goffman's work.[21]

The key elements of Butler's theory—her suggestion that selves are radically ungrounded and thoroughly constituted by social norms; that identity is "constituted in time"; her entire account of "the mundane way in which bodily gestures, movements, and enactments of various kinds constitute the illusion of an abiding gendered self"[22]—are suggested strongly both in Goffman's account of self and role and in his specific reflections on gender. His work on the "presentation of self" as well as his discussion, late in his career, of the social reproduction of gender inequality focus on the way that identity is constituted in time, through the repetition of gestures and social acts, and on the mundane social performances that make cultural gender roles appear as essence. Furthermore Goffman offers an ecological view of the self that places it in dynamic context, understanding individual behavior to be situated not only in time but also in space. And his attention to concrete social interaction and to particular social spaces does not preclude attention to language and textuality, as is suggested by his reference to the syntax of social interaction as well as the extreme reflexivity of his account of individual agency ("if we are to wind him up . . ."). On the one hand, then, Butler's dismissal of Goffman might be seen as a predictable moment of strategic misreading. On the other hand, it is significant because it constitutes a missed connection between a socially grounded account of performance and a linguistically oriented account of performativity.

Although any mention of Goffman drops out in the revisions for *Gender Trouble*, what does survive is a discussion of Esther Newton's *Mother Camp*. Newton's drag ethnography drew heavily on Goffman's understanding of stigma, of front stage and back stage, and on the performance of social roles. The topic of Newton's ethnography as well as its political stance against compulsory gendering make it a more obviously salient example for Butler. However, Goffman's crucial methodological influence in *Mother Camp*—legible in the account of gender as determined by social location—is missing. While drag is an important topic, Goffman's ecological treatment of this material drops out of Butler's discussion, and out of the mainstream of queer studies.

The complex relations between the self, agency, and the influence of the social world play out in Goffman's discussion of gender: not women and their moments but moments and their women. In his late book *Gender Advertisements* (1979) and in the essay "The Arrangement between the Sexes" (1977), he considers the question of institutional reflexivity, which is the term he uses to explain how "irrelevant biological differences" between the sexes are "elaborated socially."[23] This attack on the naturalness of expression does not depend on a straightforward linear account of the social construction of gender; instead he emphasizes the way that social and cultural norms retroactively produce the illusion of natural sexual difference. Considering the case of the "cultural matter" of "toilet segregation" in the 1977 essay, Goffman argues that this practice is "presented as a natural consequence of the difference between the sex-classes, when in fact it is rather a means of honoring, if not producing, this difference."[24] In *Gender Advertisements*, Goffman launches a broad argument against the "doctrine of natural expression," which underlies not only our understanding of gender but also of "intent, feeling, relationship, information state, health, social class, etc." He writes, "What the human nature of males and females really consists of, then, is a capacity to learn to provide and to read depictions of masculinity and femininity and a willingness to adhere to a schedule for presenting these pictures ... One might just as well say there is no gender identity. There is only a schedule for the portrayal of relationship."[25]

While Butler focuses on the stylized repetition of gendered acts, Goffman, influenced by Durkheim, considers the consolidation of gendered existence a matter of social ritual. This view of ritual action aimed toward the maintenance of social order leads to a view that depends on the performance of roles but does not presuppose, as Butler intimates, an autonomous, willing self. In fact Goffman's account of performance is quite different, as he suggests that institutions entail scenes that command social performance by compulsorily gendered actors. He writes, "Deep-seated institutional practices have the effect of transforming social situations into scenes for the performance of genderisms by both sexes, many of these performances taking a ritual form which affirms beliefs about the differential human nature of the two sexes even while indications are provided as to how behavior between the two can be expected to be intermeshed."[26] Goffman's focus on the centrality of the scene in "the practice between the sexes of choreographing behaviorally a portrait of a relationship" means that he understands sexual difference as unfolding in socially conditioned time and space.[27]

Goffman treats the difference between the sexes as a portable social ritual. In "The Arrangement between the Sexes," he writes:

> Gender, not religion, is the opiate of the masses. In any case, we have here a remarkable organizational device. A man may spend his day suffering under those who have power over him, suffer this situation at almost any level of society, and yet on returning home each night regain a sphere in which he dominates. And wherever he goes beyond the household, women can be there to prop up his show of competence. It is not merely that your male executive has a female secretary, but (as now often remarked) his drop-out son who moves up the hierarchy of alternative pub-

lishing or protest politics will have female help, too; and had he been disaffected enough to join a rural commune, an appropriate division of labor would have awaited him. And should we leave the real world for something set up as its fictional alternative, a science fiction cosmos, we would find that here, too, males engage in the executive action and have females to help out in the manner of their sex. Wherever the male goes, apparently, he can carry a sexual division of labor with him.[28]

Through his account of the reproductive work of social scenes, and his conjuring of several highly particularized examples of such scenes, Goffman explains how the deep force of institutional gender difference ("division of labor") is also a pop-up road show, a spectacle of difference that can be staged anywhere. The particularity of these scenes is important, since each new, apparently improvised scene gives the look and feel of spontaneity and nature to what is a highly ritualized and scripted social performance. Here again Goffman minimizes the difference between social and textual worlds: rather than treating science fiction novels and their fabricated worlds as discourse, he treats them as sites for the production of real social difference.

....

Goffman's blurring of fictional and actual worlds and his focus on particular spaces as the location of difference are crucial in his treatment of social stigma. His work in *Stigma: On the Management of Spoiled Identity* (1963), though particularly attentive to sexuality, situates him as part of an important methodological background for queer studies. The book comes out of a course that Goffman taught at UC-Berkeley. In the spring of 1961 he taught the sociology department's course in deviance studies, and he constructed a course that reflected the dominant understanding of deviance but also pushed back against it. The course drew its examples from urban, aberrant populations familiar from deviance studies: criminals, alcoholics, homosexuals, drug addicts, people with a range of physical and mental disabilities, homeless people, as well as (to a lesser extent) immigrants, people of color, and ethnic minorities. Goffman draws on the image of aberrant populations gathered together in the modern city from traditional studies of deviance; he also disregards collective movements for transforming the conditions of socially oppressed groups, as is clear in his offhand reference to the "well-known" "problems associated with militancy."[29] However, he departs from deviance studies in his account of the contingency of identity, his cunning refusal to credit the ideal of normalcy, and his highly comparative method. At the end of *Stigma*, Goffman argues that stigmatized populations should not be considered separate entities but rather that shared dynamics of stigmatization should be emphasized rather than the problems of distinct populations.[30] Both in its corrosive attitude toward identity and in its insistence on a general category of social marginality, *Stigma* resonates with key concerns of the contemporary field of queer studies.

Goffman's method of comparison is highly abstract in its disregard for the difference between different identity groups, as well as differences of nationality, history, scale, and place; it also does not attend to the differences between fictional and nonfictional accounts and draws on a mostly literary archive. At the same time, it is concrete and specific in its focus on particular social scenes and particular moments of social interaction. Because of his treatment of literary texts as real social material, it is tempting to consider *Stigma* itself as a model for coalitional politics. The outsider narratives gathered in the book's footnotes could be seen as a kind of textual collectivity, where fictional and real social others mix. Several of the sources that Goffman cites also address stigma across a wide range of social locations; many of these sources ask, alongside Goffman, the question of what these situations have in common. There are interwoven stories of friends, coworkers, inmates, acquaintances, and co-conspirators; top-down accounts of patients and prisoners as well as case studies written by deviant subjects themselves. These texts offer unusual models of intimacy between deviants while repeatedly running up against taken-for-granted notions of the power relations that inform genres like the case study or the psychiatric report. All of these texts are informed by the model of deviance studies, which seems a dated framework today. However, while some suppositions of the field have gone by the wayside, its methods are still vital: the focus on concrete interactions in particular contexts; the microanalysis of the multiple forces at play in social scenes; a lack of attention to the psychological sources of social behavior; and their attention to the situated particularity of individual actors rather than to general categories.

Through the extractions he makes from literary and fictional texts, *Stigma* offers a model of coalition that remains relevant today. One of his key sources is *Underdogs: Eighteen Victims of Society*, first published in England in 1961 and reprinted a year later in the United States under the title *Underdogs: Anguish and Anxiety. Eighteen Men and Women Write Their Own Case Histories*. The book itself provides the kind of digest or compilation of outsider experience that structures *Stigma* and suggests a widespread interest in comparing forms of social exclusions in the period. In 1960 Philip Toynbee, then the principal literary reviewer at the *Observer*, placed advertisements in several major newspapers in England in which he asked people to send in their "underdog confessions." In his introduction he describes receiving over five hundred replies in the first two weeks; in the end he selected eighteen underdog stories to publish. The fact that Toynbee was overwhelmed with underdog confessions in response to his appeal might support Foucault's claims about the incitement to discourse and the embrace of confession as a dominant genre of modernity. But the existence of this underdog archive might also lead us to challenge Foucault's understanding of the power dynamics of the clinic and of the case study. Like several of Goffman's sources, *Underdogs* is made up of self-authored case histories. These are capsulations of social suffering, failure, and alienation that are written not by a psychologist, medical doctor, or criminologist but by the subjects themselves. These examples of "own stories" or "case histories written by themselves" frustrate our expectations about the politics of authorship and authority. These instances of self-proclaimed underdogs serving up digest versions of themselves in the genre of social problem literature suggest something other than a simple internalization of oppressive social forces. Instead they indicate the plasticity of the case study form, the felt need to articulate experiences of social suffering, and the significance of narrative in representing the specific dynamics of stigmatization.

Like Goffman's *Stigma*, *Underdogs* brings together a range of experiences of social exclusion. Some of the differences represented in the book later went on to form the basis for social movements, while others did not. Toynbee's collection deals with issues of homelessness, disability, domestic violence, homosexuality, and illegitimacy, and it includes confessions from a pederast, a mother of four young children during wartime, and a ghostwriter with frustrated literary ambition. As in *Stigma*, race, ethnicity, and gender get relatively little attention in relation to more miscellaneous forms of underdog experience. Toynbee's aim in collecting these narratives is to shed new light on a wide variety of suffering and to raise the question of what can make an individual into an underdog. His emphasis on unexpected forms of discrimination leads Toynbee to emphasize outliers in the field of difference. As he writes in his introduction, "The resulting book, then, is in no sense a comprehensive survey of our underdogs; it is not even a representative selection from the main complaints which have been made. But it does contrive, I think, to deal with the familiar in a new way and to reveal a great deal of suffering which we seldom contemplate."[31]

Like Goffman, Toynbee organizes highly diverse narratives in relation to a general category, the underdog. In each of Toynbee's collected cases, the designation is up for grabs; each writer spends some time defining what it means to be an underdog and arguing that his or her experience is adequate qualification for underdog status. The authors speculate about the relationship of their form of disadvantage to others. In one example, the anonymous author N. O. Goe begins his confession, called "The Stricture," with a reflection on the relative obscurity of his condition:

> This title, which so interestingly looks as though it might be that of a poem by Donne or a story by Henry James, simply means what The Concise Oxford Dictionary says: "STRICTURE (Path.) morbid contraction of some canal or duct in the body." The matter is, in fact, very down to earth, and in every sense of the word, vulgar; and some may well think it trivial. But while I agree that, compared with other disadvantages, such as physical deformity, the lack of one or more of the five wits, or a sexual deviation, the stricture scarcely ranks high, nevertheless it can cause a certain sense of shamed inferiority, as well as bodily discomfort, and may have a considerable influence on a person's life.[32]

By framing this medical condition in terms of the dynamics of stigma—what makes the stricture a difficult condition to live with is primarily "a sense of shamed inferiority," even more than "bodily discomfort"—one sees the definitional flexibility that the underdog status allows. Having a stricture does not necessarily lead one into a grouping of those with strictures; rather his connection is to a less specific, expansive group, who are negatively rather than positively defined—those, who through unexpected turns in their life course, have been converted into underdogs.

For Toynbee, the capaciousness of the category *underdog* constitutes its value. He points out that this category captures better the way social exclusion need not be tied to moral or constitutional unfitness. He writes, "A book of this kind could only have been produced, with any hope of welcome, in a society which no longer equates failure with moral error, or criminality with wickedness."[33] Disarticulating pathology from underdog status allows Toynbee's authors to describe themselves as underdogs but not as wholly other. Underdog, as its name would suggest, is not a fixed category of identity but rather a relational or positional—and at least potentially a temporary—designation. For Toynbee, to see the contributors to the book as underdogs is a mark of social progress, evidence of an unwillingness to ascribe blame, and even as a kind of secular grace. He writes, "What has certainly happened in the last hundred years is that more of us have adapted the famous heart-cry of John Bradford. There, but for some accident of upbringing or circumstance, go we ourselves. And the fact that almost all of us sometimes regard ourselves as underdogs is not necessarily a foolish indulgence or due to a fit of meaningless depression. We are given, at these moments, an opportunity to ally ourselves in spirit with those who are more constantly unfortunate."[34] In contrast to the standard perspective of deviance studies, which imagines passive victims awaiting rescue from above, Toynbee envisions a form of coalition based on lateral thinking across difference. Partial identification—rather than pity for the wholly other—is the form of response that Toynbee imagines to these stories of failure.[35]

There are shortcomings in Toynbee's collection of underdog confessions, just as there are in Goffman's *Stigma*. The fact that the category of underdog might include potentially anyone who feels excluded indicates its limited critical force. In addition, the fact that race, gender, and ethnicity get little attention in *Stigma* (and almost none in *Underdogs*) indicates the difficulty of accounting for hierarchy and oppression outside a model of statistical minority or deviance in these studies. We might read these books as cautionary examples about the difficulties of taking on near universal categories of otherness, of disregarding pervasive (rather than exceptional or novel) forms of inequality. Similar debates have clustered around the term *queer*, another quasi-universal category of social marginality. However, while these texts might be read as cautionary tales about the dangers of comparison, I think they also suggest the potential usefulness of a general theory of stigma grounded in highly particular accounts of social marginality. Goffman's incorporation and revision of the deviance studies paradigm lays the groundwork for renewing *queer* as a term for a coalitional politics of stigma.

....

Having elaborated the resources of Goffman's methodology for contemporary sexuality studies, I want to close by talking about his influence in a particular historical instance by considering the significance of his method for Laud Humphrey's *Tearoom Trade: Impersonal Sex in Public Places*. *Tearoom Trade*, first published as a dissertation in 1968 and then as a book in 1970, is a classic example of interactionist microsociology. Working as a participant observer, Humphreys meticulously mapped the operations, gestures, glances, and sexual acts of men having sex in public restrooms in the 1960s. It is an important case study in method, both because it was the subject of an extended and public controversy about research ethics and because its method is curiously divided between a minimalist account of visible behavior and biographical and psychological profiling through the use of interviews and surveys. The first part of the book exemplifies the key aspects of Goffman's method of observation and description; it therefore offers a model of how we might account for concrete, social differences in power while avoiding many of the pitfalls of identity. The second part fills in the psychological profile of a handful of Humphreys's actors. This departure from the observational method entails a shift in ideology as well; the psychological second half of the book serves as a negative example and thus serves to make all the more visible the value of the ecological account of stigma in the first part of the book.

The anonymity and impersonality desired by the men who frequent the tearooms is reflected in Humphreys's methodology. *Tearoom Trade* opens in a discursive, dry register apparently at odds with the explicit erotic material that Humphreys discusses in the course of his account of "sexual encounters without involvement."[36] Through the early sections of the book, Humphreys offers what he refers to as an ecological account of the interactions of men in search of "kicks" in anonymous tearoom settings. Before he pursued this study, he served as a pastor, which is the reason he gives for why he is not shocked by the activities that he observes. But for his work in *Tearoom Trade*, he writes that he began to "listen to sexual deviants with a scientist's rather than a pastor's ear."[37] For most of the text tearoom participants are treated as interactants, players in a game that is rule-bound and that unfolds in a delimited space and time. Drawing on Goffman's understanding of the "interaction membrane," Humphreys details how individuals are drawn into play, how interactions are initiated, what its phases are, and what constitute closing moves. His accounts of these interactions—complete with schematic diagrams detailing the placement and movements of the actors—might easily be taken for records of chess matches, were it not for the way they are intermittently punctuated by mentions of fellatio and hand play. There is no mention in these accounts of the biographies or internal fantasy lives of the actors. Instead, Humphreys tracks their mere visible appearance and their moves in a game. The word *private* appears in scare quotes in descriptions of these sexual encounters in public. People are backgrounded in this account; what matters is the shared social space and the events that it makes possible. This ecological understanding of the space is reflected in the participants' own account of their experience. "I have noted more than once," Humphreys writes, "that these men seem to acquire stronger sentimental attachments to the buildings in which they meet for sex than to the persons with whom they engage in it."[38]

According to Humphreys, there are two important methodological gains in his choice of the tearoom as a subject: "These facilities constitute a major part of the free sex market for those in the homosexual subculture—and for millions who might never identify with the gay society. For the social scientist, these public toilets provide a means for direct observation of the dynamics of sexual encounters *in situ*; moreover, they facilitate the gathering of a representative sample of secret deviants, for most of whom association with the deviant subculture is minimal."[39] This account of the benefits of the tearoom example for the social scientist recapitulates the central division in the book, between naturalistic observation of interaction in the field and the study of the lives of secret deviants. Humphreys gathered data on the "tearoom purlieu" by means of silent observation *in situ* (while posing as a "watchqueen," both lookout and voyeur, in the restroom).[40] In order to gather data on the sociological background, family life, sexual identification, and psychological profile of his interactants, he engaged in a process that involved writing down car license numbers, cross-referencing them in police license registries, and then conducting in-depth interviews under the cover of a social health survey that he was directing simultaneously. While one might argue that neither Humphrey's research in the tearooms nor his follow-up interviews were consensual, the interviews conducted in the home were gathered under false pretenses and were more invasive than the observation of anonymous sex play.

In a 2005 article arguing that thick description has been overvalued and that thin description can also yield rich data and important analytic insights, Wayne H. Brekhus, John F. Galliher, and Jaber F. Gubrium consider Humphreys's "naturalist" work in *Tearoom Trade* and praise his detailed account of social practice: "The hallmark of naturalistic work is the presentation of richly scenic data, not exclusively the frequency, distribution, and patterned relationships evident in research material. *Tearoom Trade* presents Humphreys as a naturalist and takes the reader into the setting in which the action unfolds. His is a 'survey' in Mayhew's sense of the term, in which a social landscape is entered into and personally observed for complex patterns of living and distinctive social worlds."[41] Brekhus, Galliher, and Gubrium highlight the distinction between the first and second half of the book, tracing Humphreys's thickening of his accounts of these men through the use of interviews and richer biographical data. They argue for the value of the descriptive minimalism of the book's first half: "The thinness of tearoom participants' conduct as compared with their otherwise highly variegated lives ensconced at considerable distance from the park setting, makes their deviant status, not their urban anonymity, a 'fact' blown way out of proportion. Humphreys felt justified in offering the following public policy recommendation: 'In order to alleviate the damaging side effects of covert homosexual activity in tearooms, ease up on it.'"[42]

Brekhus, Galliher, and Gubrium draw an ethics out of Humphrey's method. What matters is not only that his account of what goes on in the tearooms is incomplete or insufficiently realized, or that it lacks feeling. Instead, by presenting the participants in the games of sexual exchange as mere players, Humphreys is able to thin out the account of deviance—to effectively void the subjectivity of these deviants, otherwise overly legible as sexual deviants, homosexuals, closet cases, sex addicts, or—one may fill in the blank. The suggestion is that once one is caught in the crosshairs of a thick psychological account of the subject, all kinds of extrapolation (psychological, moral, political) are allowed. This type of speculation and projection is excluded in the natural history of the tearoom, resulting in a different account of subjectivity, a different ethics, and even a different set of policy recommendations. Of course, one might argue through recourse to biography that it was Humphreys's later self-identification as a gay man that informed his sympathetic attitude toward the men he observed in the restrooms of these public parks. But the lesson of *Tearoom Trade*, and its ultimate value for sexuality studies, is that the politics is in the method, not the attitude. Humphreys's book shows the promise of Goffman's descriptive, observational method; in its attention to visible behavior, its disinterest in psychology, and its precise accounting of the dynamics of everyday life, it emphasizes the interactional and social parameters of sexuality, not the desires of the reader. In such a framework, both sympathy and censure are beside the point.

....

In the contemporary moment, the system of sexual stratification with which we have been familiar is in flux. New civic inclusions and a mainstream gay and lesbian platform of patriotism, parenting, and prosperity have made it difficult to see how nonnormative sexuality and stigma are linked. In fact the changing status of gay life in the global context has meant that singular attention to the stigmatization of sexual minorities can be used in the service of other projects of domination: one might point to the linking of secularism, anti-immigrant sentiment, and antihomophobia in Dutch citizenship tests; the embrace of LGBT rights by the Israeli state as an example of what has been called the "pinkwashing" of human rights abuses in Palestine and elsewhere; or the fact that multinational corporations such as Lockheed Martin and Goldman Sachs have been leaders in providing benefits to gay, lesbian, and transgender employees. Many scholars have responded to this situation by turning their attention away from sexuality and sexual communities altogether, focusing instead of the legacies of liberalism, racialization, or prison abolition as more productive and critical sites to engage sexuality as a structuring force in modernity.[43] I want to argue that, despite the uses to which a singular focus on homophobia can be put in this new climate, attention to the specific dynamics of sexual and gender stigma is still important. The history of gay liberationist, transgender, and queer political thought demonstrates the potency of stigma as an optic for making visible specific dynamics of inequality and exclusion. Paying attention to stigma led Rubin to see the feminist Sex Wars and the AIDS crisis in the context of a longer history of sex panics and to imagine novel alliances. Similarly Cathy Cohen's attention to stigma allowed her to see punks, bulldaggers, and welfare queens as figures who share significant features by virtue of their position at the outer limits of the sexual field.

By focusing on the microdynamics of social marginality, it is possible to be more specific about the processes of normalization that shape contemporary gay and lesbian life. In queer polemics about marriage, military service, gay cultural imperialism, gay gentrification, pink dollars, and other signs of assimilation, we tend to forget the significance of the ongoing stigmatization of nonnormative genders and sexualities, as well as of nonnormative sexual practices. Rubin offered an account of the relation between forms of privilege and stigmatization in "Thinking Sex" that is perhaps even more relevant today than when she wrote it: "The system of sexual oppression cuts across other modes of social inequality, sorting out individuals and groups according to its own intrinsic dynamics. It is not reducible to, or understandable in terms of, class, race, ethnicity, or gender. Wealth, white skin, male gender, and ethnic privileges can mitigate the effects of sexual stratification. A rich, white male pervert will generally be less affected than a poor, black, female pervert. But even the most privileged are not immune to sexual oppression."[44] Reading Rubin's words today reminds us to attend to the specificity of the sexual field and to attend to the dynamics of stigmatization that structure it.

It remains difficult to articulate the relationship between domination in the sexual field and other forms of privilege; the past two decades of wrestling with the term *queer* makes this difficulty visible as a symptom but does not solve it, and it is possible that the fundamental ambiguity of *queer*'s relation to power may never be resolved. The vocabularies of homonormativity and queer liberalism have given us frameworks in which to address emergent power blocs and new forms of complicity. These terms also help us to avoid the error of exaggerating the material effects of sexual stigma in contexts in which they are minimal. But the current restructuring of the sexual field is not a reason to discount the significance of stigma for gays, lesbians, transgender people, and a range of others who might be called queer. As I have tried to show, there is a long history of identifying through stigma, through quasi-universal and flexible categories like "outsider" and "underdog." Partial identifications through such general categories raise thorny questions about the limits of analogy, divergent histories, and scale. The only way through such difficulties is forward, however; by refusing to engage the problem of shared stigma we may foreclose crucial alliances.

Notes

Thanks to audiences at the University of Texas–Austin, UCLA, and the University of Maryland for their comments on earlier versions of this essay. Thanks also to Jason Potts and Daniel Stout for their patience and care in bringing this piece to publication.

1. Epstein, "Thinking Sex Ethnographically," 86.
2. Rubin makes this point herself in a retrospective essay on "Thinking Sex" when she notes the "protoqueerness" of the essay and its commitment to coalitional politics. Gayle Rubin, "Blood under the Bridge: Reflections on 'Thinking Sex,'" in *Pleasure and Danger*, 40.
3. Marcus, "*Queer Theory for Everyone*: A Review Essay." Marcus's take on the field features an unusually diverse mix of disciplines and approaches.
4. The recent publication of Rubin's essay collection *Deviations* formalizes and makes more visible this persistent critique. The volume includes Rubin's important essay "Studying Sexual Subcultures: Excavating the Ethnography of Gay Communities in Urban North America," in which she argues for the significance of ethnographic research to building queer studies, as well as her interview with Judith Butler ("Sexual Traffic"), in which, citing the influence of Jeffrey Weeks, Mary McIntosh, Kenneth Plummer, and others, she notes "how quickly people forget even recent history." Gayle S. Rubin, *Deviations: A Gayle Rubin Reader* (Durham: Duke University Press, 2011), 295. In addition to Rubin's reflections, a range of other scholars have attempted such a correction, including John D'Emilio, Escoffier, Arlene Stein, Weeks, Plummer, Gagnon, Simon, Kath Weston, Epstein, Peter M. Nardi, and Beth E. Schneider. The frustration that this forgetting engenders is audible in a 1998 reflection on the legacy of Mary McIntosh's 1968 essay, "The Homosexual Role," by Jeffrey Weeks. He writes, "It is frustrating for those of us who have been toiling in this particular vineyard since the turn of the 1960s and 1970s to have our early efforts in understanding sexuality in general, and homosexuality in particular, refracted back to us through post-Foucauldian abstractions . . . and then taken up as if the ideas are freshly minted." Jeffrey Weeks, "The 'Homosexual Role' after 30 Years: An Appreciation of the Work of Mary McIntosh," *Sexualities* 1.2 (1998): 132.
5. Jeffrey Escoffier, *American Homo*, 103. Escoffier makes this point in an essay, "Inside the Ivory Closet: The Challenge Facing Lesbian and Gay Studies," which was first pub-

lished in OUT/LOOK in 1990. He attempts to map the institutional and historical conditions determining the production of scholarly knowledge about sexuality, arguing that uneven institutionalization of the field has had profound effects on its research agenda. Humanities scholars in sexuality studies have on the whole fared better in the academy than those working in the social sciences. The resentment that is audible in many critiques of queer theory is not only a matter of disciplinary and intellectual differences, although it is that; it is also a response to real material differences. Critical responses to Escoffier's piece on queer theory did not engage the sociological framing of his argument; factors such as relative institutional privilege are not readily incorporated into queer theoretical discussions that are primarily conceptual and discursive. As Lisa Duggan points out in her careful account of responses to Escoffier's essay ("The Discipline Problem"), the objectifying force of Escoffier's argument was largely ignored; Eve Kosofsky Sedgwick, as Duggan notes, simply branded his thinking "anti-intellectual." Sedgwick cited in Lisa Duggan, "The Discipline Problem," in Duggan and Nan D. Hunter, *Sex Wars: Sexual Dissent and Political Culture* (New York: Routledge, 1995), 200.

6. Lynne Huffer has recently surveyed this territory in *Mad for Foucault*, arguing that a richer account of sexuality and social exclusion can be derived from Foucault's early work on madness than from *The History of Sexuality*.

7. Warner, introduction to *Fear of a Queer Planet*, xxvi.

8. Cohen brings together figures marked both by unequal relations to state and economic power and by specifically sexual stigma. Although she does not dispense with the categories of race, class, sexuality, and gender, she builds her politics in relation to highly specific figures. Instead of arguing for rights for groups defined on the basis of large-scale categories, she imagines connections forged through stigma between much smaller and more miscellaneous groupings. For a related discussion of "Punks, Bulldaggers, and Welfare Queens," see Heather Love, "Queers ＿＿＿＿＿＿＿ This," in *After Sex? On Writing Since Queer Theory*, edited by Janet Halley and Andrew Parker (Durham: Duke University Press, 2010).

9. Puar, *Terrorist Assemblages: Homonationalism in Queer Times* (Durham: Duke University Press, 2007); Susan Stryker, "My Words to Victor Frankenstein"; Mel Chen, *Animacies: Biopolitics, Racial Mattering, and Queer Affect* (Durham: Duke University Press, 2012).

10. Goffman warns of the dangers of excessive self-consciousness in the introduction to *Frame Analysis*: "Methodological self-consciousness that is full, immediate, and persistent sets aside all study and analysis except that of the reflexive problem itself, thereby displacing fields of inquiry instead of contributing to them" (12).

11. For an account that highlights the importance of the game to Goffman's method, see Clifford Geertz, "Blurred Genres: The Refiguration of Social Thought," in *Local Knowledges*.

12. I am grateful for Richard W. Burkhardt's account of the confrontation between U.S. behavioral research and European ethology in *Patterns of Behavior*.

13. A crucial exception is Michael Trask's recent book, *Camp Sites*, which brilliantly traces the links between dramaturgical sociology (including Goffman's) and postwar U.S. queer culture. Trask's focus on the dramaturgical view of the self (and its specific relation to Butler's work on performativity) has influenced my argument here; see below for a discussion of Goffman and Butler in particular.

14. In a recent slash-and-burn piece on the state of the field of sexuality studies, Camille Paglia argues that Goffman was also forgotten (or suppressed) by Foucault. In a highly polemical denunciation of the field as narrow and jargon-filled, Paglia refers to Goffman as "the great Canadian-American sociologist whose work in such pioneering books as *The Presentation of Self in Everyday Life* (1959) was one of Foucault's primary and deviously unacknowledged sources." Camille Paglia, "Scholars in Bondage: Dogma Dominates Studies of Kink," *Chronicle of Higher Education: The Chronicle Review*, 20 May 2013, online.

15. Butler, *Gender Trouble*, 520.

16. Butler, *Gender Trouble*, 526.

17. Butler, *Gender Trouble*, 528.

18. Butler, *Gender Trouble*, 528.

19. My account of the relation between Goffman's dramaturgical view of the self and Butler's performative view of gender is indebted to Trask's essay "Patricia Highsmith's Method." Trask acknowledges that the difference between Butler and Goffman (for him a representative of midcentury sociologists' broader concern with role playing) is political, though he does not fault Goffman for his failures as a social critic. In a broader argument about the value of authenticity in the new social movements, Trask argues that, in spite of her antifoundationalism, Butler's commitment to political agency entails a commitment to authentic selfhood. For Trask, sociologists of the 1950s understood social actors as "already attuned to the fictive or rehearsed quality of their identities" (589) and did not see possibilities for social subversion in the exposure of that fact. Ultimately, he concludes, "Butler appears less committed to repudiating authenticity or identity than to making these categories as inclusive as possible" (590). For other accounts of the relation between Goffman and Butler from a range of perspectives, see Grahame F. Thompson, "Approaches to 'Performance': An Analysis of Terms," *Screen* (1985): 78–90; Nicky Gregson and Gillian Rose, "Taking Butler Elsewhere: Performativities, Spatialities, and Subjectivities," *Environment and Planning D: Society and Space* 18 (2000): 433–52; Philip Auslander, introduction to *Performance: Critical Concepts in Literary and Cultural Studies* (London: Routledge, 2003).

20. Goffman, *Interaction Ritual*, 2–3.

21. Consider, for instance, the ending of *The Presentation of Self in Everyday Life*, the text that grounds widespread claims about Goffman's dramaturgical understanding of the self and social action. In the final pages he admits that his employment of the "language of the stage" as an attempt to "press a mere analogy so far was . . . a rhetoric and a maneuver." After suggesting that this kind of metaphor should not "be taken too seriously," he writes, "And so here the language and mask of the stage will be dropped. Scaffolds, after all, are meant to build other things with, and should be erected with an eye to taking them down" (254).

22. Butler, *Gender Trouble*, 519.

23. Goffman, "The Arrangement between the Sexes," 319.

24. Goffman, "The Arrangement between the Sexes," 316. The rhetoric of temporal inversion recurs throughout the essay, as in the following passage: "It is common to conceive of the differences between the sexes as showing up against the demands and constraints of the environment, the environment itself being taken as a harsh given, present before the matter of sex differences arose. Or, differently put, that sex differ-

ences are a biological given, an external constraint upon any form of social organization that humans might devise. There is another way of viewing the question, however. Speculatively one can reverse the equation and ask what could be sought out from the environment or put into it so that such innate differences between the sexes as there are could count—in fact or in appearance—for something" (313).

25. Goffman, *Gender Advertisements* (Cambridge: Harvard University Press, 1979), 7, 8.
26. Goffman, *Gender Advertisements*, 325.
27. Goffman, *Gender Advertisements*, 8.
28. Goffman, "The Arrangement between the Sexes," 315.
29. Goffman, *Stigma*, 114. For a critique of deviance studies and an account of its failure to survive the rise of the new social movements, see John Kitsuse, "Coming Out All Over: Deviants and the Politics of Social Problems," *Social Problems* 28.1 (October 1980): 1–13. As Kitsuse notes, many of the deviants of the 1960s had become by the 1970s "active and visible practitioners of the arts of social problems" (3).
30. Goffman writes, "I have argued that stigmatized persons have enough of their situations in life in common to warrant classifying all these persons together for purposes of analysis. An extraction has thus been made from the traditional fields of social problems, race and ethnic relations, social disorganization, criminology, social pathology, and deviancy—an extraction of something all these fields have in common. These commonalities can be organized on the basis of very few assumptions regarding human nature. What remains in each one of the traditional fields could then be re-examined for whatever it is that is really special to it, thereby bringing analytical coherence to what is not purely historic and fortuitous unity. Knowing what fields like race relations, aging, and mental health share, one could then go on to see, analytically, how they differ. Perhaps in each case the choice would be to retain the old substantive areas, but at least it would be clear that each is merely an area to which one should apply several perspectives, and that the development of any one of these coherent analytic perspectives is not likely to come from those who restrict their interest exclusively to one substantive area" (*Stigma*, 146–47). I discuss this passage at greater length in Heather Love, "Feeling Bad in 1963," in *Political Emotions: Affect and the Public Sphere*, edited by Ann Cvetkovich, Ann Reynolds, and Janet Staiger (New York: Taylor and Francis, 2010).
31. Toynbee, *Underdogs*, 9.
32. Toynbee, *Underdogs*, 147.
33. Toynbee, *Underdogs*, 14.
34. Toynbee, *Underdogs*, 14.
35. In his introduction, Toynbee suggests that pity is an acceptable but not required form of response to these underdog stories. He argues, "The underdog is someone who deserves our pity if only because he pities himself." But he adds, addressing those "neo-Nietzscheans who abominate the whole emotion," "Let them read this book, then, without compassion: the contributors have supplied their stories and it is not for the editor to decree the reception which they deserve" (11–12).
36. Humphreys, *Tearoom Trade*, 2.
37. Humphreys, *Tearoom Trade*, 24.
38. Humphreys, *Tearoom Trade*, 14.
39. Humphreys, *Tearoom Trade*, 21.
40. Humphreys, *Tearoom Trade*, 12.

41. Brekhus et al., "The Need for Thin Description," 876.
42. Brekhus et al., "The Need for Thin Description," 876.
43. For one example of this kind of call to shift the object of sexuality studies, see Eng et al., introduction to "What's Queer about Queer Studies Now?"
44. Rubin, "Thinking Sex," 293.

chapter 13

Our I. A. Richards Moment:
The Machine and Its Adjustments

Frances Ferguson

The word *practical* in I. A. Richards's *Practical Criticism* has sometimes seemed misleading. How could any version of literary criticism be practical? Richards himself seems to have worried about this issue, especially in *Principles of Literary Criticism*, the work that immediately preceded *Practical Criticism*. In *Principles*, Richards felt obliged to argue for the practicality of criticism by reviewing the claims of poetry and attempting to answer the "central question, What is the value of the arts, why are they worth the devotion of the keenest hours of the best minds, and what is their place in the system of human endeavours?"[1] Such concerns, clearly, have not gone away. Yet Richards, I'll argue, is of great practical use in ways that extend past our views on poetry—and that justify Richards's sense that his kind of criticism might function to alter our interactions with the world.

Take the following case. Someone you don't know sends an email. It appeals to generosity or greed and offers financial rewards for help. The author usually identifies himself as Nigerian, and his message is laced with misspellings. We know about such emails. We have a name for them, phishing, and marvel that they are so inexpertly composed as to contain misspellings and grammatical lapses. Yet a researcher at Microsoft sees another possibility. He suggests that the apparent haplessness and the self-identification as someone who comes from a country known for mail and email scams is itself strategic—that the phisher is trying to select a manageable audience, to eliminate the "false positives . . . that are attacked but yield nothing."[2] At least one commentator has ventured that there is no way of actually confirming the researcher's hypothesis, and he's probably right about that. But what Richards would find appealing in this interpretive scenario is that one only has to read it to see that the researcher's is a better reading than the one we are initially inclined to. Instead of assuming a clumsy con man who is actually from Nigeria, it projects an author clever enough to identify himself as someone who might be suspected of phishing in order to weed out uncooperative correspondents. And this better reading does not rest on a principled generosity that enjoins us always to read everything as if it were highly deserving of our attention and credit. Nor does it rest on an appeal to what other people agree on. It gets traction from the mere act of comparison. A comparison of one's dismissive interpretation with the method-in-the-madness or the method-in-the-clumsiness interpretation provides the only evidence there might be for the superiority of one to the other.

It is just such acts of comparison that Richards seeks to inspire in the Cambridge students who are the informants in his experiment in *Practical Criticism*, a book that collected his commentary on the commentaries that a number of Cambridge undergraduates provided on thirteen poems. Enjoining the students to read each poem repeatedly over the course of a week, he notes that some readers "recorded as many as ten or a dozen readings."[3] What he does in encouraging multiple readings is not merely to recommend close attention or interpretative generosity. He also provides students with the experience of making judgments on the basis of the confidence that they can develop about meanings that could not be confirmed by consulting either an author or an interpretative community. His model of reading, one that continually asks us to remember and compare what we just thought about the meaning of a poem or a conversation with what we now think, introduces the notion of style into reading itself. Although we can't say exactly where the idea that the phisher might not be an inept Nigerian but a clever pseudo-Nigerian came from, we immediately recognize its appeal. Even though the article venturing the hypothesis is written by a Microsoft researcher in distinctly nonliterary language, it makes itself felt as a bit of found literature. (The article was immediately taken up and re-reported by various publications.) The pleasure it generates is lodged not merely in a text but in the act of critical reading itself.

Richards's project deserves our continuing attention, I suggest, because of the way it mobilizes our attention to the importance of style in reading. Already in the 1920s Richards advances such a notion of style in reading, in criticism that anticipates much of what Jacques Rancière gets at in his ongoing account of dissensus. In a series of books and essays, Rancière has insisted upon the importance of disagreement or dissensus. He has, on the one hand, seen dissensus as the essence of politics. In this mode he has used the notion as the basis for an abstract modeling of politics and has made politics susceptible to a schematic and spatial representation that involves minimal attention to specific political content or issues. He has, on the other hand, suggested how the literary practices of high modernism made literary content itself dissident as writers like Baudelaire and Flaubert wrested it from the hierarchies of classical decorum and made it bespeak a project of radical equivalences. In this account Baudelaire might write a poetry that deliberately treats garlic and rubies as on the same plane, and Flaubert might accord as much attention to an Emma Bovary as a hero or a queen would have commanded in an earlier regime of literary hierarchies that aimed to match content with style. Dissidence, in Rancière's description of its literary aspect, may run counter to the stated political views of authors. It appears not in political themes or views but rather in style itself, as hierarchical ways of dividing the world of aesthetic representation are turned on their axes and distinctions are made to be equivalences.

Although Rancière addresses questions of political agency more actively than Richards does, his way of routing political views through authorial style and its perceptibility, his emphasis on style, helps locate the terms and importance of Richards's treatment of communication and of Richards's sense that literary criticism offers a royal road to understanding communication and its perils. Rancière, first, enables us to see the importance of realizing that disagreement is not a problem that needs to be eliminated. Criticism of the past half century has organized itself around agreement. Moreover his treating literature as a model for political issues (rather than a venue for their expression) chimes with Richards's ways of suggesting how literature does not function as a world apart from the social and political world but instead can show us how we go wrong on many occasions, some of which have little or nothing to do with literature as such. And whether this is an aspect of the second point or an additional one, Rancière helps us to see how aspects of communication that seem very far removed from doctrinal statements continually introduce differences and disagreements into our discussions.

I focus on two kinds of assertion that might appear to be in some tension with one another when Richards describes the study of language and literature as part of a project of communication. He repeatedly asserts that one of the most basic facts about human beings is that they communicate with one another. Yet communication does not for him resolve itself into agreement. Richards continually identifies mistakes (and thus might seem to hold up an implicit model of unmistaken communication). But the nature and importance of the mistake only comes into view once we take in Richards's view of the standing that individual judgment has for him. No one, he insists, has to yield her judgment to majority opinion or authority in talking about the meaning of conversations or examples from literature. He introduces the notion of the pseudo-statement, which he attaches to poetry, by contrast with the statements of science, so as to get at the limits on the universality of understanding in poetry. "Poetry," he thinks, is "our best evidence as to how other men feel about things; and as we read it, we discover not so much how life seems to another, as how it is for ourselves."[4] Poems thus look like more massive instances of the sort of malleability we see in metaphor. While we need to catch an association between lions and courage to catch the meaning of a phrase like "Achilles is lion-hearted," the path we follow in tracking the metaphor is less straightforward than positivist descriptions might have it. While a critic like Paul de Man will sometimes describe this situation by attributing it to literary language in particular, Richards continually insists that literature never achieves such independent standing.[5] The names of poems do not designate definite things for him. Instead they are markers for experiences.

In his work with C. K. Ogden in *The Meaning of Meaning*, Richards comes very early to an understanding of the nonidentity of literary texts (and aesthetic objects more generally) with themselves. Pursuing an insight analogous to (but not to be identified with) Saussure's distinction between a sign's physical properties (its appearance as an acoustic or visual image) and its conceptual aspect, he and Ogden argue that G. E. Moore was wrong to imagine that the goodness we ascribe to aesthetic objects ought to be seen as a nonsensuous and implicit property of objects. A statement like "This ball is red" represents a belief that is attributable to a property of the ball, but the burden of a sentence like "This red ball is beautiful" or "*The Waste Land* is good" falls on the attitude of the speaker. Ogden and Richards, that is, analyze statements of the kind "x is good" as statements of judgment—that is, as statements of consciousness or subjective statements. They insist, moreover, that such judgments relate to the objects themselves only in an oblique and variable fashion. Linguistic objects and literature may, without any change in our understanding of their physical properties, inspire different judgments in different people and even in the same person at different times.[6]

When Richards begins to elaborate on the implications of the views he and Ogden expound in *The Meaning of Meaning*, he is remarkably consistent in applying the distinction between beliefs (about properties in objects and what he tends to refer to as technique in poems) and attitudes (judgments of poems or other aesthetic objects that are not entirely attributable to the properties of the objects themselves). In our confusion about the two kinds of apprehension, we frequently think that our opinions matter to statements of the kind scientists make (and in the grip of such a thought we lament the fact that fewer than half of the American people believe in the theory of evolution), and simultaneously we minimize the extent to which opinions matter to the kind of pseudo-statements we make in relation to literature. In conversation and in dealing with literature, Richards thinks, people are apt to do something like picking up words, phrases, and poems by the wrong handle. And their misunderstandings tend to arise from an excessive proficiency in finding meaning: "Whenever we hear or read any not too nonsensical opinion, a tendency so strong and so automatic that it must have been formed along with our earliest speech-habits, leads us to consider *what seems to be said*."[7] That version of meaning in turn leads to our coding meanings in terms of our agreement or disagreement: "We are in fact so anxious to discover whether we agree or not with what is being said that we overlook the mind that says it."[8] On Richards's view, we objectify speech and writing without attending to the ways our codings corral the meanings or pausing to notice how being in or out of sympathy with our interlocutors affects what we think particular strings of words mean. Richards observes as well how our good mood or sleep deprivation changes what we hear and read. Composition handbooks might impress on us the desirability of clear pronoun reference or good grammar as hedges against such misunderstanding, but Richards insists that the producer of an utterance or a poem can never be careful enough. As long as auditors and readers are humans, they are going to be unreliable instruments—and from an excessive obligingness rather than the reverse. We start, he thinks, from a disposition to agree and the conviction that it is socially necessary: "The Wills of Gods, the Conscience, the Catechism, Taboos, Immediate Intuitions, Penal Laws, Public Opinion, Good Form, are all more or less ingenious and efficient devices with the same aim—to secure the uniformity which social life requires."[9] Whereas someone like Vladimir Propp of the *Morphology of the Folktale* consolidates a variety of different actions into various single functions, Richards emphasizes all the aspects of meaning that are obscured by processes of social synonymization.

In the decades after Richards's work of the 1920s, a series of critics and theorists would seek to minimize the importance of what he takes to be perhaps the most important fact about language and literature—namely, that they are directed toward humans. Yet Richards develops his "psychological theory of value" around the variability and unreliability that humans show.[10]

Everywhere he looks he encounters evidence that perceptions of value differ across cultures, between individuals, and even within persons. Anthropological studies make it possible for him to demonstrate how widely value judgments vary from one culture to another, but he also relies on the kind of knowledge that anyone might have at her disposal: "Any observant child . . . might discover in the home circle how widely people disagree." Moreover he insists on the importance of what we might think of as internal relativism: "Fortunately for psychology we can each find wide enough differences in ourselves from hour to hour. Most people in the same day are Bonaparte and Oblomov by turns."[11]

What Richards claims as psychology's fortunate ground in establishing what he sometimes calls a science of criticism is its flexibility in tracking the fluctuating values of human behavior, including linguistic and literary behavior. His version of literary psychology aims to recognize broad consistencies in people's ways of interpreting literature. He is, in particular, alert to the ways we are likely to mislead ourselves. We rely on our past experience and our expectations so thoroughly as to have a hard time reading the text in front of us. Even Hume, despite all his acuity in tracking the modes and fields of application of various emotions, looks, under the kind of gaze Richards might extend, like someone who was attempting to consolidate verbal comprehension and sound literary judgment more extensively than experience warrants. Hume's mild identification of some people as better judges of literature and art than others appears to stop short, focusing on these people by comparison with those rather than attending to the variations in response that even the most reliable judges exhibit. He operates with a whole-person standard, by contrast with Richards.

Richards's aim in locating various different sorts of verbal behavior is to name the behavior and, in naming it, to make it susceptible to change. The usefulness of what he calls "an alienist's attitude" (the approach of a psychoanalyst) is that it does not merely record a series of first-person evaluations and interpretations of poetry.[12] Instead it calls for a further and, implicitly, self-reflexive judgment on the worth of such attitudes. We never really lose sight of "ulterior ends," he observes in arguing against A. C. Bradley's description of the aesthetic as "a world by itself, independent, complete, autonomous."[13] "Fundamentally, though this is an unfair way of putting it, when any person misreads a poem it is because, *as he is at that moment, he wants to.*"[14] The question we have to address here is how the judgment on judgment is to be made. How can we evaluate the various motives that lead us to read less well than we might?

A survey of some key alternative positions—principally those of some of the most prominent New Critics—may help us to focus that question. To W. K. Wimsatt, Monroe Beardsley, and Cleanth Brooks, Richards's project looked like the rankest sort of affectivism. They thought that Richards reduced literary meaning to a matter of response and thus opened the door to the possibility that one could never say anything about literature that amounted to more than simple readerly projection. They therefore thought that literary meaning and literary value appeared in Richards's scheme as a pure subjectivism. It could, they believed, only issue in an absolute relativism in which each person, in claiming to be judging through the lens of emotions that each treated as an absolute warrant for valuing and understanding particular poetic objects, essentially took literature and criticism out of the public sphere.

I shall have more to say later about the positions they developed against this perceived threat and how they related to Richards's own work. For the moment, however, it may suffice to say that Richards had a much more capacious account of psychology—and a less substantial notion of the solidity of words and text—than they. A much more recent example may serve to illustrate the sort of point toward which Ogden and Richards, first, and Richards alone, later, drove. My exhibit is a *New York Times* story about the difficulty that a number of people have in remembering the passwords to their various online accounts. Although the article features many celebrities, almost anyone would testify as feelingly as they do to the difficulties of remembering their passwords and the clues that are supposed to enable them to reconnect with their accounts when they have forgotten their passwords. The difficulty is that computer systems, being computer systems and correspondingly rigid, do not recognize and allow for the lack of rigidity that the respondents' memories abundantly display. One respondent tries to remember whether he was thinking, at the time he answered the security question, about the name of his first girlfriend, about the first person he slept with, or the first person with whom he was infatuated even when his affections went unrequited. Another worries that his first teacher might have been either his kindergarten teacher or his teacher in what he calls "real school," and then points out that his first-grade teacher married halfway through the school year and acquired a new name. Which name was he thinking of when he answered the security question? The password is rigid: It requires that a user reproduce letters, numbers, and symbols, capitalized and lowercase letters in exactly the same sequence in which she first entered it, and is recoverable only through a process of producing answers to security questions that is itself rigid. Computer systems do not hear place-names that mention a city and a state if they are calling for the name of a city alone. And the problem manifests itself in a variety of ways. One respondent tries to capture rigidity in a different form. She recommends using the first letters of song lyrics as a foolproof way of arriving at passwords, and then confesses that she can't ever remember whether the Beatles sang "Hey Jude, don't make it bad" or "Hey Jude, don't make it sad." One might arrive at a highly individualized psychoanalytic account of why each of the informants chose the passwords and the questions and answers they did, but the basic point that would give support to Richards's views is that we can see a pattern of divergence between a string of letters, numbers, and symbols and the image of it that appears in memory.[15] The problem that Richards and Ogden isolate and that the newspaper story illustrates is that our means of recapturing even factual bits of information shift that information and our access to it.

The variation between the rigid term (the user name, the password, and the answer to a security question) and an informant's memory would have been of interest to Richards simply because it shows how readily one might arrive at the possibility of varying names for what we take to be the same thing. While a computer enforces rigidity (down to, and including, spacing and marks of punctuation), natural language does not. The same object may be termed the morning star and the evening star.[16] And such variation does not rely on the kind of affectivism that Wimsatt and Beardsley assimilated Richards's position to when they depicted affect as any kind of emotion that might not readily be shared by another person in different circumstances. What they called "the objective way" in criticism made poetic objects stand in for the possibility of substantial general agreement. It demanded the creation of especially tightly wound objects—versions of poetic texts that pushed variants to the side, dictionaries that they described as offering possibilities "internal" to the poem because they were public.[17] Representing authorial and readerly psychology only in examples of suspiciously heightened transport (from Longinus to Housman), they offered an account of literary interpretation that created entrance requirements and made a reader abandon her irrelevant attitudes at the door. Reading literature seemed almost to involve signing a contractual agreement about what one would and would not notice.

Richards's practice in both *Principles of Literary Criticism* and *Practical Criticism* entered a wider range of literary response into the record. He licensed some of Wimsatt and Beardsley's suspicion of his psychology when he made room for a wide range of motivations that were centered in persons and said, for instance, "The personal situation of the reader inevitably (and within limits rightly) affects his reading, and many more are drawn to poetry in quest of some reflection of their latest emotional crisis than would admit it if faced with such a frank declaration as that in 11.2" (one of the protocols in Practical Criticism, in which the respondent says that the poem's "reflective, conversational manner *awakens a quiet mood, rather than a rapture, and since rapture is what I want of poetry, it is lacking to me*").[18] In statements like this, Richards made considerable allowance for the ways people use poetry instrumentally, to further their own emotions rather than to observe the language as if from a distance. He even went so far as to observe that one's ostensible human objects might virtually vanish under the powerfully instrumentalizing force of emotions: "Very few people, for example, fall in love for the first time without becoming enthralled by their emotions merely as a novel experience . . . and [indeed] become absorbed in them often to the exclusion of genuine interest in the loved object."[19]

Writing well before the computer age had set in, Richards had his own description for the problem of rigidity: it was using language as if it consisted of nothing but proper names, by which he meant that the names referred to one and only one person or thing.[20] He thought, moreover, that the problem with such a picture of language was that it imagined that there was a unique linguistic object available for retrieval. The ongoing development of language, its continually adding new words and giving new resonance to others, served as evidence against that picture: "No one who uses a dictionary—for other than orthographic purposes—can have escaped the shock of discovering how very far ahead of us our words often are. How subtly they already record distinctions towards which we are still groping."[21] The kinds of lexical shifts that Raymond Williams would catalogue in *Culture and Society* and particularly in *Keywords* were the sorts of things he aimed to tap in thinking about the relation between our sense of our use of individual words (What did we know and when did we know it?) and our sense of the resonances the language has on offer. It was an account that treated the dictionary as provoking an oscillation between one's consciousness of a moment of consciousness and a larger and entirely impersonal registration of consciousness. In that, it complemented the awareness that Richards provoked of an individual's own shifts of consciousness—her reading that poem when she was Napoleon, her reading it when she was Oblomov. The experience of reading poetry could not be captured by models of an archive or a channel (since one's emotions and experiences were not, Richards thought, merely an orderly continuation of one's past experience).[22]

By providing a notion of communication that did not always define itself in terms of success, Richards produced a practical criticism that was, as Wimsatt and Beardsley recognized, not focused on a textual object. He was perfectly content to count ignoble personal inclinations among the motives that drew people to literary texts, and he was willing to suggest that texts, being made up of words, were never going to be any more stable than the words they were made of. Indeed the project of evaluation which he thought of as central to literary criticism needed to face up to the distinction he and Ogden had earlier drawn between beliefs about the properties of the object and the attitudes one expressed about it in judging it.

Wimsatt, writing with Beardsley and writing alone, treated Richards's emphasis on emotive aspects of poetry as a simple distortion of meaning. He did not explicitly take up Moore's argument that the goodness or beauty of aesthetic objects was an actual—if supersensible—property of the objects, but at every point described the meaning of individual poems and the meaning of the images that they deployed as implicit statements about the properties of the poems and the images. Metaphor and simile thus seemed to him to suggest lines of connection that worked almost like algebraic equations, and he was willing to create narrative descriptions of motivations that would further specify what might cause such connections. Literary works, he and Beardsley thought, drew on a "repertoire of suggestive meanings which here and there in history—with somewhat to start upon—a Caesar or a Macbeth—have created out of a mere case of factual reason for intense emotion a specified, figuratively fortified, and permanent object of less intense but far richer emotion."[23] Poetry could not, he and they said, ever be "a poetry of pure emotion." It was, even when it took up symbols rather than actualities, always a "poetry about things," and they endorsed C. S. Lewis's assertion that it was impossible to override the properties of things: "The Romance of the Rose could not, without loss, . . . be rewritten as The Romance of the Onion."[24]

It might seem plausible enough to look at symbols and metaphors in terms of properties, but it was harder for Wimsatt and Beardsley to say what the properties of a poem were, particularly when a poem appeared in various forms.[25] How was one to know when one was looking at a poem, and in particular a good poem? They took it as "axiomatic" that "judging a poem is like judging a pudding or a machine. One demands that it work."[26] The pronouncement sounds like a direct riposte to one of Richards's most famous and most often repeated lines: "A book is a machine to think with."[27] Richards had modeled the observation on Le Corbusier's maxim that a house is a machine for living, which he credited James Wood with having introduced him to.[28] Yet the differences between the two treatments of the machine are very substantial. Wimsatt and Beardsley took a poem to be a product, an object whose various properties enabled it to work. Richards, immediately after adapting Le Corbusier, had gone on to suggest the class of machines and then to rule out certain kinds of machines, saying, "But it need not, therefore, usurp the functions either of the bellows or the locomotive."[29] Wimsatt and Beardsley's machine might be objective, but what this meant for them was that it had properties. That is, they talked about poems as if they were objects with properties about which one might have beliefs that accounted for one's responses to the poem. They rejected any of the sidelong movement that Richards saw as interrupting the process of making descriptive statements about properties and treating poetry as a species of statement that could never satisfactorily be explained in terms of such properties. They could thus disqualify the footnotes to The Waste Land as not really part of the poem because the footnotes seemed too much a personal record of Eliot's own reading.[30]

At the same time that the New Critics' objective way of criticism seemed to set narrow boundaries to poetic objects, however, their poetic objects began to swell from within. Thus Cleanth Brooks insisted that the language of poetry was, on the one hand, distinct from language in general and was, on the other, the language of paradox and ambiguity. Brooks might restrict the sphere of poetry, just as Wimsatt and Beardsley restricted interpretation to poetic objects that seemed to be narrowly defined, but these straitened objects began filling with more and more possibilities as the range of meanings was unrestricted. While Richards hewed to the observation that the words in literary works could never serve as absolutely rigid designators, the New Critics stabilized the instability of the words in literature by designating the language used in literature as a distinctly literary language. Once words entered the precincts of a poem, they were able to grasp and hold as many competing and irreconcilable meanings as a reader might attach to them.

Although Wimsatt and Beardsley used a utilitarian language of "work" in "The Intentional Fallacy," one of their central aims was to free poems from utility, so that Wimsatt could, early and late, affirm that "a poem is a verbal expression which has no end except to be known."[31] And detaching poems from purposes ended up producing a theoretical position that had to import a notion of drama, with its attendant notions of setting and tone, in order to make it realistic to read a poem as anything other than a variorum in process, in which every word called up all the possible meanings one might associate with it. The peculiar outcome was that Brooks, alone and with his interpretative collaborator, Robert Penn Warren, needed to provide positive examples of criticism, since they were taking various things like tone to be internal attributes of poems in a way that might have appeared to license some of the less extravagant versions of the emotivism that Wimsatt and Beardsley decried.

It was therefore highly instructive when Wimsatt wrote the essay "I.A.R.: What to Say about a Poem," in which he described an essay he had written. He had, he says, "conceived [it] as a teacher's concern about a poem," and he "foisted [his] title" and some of his line of thought upon Richards in the later essay on the grounds that Richards is "by his own profession and in his conspicuous achievement, a critic of and for teachers of poetry."[32] Wimsatt's essay is learned, witty, and decorously alert to its place in a Festschrift for Richards, but his gesture toward the pedagogical imperatives that he takes Richards to share with him may help us see where Richards parts company with both the New Critics and much of the criticism following them. Wimsatt catalogues "the kind of things that a teacher of poetry has to say—analytic, interpretive, explicatory (celebratory, perhaps, rhapsodic—at the same time, more or less sober), reliable, internally oriented to the poem itself—and in these ways distinguishable from the various kinds of things that other kinds of writers, journal essayists, reviewers, historians, biographers, might legitimately say."[33] In his remarks we can catch an intimation of the progress through which the "poem itself" came to be what Stanley Fish would call "literature in the reader." Literary criticism was a specific way of dealing with literature that aimed to attend more actively than other professions might with that "poem itself," and teaching involved producing communities of agreement and identifying procedures under whose banner they could fly.

The pedagogical motive justified the genially tendentious questions that Brooks and Warren set in their many editions of *Understanding Poetry* and *Understanding Fiction*: you too, as a student, can come to ask the same kinds of questions and to identify the same sets of technical matters (rhyme schemes and their names, similes and metaphors and other rhetorical figures, etc.) that your teacher asks about and identifies. What Wimsatt and Beardsley termed the objective way in criticism, that is, was always an interpretive community waiting to develop. And recent projects like Terry Eagleton's *How to Read a Poem* and Lisa Zunshine's more apparently expansive cognitivist criticism have continued such a process. Eagleton complains that the young no longer know how to read and rolls up his sleeves to produce readings that confirm a reader in the thought that this business of interpretation is a more straightforward matter than one might have thought. He grants with one hand, "So we can misinterpret, say, the tone of a poem," and surveys things that imagined readers might think, but he ultimately settles on a characterization of the poem that puts considerable stress on its distance from other readings: "But there is also something moving, as often with Yeats, about the bold, apparently artless directness of the lines [of 'A Dialogue of Self and Soul'] and their jubilant, chant-like refrain."[34] We are united in reading—and particularly in reading as he reads. Zunshine, analyzing narrative patterns, notes the connections between a joke she understood as a child and the plays on identity that operate in *Amphytrion* and Dryden's *Amphytrion, or The Two Sosias*. In all these "a character is persuaded that if somebody looks exactly like him, or even just wears his clothing, it must be him."[35] While Eagleton conjures up imagined readers with whom he differs, Zunshine finds fundamental cognitive consonance in her own experience and that of other people. She understands the joke that underwrites Dryden's play because she recognizes that she understood the same joke when she was a child. In her view, the child is father of the man, and what it means to understand literature is to model oneself on oneself, to form an interpretive community with oneself and implicitly with other persons who also understand such jokes. The discovery of the basic faculties and predispositions that narratives present helps us to establish our commonalities.

All of the critics I've cited, from Wimsatt and Brooks and Warren through Fish and Eagleton and Zunshine, discover preexisting or implicit agreement or build it where they don't. They help us to establish by contrast a recurrent feature of Richards's thought: that literature is a kind of disagreement from within. Seeing the self-qualification within expression represents Richards' alertness to the metaphorical aspects of language and to literature's capacity for representing it. A poem may be a machine to think with, but Richards cautions against our employing such machines as if we could simply and straightforwardly put them to use: we shouldn't, he says, pedal off as if riding a bicycle or spew hot air as if pumping a bellows or race down straight lines of track as if riding the rails. His way of continually adjusting a thought highlights the importance of an exchange that Wimsatt called attention to: someone whom Richards described as an "influential teacher" had written to him during World War II and had in the process deplored the way people were talking, saying, "Whenever business is seriously threatened, it appears that truth, justice, freedom, religion, democracy, ethics, and everything else are all crumbling." Wimsatt wryly observed that Richards's correspondent "no doubt . . . had expected a response of warm sympathy," and then went on to quote what Richards had written instead: "These great words, *justice, freedom*, and the others, it seems, mean primarily . . . that someone is getting at him. Interpretation and understanding mean debunking."[36] Even though Richards's correspondent takes himself to be a discerning observer of the fatuities of public discourse—and even though Richards himself might find that discourse empty—he objects to his correspondent's all too complacent expectation of agreement.

Reading an anecdote like this one, we too might object to the words of Richards's correspondent, but we might equally wonder how anyone carried on a correspondence or a conversation with Richards. We might ask why Richards holds his interlocutor to an improbably high standard and does not allow social niceties to prevail. Why does he not extend the sympathy that would make his correspondent's words understandable, if only as examples of the large, vague social meanings that he grants we rely on most of the time? The answer lies, I think, in his seeing *Practical Criticism* as what he calls an experiment in verbal behavior—and in using poetry as an arena in which one can look at verbal behavior without completely collapsing it into the social situation. He issued "printed sheets of poems—ranging in character from a poem by Shakespeare to a poem by Ella Wheeler Wilcox—to audiences who were requested to comment freely in writing upon them. The authorship of the poems was not revealed, and with rare exceptions, it was not recognized."[37] Wimsatt offers that Richards holds up a "high ideal of understanding," and he notes the scarcity of "a certain few [successful] opinions (fewer than twenty, I should say, in the total of about 385 protocols)" written by Cambridge students encountering five clearly bad poems, five clearly good poems, and three problematic poems that were both unsigned and undated. Wimsatt speaks of "the crowded galleries of this modern Dunciad," and in doing so affiliates the protocol-writers with the critical and moral limitations of the personae whose actual names shine through in Pope's satire or any other.[38]

Wimsatt's perfectly plausible characterization sounds slightly inaccurate, however, if we linger over it. For Richards's approach, for all its wit, has very little satire to it. Satire is designed to name and shame, to hold up error and make it appear as such. And while it is designed to correct, it is also designed to make failings and errors look nameable and blamable in someone else. Richards does not merely lace his text with remarks like "Whether we know and intend it or not, we are all jugglers when we converse, keeping the billiard-balls in the air while we balance the cue on our nose."[39] He continually extends the critical judgments he makes about the student protocols to "us" and refrains from naming any of his informants. In asking his informants to write about poems that lack the usual textbook identifications of author and date, he does not encourage them to arm themselves with the approval they expect to extend to Milton or Shakespeare or the scorn they are poised to heap upon the less canonized. At the same time, he bathes his informants' remarks in the waters of Lethe. His informants are not so much persons as roles. They represent the expensively educated young reader at a certain stage of development. A named reader might be tempted to explain and defend his readings. An unnamed reader is someone without a particular identity; she somewhat resembles Catherine Gallagher's account of novelistic character, the generalizable person who is Nobody and thus everybody.[40] Richards's suggestion is that neither guilt nor shame attaches to persons without names and that the experiment he is conducting runs more smoothly on that account: "We are quicker to detect our own errors when they are duplicated by our fellows, and readier to challenge a pretention when it is worn by another."[41]

Richards does not simply put his informants on the spot and make them yield up commentary on the poems. He assembles groups of responses clustered around the same poem in such a way as to make the respondents themselves seem almost like characters in a novel (considered in a different light than that of Gallagher's Nobody)—that is, with distinct personalities and ways of taking up the poems that are their putative objects of attention. Their responses are not important for being right or wrong or more or less closely aligned with positions that Richards might be expected to have. Indeed, as Wimsatt points out, Richards seems particularly unhappy with the responses that seem to attempt to ape or converse directly with Richards and "to employ the raw idiom of the Richards methodology."[42] Those eager informants, ready with phrases like "Failure of communication, as after the 20th reading *the nature of the addressee* was still obscure" (5.1), "I find it impossible to recreate the poet's experience" (6.33), and "This one seems to me a successful communication of an experience whose value is dubious, or which at most is valuable only on a small scale" (13.1), do not meet with direct criticism of their remarks. Richards simply responds to 5.1 with the following: "The interesting assumption that the 'unimpeachable body' must be a woman's, not a man's, may be noted in passing. It frequently reappears." He quotes many protocols in support of the frustration that 6.33 expresses at Gerard Manley Hopkins's "Spring and Fall, to a Young Child," and observes that "the unfortunate readers bray, snort, and bleat, so overmastering is their contempt." He characterizes 13.1 as "a writer who finds only a stock experience in the poem" (Longfellow's "In the Churchyard at Cambridge") and is "only mildly disappointed"—by comparison with others who express increasingly outraged objections to the poem's triteness. He sums up the range of criticism thus: "If the easiest way to popularity is to exploit some stock response, some poem already existent, fully prepared, in the reader's mind, an appearance of appealing to such stock responses, should the reader happen to have discarded them, is a very certain way of courting failure."[43]

As the discussion of the Longfellow poem may serve to demonstrate, Richards's informants treat the poets behind the poems as if they had motives that can only be described as social motives, and they respond as social beings. Moreover they obscure the obligingness of their own responses by their vigilance in discerning in the poet a desire to oblige. Well-guarded social beings, superior to triteness and ingratiation, they demonstrate how little the reading of poetry actually participates in a distinct and autonomous world. Reading the protocols is a bit like reading the excursuses into criticism that pepper Austen's *Emma*. Some of the informants sound a bit like Augusta Hawkins Elton, for whom poetry has such a vague meaning that she can quote bawdy lines about a bull from John Gay as if they were an anodyne tribute to love. More sound like the Emma Woodhouse who sets herself up as a textual scholar when she admits that Robert Martin's letter to Harriet Smith is a good one and then proceeds to suggest that his sisters must have helped him write it. The moral of her story and that of many of the protocol-writers is that an attitude of superiority toward what one is reading is virtually always socially appropriate.

Criticism for Richards is, then, a judgment of our judgments. And when he calls "the arts . . . our storehouse of recorded values" he is not particularly interested in identifying a canon of indisputably great works.[44] Rather the arts assist us in comparing our experiences, among ourselves but also at various different moments in our lives as individuals. John Stuart Mill made it seem as if eloquence and poetry were distinctly different uses of language when he pronounced that eloquence is heard while poetry is overheard. For

Richards, however, the public function of poetry and of the arts generally isn't about others; it's about making it possible for us as readers, as critics to hear ourselves. Hence Richards's appeal to the image of the "alienist," the person who embodies the question "Did you hear yourself?" This is why Richards's work has a strongly ethical tone. Novels like Austen's may depict self-satisfaction and complacency that operate in relation to other people and less and more public writing, but Richards's criticism does as well. In the process it makes it possible to see how one might use a lifetime of reading not merely to know more but to know better than one had before.

Notes

1. Richards, Principles of Literary Criticism, 7.
2. Cormac Herley, "Why Do Nigerian Scammers Say They Are from Nigeria?," Microsoft Research, June 2012, accessed 29 June 2012, Research.microsoft.com/apps/pubs/default.aspx?id+167712.
3. Richards, Practical Criticism, 4.
4. Richards, Poetries and Sciences, 50.
5. See, in particular, Paul de Man, "Metaphor (Second Discourse)," in Allegories of Reading, 135–59. The important and extraordinary move in de Man's chapter involves focusing his account of Rousseau on the relationship between particular instance and general term as an instance of metaphor. Metaphor thus appears in the form of the movement between the general term and its examples rather than anything like a transfer of properties from one term (a lion) to another (a person with such daring and strength of heart as to resemble a lion in that respect).
6. Charles L. Stevenson is especially effective in laying out this aspect of Richards and Ogden's thinking. See his "Richards on the Theory of Value" and Ethics and Language.
7. Ogden and Richards, The Meaning of Meaning, 6.
8. Richards, Practical Criticism, 6
9. Richards, Principles of Literary Criticism, 56.
10. See Richards's chapter of the same name in Principles of Literary Criticism, 44–57.
11. Richards, Principles of Literary Criticism, 44–45, 52.
12. Richards, Practical Criticism, 7.
13. Richards, Principles of Literary Criticism, 74.
14. Richards, Practical Criticism, 229.
15. Critics like William Empson have sometimes been criticized for producing commentaries on versions of texts that existed only in the imperfect medium of their memories. Empson and many others may have misremembered a version of various texts, but Richards and Ogden, I argue, introduced the problem as one that could not be solved merely by regularly consulting the most authoritative versions of texts available. See "Computer Passwords Grow Ever More Complicated," New York Times, 22 June 2012.

16. See Gottlob Frege for the classic discussion of *Sinn* (sense) and *Bedeutung* (reference).

17. W. K. Wimsatt and Monroe Beardsley, "The Intentional Fallacy," in Wimsatt, *The Verbal Icon*, especially 10–14.

18. Richards, *Practical Criticism*, 141.

19. Richards, *Practical Criticism*, 248.

20. Richards, *Principles of Literary Criticism*, 22.

21. Richards, *Practical Criticism*, 208.

22. Richards, *Principles of Literary Criticism*, 104–5.

23. W. K. Wimsatt and Monroe Beardsley, "The Affective Fallacy," in Wimsatt, *The Verbal Icon*, 37.

24. Wimsatt and Beardsley, *The Verbal Icon*, 38.

25. The New Criticism needed to treat only one version of a text, lest it introduce the notion that a poem was mutable. Jerome J. McGann has long called attention to the ways in which textual editing and its attention to textual variants were discounted in New Criticism. See "How Poems Come About: Intention and Meaning," in Cleanth Brooks and Robert Penn Warren, *Understanding Poetry* (New York: Holt, Rinehart and Winston, 1960), 514–550. For Brooks and Warren the practice of an ordinary reader (rather than a textual scholar) necessitates settling on one text and seeing other instances of that text as deficient forms of that text. For an account of the importance of understanding different versions of a text as distinct, see Jerome J. McGann, A Critique of Modern Textual Criticism (Charlottesville: University of Virginia Press, 1992) and "Keats and the Historical Method in Criticism," MLN (1979), 988–1032.

26. Wimsatt and Beardsley, "The Intentional Fallacy," in Wimsatt, *The Verbal Icon*, 4.

27. Richards, *Principles of Literary Criticism*, 1.

28. Brower, "I. A. Richards Interviewed," 28. *I. A. Richards: Essays in His Honor*, ed. Reuben Brower, Helen Vendler, and John Hollander (New York: Oxford University Press, 1973), 17–41.

29. Richards, *Principles of Literary Criticism*, 1.

30. One of Wimsatt and Beardsley's examples deserves particular mention. They devote substantial attention to John Livingstone Lowes's *The Road to Xanadu*, an extensive examination of the reading that, Lowes argues, provided the raw materials for Coleridge's incomplete poem "Kubla Khan." See Wimsatt and Beardsley, "The Intentional Fallacy," in Wimsatt, *The Verbal Icon*, 11–12. At same time, however, they make no mention at all of an impressively convincing brief discussion in which Richards shows the similarities between "Kubla Khan" and Book IV, ll. 223–83 of *Paradise Lost*. See Richards, *Principles of Literary Criticism*, 30–31.

31. Wimsatt, "I.A.R.," 117.

32. Wimsatt, "I.A.R.," 101.

33. Wimsatt, "I.A.R.," 101.

34. Eagleton, *How to Read a Poem*, 114–15.

35. Zunshine, *Strange Concepts and the Stories They Make Possible*, 1–2.

36. Wimsatt quotes from Richards's College English Association Chap-Book, *A Certain Sort of Interest in Language* of October 1941 ("I.A.R.," 102).

37. Richards, *Practical Criticism*, 3.

38. Wimsatt, "I.A.R.," 105, 106–7, 107.

39. Richards, *Practical Criticism*, 174.
40. Catherine Gallagher, *Nobody's Story: The Vanishing Acts of Women Writers in the Marketplace, 1670–1820* (Berkeley: University of California Press, 1994).
41. Richards, *Practical Criticism*, 315.
42. Wimsatt, "I.A.R.," 107.
43. Richards, *Practical Criticism*, 61, 84, 157.
44. Richards, *Principles of Literary Criticism*, 32.

chapter 14

Needing to Know (:) Theory / Afterwords

Ian Balfour

> It is in names that we think.
> —Hegel, Encyclopedia, § 462

To be antitheory is to be anti-intellectual. There is no discourse in the humanities and social sciences that is not in some measure theoretical, if by theory we mean a discourse of or entailing a certain generality, addressing or invoking substantially something beyond one or more entities immediately in question. Our engagement with theory might be explicit or implicit, conscious or not; in any event, theory is always at work. Were we to call those entities engaged "examples" of this or that, we would also already be in the realm of theory. An example is an example of something more, other, and larger than it; the discourse of examples necessarily has a measure of generality, if not universality, a term from which even Adorno—with his relentless emphasis on the fragmentary, the negative, the partial—does not shy away. It is thus not a question of whether or not to do theory, whether to take sides for or against it, but only a question of *how* one does it: how intensively, how self-consciously, how explicitly, how usefully, how well.

Of course, "theory"—or "Theory"—as it has usually been understood and called in the past few decades, means something more pointed; indeed it tends to denote or to connote a discourse identified with or indebted to French or Continental philosophy, with the usual named suspects being approximately, up to a while ago, one or more of (in alphabetical order) Althusser, Barthes, Deleuze, Derrida, Fanon, Foucault, Lacan, and Kristeva, or, more recently, in the era of "theory after theory": Agamben, Badiou, Butler, Nancy, Negri, Rancière, Sedgwick, Spivak, Žižek.[1] One can see from especially that first series of luminaries (yes, a star system) that if in France philosophy had not been taught in high schools, the entire course of theory in the recent West and North might have been different, not least in geographical terms. With the ratcheted-up pace of globalization has come a degree of decentering of theory across the combined and unequal "development" of nations and the work of their intellectuals. A Slovenian philosopher and cultural critic such as Žižek has been able to attain great currency, though one wonders if he would have if, in addition to being smart and provocative, he had not been so fluent in Hegel, Lacan, and company. There are, to be sure, major intellectuals (and theoretically minded ones) scattered all over the globe, only some of whom end up in the vortex that is the United States. There are likely lots I don't know about (my ignorance is partly just mine, partly a symptom of the problem), but some of them would be Kojin Karitani, Roberto Schwarz, Roberto Unger (first Brazil, then USA). . . . The list should go on. And on. But, in practice, it has not.[2]

There cannot *not* be some sort of canon of "theory" across the humanities and social sciences, even if it is what Jameson has dubbed in just such a context "disposable."[3] No one has world enough and time to do justice to all the first-rate theoretical work, even in one's own discipline and linguistic sphere(s). One virtue of having a canon is that if a critical mass of people is versed in it, then they are all, more or less, on the same page in terms of their frames of reference. It facilitates some work and some sorts of understanding. Yet the editors of this volume contend there has been something amiss with the way theory has been prosecuted of late. They are surely right that the canon of high theory was unduly constricted, with a few big names fetishized. Thinking outside the envelope of what narrowly counted as "Theory," some of the various hands of this volume return to compelling theorists of eras past, thinkers whose names students are likely to recognize but whose books they are unlikely to have read. The figures invoked, variously venerable and influential, are often ones whose productive high points stretch as far back as the 1920s or 1930s: Alfred North Whitehead, I. A. Richards, C. L. R. James, Ernst Bloch. Only Irene Tucker really reaches seriously far back, to Kant, a theorist who can't be accused of not being canonical. Yet her return to a charged moment in Kant, locating the specificity of skin for the recognition of race just at a time when the Enlightenment was proclaiming the essential humanity, the sameness, of all humans, presents us with the shock of the old and a pregnant, uncanny genealogical moment to cast a light (or maybe a shadow) on the vexed racial dynamics in America of the civil rights era and beyond. Much closer to our historical home but no longer a central part of the "canon" except in terms of the histories of the disciplines, is someone such as Erving Goffman. Other thinkers invoked are hardly household names. Of the Russian formalists we know of Shklovskii and two or three others, but how many of us had heard of, much less read, their precursor, Aleksandr Veselovskii, strategically mobilized to good use in Simon Jarvis's elaboration of a historical poetics?[4] And surely I am not the only humanities professor of almost any vintage not to have read George Ainslie, whose fascinating account of hyperbolic discounting and intertemporal bargaining and related concepts forms the basis for William Flesch's revelatory contribution, one payoff of which is a better understanding of literature on the far side of the foray into psychology and behavioral economy.

Other contributors chose to engage areas that have tended to be neglected for one reason or another as aside from or even beneath the concerns of high theory: animation as the poor relation of mainstream cinema in Karen Beckman's treatment; the materialities of texts and textual history in Jordan Stein's diagnosis; or prosody in Simon Jarvis's analysis of the stakes in and around Pope's poetry and for what counts as thinking in verse. Here we come upon one of the volume's great strengths: the articulation of empirical, material analysis with any number of pressing theoretical concerns. Walter Benjamin was fond of quoting a passage from Goethe that he took to heart: "There is a delicate empiricism which so intimately involves itself with the object that it becomes pure theory."[5] I doubt that all the authors in this volume would agree that their objects of scrutiny have turned, under their gaze, to "pure theory," but in essay after essay one sees how even just properly describing the matters at hand requires theoretical perspectives and how taking the measure of any number of given instances prompts one to think beyond the objects immediately to (intellectual) hand. Most of the essays are indeed examples of the necessity and difficulty of doing justice to theoretical and historical matters at the same time, a long-standing agenda set by Hegel's philosophy, but an agenda often more honored, over the past two centuries, in the breach than in the observance or, should we say, the observation. Goethe's "delicate empiricism" is much on display throughout this volume, an empiricism that construes its various objects as bound up in some larger nexus, if not quite the downright totality of things.

The specter of totality is raised by the very multiplicity of approaches, objects, and practitioners of theory represented in this volume. We find ourselves in a precarious moment when it comes to what might be considered a brand new totality. No sooner had we finished learning the hard lesson of poststructuralism that absolutely everything was under the sway of difference (still true), when the need to know the totality, if only to register its differential force, impressed itself in the world and on the scene of world theory and any number of seemingly local analyses. Jameson has been the most eloquent proponent of "back to totality" in his *Valences of the Dialectic*, his little book on the *Phenomenology*, the reading of *Capital* I, and any number of shorter interventions (though one thinks also of Joshua Clover's volume of poems, *The Totality for Kids*). It's as if we have to hold in our heads simultaneously Hegel's "The true is the whole" (*Phenomenology*) and Adorno's riposte to and inversion of it: "The whole is the untrue" (*Minima Moralia*); we have to think and write in the spirit of their ramifications, in other words, even if they pull in opposite directions. Jameson, as a voracious reader and preternaturally good absorber and synthesizer of culture and history, is able to pull this off far better than most in his responses to this new demand to address the new, thoroughly globalized totality. But the imperative now presents itself categorically. To everyone.

The editors locate a peculiarly distressing symptom of what has been amiss in "Theory" in the tendency for such discourse to present itself as oracular, which I take to refer to the penchant for the paradox, the gnomic utterance, the conceptual sound bite, the sweeping rhetorical gesture that can claim to do away, in nothing more than a few keystrokes, with centuries, sometimes millennia, of misguided thinking or worse. And if the writings of the canonical theorists were not already unduly oracular in their own right, they seem to have been made all the more so by the way they were cited, circulated, and taught. Now an oracular sentence can often be far more engaging and fun to read than a modest, plain one. Extravagance gets our attention. Even claims soon to be recognized as hyperbolic can give us pause, a pause to think. I once heard the great Dante scholar John Freccero say after hearing a perfectly fine but un-thought-provoking talk, "anyone can say something that is true." The implication, I took it, was that intellectual work should prod and prompt us to reflect further and that the risky, extravagant formulation, while perhaps not being entirely of the order of truth when examined in the cold light of day or under a microscope, might be more productive of intellectual work than the more circumspect, perfectly accurate one. It was partly those oracular formulations—and the reception of them as oracles—that made those not well disposed to Continental philosophical discourse and especially its poststructuralist scions collectively roll their eyes and whine about willful obscurantism. (Let's leave "aside" the fact that many parables of Jesus and many propositions of analytical philosophy, to say nothing of symbolic logic, are very hard, especially for the noninitiate, to understand.) The various hands in this collection by and large eschew the all-or-nothing, "excessorized," as it were, language of high poststructuralism, though Elisabeth Povinelli's repeated use of the terms *extinguish* and *extinguishment* in her incisive essay have a radical, absolute force, and her choice of those terms could not be more deliberate. Once again, if we take the explicit advance and the example of these authors, we have to write differently now, we have to write theory and theorized empirical work in a new way.

Walking one day through a section of Toronto called Kensington Market, an area populated more than not by students, anarchists, owners and employees of small shops, and ex-hippies, I saw a twenty-something woman sporting a T-shirt with the motto "No Theory, No Cry." There's no denying it's a witty rewriting of Bob Marley's memorable, provocative refrain "No Woman, No Cry." But if we are correct, there is no such thing as "No Theory." Perhaps what she meant to say, had there been room enough on the T-shirt, was something close to the spirit of our editors and implicitly the contributors: "No Apocalyptic Theory," "No Oracular Theory," "No Theory That Pretends to Deliver Wholesale Change." All of these could be followed by "No Cry." Once again it is a matter of *how* to do theory, not whether or not to do it. Even Hegel, the arch-"theorist," would say, in his *Lectures on the Philosophy of History*, "We must proceed . . . empirically."[6] There can be differences of approach, differences of rhetoric, and vastly different objects of study, but some sort of theory will and should be a constant. If in Kant's era everybody was a critic—Kant himself maintained it was an "age of criticism"—then perhaps in ours everyone is a theorist. Theory is not the opposite of the empirical but the medium in which it is thought. A lot turns on just how the two are articulated.

Notes

1. In the ultrafamous essay "Against Theory" by Walter Benn Michaels and Steven Knapp, "theory" means something even more pointed: "the attempt to govern interpretations of particular texts by appealing to an account of interpretation in general." Steven Knapp and Walter Benn Michaels, "Against Theory," *Critical Inquiry* 8.4 (1982): 723. Notable is the relatively small proportion in either list of hardcore Marxists and historical materialists. This is not because theory is not crucial to the whole tradition from Marx to, say, David Harvey. Certainly Fredric Jameson, for one, is powerful and subtle as a theorist and is as fluent in the history of theory as anyone around. The tendency not to call these thinkers theorists seems to derive partly from the fact that "theory" is not predominantly what they do and perhaps that the tradition of Marxism tends to privilege praxis over theory. In an earlier dispensation, would Gramsci count as a theorist? His thinking is overwhelmingly geared toward Italian matters, but it has proved useful to any number of thinkers in non-Italian contexts, if sometimes only via analogy.

2. We are dealing here primarily with "theory" as it operates in the English-speaking world and especially in North America. As such, the possibilities of theory are limited by

what appears in translation. If "theory" has a claim to traveling better than work in area studies or of a decidedly circumscribed character, not all theory travels equally well: work in Mandarin, Japanese, Arabic, and even Russian lag far behind counterparts in French or German with respect to their availability in the English-speaking world.

3. See Fredric Jameson, "Periodizing the 60s," in *The Ideologies of Theory*, 2: 193.

4. Translations of the work of Veselovskii (also transliterated as Veselovsky) are scarce but on the rise. One newly translated text can be found in "Envisioning World Literature in 1863."

5. Benjamin, "Little History of Photography," 520.

6. Hegel, *The Philosophy of History*, 10.

bibliography

Abel, Elizabeth. *Signs of the Times: The Visual Politics of Jim Crow.* Berkeley: University of California Press, 2010.
Adorno, Theodore. *Ästhetische Theorie.* Frankfurt am Main: Suhrkamp, 1970.
———. *Minima Moralia.* Frankfurt am Main: Suhrkamp, 1980.
———. *Negative Dialektik.* Frankfurt am Main: Suhrkamp, 1975.
———. *Noten zur Literatur.* Frankfurt am Main: Suhrkamp, 1974.
———. *Vorlesung zur Einleitung in die Soziologie.* Frankfurt am Main: Junius, 1973.
Agamben, Georgio. *Profanations.* New York: Zone Books, 2007.
———. *What Is an Apparatus? And Other Essays.* Translated by David Kishik and Stefan Pedatella. Stanford: Stanford University Press, 2009.
Ainslie, George. *The Breakdown of Will.* Cambridge: Cambridge University Press, 2001.
Alderson, Simon. "Alexander Pope and the Nature of Language." *Review of English Studies* 47 (1996): 23–34.
———. "Iconic Forms in English Poetry of the Time of Dryden and Pope." PhD diss., University of Cambridge, 1993.
Allen, Danielle S. *Talking to Strangers: Anxieties of Citizenship Since Brown v. Board of Education.* Chicago: University of Chicago Press, 2004.
Alpers, Svetlana, and Michael Baxandall. *Tiepolo and the Pictorial Intelligence.* New Haven: Yale University Press, 1994.
Andrew, Dudley. *What Cinema Is!* West Sussex, U.K.: Wiley, 2010.
Andrew, Dudley, with Hervé Joubert-Laurencin. *Opening Bazin: Postwar Theory and Its Afterlife.* Oxford: Oxford University Press, 2011.
Andrews, William L. "Editing 'Minority' Texts." In *The Margins of the Text,* edited by D. C. Greetham, 45–55. Ann Arbor: University of Michigan Press, 1997.
Appiah, Anthony. "The Uncompleted Argument: DuBois and the Illusion of Race." In *"Race," Writing and Difference,* edited by Henry Louis Gates, 21–37. Chicago: University of Chicago Press, 1985.
Audra, Émile, and Aubrey Williams eds. *The Poems of Alexander Pope.* Vol. 1: *Pastoral Poetry and An Essay on Criticism.* London: Methuen, 1961.
Baldwin, James. *Notes of a Native Son.* Boston: Beacon Press, 1984.
Barbaras, Renaud. "Les Trois Sens de la Chair: Sur une impasse de l'ontologie de Merleau-Ponty." *Chiasmi International* 10 (2008): 19–32.
Barnard, John, ed. *Pope: The Critical Heritage.* London: Routledge Kegan Paul, 1973.

Barthes, Roland. *Empire of Signs*. New York: Hill and Wang, 1983 (French edition: *L'Empire des signes*. Geneva. Skira, 1970).

———. *The Neutral*. New York: Columbia University Press, 2005.

———. *Le Neutre: Cours au Collège de France (1977–1978)*. Paris: Éditions du Seuil, 2002.

———. *La Préparation du Roman I et II. Notes de cours et de séminaires au Collège de France 1978–1979 et 1979–1980*. Edited by Nathalie Léger. Paris: Éditions du Seuil, 2003.

Bazin, André. "Fantasia." *Parisien Libéré* 697 (8 November 1946).

———. "Pinocchio." *Parisien Libéré* 555 (30 May 1946).

———. *What Is Cinema?* Vol. 1. Translated by Hugh Gray. Berkeley: University of California Press, 1972.

———. *What Is Cinema?* Vol. 2. Translated by Hugh Gray. Berkeley: University of California Press, 2005.

Beckett, Samuel. "The Expelled." In *Samuel Beckett: The Complete Short Prose. 1929–1989*, edited by S. E. Gontarski, 46–60. New York: Grove Press, 1995.

Beckman, Karen. "Introduction." *Animating Film Theory*. Durham: Duke University Press, 2014.

———. *Crash: Cinema and the Politics of Speed and Stasis*. Durham: Duke University Press, 2010.

Bendazzi, Giannalberto. *Cartoons: One Hundred Years of Cinema Animation*. London: John Libbey, 1994.

Benjamin, Walter. "Little History of Photography." In *Selected Writings: 1931–1934*, vol. 2, edited by Michael W. Jennings et al., 507–30. Cambridge: Harvard University Press, 1999.

Berman, Russell A. "An Agenda for the Future." *MLA Newsletter* 43 (2011): 2–3.

Best, Stephen, and Sharon Marcus. "Surface Reading: An Introduction." *Representations* 108 (2009): 1–21.

Bloch, Ernst. *Erbschaft Dieser Zeit*. Zürich: Verlad Oprecht and Helbling, 1935.

———. *Heritage of Our Times*. Translated by Neville Plaice and Steven Plaice. Cambridge, U.K.: Polity Press, 1991.

———. *The Principle of Hope*. 1959. Translated by Neville Plaice, Stephen Plaice, Stephen Knight, and Paul Knight. Vols. 1–3. Cambridge, Mass.: MIT Press, 1986.

Bloch, Ernst, Georg Lukacs, Bertolt Brecht, Walter Benjamin, and Theodor Adorno. *Aesthetics and Politics*. London: Verso, 1980.

Bogues, Anthony. *Caliban's Freedom: The Early Political Thought of C. L. R. James*. London: Pluto Press, 1997.

Bordwell, David. "Historical Poetics of Cinema." In *The Cinematic Text: Methods and Approaches*, edited by R. Barton Palmer, 369–98. Athens, Ga.: Arms Press, 1989.

Bordwell, David, and Kristin Thompson. *Film Art: An Introduction*. 7th edition. New York: McGraw-Hill, 2004.

Bowers, Fredson. *Textual and Literary Criticism*. Cambridge: Cambridge University Press, 1966.

Braidotti, Rosie. *Transpositions: On Nomadic Ethics*. London: Polity Press, 2006.

Braudy, Leo, and Marshall Cohen, eds. *Film Theory and Criticism: A Reader*. 7th edition. New York: Oxford University Press, 2009.

Brekhus, Wayne H., John F. Galliher, and Jaber F. Gubrium. "The Need for Thin Description." *Qualitative Inquiry* 11 (2005): 861–79.

Brower, Reuben. "I. A. Richards Interviewed," in *I. A. Richards: Essays in His Honor*. New York: Oxford University Press, 1973.

Brown, Matthew P. "Book History, Sexy Knowledge, and the Challenge of the New Boredom." *American Literary History* 16 (2004): 688–706.

Buchan, Suzanne. *Animated "Worlds."* Eastleigh, U.K.: John Libbey, 2006.

Buck-Morss, "Hegel and Haiti." *Critical Inquiry* 26.4 (2000): 821–65.

Buhle, Paul, ed. *C. L. R. James: His Life and Work*. London: Allison and Busby, 1986.

Burkhardt, Richard W. *Patterns of Behavior: Konrad Lorenz, Niko Tinbergen, and the Founding of Ethology*. Chicago: University of Chicago Press, 2005.

Butler, Judith. *Frames of War: When Is Life Grievable?* New York: Verso, 2009.

———. *Gender Trouble: Feminism and the Subversion of Identity*. New York: Routledge, 1990.

———. *Precarious Life: The Powers of Mourning and Violence*. New York: Verso, 2004.

———. *The Psychic Life of Power: Theories in Subjection*. Palo Alto, Calif.: Stanford University Press, 1997.

Cameron, Sharon. *Impersonality*. Chicago: University of Chicago Press, 2007.

Cavell, Stanley. "What Becomes of Things on Film." In *Cavell on Film*, edited by William Rothman, 1–10. Albany: State University of New York Press, 2005.

———. *The World Viewed: Reflections on the Ontology of Film*. Enlarged edition. Cambridge: Harvard University Press, 1979.

Césaire, Aimé. *Discourse on Colonialism*. Translated by Joan Pinkham. New York: Monthly Review Press, 1972.

Chakrabarty, Dipesh. *Provincializing Europe: Postcolonial Thought and Historical Difference*. Princeton: Princeton University Press, 2000.

Chambers, Ephraim. *Cyclopaedia: Or an Universal Dictionary of Arts and Sciences*. 2 vols. London, 1738.

Chaudhary, Zahid. "Subjects in Difference: Walter Benjamin, Frantz Fanon, and Postcolonial Theory." *Differences* 25 (2012): 151–83.

Cholodenko, Alan. "Animation—Film and Media Studies' 'Blind Spot.'" *Society for Animation Studies Newsletter* 20.1 Spring (http://gertie.animationstudies.org/).

———. "(The) Death (of) the Animator, or: The Felicity of Felix." Part 1. "Animated Dialogues," special edition of *Animation Studies*, 2007. http://journal.animationstudies.org/the-death-of-the-animator-or-the-felicity-of-felix-part-i/.

———. "(The) Death (of) the Animator, or: The Felicity of Felix." Part 2. *Animation Studies* 2 (2007). Accessed 9 May 2011. http://journal.animationstudies.org/category/volume-2/the-death-of-the-animator-or-the-felicity-of-felix-part-2/.

———, ed. *The Illusion of Life: Essays on Animation*. Sydney: Power Publications, Australian Film Commission, 1991.

———, ed. *The Illusion of Life II: More Essays on Animation*. Sydney: Power Publications, 2007.

Cohen, Cathy J. "Punks, Bulldaggers, and Welfare Queens: The Radical Potential of Queer Politics?" In *Black Queer Studies: A Critical Anthology*, edited by E. Patrick Johnson and Mae G. Henderson, 21–51. Durham: Duke University Press, 2005.

Cohen, Lara Langer, and Jordan Alexander Stein, eds. *Early African American Print Culture*. Philadelphia: University of Pennsylvania Press, 2012.

Colebrook, Claire. "Extinct Theory." In *Theory After 'Theory,'* edited by Jane Elliott and Derek Attridge, 62–72. London: Routledge, 2011.

Corrigan, Timothy, Patricia White, and Meta Mazaj, eds. *Critical Visions in Film Theory*. New York: Bedford/St. Martin, 2004.

Crafton, Donald. *Before Mickey: Animated Film 1898–1928*. Chicago: University of Chicago Press, 1993.

———. "Collaborative Research, Doc?" *Cinema Journal* 44 (2004): 138–43.

———. *Émile Cohl: Caricature and Film*. Princeton: Princeton University Press, 1990.

Culler, Jonathan. "Afterword: Theory Now and Again." *South Atlantic Quarterly* 110 (2011): 223–30.

Daniel, Samuel. *The Works of Mr. Samuel Daniel*. 2 vols. London, 1718.

Darwin, Charles. "On the Races of Man." 1871. In *From So Simple a Beginning: The Four Great Books of Charles Darwin*. New York: Norton, 2006.

Deleuze Gilles. *Foucault*. Translated by Sean Hand. Minneapolis: University of Minnesota Press, 1988.

Deleuze, Gilles, and Félix Guattari. *A Thousand Plateaus*. Translated by Brian Massumi. Minneapolis: University of Minnesota Press, 1987.

de Man, Paul. *Allegories of Reading: Figural Language in Rousseau, Nietzsche, Rilke, and Proust*. New Haven: Yale University Press, 1979.

Dubois, Laurent. *Avengers of the New World: The Story of the Haitian Revolution*. Cambridge: Harvard University Press, 2004.

Duff, David. "Maximal Tensions and Minimal Conditions: Tynianov as Genre Theorist." *New Literary History* 34 (2003): 553–63.

Durst, David C. "Ernst Bloch's Theory of Nonsimultaneity." *Germanic Review* 77 (2002): 171–94.

Eagleton, Terry. *After Theory*. New York: Basic Books, 2003.

———. *How to Read a Poem*. Oxford: Blackwell, 2007.

Eikhenbaum, Boris. "Concerning the Question of the Formalists: A Survey and a Reply." In *The Futurists, the Formalists, and the Marxist Critique*, edited by Christopher Pike and translated by Christopher Pike and Joe Andrew, 49–62. London: Links, 1979.

———. "Melodika Russkogo Liricheskogo Stikha." In *O Poezii*, 327–511. Leningrad: Nauka, 1969.

———. "The Theory of the 'Formal Method.'" In *Russian Formalist Criticism: Four Essays*, translated and edited by Lee T. Lemon and Marion L. Reis, 99–140. Lincoln: University of Nebraska Press, 1965.

Elliott, Jane, and Derek Attridge. "Introduction: Theory's Nine Lives." In *Theory After 'Theory,'* edited by Jane Elliott and Derek Attridge, 1–16. London: Routledge, 2011.

Empson, William. *Argufying: Essays on Literature and Culture*. Iowa City: University of Iowa Press, 1987.

———. "The Faces of Buddha." In *Argufying: Essays on Literature and Culture*. Iowa City: University of Iowa Press, 1987.

Eng, David L., Judith Halberstam, and José Esteban Muñoz, eds. "What's Queer about Queer Studies Now?" Special issue of *Social Text* 84–85 (2005): 1–17.

Epstein, Steven. "Thinking Sex Ethnographically." *GLQ* 17 (2010): 85–88.

Erber, Pedro. "Contemporaneity and Its Discontents." *Diacritics* 41.1 (2013): 29–48.

Esposito, Roberto. *Bios: Biopolitics and Philosophy*. Translated by Timothy Campbell. Palo Alto, Calif.: Stanford University Press, 2008.

Fabian, Johannes. *Time and the Other: How Anthropology Makes Its Object.* New York: Columbia University Press, 1983.

Fanon, Frantz. *The Wretched of the Earth.* New York: Grove Press, 2005.

Farred, Grant. "'Science Does Not Think': The No-Thought of the Discipline." *South Atlantic Quarterly* 110 (2011): 57–74.

Fechner, Gustav. *Elements of Psychophysics.* Translated by H. Adler. New York: Holt, Rinehart and Winston, 1966.

Fink, Eugen. "Vergegenwärtigung und Bild." In *Studien zur Phänomenologie, 1930–1939.* The Hague: Nijoff, 1966.

Fischer, Sibylle. *Modernity Disavowed: Haiti and the Cultures of Slavery in the Age of Revolution.* Durham: Duke University Press, 2004.

Flesch, William. *Comeuppance.* Cambridge, Mass.: Harvard University Press, 2009.

Foucault, Michel. *The Birth of Biopolitics.* Edited by Michel Senellart. Translated by Graham Burchell. Chippenham, U.K.: Palgrave Macmillan, 1988.

———. *Ethics: Subjectivity and Truth.* Edited by Paul Rabinow. New York: New Press, 1990.

———. *The History of Sexuality: An Introduction.* Vol. 1. Translated by Robert Hurley. New York: Vintage, 1990.

———. *Security, Territory, Population: Lectures at the College de France 1977–78.* Edited by Michel Senellart. Translated by Graham Burchell. New York: Picador, 2004.

———. *"Society Must Be Defended": Lectures at the College de France, 1975–1976.* Translated by David Macey. New York: Picador, 2003.

Foxon, David. *Pope and the Early Eighteenth-Century Book Trade.* Revised and edited by James McLaverty. Oxford: Clarendon Press, 1991.

Frankfurt, Harry. *The Importance of What We Care About.* New York: Cambridge University Press, 1988.

Fraser, Nancy. *Unruly Practices: Power, Discourse and Gender in Contemporary Social Theory.* Cambridge, U.K.: Polity, 1989.

Fraser, Nancy, and Axel Honneth. *Redistribution or Recognition? A Political-Philosophical Exchange.* Translated by Joel Golb, James Ingram, and Christiane Wilke. New York: Verso, 2003.

Freud, Sigmund. *Beyond the Pleasure Principle.* Volume 18. Edited and translated by James Strachey. *The Standard Edition of the Complete Psychological Works.* London: The Hogarth Press, 1955.

Furuhata, Yuriko. "Rethinking Plasticity: The Politics and Production of the Animated Image." *Animation* 6 (2011): 25–38.

———. "Returning to Actuality: Fûkeiron and the Landscape Film." *Screen* 48 (2007): 345–62.

Galloway, Alexander R. *Gaming: Essays on Algorithmic Culture.* Minneapolis: University of Minnesota Press, 2006.

———. "Origins of the First-Person Shooter." In *Gaming: Essays on Algorithmic Culture.* Minneapolis: University of Minnesota Press, 2006.

Gates, Henry Louis, Jr. "African American Studies in the 21st Century." *Black Scholar* 22 (2001): 3–9.

———. "Goodbye, Columbus? Notes on the Culture of Criticism." *American Literary History* 3 (1991): 711–27.

———. *The Signifying Monkey: A Theory of African-American Literary Criticism*. New York: Oxford University Press, 1988.
Geertz, Clifford. *Local Knowledges: Further Essays in Interpretive Anthropology*. New York: Basic Books, 1983.
Gessner, Robert. "Some Notes on Cinematic Movements." *Journal of the Society of Cinematologists* 3 (1963): 1–5.
Geuss, Raymond. "Is Poetry a Form of Knowledge?" *Arion* 11 (2003): 1–3.
Ghosh, Jayati. *Impact of Globalization on Women: Women and Economic Liberalization in the Asian and Pacific Region*. Women in Development Discussion Paper Series No. 1. United Nations Economic and Social Commission for Asia and the Pacific, 1999.
Gildon, Charles, *The Complete Art of Poetry*. 2 vols. London, 1718.
Goffman, Erving, "The Arrangement between the Sexes." *Theory and Society* 4 (1977): 301–31.
———. *Frame Analysis: An Essay on the Organization of Experience*. Boston: Northeastern University Press, 1974.
———. *Interaction Ritual: Essays on Face-to-Face Behavior*. New York: Pantheon Books, 1967.
———. *The Presentation of Self in Everyday Life*. New York: Anchor Books, 1959.
———. *Stigma: On the Management of Spoiled Identity*. Englewood, N.J.: Prentice Hall, 1963.
Goodman, Steve. *Sonic Warfare: Sound, Affect, and the Ecology of Fear*. Cambridge, Mass.: MIT Press, 2009.
Graff, Gerald. *Professing Literature: An Institutional History*. Chicago: University of Chicago Press, 1987.
Greetham, David. "[Textual] Criticism and Deconstruction." *Studies in Bibliography* 44 (1991): 1–30.
Guillory, John. *Cultural Capital: The Problem of Literary Canon Formation*. Chicago: University of Chicago Press, 1993.
Gunning, Tom. "The Discovery of Virtual Movement." Lecture given at the Penn Humanities Forum, 3 November 2010. Accessed 12 May 2011. http://www.phf.upenn.edu/1011/gunning.shtml.
———. "Moving Away from the Index: Cinema and the Impression of Reality." *differences* 18 (2007): 29–52.
Ha, Marie-Paul. *Figuring the East: Segalen, Malraux, Duras, and Barthes*. Albany: State University of New York Press, 2000.
Halberstam, Judith. "The Anti-social Turn in Queer Studies." *Graduate Journal of Social Science* 5 (2008): 140–56.
———. *The Queer Art of Failure*. Durham: Duke University Press, 2011.
Hamilton, Andy. "Ernst Mach and the Elimination of Subjectivity." *Ratio* 3 (1990): 117–35.
Hamrick, William S., and Jan van der Veken. *Nature and Logos: A Whiteheadian Key to Merleau-Ponty's Fundamental Thought*. Albany: State University of New York Press, 2011.
Hansen, Mirian. "Of Mice and Ducks: Benjamin on Adorno and Disney." *South Atlantic Quarterly* 93 (1993): 27–61.
Hardt, Michael. "The Militancy of Theory." *South Atlantic Quarterly* 110 (2011): 19–35.

Hardt, Michael, and Antonio Negri. *Empire*. Cambridge: Harvard University Press, 2001.
Hartog, François. *Régimes d'historicté: Présentisme et expérience du temps*. Paris: Seuil, 2003.
Hegel, Georg F. *Enzyklopaedie der philosohischen Wissenschaften*. Vol. 10 in *Werke in 20 Bänden*. Edited by E. Moldenhauer and K. M. Michel. Frankfurt am Main: Suhrkamp, 1970.
———. *Die Phänomenologie des Geistes*. Vol. 3 in *Werke in 20 Bänden*. Edited by E. Moldenhauer and K. M. Michel. Frankfurt am Main: Suhrkamp, 1976.
———. *The Philosophy of History*. Translated by J. Sibree. Amherst, Mass.: Prometheus Books, 1991.
Heidegger, Martin. *Being and Time*. Translated by J. Macquarrie and E. Robinson. New York: Harper and Row, 1962.
Hinton, Leanne, Johanna Nichols, and John J. Ohala, eds. *Sound Symbolism*. Cambridge: Cambridge University Press, 1994.
Hirschman, Albert O. "Against Parsimony." *AEA Papers and Proceedings* 74 (1984): 89–96.
Huffer, Lynne. *Mad for Foucault: Rethinking the Foundations of Queer Theory*. New York: Columbia University Press, 2009.
Humphreys, Laud. *Tearoom Trade: Impersonal Sex in Public Places*. New Brunswick, N.J.: Aldine Transaction, 1970.
Jackson, Leon. "The Talking Book and the Talking Book Historian: African American Cultures of Print—The State of the Discipline." *Book History* 13 (2010): 251–308.
James, C. L. R. *The Black Jacobins: Toussaint L'ouverture and the San Domingo Revolution*. New York: Vintage, 1989.
———. "Lectures on The Black Jacobins" *Small Axe* 8 (2000): 65–112.
———. *A History of Negro Revolt*. London: Fact, 1938.
———. *World Revolution 1917–1936: The Rise and Fall of the Communist International*. New York: Pioneer, 1937.
James, William. *A Pluralistic Universe*. Rockville, Md.: Arc Manor, 2008.
Jameson, Fredric. *The Ideologies of Theory*. Minneapolis: University of Minnesota Press, 1989.
———, ed. *Aesthetics and Politics*. London: Verso. 2007
Jarvis, Simon. *Adorno: A Critical Introduction*. Cambridge, U.K.: Polity Press, 1998.
———. "Bedlam or Parnassus: The Verse Idea." *Metaphilosophy* 43 (2012): 71–81.
———. *Wordsworth's Philosophic Song*. Cambridge: Cambridge University Press, 2007.
Jay, Martin. *Marxism and Totality: The Adventures of a Concept from Lukács to Habermas*. Berkeley: University of California Press, 1984.
Jeffrey, Richard. *The Logic of Decision*. 2nd edition. Chicago: University of Chicago Press, 1983.
Jehlen, Myra, and Maureen Quilligan. "Guest Column." *PMLA* 101 (1986): 771–72.
Johnson, Samuel. *The Lives of the Poets*. Edited by Roger Lonsdale. Oxford: Clarendon Press, 2006.
Jones, Judith. *Intensity: An Essay in Whiteheadean Ontology*. Nashville, Tenn.: Vanderbilt University Press, 1998.
Jones, T. E. "Plato's *Cratylus*, Dionysius of Halicarnassus, and the Correctness of Names in Pope's Homer." *Review of English Studies* 53 (2002): 484–99.
Joubert-Laurencin, Hervé. *La Lettre Volante: Quatre essays sur le cinema d'animation*. Paris: Presses de la Sorbonne Nouvelle, 1997.
Kahneman, Daniel. *Thinking Fast and Slow*. New York: Farrar, Straus and Giroux, 2011.

Kant, Immanuel. *The Conflict of the Faculties*. Translated by Mary J. Gregor. Lincoln: University of Nebraska Press, 1992.

Kennedy, John F. "The President's Civil Rights Message." *Ebony*, September 1963.

Knapp, Steven, and Walter Benn Michaels. "Against Theory." *Critical Inquiry* 8 (1982): 723–42.

Kojève, Alexandre. "In Place of an Introduction." In *Introduction to the Reading of Hegel*, edited by Allan Bloom, 3–30. New York: Basic Books, 1969.

Koselleck, Reinhart. *Futures Past: On the Semantics of Historical Time*. 1979. Translated by Keith Tribe. New York: Columbia University Press, 2004.

Lamarre, Thomas. *The Anime Machine: A Media Theory of Animation*. Minneapolis: University of Minnesota Press, 2009.

Le Grand Robert de la langue française. Edited by Alain Rey. Paris: Dictionnaires Le Robert, 2001.

Leslie, Esther. *Hollywood Flatlands: Animation, Critical Theory and the Avant-Garde*. London: Verso, 2002.

Lloyd, David. *Irish Times: Temporalities of Modernity*. Dublin: Field Day, 2008.

Mack, Maynard, ed. *The Last and Greatest Art: Some Unpublished Poetical Manuscripts of Alexander Pope*. Newark: University of Delaware Press, 1984.

———, ed. *The Poems of Alexander Pope*, vol. 3, part 1: *An Essay on Man*. London: Methuen, 1958.

Macksey, Richard, and Eugenio Donato. "The Space Between—1971." In *The Structuralist Controversy*, edited by Richard Macksey and Eugenio Donato, xv–xx. Baltimore: Johns Hopkins University Press, 1972.

Macksey, Richard, René Girard, and Jean Hyppolite. "Concluding Remarks." In *The Structuralist Controversy*, edited by Richard Macksey and Eugenio Donato, 319–22. Baltimore: Johns Hopkins University Press, 1972.

Manovich, Lev. *The Language of New Media*. Cambridge, Mass.: MIT Press, 2001.

Lev Manovich, "What Is Digital Cinema?" (1995). Accessed 13 October 2013. http://manovich.net/TEXT/digital-cinema.html.

Marcus, Sharon. "Queer Theory for Everyone: A Review Essay." *Signs: Journal of Women in Culture and Society* 31.1 (2005): 191–218.

Marx, Karl. "Contribution to the Critique of Hegel's Philosophy of Right. Introduction" (1843). In *Early Writings*, translated by Rodney Livingstone and Gregor Benton. Harmondsworth, U.K.: Penguin, 1975.

Maslov, Boris. "The Semantics of *Aoidos* and Related Compounds: Towards a Historical Poetics of Solo Performance in Archaic Greece." *Classical Antiquity* 28 (2009): 1–38.

McGann, Jerome. *A Critique of Modern Textual Criticism*. Chicago: University of Chicago Press, 1983.

McGill, Meredith L. *American Literature and the Culture of Reprinting, 1834–1853*. Philadelphia: University of Pennsylvania Press, 2003.

McKenzie, D. F. *Bibliography and the Sociology of Texts*. Cambridge: Cambridge University Press, 1986.

McLaverty, James. *Pope, Print and Meaning*. Oxford: Oxford University Press, 2001.

Merleau-Ponty, Maurice. *The Phenomenology of Perception*. Translated by Colin Smith. London: Routledge, 2002.

———. *The Visible and the Invisible*. Translated by A. Lingis. Evanston, Ill.: Northwestern University Press, 1968.

Miéville, China. *The City and the City*. New York: Random House, 2009.

Miller, D. A. *Bringing Out Roland Barthes*. Berkeley: University of California Press, 1992.

Mitchell, W. J. T. "Medium Theory: Preface to the 2003 Critical Inquiry Symposium." *Critical Inquiry* 30 (2004): 324–35.

Mulvey, Laura. "Visual Pleasure and Narrative Cinema." *Screen* 16 (1975): 6–18.

Nietzsche, Friedrich. *Untimely Meditations* (1873–76). Translated by R. J. Hollingdale. Cambridge: Cambridge University Press, 1997.

Ngai, Sianne. *Ugly Feelings*. Cambridge: Harvard University Press, 2007.

Noxon, Gerald. "Cinema and Cubism (1900–1915)." *Journal of the Society of Cinematologists* 2 (1962): 23–33.

———. "Pictorial Origins of Cinema Narrative: The Illusion of Movement and the Birth of the Scene in the Paleolithic Cave Wall Paintings of Lascaux." *Journal of the Society of Cinematologists* 4/5 (1964–65): 20–26.

Ogden, C. K., and I. A. Richards. *The Meaning of Meaning*. San Diego: Harcourt Brace Jovanovich, 1989.

Osborne, Peter. "Philosophy after Theory: Transdisciplinarity and the New." In *'Theory After Theory,'* edited by Jane Elliott and Derek Attridge, 19–33. London: Routledge, 2011.

Pattai, Daphne, and Will H. Corral. Introduction. In *Theory's Empire*, edited by Daphne Pattai and Will H. Corral, 1–18. New York: Columbia University Press, 2005.

Phongpaichit, Pasuk. *From Peasant Girls to Bangkok Masseuses*. Geneva: International Labour office, 1982.

Pilling, Jayne. *Animation 2D and Beyond*. London: Rotovision, 2001.

———. *Women and Animation*. London: BFI, 1992.

Poovey, Mary. "Recovering Ellen Pickering." *Yale Journal of Criticism* 13 (2000): 437–52.

Price, Leah. *The Anthology and the Rise of the Novel: From Richardson to George Eliot*. Cambridge: Cambridge University Press, 2005.

Prins, Yopie. "Historical Poetics, Dysprosody, and the Science of English Verse." *PMLA: Publications of the Modern Language Association of America* 123.1 (2008): 229–34.

Propp, Vladimir. *The Morphology of the Folktale*. Austin: University of Texas Press, 1973.

Punpuing, Sureeporn. "Female Migration in Thailand: A Study of Migrant Domestic Workers." In *Perspectives on Gender and Migration: From the Regional Seminar on Strengthening the Capacity of National Machineries for Gender Equality to Shape Migration Policies and Protect Migrant Women, Bangkok, 22–24 November 2006*. Bangkok, Thailand: United Nations Economic and Social Commission for Asia and the Pacific, 2007.

Rabinbach, Anson. "Unclaimed Heritage: Ernst Bloch's *Heritage of Our Times* and the Theory of Fascism." *New German Critique* 11 (1997): 5–21.

Rancière, Jacques. *Disagreement: Politics and Philosophy*. Edited by Julie Rose. Minneapolis: University of Minnesota Press, 2004.

———. *Dissensus: On Politics and Aesthetics*. Translated and edited by Steven Corcoran. London: Continuum, 2010.

Rasch, William. "Theory after Critical Theory." In *Theory After 'Theory,'* edited by Jane Elliott and Derek Attridge, 49–61. London: Routledge, 2011.

Reinke, Steve. "The World Is a Cartoon: Stray Notes on Animation." In *The Sharpest Point: Animation at the End of Cinema*, edited by Chris Gehman and Steve Reinke, 9–26. Toronto: YYZ Books, 2005.

Richards, I. A. *Poetries and Sciences: A Reissue of Science and Poetry (1926, 1935) with Commentary*. London: Routledge and Kegan Paul, 1970.

———. *Practical Criticism*. New York: Harcourt, Brace and World, 1956.

———. *Principles of Literary Criticism* (1925). New York: Harcourt, Brace and World, 1965.

Richardson, Jonathan. *An Essay on the Theory of Painting*. London: William Bowyer, 1715.

Robinson, Cedric. *Black Marxism: The Making of the Black Radical Tradition*. Chapel Hill: University of North Carolina Press, 2000.

Rodowick, David. *The Virtual Life of Film*. (Cambridge: Harvard University Press, 2007).

———. "The World, Time." In *Afterimages of Gilles Deleuze's Film Philosophy*, edited by D. N. Rodowick, 97–114. Minneapolis: University of Minnesota Press, 2010.

Rooks, Noliwe. *White Money / Black Power: The Surprising History of African American Studies and the Crisis of Race in Higher Education*. Boston: Beacon Press, 2007.

Rothberg, Michael. *Multidirectional Memory: Remembering the Holocaust in the Age of Decolonization*. Palo Alto, Calif.: Stanford University Press, 2009.

Rowell, Charles H. "An Interview with Henry Louis Gates, Jr." *Callaloo* 14 (1991): 444–63.

Rubin, Gayle. "Thinking Sex: Notes for a Radical Theory of the Politics of Sexuality." In *Pleasure and Danger: Exploring Female Sexuality*, edited by Carole S. Vance, 267–319. Boston: Routledge and Kegan Paul, 1984.

Rudy, Jason R. "On Cultural Neoformalism, Spasmodic Poetry, and the Victorian Ballad." *Victorian Poetry* 4 (2003): 590–96.

Rumbold, Valerie, ed. *The Dunciad in Four Books*. London: Longman, 1999.

Russell, Bertrand. "The Ultimate Constituents of Matter." In *Realism and the Background of Phenomenology*, edited by R. Chisholm, 223–37. Glencoe, Ill.: Free Press, 1960.

Samuelson, Paul. "A Note on Measurement of Utility." *Review of Economic Studies* 4 (1937): 155–61.

Scott, David. *Conscripts of Modernity: The Tragedy of Colonial Enlightenment*. Durham: Duke University Press, 2004.

Sedgwick, Eve Kosofsky. *Epistemology of the Closet*. Berkeley: University of California Press, 1990.

———. *Touching Feeling*. Durham: Duke University Press, 2003.

———. *The Weather in Proust*. Edited by Jonathan Goldberg. Durham: Duke University Press, 2011.

Sesonske, Alexander. "The World Viewed." *Georgia Review* 28 (1974): 561–70.

Shaitanov, Igor. "Aleksandr Veselovskii's Historical Poetics: Genre in Historical Poetics." *New Literary History* 32 (2001): 429–43.

Shaviro, Steven. *Without Criteria: Kant, Whitehead, Deleuze, and Aesthetics*. Cambridge, Mass.: MIT Press, 2009.

Sherburn, George, ed. *The Correspondence of Alexander Pope*. Oxford: Clarendon Press, 1956.

The Simpsons. "The Scorpion's Tale." Episode 479, 6 March 2011.

Skrbina, David. *Panpsychism and the West*. Cambridge, Mass.: MIT Press, 2005.
Sobchack, Vivian. "Final Fantasies: Computer Graphic Animation and the [Dis]Illusion of Life." In *Animated "Worlds,"* edited by Suzanne Buchan, 171–82. Eastleigh, U.K.: John Libbey, 2006.
———. *Meta-Morphing: Visual Transformation and the Culture of Quick-Change*. Minneapolis: University of Minnesota Press, 2000.
Spence, Joseph. *Observations, Anecdotes, and Characters of Books and Men: Collected from Conversation*. Edited by James M. Osborn. Oxford: Clarendon Press, 1966.
Spinoza, Baruch. *Ethics*. Translated by G. H. R. Parkinson. New York: Oxford University Press, 2000.
Stam, Robert, and Toby Miller, eds. *Film and Theory: An Anthology*. Malden, Mass.: Blackwell, 2000.
Starr, Cecile. *Experimental Animation: Origins of a New Art*. New York: Da Capo, 1976.
Stevenson, Charles L. *Ethics and Language*. New Haven: Yale University Press, 1944.
———. "Richards on the Theory of Value." In *I. A. Richards: Essays in His Honor*, edited by Reuben Brower, Helen Vendler, and John Hollander, 119–34. New York: Oxford University Press, 1973.
Stryker, Susan. "My Words to Victor Frankenstein," *GLQ* 1, no. 3 (1994): 237–54.
Surin, Kenneth. "Introduction: 'Theory Now'?" *South Atlantic Quarterly* 110 (2011): 3–17.
Sutherland, John. "Publishing History: A Hole at the Centre of Literary Sociology." *Critical Inquiry* 14 (1988): 574–89.
Tarlinskaia, Marina. *English Verse: Theory and History*. The Hague: Mouton, 1976.
Terada, Rei. "The Frailty of the Ontic." *South Atlantic Quarterly* 110 (2011): 37–55.
Tibbetts, John. Review. *Cinema Journal* 8 (1969): 32–33.
Tillotson, Geoffrey, ed. *The Poems of Alexander Pope*, vol. 2: *The Rape of the Lock and Other Poems*. New Haven: Yale University Press, 1962.
Toynbee, Philip. *Underdogs: Anguish and Anxiety. Eighteen Men and Women Write Their Own Case Histories*. New York: Horizon Press, 1962.
Trask, Michael. *Camp Sites: Sex, Politics, and Academic Style in Postwar Culture*. Stanford: Stanford University Press, 2013.
———. "Patricia Highsmith's Method." *American Literary History* 22 (2010): 584–614.
Traverso, Enzo. *L'histoire come champ de bataille: interpréter les violences du xxe siècle*. Paris: La Découverte, 2010.
Trotsky, *History of the Russian Revolution*. Translated by Max Eastman. Vol. 1. New York: Simon and Schuster, 1932.
Trouillot, Michel-Rolph. *Silencing the Past: Power and the Production of History*. Boston: Beacon Press, 1995.
Tucker, Herbert. *Epic: Britain's Heroic Muse 1790–1910*. Oxford: Oxford University Press, 2008.
———. "The Fix of Form: An Open Letter." *Victorian Literature and Culture* 27 (1999): 531–35.
Tynianov, Yuri. *Arkhaisty i Novatory*. Edited by Dmitri Tschiżewskij. Slavische Propyläen, 31. Munich: Wilhelm Fink Verlag, 1967.
———. *The Problem of Verse Language*. Edited and translated by Michael Sosa and Brent Harvey. Ann Arbor, Mich.: Ardis, 1981.
Velleman, J. David. *Self to Self*. New York: Cambridge University Press, 2005.

Veselovsky, A. N. "Envisioning World Literature in 1863: From the Reports on a Mission Abroad." Translated by Jennifer Flaherty. Edited by Boris Maslov, with an introductory note by Maslov. PMLA 128.2 (2013) 439-51.

Warren, Kenneth W. *What Was African American Literature*. Cambridge, Mass.: Harvard University Press, 2011.

Warner, Michael. *Fear of a Queer Planet: Queer Politics and Social Theory*. Minneapolis: University of Minnesota Press, 1993.

Wellek, Rene. *A History of Modern Criticism: 1750–1950. The Later Nineteenth Century*. New Haven: Yale University Press, 1965.

Wells, Paul. "Battlefields for the Undead: Stepping Out of the Graveyard," *Animation Studies—Animated Dialogues*, 7 July 2007. Accessed 9 May 2011. http://journal.animationstudies.org/2009/07/07/paul-wells-battlefields-for-the-undead/#more-64.

———. "Notes toward a Theory of Animation" In *Understanding Animation*, 35–67. New York: Routledge, 1998.

Wenzel, Jennifer. *Bulletproof: Afterlives of Colonial Prophecy in South Africa and Beyond*. Chicago: University of Chicago Press, 2009.

———. "Remembering the Past's Future: Anti-Imperialist Nostalgia and Some Versions of the Third World." *Cultural Critique* 62 (2006).

Whitehead, Alfred North. *Process and Reality: An Essay in Cosmology*. Edited by D. R. Griffin and D. W. Sherburne. New York: Free Press, 1979.

Wilder, Gary. "Untimely Vision: Aimé Césaire, Decolonization, Utopia." *Public Culture* 21.1 (2009): 101–40.

Williams, Raymond. *Culture and Society, 1780–1850*. New York: Harper and Row, 1966.

———. *Keywords: A Vocabulary of Culture and Society*. New York: Oxford University Press, 1985.

Willoughby, Dominique. *Le cinema graphique: Une histoire des dessins animés. Des jouets d'optique au cinema numérique*. Paris: Éditions Textuel, 2009.

Wimsatt, W. K. "I.A.R.: What to Say about a Poem." In *I. A. Richards: Essays in His Honor*, edited by Reuben Brower, Helen Vendler, and John Hollander, 101–17. New York: Oxford University Press, 1973.

———. *The Verbal Icon*. Lexington: University of Kentucky Press, 1967.

Wimsatt, William K., and Monroe C. Beardsley. "The Intentional Fallacy." *Sewanee Review* 54 (1946): 468–88.

Wolfe, Cary, "Theory as a Research Program—The Very Idea." In *Theory After 'Theory,'* edited by Jane Elliott and Derek Attridge, 34–48. London: Routledge, 2011.

Women and Globalization. http://www.unescap.org/sdd/publications/gender/Pub_globalization.pdf. Accessed 13 October 2013.

Wordsworth, William. "Essay, Supplementary to the Preface." In *Shorter Poems, 1807–1820*. Edited by Carl H. Ketcham, 642–57. Ithaca: Cornell University Press, 1989.

Zhirmunsky, Viktor. *Kompozitsiya liricheskikh stikhotvorenij*. Petersburg: Opoyaz, 1921.

Zunshine, Lisa. *Strange Concepts and the Stories They Make Possible: Cognition, Culture, Narrative*. Baltimore: Johns Hopkins University Press, 2008.

contributors

IAN BALFOUR teaches English at York University. He is the author of several books, including The Rhetoric of Romantic Prophecy (2002). He has coedited with Atom Egoyan Subtitles: On the Foreignness of Film (2004) and with Eduardo Cadava And Justice for All? The Claims of Human Rights for SAQ. He has taught at Cornell as the M. H. Abrams Distinguished Visiting Professor and held visiting professorships at Williams College, the Johann Wolfgang Goethe University in Frankfurt, Stanford, and the University of Toronto. He is currently finishing a book on the sublime.

KAREN BECKMAN is the Elliot and Roslyn Jaffe Professor of Cinema and Modern Media in the department of the History of Art at the University of Pennsylvania. She is the author of Vanishing Women: Magic, Film and Feminism (Duke University Press, 2003); Crash: Cinema and the Politics of Speed and Stasis (Duke University Press, 2010), and is working on a new book, Animation and the Contemporary Art of War. She is the co-editor (with Jean Ma) of Still Moving: Between Cinema and Photography (Duke University Press, 2008) and (with Liliane Weissberg) of On Writing With Photography (2013), and editor of Animating Film Theory (Duke University Press, 2014).

PHENG CHEAH is a professor of rhetoric at the University of California, Berkeley, where he has taught since 1999. He has published extensively on the theory and practice of cosmopolitanism and is the author of Inhuman Conditions: On Cosmopolitanism and Human Rights (2006) and Spectral Nationality: Passages of Freedom from Kant to Postcolonial Literatures of Liberation (2003) and the coeditor of Cosmopolitics: Thinking and Feeling Beyond the Nation (1998). He is also the co-editor of Thinking through the Body of the Law (1996); Grounds of Comparison: Around the Work of Benedict Anderson (2003); and Derrida and the Time of the Political (Duke University Press, 2009). He is completing a book on theories of the world and world literature from the postcolonial world in an age of financial globalization and a related book on globalization and the three Chinas, as seen from the perspectives of the independent cinema of Jia Zhangke, Tsai Ming-Liang, and Fruit Chan.

FRANCES FERGUSON teaches in the English Department at the University of Chicago. She works on eighteenth- and nineteenth-century literature and literary theory and is currently completing studies on the rise of mass education and on reading and practical criticism.

WILLIAM FLESCH teaches literature, film, and sometimes philosophy at Brandeis and writes regularly for the *Los Angeles Review of Books* and TLS.

ANNE-LISE FRANÇOIS is an associate professor of English and comparative literature at University of California, Berkeley. Her first book, *Open Secrets: The Literature of Uncounted Experience* (2008), was awarded the 2010 René Wellek Prize by the American Comparative Literature Association. Her current book project sharpens the critique of Enlightenment models of heroic action, productive activity, and energetic accumulation begun in *Open Secrets*.

MARK B. N. HANSEN is a professor of literature and the director of Undergraduate Studies, Literature in Duke University's Art, Art History and Visual Studies Department. Over the past decade he has sought to theorize the role played by technology in human agency and social life. He is the author of *Embodying Technesis: Technology beyond Writing* (2000), *Bodies in Code: Interfaces with New Media, New Philosophy for New Media* (2004), and *Feed Forward: On the "Future" of 21st Century Media* (2013).

SIMON JARVIS is the Gorley Putt Professor of Poetry and Poetics at the University of Cambridge. He is the author of *Wordsworth's Philosophic Song* (2007) as well as of many essays on literary theory and the poetics of verse.

HEATHER LOVE is the R. Jean Brownlee Term Associate Professor at the University of Pennsylvania. She is the author of *Feeling Backward: Loss and the Politics of Queer History* (2007), the editor of a special issue of GLQ on the scholarship and legacy of Gayle Rubin ("Rethinking Sex"), and the coeditor of a special issue of *New Literary History* ("Is There Life after Identity Politics?"). She has current projects on new reading methods in literary studies, the sociologist Erving Goffman, and pedagogy and mentorship in queer studies.

NATALIE MELAS is an associate professor in comparative literature at Cornell University. She has published essays on the fate of the humanities in the contemporary university, on incommensurability, on Joseph Conrad, and on French Caribbean literature; her book, *All the Difference in the World: Postcoloniality and the Ends of Comparison*, is published by 2007. Her current project addresses the formation of alternative modernities in the broken link between modernism and colonialism.

JASON POTTS teaches at St. Francis Xavier University and publishes articles on American literature and literary theory. His current book project examines the development of meritocratic thinking in late nineteenth- and early twentieth-century American literature.

ELIZABETH A. POVINELLI is a professor of anthropology and gender studies at Columbia University, where she is also chair of the Department of Anthropology. Her works focuses on the critique of late liberalism, with a special focus on settler colonialism. She is the author of four books—*Labor's Lot* (1994), *The Cunning of Recognition* (Duke University Press, 2002), *The Empire of Love* (Duke University Press, 2002), and *Economies of Abandonment* (Duke University Press, 2011)—and numerous essays and articles published in major journals in anthropology, cultural studies, gender studies, and critical art. She is currently completing a graphic book about generational memory.

EVE KOSOFSKY SEDGWICK (1950–2009) was a Distinguished Professor of English at the CUNY Graduate Center. Her books include *Epistemology of the Closet*; *Between Men*; *A Dialogue on Love*; *Touching Feeling* (Duke University Press, 2003); *Fat Art, Thin Art* (Duke University Press, 1994); and *The Weather in Proust* (Duke University Press, 2011).

JORDAN ALEXANDER STEIN is the author of journal articles in *American Literary History*, *American Literature*, and ESQ. With Justine S. Murison he co-edited a special issue of *Early American Literature* on "Methods for the Study of Religion" in 2010, and with Lara Langer Cohen he co-edited *Early African American Print Culture* (2012).

DANIEL STOUT is an assistant professor at the University of Mississippi. His current project is a book-length study of collectivity, corporate personhood, and justice in the nineteenth-century British novel.

IRENE TUCKER is a professor of English at University of California, Irvine, and the author of *A Probable State: The Novel, the Contract and the Jews* (2000) and *The Moment of Racial Sight: A History* (2012).

index

abjection, 122
access, 190; experimentation and, 223; Fechner and, 222; to modes of cinematic analysis, 192; to sensory dimensions of experience, 220, 221
Addison, Joseph, 211
adjacency, 13
Adorno, Theodor: *Aesthetic Theory*, 100; affinity of, to James's American writings, 76n21; critical theory and, 101, 280; historical aesthetics and, 100; historical poetics and, 15; totality and, 283
aesthetics, 14, 170, 266, 270; evaluation of, 11; historical, 100; Kant and, 145; rupture of, 15; study of literature and, 164; terms of, 163; therapeutic turn and, 211n9; of verse, 112
affects: affectivism and, 267, 268; Sedgwick on, 47, 49, 54n38
Africa, 65–72; Bloch and, 64
African American literary studies, 170–173; bibliography and, 160–62, 170
African Americans, 157n4; admitted to University of Alabama, 143; capacity of, for development, 68–69; culture of, 16; history of racism and, 32n1; literature of, 157n4, 160–76; periodicals of, 167; texts of, 166
Agamben, Giorgio, 38, 54n42, 73n3, 74n8, 280
agency, 2, 224, 231, 240; of contrast, 229; critical, 45; individual, 243–45;

ontology and, 12; perception and, 225; political, 258n19, 263
Ainslie, George, 199–217, 282; as behavioral economist and psychiatrist, 199; *Breakdown of Will*, 206–8; *Picoeconomics*, 217n25; on pleasure and reward, 217n24; theory of hyperbolic discounting and intertemporal bargaining of, 17
Akenside, Mark, *Pleasures of the Imagination*, 109
Alderson, Simon, 107
alliteration, Pope and, 103
altercide, 14, 79, 87, 91, 93n37
Althusser, Louis Pierre, 78, 80, 81, 82, 92n5, 129–30, 280
ambivalence: Bond and, 106; "Hansel and Gretel" and, 207; Johnson and, 109; Pope and, 103, 114; in readers' responses, 102; source of, 107
anachronism, 61–62, 64–65, 71
Andrew, Dudley, 186–87, 194n30, 194n31; *Opening Bazin*, 189
Andrews, William L., 161, 167
Animated Media Scholarly Interest Group, 180
Animation, 191
animation, 16–17, 179, 181, 190; absence of, in film theory, 177, 178, 191, 192, 192n1, 282; affective landscape of, 185; as cartoons not movies, 184; historical precedents of, 183, 192; importance of animators' writings and, 192; as modernist medium, 181, 193n18; in

animation (continued)
  opposition to cinema, 180, 181, 182; studies of, 177–82, 187, 191, 192; theory, 190
anticolonial movement, 56, 58–59, 66, 70, 73
antiprogressism, 58
antipsychiatry movement, 239
anti-Semitism, 29, 32n1
anti-Theory, 5–6, 280
anxiety, 51; narrative, 209
appetite, 39, 53n20, 209
Appiah, Anthony, on race, 144
arbitrary signification, race construction as, 143, 144
archaisms, 61–62, 64
archives, 14; African American, 166, 167, 172; literary, 248; research in, 161; theory of citation and, 168; of underdog, 249
Arp, Bill, 206
Aristotle, 44, 105
art, 101, 107; fine, 178; history of, 189, 190; poetry and, 105; Pope and, 108; relationship between film, painting, and sculpture, 181; verse as, 101, 103, 112
artisan, 53, 102, 105
asceticism, 35–36, 203, 214–15n8
Asia, 48, 49, 125, 126, 137. *See also names of individual countries*
aside-ness, 13
assonance, 103
ataraxia (rest), in classical skepticism, 35
attention, intellectual, 4, 9, 10, 13, 20
Attridge, Derek, and Jane Elliott, *Theory After 'Theory'*, 1–4, 11, 13, 19, 22n13, 24n38
Austen, Jane, 211, 276
author, authorship, 102, 112, 164, 171, 274; becoming an artisan, 102; books as products solely of, 172; intentions of, 162, 175n13; nineteenth-century black women as, 165; politics of, 249; Pope as, 104, 109
automatism, 100

authority, 2, 17, 49, 82, 158n8, 249, 264; narrative, 37; pedagogical, 38; of physician, 148
autopsy, autopsies, 147–48, 151, 158n8
avant-garde, 6, 9, 179, 20n4

Badiou, Alain, 280
Baker, Houston, 161, 167
Bakhtin, Mikhail, 99
Balint, Michael, 47, 53–54n32, 54n38
bargaining, bargains, 208, 210; games of, 206; noncausal, 211–13; studies of, 199. *See also* intertemporal bargaining
Barthes, Roland, 14, 34–50, 280; as agonistic critic, 34; on desire, 53n20; draws on Asian culture, 36, 38, 48–49, 52n9; figures of, 36, 38–40, 47, 48, 51n5; homosexuality and, 43; *Le Neutre*, 36–41, 45–47, 51n5, 51n7, 52n9, 53n28, 54n34, 54n37; reading of *Pélleas et Mélisande*, 41–44, 53n21; style of, 39; writings of, on haiku, 38–40, 50, 52n13, 52n16
Bataille, George Maurice Victor, 80
Bazin, André, 182, 188, 189, 186; aesthetic of discovery, 185; animation and, 194n30; *What Is Cinema?*, 189; writings of, 186, 188, 194n31
Beardsley, Monroe C., 267–68, 270, 272; Wimsatt and, "The Intentional Fallacy," 162, 271
Beckman, Karen, 16–17, 282
being, 81, 91, 122, 224, 233, 235n20, 235n24; *conatus* and, 79, 88; essence of, 83, 85; modes of, 15, 47, 80, 91; persevere in, 85, 87, 90; -in-the-world, 221, 234
Benjamin, Walter, 8, 74n12, 282
Berman, Russell A., 173
Bersani, Leo, 84
Best, Stephen, on surface reading, 44–46
bibliography, bibliographic studies, 163, 169; critical, 172; descriptive, 174n4; dismissal of, 168; interpretive formulations and, 162, 164, 173; literary analysis and, 160; not valued in English departments, 165; recovery of texts and, 161

304 Index

bienveillance, 36, 38, 47, 51n5
binary thinking, 45–46, 169
biology, 53n32, 87, 130–32, 215n12, 245, 259n24; of homosexuality, 31; race and, 68, 144
biopolitics, 7; of human capital, 118, 137; of recognition, 117–42; as response to life, 135–40; technologies of, 129, 130–35, 137, 139
biopower, 83, 130–36, 129, 139; analytics of, 118; recognition model and, 16
black studies programs, 160–61
black theory, 168
Bloch, Ernst, 14, 56–73, 75n21, 76n22, 281; African politics and, 64; Caribbean and, 64; comparisons by, 71; *Heritage of Our Times*, 60, 61, 64, 65, 74n11, 74n12; noncontemporaneity, 61–65, 69, 71–72, 74n9, 74n11, 75n13, 75n20; *The Principle of Hope*, 72; refuge in Switzerland, 61; *The Spirit of Utopia*, 74n9; on utopia, 71–72
body, bodies, 158n11, 235n22; administration of, 78; anti-, 82, 89, 90; autonomy of, 147; Christians and, 87, 89; discipline and, 130, 131; embodiment and, 16, 132; implicit positivity and, 83; inaccess to, 159n13; internal similarity of, 145–46, 147; materiality of, 118, 129, 131; minds and, 88; pleasures and, 79, 80, 82; rights and, 135; standardized, 148, 155–56, 158n8; surface of, 132; withness of, 227, 231
Bond, William, 105, 106
book, books, 102, 149–50, 160, 166–74; beginning of, 51; collectors of, 167, 175n17; history of, 163, 174n4; as machine to think with, 270; text-, 164, 165, 173, 179
Boone, Joseph, 163
Bordwell, David, 98, 178; *Film Art: An Introduction*, 179
Braidotti, Rosie, positivity and, 83
Braudy, Leo, and Marshall Cohen, *Film Theory and Criticism*, 182
Brekhus, Wayne H., 253–54

Brooks, Cleanth, 267, 271–73, 278n25
Brown, Matthew P., 172
Buchan, Suzanne, 180–82
Buddha, 34–37, 38, 39, 44. *See also* Zen Buddhism
Buffon, Georges Louis Leclerc, comte de, 145
Burch, Noël, 191
Butler, Judith, 280; *Gender Trouble*, 240, 242–43, 245; Goffman and, 242–45, 258n19; interviews with, 256n4; on neo-imperial warfare, 124; on performativity, 242–46, 257n13, 258n19; recognition model and, 15–16, 121–24, 129, 132; on violence and power, 121, 123, 129

Cameron, Sharon, on Buddha's face, 36
Canguilhem, Georges, as Foucault's teacher, 237
canon, 2, 170, 275; attention organized by, 21n8; canonicity and, 2, 11; canonization of theory and, 23n16, 162, 276, 281, 283; decanonization and, 1; literary, 10, 24n32, 165–66; of oracular figures, 3; wars and debates of, 11, 24n32, 162, 171, 172
capital, capitalism, 50, 58, 62, 82, 129, 137; advanced, 66; anti-, 75n20; contemporaneity and, 63, 64, 71; industrial, 2, 47–48, 49, 123; organization of, 92n9; pre-, 65, 69; rise of, 135; social, 138; triumph of, 57; workers in, 48–49. *See also* global capitalism; human capital
Carby, Hazel, 161
Caribbean, 64–66. *See also* Haiti; San Domingo
Carpentier, Alejo, 72
case study, studies, 5, 17, 101, 161, 248–49, 251
categories, categorization: complicated, 19; disciplinary, 1; false, 31; flexible, 18, 256; of otherness, 251; predictable, 22, 257n8; racial, 71, 144; reader's identification with, 51–52n8; social, 86; of texts, 168

Index   305

causality, 154, 227, 229, 233n3; causal decision theorists and, 217n25; efficacy of, 220, 224–28, 231; Foucault and, 129–30; in humoral model, 148, 151; interactions of, 235n26; laws of, 223. *See also* bargaining, bargains: noncausal

Cavell, Stanley, 183, 215n11; on cartoons, 184; Center for Cultural Analysis, 98; memories and, 215; on power of film, 208; Sesonske and, 184, 185

Césaire, Aimé, 74n7, 77n77

Chakrabarty, Dipesh, 60, 64, 74n8

Chambers, Ephraim, 105

Chartier, Roger, 163

Cheah, Pheng, on power, 15–16, 24n30

Chicago School of economists, 117, 237, 239

China, 48, 285

Cholodenko, Alan, 178, 179, 180; film theory and, 179, 181, 187, 192; Manovich and, 187; neglect of, 194n33

chronology, chronologies, 13, 14, 23n26, 71

cinema, 177–98; animation and, 177, 179, 181, 182, 185–88, 190, 192, 282; art history and, 190; biographical approaches to, 180; components of, 181; digital, 183, 185; evolution of, 183; incorporation of digitally based moving image culture by, 182; live-action, 190; mainstream, 179; in opposition to animation 180; photographic theories of, 177; politics of translation and, 189; postwar French filmmakers and, 190; professional organizations of, 180–82; studies of, 177, 178, 179, 181, 182, 189; theory of, 182, 185–86; traits of, 180

Cinema Journal, 180, 181

Civil Rights Movement, 143, 157n4, 160, 281

class, 22n15, 32–33n1, 33n1, 66, 67, 69

Clementi, Tyler, 84, 88

climate, skin color and, 154–55

closeted subject, 37

Clover, Joshua, 283

cognition, 35, 38, 101, 111; cognitive science and, 23n17; cognitivist criticism and, 273; maps of, 51n8; theory of, 214n2

Cohen, Cathy J., 239, 255, 257n8

Cohen, Lara Langer, 172

Cohen, Marshall, 182

collectivity: collective life and, 119; collective minds and, 232n2; collective stigma and, 239; collective subjects and, 129, 130; models of, 239, 240; norms and, 120, 121; social, 84, 238; textual, 248

colonialism, 64, 69, 70–71, 77n39, 81

Colebrook, Claire, 6–8, 23n26

communication, 18, 117, 119, 126, 263, 270, 275

communism, 61

comparison, in criticism, 60, 248, 251, 262

compartmentalization, 29, 31

complexity, 12, 72, 79, 111, 136, 145, 157, 228; of causality, 129; of consciousness, 233n6; Goffman and, 243, 244, 245; of history, 190; of humans, 226; of material reality, 133

conatus (striving to persevere in being), 15, 79, 83, 84; perseverance and, 88, 90, 91

concrescence, 228–30

Congreve, William, misquoted, 162–63

Consciousness, 119, 129, 130–31, 235n24; formation of, 131; intersubjective constitution of, 122; oppression and, 16; perceptual, 219; self-, 257n10; shifts of, 269; statements of, 264; universal, 222, 233–34n6

consent, 47–48, 127, 129, 212

contemporaneity, 19, 57–61, 70, 72, 73n3; Agamben on, 74n8; Bloch and, 62–63, 69; capitalist, 64; interplay between noncontemporaneity and, 14, 57, 63, 72, 74n11; modernity's, 68; precapitalist, 65; unified, 73. *See also* noncontemporaneity

Corral, Will H., and Daphne Pattai, *Theory's Empire*, 5–6, 22–23n15, 23n16 correctness, 106–8, 114; interventions and, 189; poet and, 10; printers and, 165; satire and, 275; theory and, 284; in verse, 108; Whitehead and, 220; writing and, 103

Corrigan, Timothy, *Critical Visions in Film Theory*, 183

Critical Inquiry, 163; special issue (2004), 5, 21n9, 24n32; symposium (2003), 169

critical methodology, 21, 153, 163, 173, 174n9

critical philosophy of Kant, 146, 148–49, 150, 153, 155

critical theory, theorists, 14–15, 79, 80, 84, 89, 90; Adorno and, 101; analytical categories of, 117; biopolitical thought and, 79; *conatus* and, 83, 91; discursive-linguistic turn of, 124, 144; German, 85, 86; liberal power and, 78; melancholy and, 7; modern, 24n32; Rasch on, 11; recognition and, 117; of society, 123; War on Terror and, 124. *See also* theory

criticism, 104, 164, 169, 272; Afro-American literary tradition and, 168; animation and, 178; cultural, 214; Foucault and, 199; Greg-Bowers method of, 164; historical poetics and, 99; judgment and, 276; literary interpretation and, 163–64; literary theory and, 160, 168, 172, 261; New Criticism theory and, 174n4; of Pope's works, 108, 109; practicality of, 261–62; priority of interpretation and, 175n16; psychology and, 18; reader-response and, 163; recovered texts and, 165; Richards and, 261, 266; theory of, 168, 284; writing of, 171

critique, 7, 56; agonistic, 34, 45; political, 121; postcolonial, 60, 64; social science, 238; of subject-formation, 130

Culler, Jonathan, 6, 23n17, 175n16

cultural analysis, in queer studies, 239

cultural history, 99

cultural studies, 100, 172

cultural theory, 1, 2, 3, 5, 20n6

culture wars, 169

currency, 13

cyborg assemblages, 220, 224, 229

Daniel, Samuel, 104

Danky, James P., 167

Darwin, Charles, 145. *See also* Literary Darwinism

decision theory, 200, 203, 213n1

deconstruction, 10, 16, 162, 163, 172

Deleuze, Gilles, 8, 19, 280; on cinema, 187; desire and, 81, 90; implicit positivities of, 83; influence of Spinoza on, 80, 92n8; as precursor to queer theory, 238

de Man, Paul, 264, 277n5

Derrida, Jacques, 9–10, 11, 19, 199, 280

Descartes, René, 227

desire, desires, 17; arrogance as, 53n20; biopower and, 134; Deleuze and, 90; dynamics of, 208; intertemporal conflicts among, 216n19; literature and, 208; narrative and, 209–10; need vs., 53n32, 54n38; pursuit of, 36, 41; renunciation of, 35–36; temporal horizons of, 201, 205, 206

developmentalism, 58, 62, 71, 72; developmental crisis and, 16; developmental logic and, 13, 59; Marxism and, 60, 66, 67, 68; modernity and, 65

deviance paradigm, 237, 240

deviance studies, 237–39, 240, 248, 251; Goffman and, 242, 247

Dickens, Charles, 211

disciplines, 6, 9, 16, 23–24n28, 160–61, 173, 237, 243

discounting. *See* hyperbolic discounting

discourse, 129, 238; of anatomical medicine, 155; black vindicationalist, 68; of development, 126; of fiction, 209; of film theory, 177, 178, 180, 182, 183, 192; Foucauldian, 239; about homosexuality, 31; of human capital, 117, 126; patriarchal, 127; philosophical, 134, 283; premodern, 61; of racial construction, 157n4; of scarcity, 35, 48; social, 243; theoretical, 21, 280, 283

disease, 133, 145, 147–48, 158n8, 207
disponible, 49–50
documentary film, 178, 179
domination, 64, 88, 119, 238, 254, 255
Donato, Eugenio, and Richard Macksey, *The Structuralist Controversy*, 19–20
Dreyfus, Albert, case of, 29–31
Dreyfus, Herbert, 81
drives and needs, Sedgwick on, 47, 48, 53n32, 54n38
Duggan, Lisa, 257n5
Durkheim, Émile, 246
dysprosody, 97

Eagleton, Terry, 2, 6, 8, 10; *How to Read a Poem*, 272–73
economics, 17, 194n33, 199, 200, 201
Edelman, Lee, 84
editions, 164; reprint, 165, 167, 170; scholarly, 169
Eikhenbaum, Boris, *Melodics of Russian Lyric Verse*, 99
Eisenstein, Sergei, 191, 192
Eliot, T. S., 271
Elliott, Jane, and Derek Attridge, *Theory After 'Theory'*, 1–4, 11, 13, 19, 22n13, 24n38
emancipation of blacks, 70, 72, 76n35
empiricism, 101, 220, 230, 238, 241, 282
Empiricus, Sextus, 49, 51n7
Empson, William, 14, 23n16, 46, 49, 277n15; "The Faces of Buddha," 34–39, 44
Encyclopedia Britannica, 29–31, 33n1
English departments, 160–61, 163, 165, 173, 174
English language, 189, 190, 194n32, 284–85n2; domination of, 48; spoken, 107
Enlightenment, 146, 155, 156, 158n7, 281
Epstein, Steve, on Rubin's "Thinking Sex," 237–38, 256n4
equality, universal, 146, 155, 156
ESCAP (Economic and Social Commission for Asia and the Pacific), 126
Escoffier, Jeffrey, 238–39, 256n4, 256–57n5

Esposito, Roberto, *Political Treatise*, 83
ethics, 15, 18, 21n9, 83, 87, 119
ethnicity, 160, 247, 249, 251, 255, 259n30
ethnography, 237, 241, 245, 256n4
Eurocentrism, 68, 73n3
Evers, Medgar, 143
exclusion, 123, 127, 139, 239, 248, 249, 250
exemplarity, 170–71, 172
existence, 120, 150; biological, 131; finitude, 90, 93n36; gendered, 246; human, 131, 132, 159n12; non-, 78; physical, 129; right of, 84, 85
experience, 6, 17, 120, 129, 145, 219; cinematic, 186, 188; classification of, 173; complexity of, 12; empiricism vs., 101; expectation and, 57; intersubjective, 213; intertemporal, 211; literary, 199, 209; of narrative, 204, 211; perceived, 218; perceptual, 226, 234n13; phenomenal, 231; prosodic, 108; sensory, 220, 221, 226, 229, 234n13; theorizing of, 227
experimental film, 178, 179, 191
experimental theory, 17
exteriority, 120, 122, 222
extinction theory, 7
extinguishment, 79, 88, 90, 91, 93n37; of life, 14–15, 83, 84, 85, 86; multiplicity and, 89; of social projects and worlds, 80, 82, 85, 86, 87; suicide and, 87

Fabian, Johannes, 60, 64
Fanon, Frantz, 80–81, 238, 280
Farred, Grant, 10, 11, 23–24n28, 24n35
fascism, 61, 65, 71, 77n39
Fechner, Gustav, 219–23, 233n5, 233n6, 234n13; as father of psychophysics, 220; *Nanna, or on the Soul-Life of Plants*, 232n2; *On the Soul Question*, 232n2
female subjects: of globalization, 117–42; interrelated types of, 125; recognition paradigm and, 127; transnational labor of, 118
feminism, 8, 10, 12, 93, 163, 180, 255
Ferguson, Frances, on Richards's work, 18, 261–79

Fichte, Johann Gottlieb, 119, 205
fiction, 208–9, 214n2
film, 177, 180, 181, 183. See also cinema
film theory, 180–83; animation and, 16, 177, 178, 183, 191, 192; anthologies of, 189; benefits of being left out of, 179; Eisenstein and, 192; history of, 192; studies of, 177, 178
Fink, Eugen, on de-presencing, 226, 231
Fish, Stanley, 272, 273
Fitzgerald, Burgo, 211
Fitzgerald, F. Scott, 214–15n8
Flaubert, Gustave, 263
Flesch, William, on Ainslie's work, 17, 199–217, 282
formalism, 49, 98, 162, 166
Forster, Georg, 154–55
Foster, Frances Smith, 161
Foucault, Michel, 10, 19, 85, 123–24, 199, 258n14, 280; abstractions of, 256n4; Barthes and, 41; biopower and, 16, 129, 130–35; critique of Althusser's writings and, 80–81; discourse and, 239, 249; focuses on subjugated knowledges, 89, 92n2; gay rights and, 83, 84, 87; *History of Sexuality*, 78, 90, 257n6; positivities of freedom and, 87; power and, 82, 92n2, 118, 249; on social marginality, 237; Western ordering of things and, 81
France, 29–31, 66–69, 70, 280
François, Anne-Lise, on minimal affirmations, 14, 34–55
Frankfurt, Harry, 203
Frankfurt School, 76n23, 120–22, 134
Fraser, Nancy, 85–86, 117, 120, 123, 124
Freccero, John, 283
freedom, 9, 84, 85, 87, 89
French language, 49, 163, 189, 190, 285n2
Freud, Sigmund, 42, 200, 204, 207, 213n1, 215n10, 216n20
Freytag's triangle, 205
Furuhata, Yuriko, 190, 191
future, futures: decisions and, 206–7; past, 56–57, 59, 71, 73; in instant, 208–13; memory and, 204; noncontemporaneity of, 69; selves, 201–2; still possible, 63; of theory, 11, 14–15

Gagnon, John, 237–39, 256n4; *Sexual Deviance*, 239
Gallagher, Catherine, 275
Galliher, John F., 253–54
Galloway, Alexander, 183
Gardner, John, 205
Gates, Henry Louis, Jr., 161, 167, 169–70; *The Signifying Monkey*, 168–69, 171; "Race," Writing and Difference, 144
gaylesbianqueer rights, 86, 87, 89, 93
gay rights, 83, 84, 87, 90
gender, 22n15, 126, 243, 245, 246; canon and, 170; history of, 32n1; identity of, 240; inequality of, 127; intersects with sexuality, 33n1; labor hierarchy and, 247; performativity of, 242
genre, genres: as aesthetic term, 163; case studies and psychiatric reports as, 248; confession as, 249; historical poetics and, 99; of modernity, 249; outside categories of, 192; prejudices of, 190; representative texts and, 171; search for new, 173
Georgia Review, 184
Germany, 61, 71, 98, 285n2. See also Nazism
Gessner, Robert, 181
Getino, Octavio, 192
Ghosh, Jayati, on labor of Asian women, 125
Gildon, Charles, 105; *Complete Art of Poetry*, 104
global capitalism, 124, 135, 140; contemporary, 117, 125; oppression of women in, 128; recognition and, 136; as striated, 137; tenaciousness of, 16, 130, 139
globalization: as beneficial for women, 126; female subjects of, 16, 117–42; global capitalist system and, 135; recognition and, 117, 134, 136; theory and, 281, 283
God, 83, 87, 89, 210

Goethe, Johann Wolfgang von, 282
Goffman, Erving, 237–60; "The Arrangement between the Sexes," 246–47; Butler and, 242–45, 258n19; canon and, 281; *Frame Analysis*, 257n10; *Gender Advertisements*, 245–46; Humphreys and, 252; influenced by Durkheim, 246; *Interaction Ritual*, 244; *The Presentation of Self in Everyday Life*, 241, 258n14, 258n21; sexuality studies and, 240–56, 258n14; on stigma, 18, 245, 247–51, 259n30; *Stigma*, 242, 247, 248, 249, 251
Graff, Gerald, 164, 175n16
Gramsci, Antonio, 81, 129–30, 284n1
Greetham, D. C., 160
Greg-Bowers method of textual criticism, 164, 175n13
Grégoire, Abbé, 70
Grenier, Jean, 49
Guattari, Félix, 8, 80, 83, 187
Gubrium, Jaber F., 253–54
Guillory, John, on canon debates, 170
Gunning, Tom, 177, 178, 192n1; "Moving Away from the Index," 177

Ha, Marie-Paule, on Barthes's haikus, 39
haiku, Barthes on, 38–40, 50, 52n13, 52n16
Haiti, 60, 65–72, 76n35, 76n36
Halberstam, Judith, 84; *The Queer Art of Failure*, 21–22n10, 185
Hansen, Mark, on Whitehead's metaphysics, 17, 218–236
Hansen, Miriam, 178
Hardt, Michael, 6–8, 23n26, 49
Harland, Sydney, 68
Hartog, François, 57
Hawthorne, Nathaniel, works of, 164
Hazlitt, William, *Essay on the Principle of Human Action*, 201–2
hearkening, 45, 234n15
Hegel, Georg Wilhelm Friedrich, 9, 19, 49, 92, 138, 280; Fichte and, 119; finitude and, 91; historical aesthetics and, 75n13, 100; Jena writings of, 140n4; *Lectures in the Philosophy of History*, 284; philosophy of, 8, 75, 80, 90, 92n5, 282; recognition in, 117, 140n3; totality and, 283; Žižek and, 281
hegemony, 81, 117, 121, 130, 237; counterhegemonic theorizing and, 22n10; hegemonic norms and, 129–30; of neoliberalism, 57; social control and, 123
Heidegger, Martin, 8; *Being and Time*, 234n15; extinguishment and, 90–91; hearing and, 224; influence of, 80; postmodernism and, 224; reflections on being, world, and thing, 81
Herbert, George, "Home," 209–10
High Theory / high theory, 2, 124–25, 282; avant-garde-ism and, 9; High Theorists and, 22n10; medium theory vs., 5; practices of, 45. See also theory; Theory
Hippolite, Jean, 20
Hipponax, epitaph of, 36
historical poetics, 97–115, 282; cultural resonance and, 101; form and, 100; formalism and, 96, 99; history of verse technique and, 115; Jarvis and, 15, 282; Maslov's definition of, 99; neoformalism and, 100; Prins and, 97, 98, 100; study of lyrical poetry as, 97
historicism, new, 199
history, historicization, 57, 71; alternative, 13; of books, 163, 172, 174n4; counterhistorical project and, 14; crisis of historicity and, 58, 73; determination of, 67; historicism and, 60, 64, 100, 157, 167, 199; of medicine, 147; of race, 157n4; of signs of racial difference, 144–45; of theory, 12
Hitchcock, Alfred, *The Lady Vanishes*, 177–78
Hitler, Adolf, 61, 70–71
homonormativity, 240, 255
homophobia, 13, 29–32, 32n1, 255
homosexuality, 30–32, 32n1, 252–53, 256n4
Honneth, Axel, 123, 136; on global capitalism, 124; on humanity, 122–23; reading of Hegel by, 140n4; on recognition, 117, 119, 120

Hopkins, Gerard Manley, 275
Hufeland, Cristoph Wilhelm, 150–51, 158n11; *Macrobiotics, Or the Art of Prolonging Human Life*, 150
human capital, 124–26, 137–39; migration and, 141n23; nonrecognition of, 123–35
humanism, 122, 134
humanities: attacks on, 10; Black Studies and, 160–61; crisis in, 4, 49; decanonization of, 1; future of, 173, 174; paradigm shifts in, 3; prejudices of, 17; queer scholars in, 238, 239; social sciences and, 18; theory as socially pertinent dimension of, 6
humanity, 140, 154, 155
human rights, 118, 122, 134, 135, 254
Hume, David, 149, 220, 266
humoral paradigm, 147, 148, 150–51, 154, 159n13
Humphreys, Laud, 18, 242; *Tearoom Trade: Impersonal Sex in Public Places*, 240, 251–54
Hurston, Zora Neale, 169
Husserl, Edmund, 226, 230, 235n20
hyperbolic discounting, 204; evolutionary reasons for ubiquity of, 215n12; examples of, 200–201, 203; experimental work on, 203; graphing of, 214n5; internal psychic conflict predicted by, 199, 200; intertemporal bargaining and, 17, 199–217

ideology, 11, 32n3, 124, 128, 134, 135, 180; colonial, 68; control by, 32n4, 129–30; critique, 45; fascist, 61; history of, 13; homophobia and, 32n1; literary studies and, 241; mystification of, 127, 129; shifts in, 252; state apparatuses of, 81
idioms, 98, 108, 162
imaginary, 7, 8, 131
immediacy, 145, 156, 228
inclusion, 118, 135, 254; dynamic of, 137; exclusion-effects and, 139; inclusionary power and, 123–35; politics of, 86. *See also* exclusion
instrument, instruments, 102, 111, 112, 125

intellectual development, 4, 8, 20, 22n13
intelligence, 53n27, 68, 113; prosodic, 15, 108, 113
intelligibility, 123, 132
intensity, Jones on, 228–29
interest, as desire, 208
interiority, 82, 132, 145, 146, 243, 244, 245
interpretation of texts, 163, 274; African American, 167–68; bibliography vs., 173; in literary studies, 166; poetry and, 273
intertemporal bargaining: Ainslie and, 206–8; fictional narratives and, 210–11; hyperbolic discounting and, 17, 199–217; strategies of, 216n19
Islamic fundamentalism, 124

Jackson, Leon, 167, 175n17
Jakobson, Roman, 208
James, C. L. R., 14, 56–73, 75–76n21, 76n25, 76n35, 281; *The Black Jacobins*, 58–60, 64–73; *A History of Negro Revolt*, 68; *World Revolution*, 68
James, Henry, 250
James, William, 222, 228, 232n2; *A Pluralist Universe*, 233–34n6
Jameson, Fredric, 57, 281–83, 284n11
Japan, 48–49, 190–91, 285n2
Jarvis, Simon, on historical poetics, 15, 97–116, 282
Jews, 29, 32n1
Jim Crow, 143, 157n4. *See also* racism
Johnson, Barbara, 167
Johnson, Samuel, 104, 106, 108–9, 111, 113–14, 212
Jones, Judith, *Intensity*, 228–29, 235n26
Jones, Tom, 107
Joubert-Laurencin, Hervé: *La Lettre Volante*, 189; with Andrew, *Opening Bazin* 189, 194n30, 194n31
Journal of the Society of Cinematologists, 181
Joyce, James, 208
judgment, 35, 270, 276
juste, justesse, 40
just noticeable difference, 220, 233n5

Kafka, Franz, *Hunger Artist*, 214n8
Kahneman, Daniel, 204
Kakuzo, Okakura, 49
Kant, Immanuel: canon and, 281; *The Conflict of the Faculties*, 150–53, 158n11; critical philosophy of, 146–50, 153, 155, 284; *Critique of Judgment*, 145; *The Critique of Pure Reason*, 159n12; *De Medecina Corporis, quae Philosophorum est*, 158n11; on skin color and race, 16, 145, 281; "On the Use of Teleological Principles in Philosophy," 154–56
Kaplan, Amy, 163
Karitani, Kojin, 281
Kennedy, John F., 143–44, 156
Kermode, Frank, 11, 24n32, 23n15
Kierkegaarde, Søren, 208, 215n10
Kiyoteru, Hanada, 191
Klein, Melanie, 200, 238
knowledge, 46, 97, 99, 130, 138, 147; applied, 8, 9; banks of, 14; discourse and, 129; organization of, 2, 65; origin point of, 223; production of, 22; reconfiguration of, by High Theory, 2; of world, 37, 51, 88
Kojève, Alexandre, 80, 92n6, 117
Koselleck, Reinhardt, futures and, 56–58, 71, 73
Kracauer, Siegfried, *Theory of Film*, 183
Kristeva, Julia, 122, 280

labor: of female subjects, 118; feminization of, 123–35; gendered division of, 246–47; international division of, 125, 137; migrant, 126, 136, 137, 138
Lacan, Jacques, 21n9, 199, 216n19, 238, 280, 281
Lady Vanishes, The, 177, 178
Laertius, Diogenes, 48, 49, 52n19
Lamarre, Thomas, 178, 195n37
language, 48, 178, 190, 192, 269, 271. See also linguistics; translation; *and names of specific languages*
Lanier, Sidney, *Science of English Verse*, 97, 98, 100
Lapsansky, Phil, 167

Latin America, 125
Lenin, Vladimir, 67
Leslie, Esther, 178
Lewis, C. S., 270
liberalism, 14, 79, 81, 82, 255
life, 85, 86, 89; biopower as response to, 135–40; capacity to produce and manage, 78, 80; claim on, 84; conflicting preferences of, 204; extinguishment of, 14–15, 79; forms of, 87, 88, 90, 91; mental, 17
linguistics, 110, 194n33, 264, 269, 281; analysis of, 17, 220; behavior of, 18, 266; discourses of, 189; divisions of, 190; gestures of, 101; norms of, 243; performativity and, 245; Saussurean, 53n27; turn of, 24n30, 124, 144. See also language
Linnaeus, Carl, 145
literary analysis, 160, 166
literary criticism, critics, 160, 162, 171, 261–79; disagreement and, 263; earlier, 23, 172; high theory and, 168; interpretation and, 163–64, 165, 172; philosophical, 199; psychoanalysis and, 213n1; teachable, 23n15; writing of, 171
Literary Darwinism, 200, 213–14n2
literary history, 99
literary studies, 6, 23n15, 160, 162, 173, 241; classrooms of, 171; interpretation in, 165, 166, 167; journals of, 163. See also African American literary studies
literary theory, theorists, 17, 98, 150; African American literature and, 168; Ainslie and, 199–200; bibliography and, 160; Gates on, 169; incorporated into English departments, 161; interpretive possibilities of, 172; in Russia, 99
literature, 264, 265; affection for, in literary studies, 6; African American, 160–76; birth of study of, 164; cognitive view of, 214n2, 272–73; desire and, 208; as disagreement from within, 273; found, 262; political issues and, 263; in reader, 272; world, 98, 99

312   Index

localism, 7, 10, 11, 46, 103, 112, 282
Locke, John, 158n8, 220
Longfellow, Henry Wadsworth, 276
L'Ouverture, Toussaint, 59, 67, 68
Love, Heather, on sexuality studies, 17–18, 93n25, 237–60
low theory, 21–22n10, 110
lyric poetry, 97, 100

Mach, Ernst, 219, 222–24, 234n13; *The Science of Mechanics*, 222
Macherey, Pierre, as Althusser's student, 92
Mack, Maynard, 101
Macksey, Richard, and Eugenio Donato, *The Structuralist Controversy*, 19–20
Maeterlinck, Maurice, *Pélleas et Mélisande*, 41–43, 53n21
Majaz, Meta, *Critical Visions in Film Theory*, 183
Marcus, Sharon, 44–46, 238, 256n3
marginalization, social, 240, 247–48, 251, 255
Marx, Karl, 49–50, 54n38, 67, 127, 134, 284n1
Marxism, Marxist ideology, 10, 44, 129–30, 284n1; classes in, 62; Foucauldianism vs., 10; freedom of proletarian figure of, 49–50, 54n38; historicism of, 60; structuralism's turn away from, 53n27; theories of revolution of, 67; Western, 76n23
Maslov, Boris, 99
Maspero, Gaston, 49
materialism, 16, 129–30, 132, 163, 166, 284n1
McGann, Jerome, 160, 278n25
McGill, Meredith, 172
McIntosh, Mary, 238, 256n4
McKenzie, D. F., 160, 166, 168; *Bibliography and the Sociology of Texts*, 162–63, 164, 172
media, 22n13; global, 124; studies of, 16, 182, 190, 192; twenty-first century, 219, 220, 221, 225, 226, 229, 232

medicine, anatomical, 145–48, 150, 155; humoral model vs., 147, 159n13; Kant and, 151–52, 153, 158n11, 159n12
medium theory, 5, 22n13
Melas, Natalie, 14, 56–77
Melville, Herman, writings of, 164
memory, 57, 152, 204, 215n11, 268
Merleau-Ponty, Maurice, 17, 218, 226, 230–32
metaphor, metaphors, 39, 64, 81, 277n5; Goffman on, 258n21; malleability in, 264; in poetry, 270, 272, 273; of theatricality, 243
metaphysics: animation and, 181; art and, 105, 107; Fechner and, 221, 222, 232n2; liberation and, 88; post-metaphysical and, 119; Shaviro and, 235n16; truth and, 81; of Whitehead, 17, 220, 224
meter, 98, 100, 105
method, methodology, 169, 174n4; African American literary studies and, 162; binarization of, 15; conservativeness of editions', 164; critical, 163; of Goffman, 245, 252; of Kant, 149; in literary studies, 6; pluralism of, 16, 161, 172–73; of Richards, 275
Michelet, Jules, 66
Mickey Mouse, 184
Miéville, China, *The City & the City*, 210
migration, 126–27, 127–28, 141n23
Mill, John Stuart, 276
Miller, D. A., 43
Miller, Toby, and Stam, *Film and Theory: An Anthology*, 182
Milner, Jean-Claude, 46, 53n27
Milton, John, 203, 215n8, 275
mimesis, 102, 103, 105, 108, 115, 167
mind, 200, 223, 234n13; body and, 158n11; levels of, 233n6; metrical, 112; nature and, 222; presence of, 152; theory of, 214n2
minimal affirmatives, 14, 34–51
Mitchell, W. J. T., 5, 22n13, 24n32
models of theory. See under names of individual models and paradigms

Index 313

modernity, modernism: colonial, 64, 68, 69, 76n35; high, 262; historical time of, 14, 72; realism vs., 75n20; scientific, 46; sexuality as structuring force in, 255; temporality of, 57, 59, 71
Modern Language Association (MLA), 24n32, 163, 173; Committee on Scholarly Editions, 164
Moore, G. E., 264, 270
monism, 223, 231
Morize, André, *Problems and Methods of Literary History*, 164
Morocco, 48
motivation studies, 199, 207–8, 241, 242, 268–70
Mulvey, Laura, 192; "Visual Pleasure and Narrative Cinema," 189
Museum of African American History, 166
music videos, 182
Mussolini, Benito, 65

Nancy, Jean-Luc, 90–91, 93n36, 280
narrative, 23n17, 37, 51–52n8, 59, 204–5, 209–12
natural history, historians, 145, 154, 254
nature, 83, 87, 90, 97
Nazism, 60, 61, 70–71
needs and drives, Sedgwick on, 47, 48, 53n32, 54n38
Negri, Antonio, 49, 280
neoformalism, 100
neoliberalism, 57, 79, 81, 117, 137
Neuter, Neutral, 41–44, 51n5, 54n37
Newcomb's problem, 212–13, 217n25
New Criticism, New Critics, 99, 174n4, 267, 271, 272, 278n25
new media, digital modes of reading, 45
newness, 8, 9, 13
Newton, Esther, *Mother Camp*, 240, 245
nextness, 13
Ngai, Sianne, *Ugly Feelings*, 185
NGOs (nongovernmental organizations), 138–39
Nietzsche, Friedrich, 8, 75n13, 83, 259n35; *The Genealogy of Morals*, 214n8

noncontemporaneity (*Ungleichzeitigkeit*), 60–65, 68–73; of Bloch, 62–63, 65, 71, 74n11, 75n13, 75n20; comparative, 56–77; interplay between contemporaneity and, 14, 57, 63, 72, 74n11; of James, 65, 68, 69; use of term, 74n9. See also contemporaneity
normativity, 117, 122; anti-, 239; commitment of, 79, 85; conventions of, 12; force of, 134; forms of, 120; hetero-, 121; homo-, 240, 255; ideals of, 139; non-, 237, 240, 254, 255; recognition paradigm and, 118; subject formation and, 119. See also norms
norms, 123, 132, 139, 245; changing social, 133; cultural, 120; hegemonic; heterosexual gender, 121–22; power of, 243; process of normalization and, 255; recognition and, 129
Norton Anthology of African American Literature, The, 169
Norton Anthology of Theory and Criticism, The, 23n16
nostalgia, 56, 64, 185
Noxon, Gerald, "Cinema and Cubism," 181

obliquity of homosexuality, 30–32
observation, 12, 18, 221–22, 241–45, 253–54, 282; of Foucault, 85; of Goffman, 252; of language, 269; in medicine, 145–48; participant, 251; Richards and, 270, 274
obsolescence, 4, 19, 58, 59, 97, 101; avoidance of, 72–73; threat of, 21n7
O'Connor, Flannery, 203
Ogden, C. K., 264, 267, 268, 270, 277n15
ontology, 89, 119, 122, 154, 222; of film, 185; Heidegger and, 224; James and, 69; replaces agency, 12; of Whitehead, 219, 225, 227, 228, 236n27
oppression: consciousness and, 16, 119, 130; implicit ontological meaning of, 119–20; as institutionalized patterns of cultural value, 123; sexual, 255; shortcoming of recognition paradigm for, 133–34. See also racism
oracular figures, 3, 8, 9, 15, 19

Orientalism, 39, 48, 49, 68, 124, 127–28
Osborne, Peter, 8–9, 11; "Philosophy after Theory," 8
Oxford-Schomburg African American Women Writers Series, 169
Oxford University, 162

paradigm shifts, 3, 20n6, 21n6, 167, 238
past, 14, 57–58, 63, 69, 73n5, 75n16
patriarchy, 127–28, 130, 169
Pattai, Daphne, and Will H. Corral, *Theory's Empire*, 5–6, 22–23n15, 23n16
perception, 12, 52n8, 191, 225, 227–28, 229, 236n27, 266; human capacity of, 218; model of, 220; principles vs., 106; of race, 145; of sound, 234n15; subjective, 223; Whitehead's model of, 17, 219, 220–22, 224, 226, 227, 235n22. *See also* sense perception; sensibility
performances, 98, 243
performativity theory, 242–43, 245
perseverance, *conatus* and, 83, 88, 90, 91
phenomenology, 218–36; Butler and, 242–43; essentialness of, 226; experience or analysis and, 220; orthodox, 219; sensation and, 221; tradition of, 231
philosophy, philosophical thinking, 12, 199, 200
Phongpaichit, Pasuk, on Thai sex workers, 127–29
photographic theory of cinema, 177
plasticity, 15, 79, 83, 90, 118, 191, 249
Plato, 101, 229
Plummer, Kenneth, 238, 256n4
PMLA, 163, 164–65
poetic justice, 211
poetics, 19, 99, 100, 101, 109; historical, 15, 97–116; history of, 98; of poets, 107; of Pope, 106
poetry, poems, 18, 270; analysis of students' commentaries on, 262; English, 112; of Herbert, 209; language of, 208; of Pope, 282; reading of, 15, 271, 276; Richards and, 261, 264–65, 268–69, 273, 277; teachers of, 272. *See also* historical poetics

politics, 79, 84, 85, 86, 89; film theory and, 180; progressive, 80, 88, 91; sexual, 87
Pope, Alexander, 103, 274; "Cecilia's Day Ode," 111; correctness and, 116; *Duniciad*, 106, 114; *Essay on Criticism*, 106, 110; *Essay on Man*, 108; *Pastorals*, 101, 104; *The Rape of the Lock*, 112; "Summer," 101, 102, 115; technical virtuosity and, 105; verse art of, 109, 113, 282; verse technique, 108, 282; versification and, 15, 107; Walsh and, 11n23
Porter, Dorothy, 167
positivity, positivism, 83, 157n4, 264; *conatus* and, 90; logical, 220, 221
postcolonial theory, 14, 59, 60, 73, 76n35, 119
postmodernism, 57, 224
poststructuralism, 174n4, 174n9, 282, 283; bibliographic scholars and, 160; linguistic turn of, 144; recognition and, 119; replaces structuralism, 12
potentiation, potentiality, 15, 90
Povinelli, Elizabeth, on extinguishment of life, 14–15, 78–93, 283–84
power, 80, 81, 82, 137; Butler on, 121; Cheah on, 15–16; *conatus* and, 84; Esposito and, 83; formal understanding of, 129–30; Foucault on, 118, 123; liberal, 78; as producer of subjectivities, 41, 130; productive, 118, 123–35; recognition in social relations and, 117, 129; silence of, 136; of U.S. imperial sovereignty, 124. *See also* biopower
pragmatism, 8, 157, 161
preferences, 203, 204, 210–11
prejudice, 17, 190
present, 8, 14, 56, 70, 71, 201–2, 206; Bloch and, 63–65, 72, 75n13; certainties of, 60; as conjuncture, 19; as crisis of historicity, 57–58; exhausted, 7; heritage of, 61; modernity's, 69; political, 83; in postcolonial theory, 14, 59, 73; theoretical, 20; withdrawal from, 63. *See also* presentism
presentism, 57–60, 73, 187

Index 315

Price, Leah, 171
primitivism, 76n22, 144, 225, 229, 232
Prins, Yopie, 97, 98, 100, 115
prisoner's dilemma, 206–7, 211, 212, 215–16n15
production, 57, 62, 81, 75n13
proletariat, 49–50, 54n38, 62–63, 67, 69, 127, 140
proper name, 1–2, 269
Propp, Vladimir, *Morphology of the Folktale*, 265
prosody, 97, 112, 282
Proust, Marcel, 29, 30, 31, 38, 204
psyche, 131, 136, 199, 200, 203
psychoanalysis, psychoanalytic theory, 10, 12, 17, 44, 119, 163, 199–200
psychology, 200; criticism and, 18; ego and, 37, 222; literary, 266; object-relations, 53–54n32; philosophical, 199; psychopathology and, 103; Richards and, 267
psychophysics, psychophysicists, 17, 218–36; as experimental project, 220, 221, 224, 233n3; nineteenth-century, 219, 229; tradition of, 231
publication, publishing industry, 2, 4, 9, 25n39, 165, 167. *See also* book, books
Pynchon, Thomas, *Gravity's Rainbow*, 205

queer studies, 18, 237, 240, 248; deviance studies and, 239; methodological background to, 247; precursors to, 238; psychology and, 241; truth of self and, 84
queer theory, 12, 23n17, 239, 240, 257n5

race, 22n15, 70, 71, 143–44, 157n4, 156; biological basis of hierarchy based on, 68; canon and, 170; deconstructive account of, 16; as drive toward stability, 146; intersects with sexuality, 33n1; modern, 145, 155; without racism, 16; temporalization of, 60, 65, 68. *See also* racism
racism, 16, 32n1, 70–71, 156; scientific, 68, 157–58n7

radicalism fatigue, 23n26
radical replacement model, 9, 23n26
Rancière, Jacques, 86, 262–63, 280
Rasch, William, on theory's self-reflexivity, 11–12
rational choice, 201, 202, 203
reader, readership, 51–52n8, 102, 167
reading, 18, 44–46, 262; close, 171, 174n4; paranoid, 37, 43, 52n19, 53n28; of poetry, 269, 271, 276
realism, 75n20, 163, 181, 183
reality, realness, 131, 149
recognition: biopolitics of, 117–42; Butler and, 15–16; constitution of subjects under, 123; criteria of, 122; as disempowerment, 123; as effect of biopower, 135–40; evolution of, 118–19; Hegel and, 140n3; as hegemonic control, 123; as important analytical category in critical theory, 117; inclusion and, 135–37; mis-, 120; non-, 123; oppression and, 133; politics of, 124, 131; power and, 118, 123, 124; revitalization of, 137; versions of, 118–23; withholding of, 139
recursive return, 9
Reich, Robert, on global living standards, 117–18
Reinke, Steve, 179; *The Sharpest Point*, 193n5
relativism, 100, 166, 266, 267
Representations, special issue devoted to surface reading, 44
repression, 78–91, 124, 135; exclusionary, 118; Freudian, 204; self-, 203; techniques of, 31
repressive hypothesis, 90; biopolitical discussions and, 79, 91; field of productivity and, 81; Foucauldian critique of, 40, 78; refusal of, 85; violence and, 80
rest, 35, 36–37, 50
revolutions: African, 69, 71–72; anticolonial, 58–59, 70; French, 66–69; Haitian, 60, 65–72, 76n35, 76n36; Russian, 66;

316 Index

San Domingo, 66; theories of, 60, 66–67, 69–70; world, 71
rhetoric, 153, 168, 169, 170, 258n21, 284; analysis of, 174n4; desire and, 208; devices of, 71; of either/or, 173; figures of, 272; of Kennedy, 144; level of, 68; of modernity, 76n35; of 99 percent, 81; of pathology, 152; sarcastic, 63; schemes of, 209; structures of, 154; of temporality, 70, 258n24
rhythm: Bloch and, 63; historical poetics and, 98, 100; of interest, 208; syllabicity and, 110, 111, 113; thinking and, 107
Richards, I. A., 261–77, 277n15, 281; *The Meaning of Meaning*, 264–65; *Practical Criticism*, 18, 261, 262, 268–70, 274; *Principles of Literary Criticism*, 261, 268–69, 278n30
Richardson, Jonathan, *Essay on the Theory of Painting*, 102
rigidity, 2, 5, 19, 208, 267–68, 269, 271
Robinson, Cedric, 67
Rodowick, David, 183, 187
Rorty, Richard, 8
Rousseau, Jean-Jacques, 277n5; *Promenades*, 45
Rubin, Gayle, 18; *Deviations*, 256n4; "Thinking Sex," 237–39, 255, 256n2
rupture: of asignifying, 194n23; of Middle Passage, 69; with past, 57, 58; political action and, 86, 87; social, 88; theoretical, 15
Russell, Bertrand, "The Ultimate Constituents of Matter," 222–24
Russia, 65, 66–67, 285n2; theory in, 99, 100, 281

Said, Edward, on Orientalism, 49
Saint Thomas Aquinas, 215n8
San Domingo, 66, 70–71
Sappho, 31
Sartre, Jean Paul, 215n1
satire, 274–75
satisfaction, 35–36, 209–10
Saussurean linguistics, 53n27, 264

scansion, 97, 100
Schickel, Richard, *The Disney Version*, 181
Schmidgen, Henning, on cyborg assemblages, 220
Schomburg, Arthur, 166
Schwarz, Roberto, 281
Scott, David, 73, 74n7; *Conscripts of Modernity*, 58–60
Sedgwick, Eve Kosofsky, 35–51, 257n5, 280; *Epistemology of the Closet*, 14, 37, 38, 51–52n8; minimal affirmatives and, 14, 35; on needs, drives, and affects, 46–49, 53–54n32, 54n38; paranoid readings and, 37–38, 41, 43, 52n19, 53n28; "Pedagogy of Buddhism," 38, 48–49; reparative reading, 45; style of, 37, 39; *Touching Feeling*, 14, 37–41, 43, 46–49, 52n19, 54n35; "Writing the History of Homophobia," 13, 29–32, 32n1
self: awareness of, 159n12; care of, 21n9; consciousness of, 1–2, 80, 119, 257n10; deception of, 208, 215n10; future, 201–2, 212; gendered, 255; interiority and, 243, 245; presentation of, 240, 242; realization of, 120; reflection of, 11, 18; reflexivity of, 245
sensation, sensing, 220; autonomy of, 218; human, 226; localized, 234n13; nonhuman, 219; nonsubjectivist monism of, 223; objective of, 221–25, 231; phenomenology and, 17; primacy of, 218–36; stimulus and, 222; without subjects, 224–29
sense perception, 225, 227; causal efficacy and, 220, 227–28, 231; of humans, 221; human synthesis of, 233n3
sensibility: embodied in concrete actuality, 225; generalized, 17, 230; general measure for, 233n5; intensification of, 17; media and, 219; nonperceptual, 224, 227, 228, 229; sensation and, 220; subperceptual, 221
Sesonske, Alexander, 184–85; *More of the World Viewed*, 183; *The World Viewed*, 183

Index 317

sexuality, 84, 86, 87, 89, 22n15; extinguishment and, 79; heteronormative, 121; history of, 32n1; meaning of, 31, 32; mortification and, 203; nonnormative, 254; radical politics of, 237; social construction of, 238; Thai sex workers and, 125, 127–28
sexuality studies, 18, 237–60
Shaftesbury, Anthony Ashley-Cooper, Earl of, 114
Shaitanov, Igor, 98, 99
Shakespeare, William, 275; *Hamlet*, 208, 212; *King Lear*, 210, 212
Shaviro, Steve, 224, 235n16
Shepard, Matthew, 84, 87
Shklovskii, Iosif, 281
signification, 16, 119, 144
Simon, William, 237, 238, 256n4; *Sexual Deviance*, 239
skepticism, 2, 37, 50, 73, 214n2; academic, 38; classical, 35, 52n9; genial, 10; of Hume, 149, 220; as literary principle, 7; of readers, 109
skin: changing idea of, 146; climate and, 154–55; color of, as immediate identifying mark of race, 16, 68, 143, 144, 145, 154–56, 281; in humoral model, 147
Skrbina, David, 222
Skype, 190
slaves, 65, 66, 67, 69–70, 80
Smith, Barbara Hernstein, 8
Sobchack, Vivian, 178
social sciences, 237, 238, 239, 242, 257n5; empirical, 240; humanities and, 18, 241, 280, 281
Society of Animation Studies (SAS), 180, 181; *Animation Studies* journal and, 180
Society of Cinema and Media Studies (SCMS), 180, 181, 190, 194n33, *Cinema Journal* and, 180, 181
Society of Cinema Studies, 182
Society of Cinematologists, 180, 193n6
sociology, sociologists, 17, 238, 258n19; Chicago school, 237, 239; dramaturgical, 257n13; Goffman and, 247, 258n14;

of homosexuality, 31; literary, 170; micro-, 18, 241, 242, 251; postwar, 240, 241, 242; queer theory and, 11; of texts, 166
Solanas, Fernando, 192
Sophists, 44, 54n34
South, developing, 125, 126
South Africa, racism in, 70–71
South Atlantic Quarterly special issue on "Theory Now," 7, 22n13
Southerland, John, 163
Spanish Civil War, 65
spectatorship, 182
Spence, Joseph, 103
Spenser, Edmund, *Faerie Queene*, 203, 215n8
Spinoza, Baruch, 15, 79, 80, 82–83, 92n5, 92n8
Spivak, Gayatri Chakravorty, 280
Stalin, Joseph, 65, 76n21
Stam, Robert, and Toby Miller, *Film and Theory: An Anthology*, 182
Stanhope, Henry, 105
status quo, 21n6, 120, 243
Stein, Jordan Alexander, on disciplinary wholeness, 16, 282
Stephenson, Ralph, *The Art of Animation*, 181
Stepto, Robert, 167
stigma, 240; Goffman and, 18, 245, 247–51; mechanics of stigmatization and, 238, 249, 250; sexual, 237, 256, 257n8; theory of, 251; in urban ecology, 239
stimulus, 97, 221, 222, 233n5
structuralism, 8, 12, 19–20, 53n27, 144
subcultures, sexual, 237, 253
subject, human, 16, 139, 149
subject formation, 119, 130, 132, 134, 136
subjectivity, subjectification, 17, 230, 254; asubjective, 219, 228; internalization of coercive norms and, 136; intersubjective constitution of, 140n3; modes of, 140; perceived experience and, 218; rational consent and, 127; subjectivism and, 267

318 Index

suicide, 78–93
superjectivity, 218, 228, 230–31
Surin, Kenneth, 6–9
Suzuki, D. T., 39, 49
syllabicity, 103, 110, 111
symposium, 5, 20, 21n9, 169

Taihei, Imamura, 191
Taoism, in Western thinking, 36, 38, 49, 52n9
Tarlinskaia, Marina, 110
Tate, Nahum, 210, 212
technique, 104, 107, 108, 113, 115
technology, 233n3; biopolitics and, 129, 130–35, 137, 139; cinema and, 177; disruptive, 20n6; governmental, 136; machinic approach to sensibility and, 225; media, 231
teleology, 59, 75n13, 145, 154; failed, 57–58; of past, 14; twenty-first century, 224–25
television, 182
temporality, 72, 150, 153, 206, 226, 230–31
Terada, Rei, 12, 15
text, texts, 160, 163; by African Americans, 166, 170; categorization of, 168; editing of, 175n15; interpretation of, 161; recovery of, 161, 167, 170; textuality and, 245; world and, 241
textual criticism, Greg-Bowers method of, 164
Thailand, sex workers in, 125, 127–28
theater studies, 242
theoretical past and present, 20
theory, 5, 8–9, 10, 12, 174n4, 284–85n2; African American literature and, 160–76; canonization of, 23n16, 281; chic negativity of, 23n26; condition of, 12, 13; as destructive of imagination and imaginary, 7; development of, 17, 280–81; domestication of, 6; double condition of, 4; future of, 6, 11; inward turn of, 21n10; life/death/life cycle of, 24n38; globalization of, 281; meaning of, 280–81, 284n1; misunderstanding of Foucault in, 118; operates as canon

of singularities, 2; pure, 282; representation-discursive turn of, 24n30; role of, 46; therapeutic turn of, 21n9; unconditionality of; as wholesale transformation, 8, 22n10; world without, 23n16. *See also names of individual theories*
Theory, 5; death of, 22n11; without humans, 7; meaning of, 280–81, 283; serial replacement of schools in, 21n7; without Theorists, 3. *See also* High Theory; theory
thick description, 157n4, 253
thinking, 107, 108, 110, 113, 114, 115, 282
Thompson, Kristin, 178; *Film Art: An Introduction*, 179
Tibbetts, John, 181
time, 56–73; desire and, 201; former future, 57; futures past, 56–57, 59; as linear, 58, 63; transcendence of, 61. *See also* temporality
Tolstoy, Leo, 49
Tomkins, Silvan, on weak theory, 45, 46
totality, in theory, 282–83
Toynbee, Philip, *Underdogs*, 18, 248–51, 259n35
transcendental deduction (Kant), 149
translation, 9; availability of, 284–85n2; of cinematic theory, 189; of French works, 49, 285n2; issues of, 190; meaning transcending, 52n16
Trinidad, 65, 68, 76n25
Trollope, Anthony, 211
Trotsky, Leon, 76n21; *The History of the Russian Revolution*, 66–69
truth, 81, 82, 83, 92n2, 101
Tucker, Herbert: *Epic: Britain's Heroic Muse 1790–1910*, 100; "The Fix of Form," 100
Tucker, Irene, 16, 281
Tynianov, Iurii Nikolaevich, 100; *Archaists and Innovators*, 99

unconscious, 107, 207, 241
Unger, Roberto, 281
UN (United Nations), 16, 126, 128, 137–38, 139

universalism, 146, 158, 239
university, 6, 9, 14, 23n16, 35, 48, 167; desegregation of, 143; graduate students at, 164, 173, 241; presses of, 165; student protests for ethnic studies at, 160
University of Jena, 140n4, 150
utility theory, 202, 271–72
utopia, 75n20, 133, 134; Bloch and, 62, 63, 64, 69, 71–72, 74n9

value, psychological theory of, 265–66
Velleman, N. David, 203, 215n10
verse, 15, 98, 103, 108; art of, 107, 112; Lanier's science of, 100; Pope and, 101, 104–6, 109–14, 282; reading of, 111; scansion of, 100, 109; Shaftesbury and, 114; technical virtuosity and, 104, 115; thinking and, 101, 107, 113–15, 282; versification and, 105
versification, 104–7, 109
Vertov, Dzgia, 192
Veselovsky, Alexander (Aleksandr Veselovskii), 15, 98, 99, 282, 285n4; *Istoricheskaia Poetika*, 98
Victorianists, 100
video games, 182, 183
violence, 23n26, 124, 144; Butler on, 121, 122, 123; domestic, 249; exclusionary, 120; as part of liberal power, 80; in poetry, 110; of social upheavals, 84; state, 81
visual art, animation as, 178
voice, 97, 112, 114, 124, 282
Vossius, Isaac, 105

Walsh, William, 103, 116n23
Warner, Michael, *Fear of a Queer Planet*, 239
War on Terror, 121, 124
Warren, Kenneth, *What Was African American Literature?*, 156, 157n4
Warren, Robert Penn, 272, 273, 278n25
weak theory, Tomkins on, 45, 46

Weber, Max, 46, 217n25, 233n5
Weeks, Jeffrey, 238, 256n4
Wellek, René, 99
Wells, Paul, 181, 191, 193n18
Wenzel, Jennifer, 76
Wesley, Dorothy Porter, 167
White, Patricia, *Critical Visions in Film Theory*, 183
Whitehead, Alfred North, 219, 220, 224, 225, 230, 236n27, 281; *Adventures of Ideas*, 227; *Process and Reality*, 220, 223, 227, 228, 235n22, 235n24; sensation and, 17, 219–36, 233n3, 235n22; *Symbolism*, 227
Whitman, Walt, as homosexual, 31
Wilde, Oscar, 30, 31, 238
will, 206–7, 214–15n8, 215n14
Williams, Eric, *Capitalism and Slavery*, 69
Williams, Raymond, 214n2, 269
Wimsatt, William K., 278n30; Beardsley and, "The Intentional Fallacy," 162–63, 271–72; "I. A. R.: What to Say about a Poem," 272; on poetry, 267–68, 270–72; on Richards, 273–75
Winnicott, Donald, 50, 53–54n32
Wolfe, Cary, 8–9, 11, 23–24n28
women, 33n1, 117–42, 126, 165. *See also* feminism; gender
Wordsworth, William, 2, 108–9, 111, 204
working through, 12
worldly sensibility, 218, 225, 226, 228, 229, 231, 235n17; forms of, 219; operation of, 236n27; world appearance and, 229–32

yes/no paradigm, as theoretical impasse, 41–43

Zen Buddhism, 36, 38, 39, 48–49, 52n9. *See also* Buddha; Taoism
Zhirmunsky, Viktor, *The Composition of Lyric Poems*, 99
Žižek, Slavoj, 280, 281
Zunshine, Lisa, 214n2, 272–73

www.ingramcontent.com/pod-product-compliance
Lightning Source LLC
Chambersburg PA
CBHW070750230426
43665CB00017B/2321